BENEATH THE MOUNTAIN

"*Beneath the Mountain* makes clear the fact that prison was a part of slavery, just as slavery was part of a prison. In doing so, it expands for readers the definition of 'unfreedom' and illuminates how, from the plantation to the prison, the struggle to emerge from beneath the mountain has required the development of a revolutionary consciousness that comes from analyzing the full scope of one's present condition and emancipating one's mind. *Beneath the Mountain* provides a stunning genealogy of ideas, showing us how unfree revolutionaries continue to build upon the genius of those who have come before them. The words of George Jackson, for example, would come to inspire Ed Mead, just as the mentorship of Russell Shoatz would provide political education to Saleem Holbrook, and, of course, the leaders of antebellum slave revolts have always inspired generations of incarcerated radical thinkers. The fact that books on plantation insurrections have come to be banned by Departments of Corrections across the country only speaks to the incredible power and potential that these speeches, testimonies, and letters possess. *Beneath the Mountain* illustrates the role these writings play in both honoring past struggles and serving as a blueprint for future generations. Most importantly, this reader provides a hopeful promise that there is a future where this centuries-long struggle for freedom will finally be realized."

—**TAMAR SARAI**, writer and reporter at *Prism*

"Who stands beneath the mountain but prisoners of war? Mumia Abu-Jamal and Jennifer Black have assembled a book of fire, each voice a flame in captivity shedding light on what John Brown called 'a most barbarous, unprovoked, and unjustifiable war' and illuminating a path to freedom. Whether writing from a place of fugitivity, the prison camp, the city jail, the modern gulag, or death row, these are our revolutionary thinkers, our critics and dreamers, our people. The people who move mountains."

—**ROBIN D. G. KELLEY,** author of *Freedom Dreams: The Black Radical Imagination*

"This collection is an irruption of state captivity in all its forms. Gathering the voices of unapologetic revolutionaries, abolitionists, anti-imperialists, and militant resisters, *Beneath the Mountain* echoes an archive of something else after the mountain has crumbled at the feet of those who dare to do what it takes to find liberation."

—**DYLAN RODRIGUEZ,** author of *Forced Passages: Imprisoned Radical Intellectuals and the U.S. Prison Regime*

"Since the days of slavery, American prisons have been Blacks' home away from home. Slaves guilty of no crime were often held in prison until they could be sold. Everything I have read indicates that two-thirds of Black and Brown persons would not be doing time if they were white. This anthology by Jennifer Black and Mumia Abu-Jamal provides more ammunition for those who would end the arbitrary holding of Blacks, Browns, and Reds in captivity."

—**ISHMAEL REED,** author of *The Haunting of Lin-Manuel Miranda*

"*Beneath the Mountain* salutes generations of revolutionaries from around the world as a wonderful example of what Frantz Fanon once called 'combat literature.' The uncompromising and bold voices in this collection speak to us, crafting a *we* with their clarity of thought, fearlessness, and determination. They invite us, teach us, challenge us, enlist us; they embolden and empower us. These are the voices of those defined not by their captivity but by their refusal to submit to oppression and their commitment to freedom. Their words resound across the many decades of struggle. They traverse space, overcoming its carceral partitioning with barbed wires, thick walls, and militarized borders. They advance our quest for dignity and collective liberation."

—**BANU BARGU,** author of *Starve and Immolate: The Politics of Human Weapons*

"*Beneath the Mountain* reminds us that ancestors and rebels have resisted conquest and enslavement, building marronage against colonialism and genocide."

—**JOY JAMES,** author of *New Bones Abolition: Captive Maternal Agency and the (After)Life of Erica Garner*

"Filled with insight and energy, this extraordinary book gifts us the opportunity to encounter people's understanding of the fight for freedom from the inside out."

—**RUTH WILSON GILMORE,** author, *Abolition Geography* and *Golden Gulag*

"This collection gives a compelling sense of insurgent spirits and critical minds enduring imprisonment and even facing death at the hands of powerful oppressors. These contributions have much to tell us about past and present realities that must be confronted. Mumia Abu-Jamal and Jennifer Black must be thanked for this precious gift—an inspiring resource for activists, scholars, and all who care about social justice and human rights."

—**PAUL LE BLANC,** editor of *Black Liberation and the American Dream*

"The book is one-of-a-kind... stunning and impeccably curated... gleaned directly from the pens of rebels who have worked toward liberation from the bowels of the US prison system."

—**ROBYN MAYNARD,** co-author of *Rehearsals for Living*

"Like America's dungeons, this book is full of caged freedom fighters, unfree radicals, and outlaw intellectuals, whose words, smuggled from behind prison bars and cages, offer a beautiful literary anti-canon of liberation."

—**DAVID CORREIA,** author of *Violent Order: Essays on the Nature of Police*

BENEATH THE MOUNTAIN

AN ANTI-PRISON READER

Edited by Mumia Abu-Jamal and Jennifer Black

CITY LIGHTS BOOKS | OPEN MEDIA SERIES

Beneath The Mountain
An Anti-Prison Reader
Edited by Mumia Abu-Jamal and Jennifer Black

CITY LIGHTS BOOKS | OPEN MEDIA SERIES

Open Media Series Editor: Greg Ruggiero
Cover illustration copyright © R. Black
Cover design by R. Black
Text design by Patrick Barber

ISBN-13: 978-0872869264

Library of Congress Cataloging-in-Publication Data

Names: Abu-Jamal, Mumia, editor. | Black, Jennifer, 1969– editor.
Title: Beneath the mountain : an anti-prison reader / edited by Mumia Abu-Jamal and Jennifer Black.
Description: San Francisco, CA : City Lights Books, [2024] | Includes bibliographical references and index. |
Identifiers: LCCN 2024005047 (print) | LCCN 2024005048 (ebook) | ISBN 9780872869264 (paperback) | ISBN 9780872869271 (epub)
Subjects: LCSH: Prisoners—United States. | Imprisonment—United States. | Liberty.
Classification: LCC HV9471 .B399 2024 (print) | LCC HV9471 (ebook) | DDC 365/.973—dc23/eng/20240214
LC record available at https://lccn.loc.gov/2024005047
LC ebook record available at https://lccn.loc.gov/2024005048

City Lights Books are published at the City Lights Bookstore
261 Columbus Avenue, San Francisco, CA 94133
citylights.com

CONTENTS

"Vast numbers of incarcerated people do the hard work of learning, often learning to read as Malcolm did, but certainly learning to use their intellects. And as a matter of fact, there's probably more intellectual greatness behind bars now than in any other place."

—ANGELA DAVIS

BENEATH THE MOUNTAIN

INTRODUCTION

UNDERSTANDING THE AMERICAN PRISON IS CENtral to understanding US history. Since its inception, the United States has been a place where race, gender, and land determined status. Those who owned property ruled, and those who didn't were disposable. That included Indigenous people, Africans, impoverished European immigrants, and women of all ethnicities. "Property = Power" might as well have been the motto of the new settler-colonial nation.

Papal support for the African slave trade began as early as 1452, when Pope Nicholas V charged Alfonso of Portugal with the Christian duty to enslave any non-Christian, which included Africans. This marked a turning point in Western history: the emergence of a carceral system of state repression designed to control Black freedom and exploit Black labor. Enslavement and incarceration went hand in hand, and all conversations regarding the emergence of incarceration in the United States must begin with slavery.

When speaking of the carceral system, we are not just referring to policing and prisons but also to the set of relations that made slavery and imprisonment morally acceptable. As we write on unceded Lenape land, we include Native American expulsion, slaughter, and forced placement on reservations within the notion of the carceral system, as reservations were created to assist with plans for "Indian removal." President Andrew Jackson pursued this legislative and legal agenda while accelerating genocidal removal through military warfare, one-sided treaties, and settler expansion. Crazy Horse died attempting to escape the open-air prison where the US intended to relocate him. The Pine Ridge Reservation originally served as a detention camp for Indigenous prisoners of war. Today, Native Americans living on reservations have the lowest life-expectancy rates in the nation, the highest poverty rates, and the lowest employment rates. For Africans forcibly exported from their homelands, the entire southlands of the United States became a vast prison where torture and death awaited those who sought the very things the so-called Founding Fathers claimed were the rights of all—life, liberty and the pursuit of happiness.

In his 1853 book, *Stroud's Slave Laws,* attorney George Stroud recounts the statutes adopted by half a dozen slave states and the bone-chilling horrors inflicted upon Black captives in the 1700s. Such horrors express the ruthlessness borne in the heart of a society of enslavers. Stroud offers some insight into the society's sense of the worth of the people it bred, trafficked, and enslaved for profit:

> Where the *life* of the slave is thus feebly protected, his *limbs,* as might be expected, share no better fate. I quote again from the act of 1740, of South Carolina. "In case any person shall willfully cut out the tongue, put out the eye, castrate, or *cruelly* scald, burn, or deprive any slave of any limb or member, or shall inflict any *other cruel punishment, other than by whipping or beating* with a *horsewhip,* cowskin, switch or small stick, or *by putting irons on, or confining or imprisoning such slave,* every such person shall, for every such offense, forfeit the sum of one hundred pounds current money." This section has, as far as I have been able to learn, been suffered to disgrace the statute-book from the year 1746 to the present hour.

We know that enslaved Black people actually had no right to report the abuses that white people perpetrated on them. The absence of such rights presaged the coming of Jim Crow, a system of racial subordination that continued to inflict racial, social, and economic marginalization on people of color in the United States.

In his book *Slavery by Another Name,* Douglas A. Blackmon describes how, beginning in the 1860s "and accelerating after the return of white political control in 1877," every southern state "enacted laws essentially intended to criminalize black life." Anti-vagrancy laws were so vague that a Black person could be arrested for almost any reason. Multiple states prohibited Black people from changing employers without permission, effectively preventing them from leaving the plantations of the whites they worked for. Through the convict-lease system, imprisoned Black people were forced to labor for free for private businesses.

When the twentieth century dawned, prisons were also considered to be places of social reform for the troublesome European immigrants from Italy and Ireland. Despite the fact that the convict-lease system in the South primarily targeted Black males, the majority of prisoners were from the majority of the larger population: white, working-class, non-Anglo-Saxon Protestants such as southern, central and eastern Europeans, and Irish.

The racial demography of the carceral system changed dramatically in the 1960s and 1970s when the eruption of Black freedom struggles and social discontent tasked the state with a new mission: social control of a rebellious community against white supremacy. This period marked the transformation of prison, which now acquired the unique ideological function of discrediting Black liberatory efforts. This period also marked the emergence of the so-called drug war, a masquerade used to justify state surveillance and criminalization of entire communities. All the while, the rhetoric of freedom and liberty was blared around the world by US propagandists, while *un*-freedom remained the lot of millions of Africans and their dusky descendants. It takes intense effort to achieve the draconian levels of mass incarceration in present-day America. It took bipartisan political wherewithal and a kind of methodical intentionality in the social targeting of a people perceived as "problematic."

When Nixon administration officials launched the war on drugs, including marijuana, the die was cast. The state raided, attacked, criminalized, and imprisoned Black people across the nation. However, "reefer madness" and drug war hysteria quickly dissipated with the mass addiction of white people to opioids in rural and suburban areas, where rehabilitation instead of imprisonment became the treatment of choice.

Well into our day, right-leaning white America continues to make the point that the history, freedom, and lives of Americans of color are a threat to the status quo. The living legacy of slavery's anti-literacy laws can be seen in the fascist anti-woke legislation, book bannings, and prohibitions against teaching the history of Americans of color. Lynchings today do not just come at the end of a noose but also via chokehold, a knee to the neck, and the slow death of imprisonment. Political power depends on a strong army to maintain control, but it also depends on the ability to confine individuals and groups; to hold people in place—literally, in chains and cages; and structurally, by maintaining rigid societal hierarchies based on race, gender, and class, enforced through doctrine, custom, law, terror, and violence.

In *Beneath the Mountain* we present a selection of writings from unfree radicals—enslaved people, political prisoners, jailed revolutionaries, labor activists, imprisoned Native

American insurgents—who contribute to the canon of contemporary abolitionist thought and anti-prison organizing. The voices collected here are meant to affirm, inform, and advance the abolitionist organizing that is already happening in the streets, the cages, and the classrooms. They aim to present a nuanced perspective, transcending a simplistic equation of "slavery = prison = profits for prison lords." The undeniable correlation between the institutions of slavery and prison and their pernicious legacy is acknowledged. However, it is our hope that readers will gain insight into the broader social role that prisons play in maintaining hierarchies and control, including their inherent elasticity. Organizer and scholar Ruth Wilson Gilmore reminds us that prisons have become catch-all solutions to social problems. In the introduction to her 2007 book *Golden Gulag,* she notes that "laws change, depending on what, in a social order, counts as stability, and who, in a social order needs to be controlled."

We call this an *anti-prison reader* to acknowledge that the development of anti-prison consciousness is foundational to the larger abolitionist project of liberation and transformation of social and political relations. This necessarily involves transitioning from current forms of policing, surveillance, and prison to restorative forms of justice that seek solutions centered on education, mutual aid, and community. At the end of the day, it's about freeing people.

Abolitionists of the past were visionaries who imagined and fought for a future without slavery. Modern-day abolitionists imagine a future free of retribution and prison as solutions. As Assata Shakur expresses in her poem,

If I know anything at all
It's that a wall is just a wall
And nothing more at all
It can be broken down.

"The rebels went to prison," writes Joy James in *Imprisoned Intellectuals*, "and passing through, or surviving incarceration, they wrote as outlaw intellectuals with unique and controversial insights into idealism, warfare, and social justice." The outlaw rebels in this volume have vital lessons to impart, especially for a nation that targets economically disadvantaged people; Indigenous, Black, and Brown people; and gender non-conforming people. They teach us about the nature of punishment and discipline, how nations wield power, why self-representation is vital, about liberation, courage, unity, agency, and the contradictions of inequality. They show us how to organize, how ideology can provide guidelines for our actions, and why cultivating the qualities of revolutionary love and hope are necessary to realize our freedom dreams.

Revolutionary love speaks to the ways we protect, respect, and empower each other while standing up to state terror. Its presence is affirmed through these texts as a necessary component to help chase away fear and to encourage the solidarity and unity essential for organizing in dangerous times and places. Its absence portends tragedy. Revolutionary love does not stop the state from wanting to kill us, nor is it effective without strategy and tactics, but it is the might that fuels us to stand shoulder to shoulder with others regardless. Perhaps it can move mountains. As we co-editors hail from Pennsylvania, our default point of reference is Philadelphia. To denote the historical and regional circumstances of the state repression and terror we are most familiar with, and to combat the ways the state tries to divide us, we convey it Philly style—with the encouragement that we move forward and organize with "love, not phear."

Each author in *Beneath the Mountain* has somehow challenged the laws, customs, and codes promoting inequality in their respective eras. Some have paid with their liberty, others with their lives. Each has contributed to the collective development of radical, anti-prison consciousness even if they did not identify themselves as "anti-prison" or "abolitionist," as these social categories have not always existed in the same way we understand them today. The words that emerge from their struggles demonstrate the continuity of emancipatory consciousness across many generations, while pointing toward a more just and egalitarian future.

We endeavor to let their raw unmediated voices speak for themselves, as self-representation is crucial. In several instances this is not possible, and the statements are conveyed by a scribe or reporter. The value of the content is worthwhile even as we acknowledge that mediation allows for the possibility of misrepresentation and bias, no matter how well-meaning or accurate the scribe strives to be.

There are many more fighters, lovers, and revolutionaries trapped beneath the mountain. This book is a good starting point, but we must keep reading, teaching, strategizing, and organizing. Revelations are found among the humbled and the burdened, the disempowered and forsaken, the poor, the oppressed, and the unfree. Our fight for liberation is a gift to humanity. We cannot predict all the challenges ahead, but we know that prisons are not an inevitable and permanent feature of society.

Following sixteen months of imprisonment, in June 1972 a jury declared Angela Davis not guilty of conspiracy, murder, and kidnapping. A few days after her courtroom victory, Angela gave a speech in Los Angeles, saying,

> Martin Luther King told us what he saw when he went to the mountaintop. He told us of visions of a new world of freedom and harmony; told us of the sisterhood and brotherhood of humankind. Dr. King described it

> far more eloquently than I could ever attempt to do. But there's also the foot of the mountain, and there are also the regions beneath the surface. And I am returning from a descent, together with thousands and thousands of our sisters and brothers, into the ugly depths of society. I want to try to tell you a little something about those regions. I want to attempt to persuade you to join in the struggle to give life and breath to those who live sealed away from everything that resembles human decency.

More than half a century later, these words could have been written this morning. The regions Angela speaks of, the deplorable depths that stand in contrast to the possibility of liberation, remain a soul-crushing hell for those sentenced to endure them. Winning the freedom of the detained, dispossessed, discarded, and disrespected unfree human beings who remain trapped beneath the mountain—and abolishing the possibility of such a fate for the generations of the future—is the ultimate cause to which this book is dedicated.

In love, not phear,
MUMIA ABU-JAMAL & JENNIFER BLACK

ONE

ONA "ONEY" JUDGE STAINES

Response to George and Martha Washington, Her Enslavers (1790s)

SHE WAS BORN BENEATH THE MOUNTAIN, AND succeeded in coming out from under it, inspired by the same revolutionary principles that drove her enslavers to rebel against the British monarchy. Oney Judge was among hundreds of people enslaved by President George Washington and First Lady Martha Washington, and one of several whom the Washingtons covertly rotated out of Philadelphia, often to Virginia, in order to evade Pennsylvania's Gradual Abolition of Slavery Act of 1780.[1] After learning that the Washingtons were going to give her to their ill-tempered granddaughter as a wedding gift, Ms. Judge began to plan her self-emancipation. One evening, while the president and First Lady were dining in their Philadelphia residence, Oney, a domestic servant, stole away mid-meal. Judge later recalled in an 1845 interview,

> Whilst they were packing up to go to Virginia, I was packing to go, I didn't know where; for I knew that if I went back to Virginia, I should never get my liberty. I had friends among the colored people of Philadelphia, had my things carried there beforehand, and left Washington's house while they were eating dinner.[2]

Despite fear of bad publicity, the Washingtons relentlessly hunted Ms. Judge. They enlisted people to locate her and placed an ad in the *Philadelphia Gazette* promising a $10 reward for her capture. Their ad described the now-free woman: "a light mulatto girl, much freckled, with very black eyes and bushy black hair, she is of middle stature, slender, and delicately formed, about 20 years of age."

Thanks to the support of an abolitionist network, including a group of free Black Philadelphians whom she befriended, Ms. Judge safely made her way to New Hampshire. When she was recognized there by a friend of the Washingtons, the president enlisted the help of a local official to find her and implored her voluntary return. Ms. Judge tersely declined. While free, she learned to read and write, married, and had three children. On two occasions she was interviewed by abolitionist newspapers in the mid-1840s. None of the hollow promises of her enslavers could offer her a better life than the one she had already made for herself. We laud her bravery, her resistance, and her resolve by honoring her response to the entreaties of the revolutionary general and first president of the United States. When beseeched to return to her position as enslaved servant, she replied succinctly,

> "I am free now and choose to remain so."[3]

TWO

NAT TURNER

The Pre-Trial Confessions as Fully and Voluntarily Made to Thomas R. Gray (1831)

WE CANNOT HIDE FROM HISTORY, NO MATTER how ugly it is. Therefore, it makes sense to include Nat Turner, who at the time of this "confession," was both enslaved and detained. Contesting these impositions, the insurgent preacher traded in the currency of the era—religious righteousness. Turner was known to have spiritual visions and prophetic dreams, some of which he interpreted as a call to uprising. Engaging Bible principles to rationalize revolt, Turner led the bloodiest slave rebellion in US history, organizing approximately seventy Black people to attack the white society that propagated human trafficking, breeding, and slavery. Turner's insurgents reportedly spared some houses—those of impoverished white families who Turner believed posed no threat. While Turner eluded immediate capture, after two months he was apprehended. In response to questions from a white lawyer named Thomas R. Gray, Turner explained the circumstances that led to his revolt. He was found guilty and executed along with his co-conspirators.

Following Turner's revolt, the South reacted against Black literacy in much the same way it has revolted against Critical Race Theory since the Black Lives Matter uprisings. Anti-literacy laws prohibiting enslaved people from learning to read and write were strengthened and more widely enforced. A literate and articulate Black man, Turner confronted the slaveocracy with what can happen when human beings are treated like livestock. How different might this account be if Turner, afforded the privilege of self-representation, had written it himself instead of our having mediation of the lawyer who transcribed his words? The role of literacy and the significance of self-representation prove to be currents throughout this book. Turner's plight raises other questions that remain relevant to this day. From an abolitionist perspective, what are the best methods to liberate ourselves from violent systemic oppression? Is the use of armed resistance ever justified? If so, when, and who decides?

Sir,

YOU HAVE asked me to give a history of the motives which induced me to undertake the late insurrection, as you call it. To do so I must go back to the days of my infancy, and even before I was born.

I was thirty-one years of age the 2nd of October last, and born the property of Benj. Turner, of this county. In my childhood a circumstance occurred which made an indelible impression on my mind, and laid the ground work of that enthusiasm, which has terminated so fatally to many, both white and black, and for which I am about to atone at the gallows.

It is here necessary to relate this circumstance. Trifling as it may seem, it was the commencement of that belief which has grown with time, and even now, sir, in this dungeon, helpless and forsaken as I am, I cannot divest myself of. Being at play with other children, when three or four years old, I was telling them something, which my mother overhearing, said it had happened before I was born. I stuck to my story, however, and related some things which went, in her opinion, to confirm it. Others being called on were greatly astonished, knowing that these things had happened, and caused them to say in my hearing, I surely would be a prophet, as the Lord had shewn me things that had happened before my birth.

And my father and mother strengthened me in this my first impression, saying in my presence, I was intended for some great purpose, which they had always thought from certain marks on my head and breast....

My grandmother, who was very religious, and to whom I was much attached; my master, who belonged to the church; and other religious persons who visited the house, and whom I often saw at prayers, noticing the singularity of my manners, I suppose, and my uncommon intelligence for a child, remarked I had too much sense to be raised, and if I was, I would never be of any service to any one as a slave.

To a mind like mine, restless, inquisitive and observant of everything that was passing, it is easy to suppose that religion was the subject to which it would be directed, and although this subject principally occupied my thoughts, there was nothing that I saw or heard of to which my attention was not directed. The manner in which I learned to read and write, not only had great influence on my own mind, as I acquired it with the most perfect ease, so much so that I have no recollection whatever of learning the alphabet, but to the astonishment of the family, one day, when a book was shewn me to keep me from crying, I began spelling the names of different objects. This was a source of wonder to all in the neighborhood, particularly the blacks, and this learning was constantly improved at all opportunities.

When I got large enough to go to work, while employed, I was reflecting on many things that would present themselves to my imagination, and whenever an opportunity occurred of looking at a book, when the schoolchildren were getting their lessons, I would find many things that the fertility of my own imagination had depicted to me before; all my time, not devoted to my master's service, was spent either in prayer, or in making experiments in casting different things in moulds made of earth, in attempting to make paper, gunpowder, and many other experiments, that although I could not perfect, yet convinced me of its practicability if I had the means.

I was not addicted to stealing in my youth, nor have [I] ever been. Yet such was the confidence of the negroes in the neighborhood, even at this early period of my life, in my superior judgment, that they would often carry me with them when they were going on any roguery, to plan for them. Growing up among them, with this confidence in my superior judgment, and when this, in their opinions, was perfected by Divine inspiration, from the circumstances already alluded to in my infancy, and which belief was ever afterwards zealously inculcated by the austerity of my life and manners, which became the subject of remark by white and black.

Having soon discovered to be great, I must appear so, and therefore studiously avoided mixing in society, and wrapped myself in mystery, devoting my time to fasting and prayer. By this time, having arrived to man's estate, and hearing the scriptures commented on at meetings, I was struck with that particular passage which says: "Seek ye the kingdom of Heaven and all things shall be added unto you."

I reflected much on this passage, and prayed daily for light on this subject. As I was praying one day at my plough, the spirit spoke to me, saying "Seek ye the kingdom of Heaven and all things shall be added unto you."

Question: What do you mean by the Spirit?

Answer: The Spirit that spoke to the prophets in former days. And I was greatly astonished, and for two years prayed continually, whenever my duty would permit. And then again I had the same revelation, which fully confirmed me in the impression that I was ordained for some great purpose in the hands of the Almighty.

Several years rolled round, in which many events occurred to strengthen me in this my belief. At this time I reverted in my mind to the remarks made of me in my childhood, and the things that had been shewn me. And as it had been said of me in my childhood by those by whom I had been taught to pray, both white and black, and in whom I had the greatest confidence, that I had too much sense to be raised, and if I was, I would never be of any use to any one as a slave.

Now finding I had arrived to man's estate, and was a slave, and these revelations being made known to me, I began to direct my attention to this great object, to fulfil the purpose for which, by this time, I felt assured I was intended. Knowing the influence I had obtained over the minds of my fellow servants—not by the means of conjuring and such like tricks, for to them I always spoke of such things with contempt, but by the communion of the Spirit whose revelations I often communicated to them—they believed and said my wisdom came from God.

I now began to prepare them for my purpose, by telling them something was about to happen that would terminate in fulfilling the great promise that had been made to me. About this time I was placed under an overseer, from whom I ran away, and after remaining in the woods thirty days, I returned, to the astonishment of the negroes on the plantation, who thought I had made my escape to some other part of the country, as my father had done before. But the reason of my return was, that the Spirit appeared to me and said I had my wishes directed to the things of this world, and not to the kingdom of Heaven, and that I should return to the service of my earthly master. "For he who knoweth his Master's will, and doeth it not, shall be beaten with many stripes, and thus, have I chastened you."

And the negroes found fault, and murmured against me, saying that if they had my sense they would not serve any master in the world. And about this time I had a vision. I saw white spirits and black spirits engaged in battle, and the sun was darkened. The thunder rolled in the Heavens, and blood flowed in streams, and I heard a voice saying, "Such is your luck, such you are called to see, and let it come rough or smooth, you must surely bare [sic] it."

I now withdrew myself as much as my situation would permit from the intercourse of my fellow servants, for the avowed purpose of serving the Spirit more fully, and it appeared to me, and reminded me of the things it had already shown me, and that it would then reveal to me the knowledge of the elements, the revolution of the planets, the operation of tides, and changes of the seasons.

After this revelation in the year 1825, and the knowledge of the elements being made known to me, I sought more than ever to obtain true holiness before the great day of judgment should appear, and then I began to receive the true knowledge of faith. And from the first steps of righteousness until the last, was I made perfect; and the Holy Ghost was with me, and said, "Behold me as I stand in the Heavens."

I looked and saw the forms of men in different attitudes, and there were lights in the sky to which the children of darkness gave other names than what they really were, for they were the lights of the Saviour's hands, stretched forth from east to west, even as they were extended on the cross on Calvary for the redemption of sinners. And I wondered greatly at these miracles, and prayed to be informed of a certainty of the meaning thereof, and shortly afterwards, while laboring in the field, I discovered drops of blood on the corn as though it were dew from heaven. I communicated it to many, both white and black, in the neighborhood, and I then found on the leaves in the woods hieroglyphic characters, and numbers, with the forms of men in different attitudes, portrayed in blood, and representing the figures I had seen before in the heavens.

And now the Holy Ghost had revealed itself to me, and made plain the miracles it had shown me. For as the blood of Christ had been shed on this earth, and had ascended to heaven for the salvation of sinners, and was now returning to earth again in the form of dew. And as the leaves on the trees bore the impression of the figures I had seen in the heavens, it was plain to me that the Saviour was about to lay down the yoke he had borne for the sins of men, and the great day of judgment was at hand. About this time I told these things to a white man—Etheldred T. Brantley—on whom it had a wonderful effect, and he ceased from his wickedness, and was attacked immediately with a cutaneous eruption, and blood oozed from the pores of his skin. And after praying and fasting nine days, he was healed, and the Spirit appeared to me again, and said, as the Saviour had been baptized so should we be also, and when the white people would not let us be baptized by the church, we went down into the water together, in the sight of many who reviled us, and were baptized by the Spirit.

After this I rejoiced greatly and gave thanks to God. And on the 12th of May, 1828, I heard a loud noise in the heavens, and the Spirit instantly appeared to me and said the Serpent was loosened, and Christ had laid down the yoke he had borne for the sins of men, and that I should take it on and fight against the Serpent, for the time was fast approaching when the first should be last and the last should be first.

Question: Do you not find yourself mistaken now?

Answer: Was not Christ crucified? And by signs in the heavens that it would make known to me when I should commence the great work, and until the first sign appeared, I should conceal it from the knowledge of men. And on the appearance of the sign—the eclipse of the sun last February—I should arise and prepare myself, and slay my enemies with their own weapons.

And immediately on the sign appearing in the heavens, the seal was removed from my lips, and I communicated the great work laid out for me to do, to four in whom I had the greatest confidence—Henry, Hark, Nelson, and Sam.

It was intended by us to have begun the work of death on the 4th July last. Many were the plans formed and rejected by us, and it affected my mind to such a degree, that I fell sick, and the time passed without our coming to any determination how to commence. Still forming new schemes and rejecting them, when the sign appeared again, which determined me not to wait longer.

THREE

JOHN BROWN

Last Letter to His Family (1859)

JOHN BROWN WAS BORN IN 1800, THE SAME YEAR AS Nat Turner. Brown admired Turner and ultimately met a similar fate, receiving a death sentence for treason, murder, and conspiring with slaves to rebel. By the time Brown put into motion his long-standing plan to launch a slave rebellion, he had become tired of tame tactics. On the reigning tendency of abolitionist pacifism, he had this to say: "Talk! Talk! Talk! That will never free the slaves. What is needed is action—action!"

An abolitionist is a person who organizes to dismantle an oppressive institution, be it slavery or the prison-industrial complex, and Brown, a man of conviction as well as action, was guided by both abolitionism and Christianity. Faithful to both doctrines, he drew moral inspiration from the precepts of Calvinist theology, which he applied to the anti-slavery mission. Captured just two days after raiding a federal armory at Harpers Ferry, Virginia, he was arrested, tried, convicted, and executed in a six-week period. This occurred despite his commanding presence at trial, where he insisted his goal was to liberate slaves, not kill slaveholders. Regardless, after a forty-five-minute deliberation, the jury returned a one-word verdict: Guilty. During the weeks he spent in jail between his capture and execution, he healed from multiple injuries, wrote letters, and gave interviews in furtherance of abolition.

In his final letter to his family, written just two days before his public hanging in Charles Town, Virginia, he affirms his faith in Christ and the abolitionist cause, and urges acceptance of his destiny. "I am waiting the hour of my public murder with great composure of mind and cheerfulness, feeling the strong assurance that in no other possible way could I be used to so much advantage to the cause of good and of humanity, and that nothing that either I or all my family have sacrificed or suffered will be lost."

John Brown was executed just two years before the Civil War began. It took a long, violent war to reckon with the "peculiar institution" of slavery, but the violence, repression, inequality, and racism at its heart persist. John Brown, who put pikes in the hands of enslaved people while he held their masters captive, paid the ultimate sacrifice to liberate souls from beneath the mountain. His words and spirit march on.

Charles Town, Jefferson County, Virginia
November 30, 1859

My dearly beloved wife, sons and daughters, every one,
As I now begin what is probably the last letter I shall ever write to any of you, I conclude to write to all at the same time. I will mention some little matters particularly applicable to little property concerns in another place.

I recently received a letter from my wife, from near Philadelphia, dated November 22, by which it would seem that she was about giving up the idea of seeing me again. I had written her to come on if she felt equal to the undertaking, but I do not know that she will get my letter in time. It was on her own account chiefly that I asked her to stay back. At first I had a most strong desire to see her again, but there appeared to be very serious objections; and should we never meet in this life, I trust that she will in the need be satisfied it was for the best at least, if not most for her comfort. I enclosed in my last letter to her a draft of fifty dollars from John Jay, made payable to her order. I have now another to send her, from my excellent old friend Edward Harris, of Woonsocket, R.I., for one hundred dollars, which I shall also make payable to her order.

I am waiting the hour of my public murder with great composure of mind and cheerfulness, feeling the strong assurance that in no other possible way could I be used to so much advantage to the cause of good and of humanity, and that nothing that either I or all my family have sacrificed or suffered will be lost. The reflection that a wise and merciful, as well as just and Holy God, rules not only the affairs of this world, but of all worlds, is a rock to set our feet upon under all circumstances—even those more severely trying ones into which our own feelings and wrongs have placed us. I have now no doubt but that our seeming disaster will ultimately result in the most glorious success; so, my dear shattered and broken family, be of good cheer, and believe and trust in God with all your heart, and with all your soul; for He doeth all things well. Do not feel ashamed on my account, nor for one moment despair of the cause or grow weary of well doing. I bless God I never felt stronger confidence in the certain and near approach of a bright morning and a glorious day than I have felt, and do now feel, since my confinement here. I am endeavoring to return, like a poor prodigal as I am, to my Father, against whom I have always sinned, in the hope that he may kindly and forgivingly meet me, though a very great way off.

Oh! my dear wife and children, would to God you could know how I have been travailing in birth for you all, that no one of you may fail of the grace of God.

Through Jesus Christ—that no one of you may be blind to the truth and glorious light of his Word, in which life and immortality are brought to light, I beseech you every one, to make the Bible your daily and nightly study, with a childlike, honest, candid, teachable spirit of love and respect for your husband and father.

And I beseech the God of my fathers to open all your eyes to the discovery of the truth. You cannot imagine how much you may soon need the consolations of the Christian religion. Circumstances like my own for more than a month past have convinced me beyond all doubt of our great need of some theories treasured up when our prejudices are excited, our vanity worked up to the highest pitch. Oh! do not trust your eternal all upon the boisterous ocean without even a helm or compass to aid you in steering. I do not ask any of you to throw away your reason; I only ask you to make a candid, sober use of your reason.

My dear younger children, will you listen to this last poor admonition of one who can only love you? Oh! be determined at once to give your whole heart to God, and let nothing shake or alter that resolution. You need have no fears of regretting it. Do not be vain and thoughtless, but sober minded; and let me entreat you all to love the whole remnant of our once great family. Try and build up again your broken walls, and to make the utmost of every stone that is left. Nothing can so tend to make life a blessing as the consciousness that your life and example bless and leave you the stronger. Still, it is ground of the utmost comfort to my mind to know that so many of you as have had the opportunity have given some proof of your fidelity to the great family of men. Be faithful unto death; from the exercise of habitual love to man it cannot be very hard to learn to love his Maker.

I must yet insert the reason for my firm belief in the divine inspiration of the Bible, notwithstanding I am perhaps naturally skeptical, certainly not credulous. I wish all to consider it most thoroughly when you read that blessed book, and see whether you cannot discover such evidence yourselves. It is the purity of heart filling our minds as well as work and actions, which is everywhere insisted on, that distinguishes it from all the other teachings, that commends it to my conscience. Whether my heart be willing and obedient or not, the inducement that it holds out is another reason of my convictions of its truth and genuineness; but I do not here omit this my last argument on the Bible that eternal life is what my soul is punting after this moment. I mention this as a reason for endeavoring to leave a valuable copy of the Bible to be carefully preserved in remembrance of me, to see many of my posterity, instead of some other book at equal cost.

I beseech you all to live in habitual contentment with moderate circumstances and gains of worldly store, and earnestly to teach this to your children and children's children after you, by example as well as precept. Be determined to know by experience, as soon as may be, whether Bible instruction is of divine origin or not. Be sure to owe no man anything, but to love one another. John Rogers wrote to his children, "Abhor that arrant whore of Rome." John Brown writes to his children to abhor, with undying hatred also, that sum of all villainies—Slavery. Remember, "he that is slow to anger is better than the mighty," and "he that ruleth in spirit than he that taketh a city." Remember, also, that "they being wise, shall shine, and they that turn many to righteousness as the stars forever and ever."

And now, dearly beloved family, to God and the work of His Grace I commend you all.

Your affectionate husband and father,
John Brown

FOUR

FREDERICK DOUGLASS

The Runaway Plot (1855)

FREDERICK DOUGLASS STANDS AS A SHINING BEAcon of abolitionist courage, resistance, and wisdom. Born into bondage in Maryland, he rose from the depths of racist degradation to become one of the most powerful voices for justice and equality in US history. Douglass escaped illiteracy and physical bondage in his youth, acts of audacious defiance that marked the beginning of his lifelong mission to advance equal rights. Once free, Douglass could have chosen to live in relative safety and obscurity, but instead he opted, like Harriet Tubman, to dedicate his life to liberating and elevating others.

Unlike Oney Judge, Frederick Douglass did not find freedom on his first attempt and was jailed after a plan to escape slavery with friends was foiled. The anguish Douglass and his five fellow conspirators experienced was caused by factors common to many beneath the mountain: lack of information about the case against them, lack of communication with the world outside, immobility, separation from community, and the destabilization of not knowing what was coming next. It's not the uniqueness of experience that makes Douglass's narrative so meaningful but rather the powerful manner in which he tells his tale. Douglass's literacy gave him an advantage over his five friends, making him the ringleader of the group, also giving him a historical advantage. Due to the illiteracy enslavers imposed on their Black property, there are countless stories we will never hear. Through Douglass we learn that prison was part of slavery, just as slavery was part of prison. Both institutions, entwined, continue to play their part in defining the compromised moral status of the nation. Freedom,

Douglass asserts, is a human right. To lose possession of your sovereignty, even briefly, is torture. And certainly, every prisoner, just like every slave, yearns to be free.

THE RUNAWAY PLOT

I AM now at the beginning of the year 1836, a time favorable for serious thoughts. The mind naturally occupies itself with the mysteries of life in all its phases—the ideal, the real and the actual. Sober people look both ways at the beginning of the year, surveying the errors of the past, and providing against possible errors of the future. I, too, was thus exercised. I had little pleasure in retrospect, and the prospect was not very brilliant. "Notwithstanding," thought I, "the many resolutions and prayers I have made, in behalf of freedom, I am, this first day of the year 1836, still a slave, still wandering in the depths of spirit-devouring thralldom. My faculties and powers of body and soul are not my own, but are the property of a fellow mortal, in no sense superior to me, except that he has the physical power to compel me to be owned and controlled by him. By the combined physical force of the community, I am his slave—a slave for life." With thoughts like these, I was perplexed and chafed; they rendered me gloomy and disconsolate. The anguish of my mind may not be written.

At the close of the year 1835, Mr. Freeland, my temporary master, had bought me of Capt. Thomas Auld, for the year 1836. His promptness in securing my services, would have been flattering to my vanity, had I been ambitious to win the reputation of being a valuable slave. Even as it was, I felt a slight degree of complacency at the circumstance. It showed he was as well pleased with me as a slave, as I was with him as a master. I have already intimated my regard for Mr.

Freeland, and I may say here, in addressing northern readers—where there is no selfish motive for speaking in praise of a slaveholder—that Mr. Freeland was a man of many excellent qualities, and to me quite preferable to any master I ever had.

But the kindness of the slavemaster only gilds the chain of slavery, and detracts nothing from its weight or power. The thought that men are made for other and better uses than slavery, thrives best under the gentle treatment of a kind master. But the grim visage of slavery can assume no smiles which can fascinate the partially enlightened slave, into a forgetfulness of his bondage, nor of the desirableness of liberty.

I was not through the first month of this, my second year with the kind and gentlemanly Mr. Freeland, before I was earnestly considering and devising plans for gaining that freedom, which, when I was but a mere child, I had ascertained to be the natural and inborn right of every member of the human family. The desire for this freedom had been benumbed, while I was under the brutalizing dominion of Covey;[4] and it had been postponed, and rendered inoperative, by my truly pleasant Sunday school engagements with my friends, during the year 1835, at Mr. Freeland's. It had, however, never entirely subsided. I hated slavery, always, and the desire for freedom only needed a favorable breeze, to fan it into a blaze, at any moment. The thought of only being a creature of the present and the past, troubled me, and I longed to have a future—a future with hope in it. To be shut up entirely to the past and present, is abhorrent to the human mind; it is to the soul—whose life and happiness is unceasing progress—what the prison is to the body; a blight and mildew, a hell of horrors. The dawning of this, another year, awakened me from my temporary slumber, and roused into life my latent, but long cherished aspirations for freedom. I was now not only ashamed to be contented in slavery, but ashamed to seem to be contented, and in my present favorable condition, under the mild rule of Mr. F., I am not sure that some kind reader will not condemn me for being over ambitious, and greatly wanting in proper humility, when I say the truth, that I now drove from me all thoughts of making the best of my lot, and welcomed only such thoughts as led me away from the house of bondage. The intense desire, now felt, to be free, quickened by my present favorable circumstances, brought me to the determination to act, as well as to think and speak. Accordingly, at the beginning of this year 1836, I took upon me a solemn vow, that the year which had now dawned upon me should not close, without witnessing an earnest attempt, on my part, to gain my liberty. This vow only bound me to make my escape individually; but the year spent with Mr. Freeland had attached me, as with "hooks of steel," to my brother slaves. The most affectionate and confiding friendship existed between us; and I felt it my duty to give them an opportunity to share in my virtuous determination, by frankly disclosing to them my plans and purposes. Toward Henry and John Harris, I felt a friendship as strong as one man can feel for another; for I could have died with and for them. To them, therefore, with a suitable degree of caution, I began to disclose my sentiments and plans; sounding them, the while, on the subject of running away, provided a good chance should offer. I scarcely need tell the reader, that I did my very best to imbue the minds of my dear friends with my own views and feelings. Thoroughly awakened, now, and with a definite vow upon me, all my little reading, which had any bearing on the subject of human rights, was rendered available in my communications with my friends. That (to me) gem of a book, the Columbian Orator, with its eloquent orations and spicy dialogues, denouncing oppression and slavery—telling of what had been dared, done and suffered by men, to obtain the inestimable boon of liberty—was still fresh in my memory, and whirled into the ranks of my speech with the aptitude of well-trained soldiers, going through the drill. The fact is, I here began my public speaking. I canvassed, with Henry and John, the subject of slavery, and dashed against it the condemning brand of God's eternal justice, which it every hour violates. My fellow servants were neither indifferent, dull, nor inapt. Our feelings were more alike than our opinions. All, however, were ready to act, when a feasible plan should be proposed. "Show us how the thing is to be done," said they, "and all else is clear."

We were all, except Sandy, quite free from slave-holding priestcraft. It was in vain that we had been taught from the pulpit at St. Michael's, the duty of obedience to our masters; to recognize God as the author of our enslavement; to regard running away an offense, alike against God and man; to deem our enslavement a merciful and beneficial arrangement; to esteem our condition, in this country, a paradise to that from which we had been snatched in Africa; to consider our hard hands and dark color as God's mark of displeasure, and as pointing us out as the proper subjects of slavery; that the relation of master and slave was one of reciprocal benefits; that our work was not more serviceable to our masters, than our master's thinking was serviceable to us. I say, it was in vain that the pulpit of St. Michael's had constantly inculcated these plausible doctrines. Nature laughed them to scorn. For my own part, I had now become altogether too big for my chains. Father Lawson's solemn words, of what I ought to be, and might be, in the providence of God, had not fallen dead on my soul. I was fast verging toward manhood, and the prophecies of my childhood were still unfulfilled. The thought, that year after year had passed away, and my best resolutions to run away had failed and faded—that I was still a slave, and a slave, too, with chances for gaining my freedom diminished and still diminishing—was not a matter to be slept over easily; nor did I easily sleep over it.

But here came a new trouble. Thoughts and purposes so incendiary as those I now cherished, could not agitate the mind long, without danger of making themselves manifest to scrutinizing and unfriendly beholders. I had reason to fear that my sable face might prove altogether too transparent for the safe concealment of my hazardous enterprise. Plans of greater moment have leaked through stone walls, and revealed their projectors. But, here was no stone wall to hide my purpose. I would have given my poor, tell-tale face for the immovable countenance of an Indian, for it was far from being proof against the daily, searching glances of those with whom I met.

It is the interest and business of slaveholders to study human nature, with a view to practical results, and many of them attain astonishing proficiency in discerning the thoughts and emotions of slaves. They have to deal not with earth, wood, or stone, but with men; and, by every regard they have for their safety and prosperity, they must study to know the material on which they are at work. So much intellect as the slaveholder has around him, requires watching. Their safety depends upon their vigilance. Conscious of the injustice and wrong they are every hour perpetrating, and knowing what they themselves would do if made the victims of such wrongs, they are looking out for the first signs of the dread retribution of justice. They watch, therefore, with skilled and practiced eyes, and have learned to read, with great accuracy, the state of mind and heart of the slave, through his sable face. These uneasy sinners are quick to inquire into the matter, where the slave is concerned. Unusual sobriety, apparent abstraction, sullenness and indifference—indeed, any mood out of the common way—afford ground for suspicion and inquiry. Often relying on their superior position and wisdom, they hector and torture the slave into a confession, by affecting to know the truth of their accusations. "You have got the devil in you," say they, "and we will whip him out of you." I have often been put thus to the torture, on bare suspicion. This system has its disadvantages as well as their opposite. The slave is sometimes whipped into the confession of offenses which he never committed. The reader will see that the good old rule—"a man is to be held innocent until proved to be guilty"—does not hold good on the slave plantation. Suspicion and torture are the approved methods of getting at the truth, here. It was necessary for me, therefore, to keep a watch over my deportment, lest the enemy should get the better of me.

But with all our caution and studied reserve, I am not sure that Mr. Freeland did not suspect that all was not right with us. It did seem that he watched us more narrowly, after the plan of escape had been conceived and discussed amongst us. Men seldom see themselves as others see them; and while, to ourselves, everything connected with our contemplated escape appeared concealed, Mr. Freeland may have, with the peculiar prescience of a slaveholder, mastered the huge thought which was disturbing our peace in slavery.

I am the more inclined to think that he suspected us, because, prudent as we were, as I now look back, I can see that we did many silly things, very well calculated to awaken suspicion. We were, at times, remarkably buoyant, singing hymns and making joyous exclamations, almost as triumphant in their tone as if we had reached a land of freedom and safety. A keen observer might have detected in our repeated singing of

O Canaan, sweet Canaan,
I am bound for the land of Canaan,

something more than a hope of reaching heaven. We meant to reach the north—and the north was our Canaan[.]

I thought I heard them say,
There were lions in the way,
I don't expect to stay
Much longer here.
Run to Jesus—shun the danger—
I don't expect to stay
Much longer here

was a favorite air, and had a double meaning. In the lips of some, it meant the expectation of a speedy summons to a world of spirits; but, in the lips of our company, it simply meant, a speedy pilgrimage toward a free state, and deliverance from all the evils and dangers of slavery.

I had succeeded in winning to my (what slaveholders would call wicked) scheme, a company of five young men, the very flower of the neighborhood, each one of whom would have commanded one thousand dollars in the home market. At New Orleans, they would have brought fifteen hundred dollars apiece, and, perhaps, more. The names of our party were as follows: Henry Harris; John Harris, brother to Henry; Sandy Jenkins, of root memory; Charles Roberts; and Henry Bailey. I was the youngest, but one, of the party. I had, however, the advantage of them all, in experience, and in a knowledge of letters. This gave me great influence over them. Perhaps not one of them, left to himself, would have dreamed of escape as a possible thing. Not one of them was self-moved in the matter. They all wanted to be free; but the serious thought of running away, had not entered into their minds, until I won them to the undertaking. They all were tolerably well off—for slaves—and had dim hopes of being set free, some day, by their masters. If any one is to blame for disturbing the quiet of the slaves and slave-masters of the neighborhood of St. Michael's, I am the man. I claim to be the instigator of the high crime (as the slaveholders regard it), and I kept life in it, until life could be kept in it no longer.

Pending the time of our contemplated departure out of our Egypt, we met often by night, and on every Sunday. At these meetings we talked the matter over; told our hopes and fears, and the difficulties discovered or imagined; and, like men of sense, we counted the cost of the enterprise to which we were committing ourselves.

These meetings must have resembled, on a small scale, the meetings of revolutionary conspirators, in their primary condition. We were plotting against our (so-called) lawful rulers; with this difference—that we sought our own good, and not the harm of our enemies. We did not seek to overthrow them, but to escape from them. As for Mr. Freeland, we all liked him, and would have gladly remained with him, as free men. LIBERTY was our aim; and we had now come to think that we had a right to liberty, against every obstacle—even against the lives of our enslavers.

We had several words, expressive of things, important to us, which we understood, but which, even if distinctly heard by an outsider, would convey no certain meaning. I have reasons for suppressing these pass-words, which the reader will easily divine. I hated the secrecy; but where slavery is powerful, and liberty is weak, the latter is driven to concealment or to destruction.

The prospect was not always a bright one. At times, we were almost tempted to abandon the enterprise, and to get back to that comparative peace of mind, which even a man under the gallows might feel, when all hope of escape had vanished. Quiet bondage was felt to be better than the doubts, fears and uncertainties, which now so sadly perplexed and disturbed us.

The infirmities of humanity, generally, were represented in our little band. We were confident, bold and determined, at times; and, again, doubting, timid and wavering; whistling, like the boy in the graveyard, to keep away the spirits.

To look at the map, and observe the proximity of Eastern Shore, Maryland, to Delaware and Pennsylvania, it may seem to the reader quite absurd, to regard the proposed escape as a formidable undertaking. But to understand, some one has said, a man must stand under. The real distance was great enough, but the imagined distance was, to our ignorance, even greater. Every slaveholder seeks to impress his slave with a belief in the boundlessness of slave territory, and of his own almost illimitable power. We all had vague and indistinct notions of the geography of the country.

The distance, however, is not the chief trouble. The nearer are the lines of a slave state and the borders of a free one, the greater the peril. Hired kidnappers infest these borders. Then, too, we knew that merely reaching a free state did not free us; that, wherever caught, we could be returned to slavery. We could see no spot on this side [of] the ocean, where we could be free. We had heard of Canada, the real Canaan of the American bondmen, simply as a country to which the wild goose and the swan repaired at the end of winter, to escape the heat of summer, but not as the home of man. I knew something of theology, but nothing of geography. I really did not, at that time, know that there was a state of New York, or a state of Massachusetts. I had heard of Pennsylvania, Delaware and New Jersey, and all the southern states, but was ignorant of the free states, generally. New York city was our northern limit, and to go there, and to be forever harassed with the liability of being hunted down and returned to slavery—with the certainty of being treated ten times worse than we had ever been treated before—was a prospect far from delightful, and it might well cause some hesitation about engaging in the enterprise. The case, sometimes, to our excited visions, stood thus: At every gate through which we had to pass, we saw a watchman; at every ferry, a guard; on every bridge, a sentinel; and in every wood, a patrol or slave-hunter. We were hemmed in on every side. The good to be sought, and the evil to be shunned, were flung in the balance, and weighed against each other. On the one hand, there stood slavery; a stern reality, glaring frightfully upon us, with the blood of millions in his polluted skirts—terrible to behold—greedily devouring our hard earnings and feeding himself upon our flesh. Here was the evil from which to escape. On the other hand, far away, back in the hazy distance, where all forms seemed but shadows, under the flickering light of the north star—behind some craggy hill or snow-covered mountain—stood a doubtful freedom, half frozen, beckoning us to her icy domain. This was the good to be sought. The inequality was as great as that between certainty and uncertainty. This, in itself, was enough to stagger us; but when we came to survey the untrodden road, and conjecture the many possible difficulties, we were appalled, and at times, as I have said, were upon the point of giving over the struggle altogether.

The reader can have little idea of the phantoms of trouble which flit, in such circumstances, before the uneducated mind of the slave. Upon either side, we saw grim death assuming a variety of horrid shapes. Now, it was starvation, causing us, in a strange and friendless land, to eat our own flesh. Now, we were contending with the waves, for our journey was in part by water, and were drowned. Now, we were hunted by dogs, and overtaken and torn to pieces by their merciless fangs. We were stung by scorpions—chased by wild beasts—bitten by snakes; and, worst of all, after having succeeded in swimming rivers—encountering wild beasts—sleeping in the woods—suffering hunger, cold, heat and nakedness—we supposed ourselves to be overtaken by hired kidnappers, who, in the name of the law, and for their thrice accursed reward, would, perchance, fire upon us—kill some, wound others, and capture all. This dark picture, drawn by ignorance and fear, at times greatly shook our determination, and not unfrequently caused us to

> Rather bear those ills we had
> Than fly to others which we knew not of.

I am not disposed to magnify this circumstance in my experience, and yet I think I shall seem to be so disposed, to the reader. No man can tell the intense agony which is felt by the slave, when wavering on the point of making his escape. All that he has is at stake; and even that which he has not, is at stake, also. The life which he has, may be lost, and the liberty which he seeks, may not be gained.

Patrick Henry, to a listening senate, thrilled by his magic eloquence, and ready to stand by him in his boldest flights, could say, "GIVE ME LIBERTY OR GIVE ME DEATH," and this saying was a sublime one, even for a freeman; but, incomparably more sublime, is the same sentiment, when practically asserted by men accustomed to the lash and chain—men whose sensibilities must have become more or less deadened by their bondage. With us it was a doubtful liberty, at best, that we sought; and a certain, lingering death in the rice swamps and sugar fields, if we failed. Life is not lightly regarded by men of sane minds. It is precious, alike to the pauper and to the prince—to the slave, and to his master; and yet, I believe there was not one among us, who would not rather have been shot down, than pass away life in hopeless bondage.

In the progress of our preparations, Sandy, the root man, became troubled. He began to have dreams, and some of them were very distressing. One of these, which happened on a Friday night, was, to him, of great significance; and I am quite ready to confess, that I felt somewhat damped by it myself. He said, "I dreamed, last night, that I was roused from sleep, by strange noises, like the voices of a swarm of angry birds, that caused a roar as they passed, which fell upon my ear like a coming gale over the tops of the trees. Looking up to see what it could mean," said Sandy, "I saw you, Frederick, in the claws of a huge bird, surrounded by a large number of birds, of all colors and sizes. These were all picking at you, while you, with your arms, seemed to be trying to protect your eyes. Passing over me, the birds flew in a south-westerly direction, and I watched them until they were clean out of sight. Now, I saw this as plainly as I now see you; and furder, honey, watch de Friday night dream; dere is sumpon in it, shose you born; dare is, indeed, honey."

I confess I did not like this dream; but I threw off concern about it, by attributing it to the general excitement and perturbation consequent upon our contemplated plan of escape. I could not, however, shake off its effect at once. I felt that it boded me no good. Sandy was unusually emphatic and oracular, and his manner had much to do with the impression made upon me.

The plan of escape which I recommended, and to which my comrades assented, was to take a large canoe, owned by Mr. Hamilton, and, on the Saturday night previous to the Easter holidays, launch out into the Chesapeake Bay, and paddle for its head—a distance of seventy miles—with all our might. Our course, on reaching this point, was, to turn the canoe adrift, and bend our steps toward the north star, till we reached a free state.

There were several objections to this plan. One was, the danger from gales on the bay. In rough weather, the waters of the Chesapeake are much agitated, and there is danger, in a canoe, of being swamped by the waves. Another objection was, that the canoe would soon be missed; the absent persons would, at once, be suspected of having taken it; and we should be pursued by some of the fast-sailing bay craft out of St. Michael's. Then, again, if we reached the head of the bay, and turned the canoe adrift, she might prove a guide to our track, and bring the land hunters after us.

These and other objections were set aside, by the stronger ones which could be urged against every other plan that could then be suggested. On the water, we had a chance of being regarded as fishermen, in the service of a master. On the other hand, by taking the land route, through the counties adjoining Delaware, we should be subjected to all manner of interruptions, and many very disagreeable questions, which might give us serious trouble. Any white man is authorized to stop a man of color, on any road, and examine him, and arrest him, if he so desires.

By this arrangement, many abuses (considered such even by slaveholders) occur. Cases have been known, where freemen have been called upon to show their free papers, by a pack of ruffians—and, on the presentation of the papers, the ruffians have torn them up, and seized their victim, and sold him to a life of endless bondage.

The week before our intended start, I wrote a pass for each of our party, giving them permission to visit Baltimore, during the Easter holidays. The pass ran after this manner:

> This is to certify, that I, the undersigned, have given the bearer, my servant, John, full liberty to go to Baltimore, to spend the Easter holidays.
>
> W. H.
>
> Near St. Michaels, Talbot County, Maryland.

Although we were not going to Baltimore, and were intending to land east of North Point, in the direction where I had seen the Philadelphia steamers go, these passes might be made useful to us in the lower part of the bay, while steering toward Baltimore. These were not, however, to be shown by us, until all other answers failed to satisfy the inquirer. We were all fully alive to the importance of being calm and self-possessed, when accosted, if accosted we should be; and we more times than one rehearsed to each other how we should behave in the hour of trial.

Those were long, tedious days and nights. The suspense was painful, in the extreme. To balance probabilities, where life and liberty hang on the result, requires steady nerves. I panted for action, and was glad when the day, at the close of which we were to start, dawned upon us. Sleeping, the night before, was out of the question. I probably felt more deeply than any of my companions, because I was the instigator of the movement. The responsibility of the whole enterprise rested on my shoulders. The glory of success, and the shame and confusion of failure, could not be matters of indifference to me. Our food was prepared; our clothes were packed up; we were all ready to go, and impatient for Saturday morning—considering that the last morning of our bondage.

I cannot describe the tempest and tumult of my brain, that morning. The reader will please to bear in mind, that, in a slave state, an unsuccessful runaway is not only subjected to cruel torture, and sold away to the far south, but he is frequently execrated by the other slaves. He is charged with making the condition of the other slaves intolerable, by laying them all under the suspicion of their masters—subjecting them to greater vigilance, and imposing greater limitations on their privileges. I dreaded murmurs from this quarter. It is difficult, too, for a slave-master to believe that slaves escaping have not been aided in their flight by some one of their fellow slaves. When, therefore, a slave is missing, every slave on the place is closely examined as to his knowledge of the undertaking; and they are sometimes even tortured, to make them disclose what they are suspected of knowing of such escape

Our anxiety grew more and more intense, as the time of our intended departure for the north drew nigh. It was truly felt to be a matter of life and death with us; and we fully intended to fight as well as run, if necessity should occur for that extremity. But the trial hour was not yet come. It was easy to resolve, but not so easy to act. I expected there might be some drawing back, at the last. It was natural that there should be; therefore, during the intervening time, I lost no opportunity to explain away difficulties, to remove doubts, to dispel fears, and to inspire all with firmness. It was too late to look back; and now was the time to go forward. Like most other men, we had done the talking part of our work, long and well; and the time had come to act as if we were in earnest, and meant to be as true in action as in words. I did not forget to appeal to the pride of my comrades, by telling them that, if after having solemnly promised to go, as they had done, they now failed to make the attempt, they would, in effect, brand themselves with cowardice, and might as well sit down, fold their arms, and acknowledge themselves as fit only to be slaves. This detestable character, all were unwilling to assume. Every man except Sandy (he, much to our regret, withdrew) stood firm; and at our last meeting we pledged ourselves afresh, and in the most solemn manner, that, at the time appointed, we would certainly start on our long journey for a free country. This meeting was in the middle of the week, at the end of which we were to start.

Early that morning we went, as usual, to the field, but with hearts that beat quickly and anxiously. Any one intimately acquainted with us, might have seen that all was not well with us, and that some monster lingered in our thoughts. Our work that morning was the same as it had been for several days past—drawing out and spreading manure. While thus engaged, I had a sudden presentiment, which flashed upon me like lightning in a dark night, revealing to the lonely traveler the gulf before, and the enemy behind. I instantly turned to Sandy Jenkins, who was near me, and said to him, "Sandy, we are betrayed; something has just told me so." I felt as sure of it, as if the officers were there in sight. Sandy said, "Man, dat is strange; but I feel just as you do." If my mother—then long in her grave—had appeared before me, and told me that we were betrayed, I could not, at that moment, have felt more certain of the fact.

In a few minutes after this, the long, low and distant notes of the horn summoned us from the field to breakfast. I felt as one may be supposed to feel before being led forth to be executed for some great offense. I wanted no breakfast; but I went with the other slaves toward the house, for form's sake. My feelings were not disturbed as to the right of running away; on that point I had no trouble, whatever. My anxiety arose from a sense of the consequences of failure.

In thirty minutes after that vivid presentiment, came the apprehended crash. On reaching the house, for breakfast, and glancing my eye toward the lane gate, the worst was at once made known. The lane gate of Mr. Freeland's house, is nearly a half a mile from the door, and much shaded by the heavy wood which bordered the main road. I was, however, able to descry four white men, and two colored men, approaching. The white men were on horseback, and the colored men were walking behind, and seemed to be tied. "It is all over with us," thought I, "we are surely betrayed." I now became composed, or at least comparatively so, and calmly awaited the result. I watched the ill-omened company, till I saw them enter the gate. Successful flight was impossible, and I made up my mind to stand, and meet the evil, whatever it might be; for I was now not without a slight hope that things might turn differently from what I at first expected. In a few moments, in came Mr. William Hamilton, riding very rapidly, and evidently much excited. He was in the habit of riding very slowly, and was seldom known to gallop his horse. This time, his horse was nearly at full speed, causing the dust to roll thick behind him. Mr. Hamilton, though one of the most resolute men in the whole neighborhood, was, nevertheless, a remarkably mild spoken man; and, even when greatly excited, his language was cool and circumspect. He came to the door, and inquired if Mr. Freeland was in. I told him that Mr. Freeland was at the barn. Off the old gentleman rode, toward the barn, with unwonted speed. Mary, the cook, was at a loss to know what was the matter, and I did not profess any skill in making her understand. I knew she would have united, as readily as any one, in cursing me for bringing trouble into the family; so I held my peace, leaving matters to develop themselves, without my assistance. In a few moments, Mr. Hamilton and Mr. Freeland came down from the barn to the house; and, just as they made their appearance in the front yard, three men (who proved to be constables) came dashing into the lane, on horseback, as if summoned by a sign requiring quick work. A few seconds brought them into the front yard, where they hastily dismounted, and tied their horses.

This done, they joined Mr. Freeland and Mr. Hamilton, who were standing a short distance from the kitchen. A few moments were spent, as if in consulting how to proceed, and then the whole party walked up to the kitchen door. There was now no one in the kitchen but myself and John Harris. Henry and Sandy were yet at the barn. Mr. Freeland came inside the kitchen door, and with an agitated voice, called me by name, and told me to come forward; that there were some gentlemen who wished to see me. I stepped toward them, at the door, and asked what they wanted, when the constables grabbed me, and told me that I had better not resist; that I had been in a scrape, or was said to have been in one; that they were merely going to take me where I could be examined; that they were going to carry me to St. Michael's, to have me brought before my master. They further said, that, in case the evidence against me was not true, I should be acquitted. I was now firmly tied, and completely at the mercy of my captors. Resistance was idle. They were five in number, armed to the very teeth. When they had secured me, they next turned to John Harris, and, in a few moments, succeeded in tying him as firmly as they had already tied me. They next turned toward Henry Harris, who had now returned from the barn. "Cross your hands," said the constables, to Henry. "I won't," said Henry, in a voice so firm and clear, and in a manner so determined, as for a moment to arrest all proceedings. "Won't you cross your hands?" said Tom Graham, the constable. "No I won't," said Henry, with increasing emphasis. Mr. Hamilton, Mr. Freeland, and the officers, now came near to Henry. Two of the constables drew out their shining pistols, and swore by the name of God, that he should cross his hands, or they would shoot him down. Each of these hired ruffians now cocked their pistols, and, with fingers apparently on the triggers, presented their deadly weapons to the breast of the unarmed slave, saying, at the same time, if he did not cross his hands, they would "blow his d—d heart out of him."

"Shoot! shoot me!" said Henry. "You can't kill me but once. Shoot!—shoot! and be d—d. I won't be tied." This, the brave fellow said in a voice as defiant and heroic in its tone, as was the language itself; and, at the moment of saying this, with the pistols at his very breast, he quickly raised his arms, and dashed them from the puny hands of his assassins, the weapons flying in opposite directions. Now came the struggle. All hands now rushed upon the brave fellow, and, after beating him for some time, they succeeded in overpowering and tying him. Henry put me to shame; he fought, and fought bravely. John and I had made no resistance. The fact is, I never see much use in fighting, unless there is a reasonable probability of whipping somebody. Yet there was something almost providential in the resistance made by the gallant Henry. But for that resistance, every soul of us would have been hurried off to the far south. Just a moment previous to the trouble with Henry, Mr. Hamilton mildly said—and this gave me the unmistakable clue to the cause of our arrest—"Perhaps we had now better make a search for those protections, which we understand Frederick has written for himself and the rest." Had these passes been found, they would have been point-blank proof against us, and would have confirmed all the statements of our betrayer. Thanks to the resistance of Henry, the excitement produced by the scuffle drew all attention in that direction, and I succeeded in flinging my pass, unobserved, into the fire.

The confusion attendant upon the scuffle, and the apprehension of further trouble, perhaps, led our captors to forego, for the present, any search for "those protections" which Frederick was said to have written for his companions; so we were not yet convicted of the purpose to run away; and it was evident that there was some doubt, on the part of all, whether we had been guilty of such a purpose.

Just as we were all completely tied, and about ready to start toward St. Michael's, and thence to jail, Mrs. Betsey Freeland (mother to William, who was very much attached—after the southern fashion—to Henry and John, they having been reared from childhood in her house) came to the kitchen door, with her hands full of biscuits, for we had not had time to take our breakfast that morning—and divided them between Henry and John. This done, the lady made the following parting address to me, looking and pointing her bony finger at me. "You devil! you yellow devil! It was you that put it into the heads of Henry and John to run away. But for you, you long-legged yellow devil, Henry and John would never have thought of running away." I gave the lady a look, which called forth a scream of mingled wrath and terror, as she slammed the kitchen door, and went in, leaving me, with the rest, in hands as harsh as her own broken voice.

Could the kind reader have been quietly riding along the main road to or from Easton, that morning, his eye would have met a painful sight. He would have seen five young men, guilty of no crime, save that of preferring liberty to a life of bondage, drawn along the public highway—firmly bound together—tramping through dust and heat, bare-footed and bare-headed—fastened to three strong horses, whose riders were armed to the teeth, with pistols and daggers—on their way to prison, like felons, and suffering every possible insult from the crowds of idle, vulgar people, who clustered around, and heartlessly made their failure the occasion for all manner of ribaldry and sport. As I looked upon this crowd of vile persons, and saw myself and friends thus assailed and persecuted, I could not help seeing the fulfillment of Sandy's dream. I was in the hands of moral vultures, and firmly held in their sharp talons, and was being hurried away toward Easton, in a south-easterly direction, amid the jeers of new birds of the same feather, through every neighborhood we passed. It seemed to me (and this shows the good understanding between the slaveholders and their allies) that everybody we met knew the cause of our arrest, and were out, awaiting our passing by, to feast their vindictive eyes on our misery and to gloat over our ruin.

Some said, I ought to be hanged, and others, I ought to be burnt; others, I ought to have the "hide" taken from my back; while no one gave us a kind word or sympathizing look, except the poor slaves, who were lifting their heavy hoes, and who cautiously glanced at us through the post-and-rail fences, behind which they were at work. Our sufferings, that morning, can be more easily imagined than described. Our hopes were all blasted, at a blow. The cruel injustice, the victorious crime, and the helplessness of innocence, led me to ask, in my ignorance and weakness—"Where now is the God of justice and mercy? and why have these wicked men the power thus to trample upon our rights, and to insult our feelings?" And yet, in the next moment, came the consoling thought, "the day of the oppressor will come at last." Of one thing I could be glad—not one of my dear friends, upon whom I had brought this great calamity, either by word or look, reproached me for having led them into it. We were a band of brothers, and never dearer to each other than now. The thought which gave us the most pain, was the probable separation which would now take place, in case we were sold off to the far south, as we were likely to be. While the constables were looking forward, Henry and I, being fastened together, could occasionally exchange a word, without being observed by the kidnappers who had us in charge. "What shall I do with my pass?" said Henry. "Eat it with your biscuit, said I;

"It won't do to tear it up." We were now near St. Michael's. The direction concerning the passes was passed around, and executed. "Own nothing!" said I. "Own nothing!" was passed around and enjoined, and assented to. Our confidence in each other was unshaken; and we were quite resolved to succeed or fail together—as much after the calamity which had befallen us, as before.

On reaching St. Michael's, we underwent a sort of examination at my master's store, and it was evident to my mind, that Master Thomas suspected the truthfulness of the evidence upon which they had acted in arresting us; and that he only affected, to some extent, the positiveness with which he asserted our guilt. There was nothing said by any of our company, which could, in any manner, prejudice our cause; and there was hope, yet, that we should be able to return to our homes—if for nothing else, at least to find out the guilty man or woman who had betrayed us.

To this end, we all denied that we had been guilty of intended flight. Master Thomas said that the evidence he had of our intention to run away, was strong enough to hang us, in a case of murder. "But," said I, "the cases are not equal. If murder were committed, some one must have committed it—the thing is done! In our case, nothing has been done! We have not run away. Where is the evidence against us? We were quietly at our work." I talked thus, with unusual freedom, to bring out the evidence against us, for we all wanted, above all things, to know the guilty wretch who had betrayed us, that we might have something tangible upon which to pour our execrations. From something which dropped, in the course of the talk, it appeared that there was but one witness against us—and that that witness could not be produced. Master Thomas would not tell us who his informant was; but we suspected, and suspected one person only. Several circumstances seemed to point SANDY out, as our betrayer. His entire knowledge of our plans—his participation in them—his withdrawal from us—his dream, and his simultaneous presentiment that we were betrayed—the taking us, and the leaving him—were calculated to turn suspicion toward him; and yet, we could not suspect him. We all loved him too well to think it possible that he could have betrayed us. So we rolled the guilt on other shoulders.

We were literally dragged, that morning, behind horses, a distance of fifteen miles, and placed in the Easton jail. We were glad to reach the end of our journey, for our pathway had been the scene of insult and mortification. Such is the power of public opinion, that it is hard, even for the innocent, to feel the happy consolations of innocence, when they fall under the maledictions of this power. How could we regard ourselves as in the right, when all about us denounced us as criminals, and had the power and the disposition to treat us as such.

In jail, we were placed under the care of Mr. Joseph Graham, the sheriff of the county. Henry, and John, and myself, were placed in one room, and Henry Baily and Charles Roberts, in another, by themselves. This separation was intended to deprive us of the advantage of concert, and to prevent trouble in jail.

Once shut up, a new set of tormentors came upon us. A swarm of imps, in human shape—the slave-traders, deputy slave-traders, and agents of slave-traders—that gather in every country town of the state, watching for chances to buy human flesh (as buzzards to eat carrion) flocked in upon us, to ascertain if our masters had placed us in jail to be sold. Such a set of debased and villainous creatures, I never saw before, and hope never to see again. I felt myself surrounded as by a pack of fiends, fresh from perdition. They laughed, leered, and grinned at us; saying, "Ah! boys, we've got you, havn't we? So you were about to make your escape? Where were you going to?" After taunting us, and jeering at us, as long as they liked, they one by one subjected us to an examination, with a view to ascertain our value; feeling our arms and legs, and shaking us by the shoulders to see if we were sound and healthy; impudently asking us how we would like to have them for masters. To such questions, we were, very much to their annoyance, quite dumb, disdaining to answer them. For one, I detested the whisky-bloated gamblers in human flesh; and I believe I was as much detested by them in turn. One fellow told me, If he had me, he would cut the devil out of me pretty quick.

These negro buyers are very offensive to the genteel southern Christian public. They are looked upon, in respectable Maryland society, as necessary, but detestable characters. As a class, they are hardened ruffians, made such by nature and by occupation. Their ears are made quite familiar with the agonizing cry of outraged and woe-smitten humanity. Their eyes are forever open to human misery. They walk amid desecrated affections, insulted virtue, and blasted hopes. They have grown intimate with vice and blood; they gloat over the wildest illustrations of their soul-damning and earth-polluting business, and are moral pests. Yes; they are a legitimate fruit of slavery; and it is a puzzle to make out a case of greater villainy for them, than for the slaveholders, who make such a class possible. They are mere hucksters of the surplus slave produce of Maryland and Virginia—coarse, cruel, and swaggering bullies, whose very breathing is of blasphemy and blood.

Aside from these slave-buyers, who infested the prison, from time to time, our quarters were much more comfortable than we had any right to expect they would be. Our allowance of food was small and coarse, but our room was the best in the jail—neat and spacious, and with nothing about it necessarily reminding us of being in prison, but its heavy locks and bolts and the black, iron lattice-work at the windows. We were prisoners of state, compared with most slaves who are put into that Easton jail. But the place was not one of contentment. Bolts, bars and grated windows are not acceptable to freedom-loving people of any color. The suspense, too, was painful. Every step on the stairway was listened to, in the hope that the comer would cast a ray of light on our fate. We would have given the hair off our heads for half a dozen words with one of the waiters in Sol. Lowe's hotel. Such waiters were in the way of hearing, at the table, the probable course of things. We could see them flitting about in their white jackets, in front of this hotel, but could speak to none of them.

Soon after the holidays were over, contrary to all our expectations, Messrs. Hamilton and Freeland came up to Easton; not to make a bargain with the "Georgia traders," nor to send us up to Austin Woldfolk, as is usual in the case of run-away slaves, but to release Charles, Henry Harris, Henry Baily and John Harris, from prison, and this, too, without the infliction of a single blow. I was now left entirely alone in prison. The innocent had been taken, and the guilty left. My friends were separated from me, and apparently forever. This circumstance caused me more pain than any other incident connected with our capture and imprisonment. Thirty-nine lashes on my naked and bleeding back, would have been joyfully borne, in preference to this separation from these, the friends of my youth. And yet, I could not but feel that I was the victim of something like justice. Why should these young men, who were led into this scheme by me, suffer as much as the instigator? I felt glad that they were released from prison, and from the dread prospect of a life (or death I should rather say) in the rice swamps. It is due to the noble Henry, to say, that he seemed almost as reluctant to leave the prison with me in it, as he was to be tied and dragged to prison. But he and the rest knew that we should, in all the likelihoods of the case, be separated, in the event of being sold; and since we were now completely in the hands of our owners, we all concluded it would be best to go peaceably home.

Not until this last separation, dear reader, had I touched those profounder depths of desolation, which it is the lot of slaves often to reach. I was solitary in the world, and alone within the walls of a stone prison, left to a fate of life-long misery. I had hoped and expected much, for months before, but my hopes and expectations were now withered and blasted. The ever-dreaded slave life in Georgia, Louisiana and Alabama—from which escape is next to impossible—now, in my loneliness, stared me in the face. The possibility of ever becoming anything but an abject slave, a mere machine in the hands of an owner, had now fled, and it seemed to me it had fled forever. A life of living death, beset with the innumerable horrors of the cotton field, and the sugar plantation, seemed to be my doom. The fiends, who rushed into the prison when we were first put there, continued to visit me, and to ply me with questions and with their tantalizing remarks. I was insulted, but helpless; keenly alive to the demands of justice and liberty, but with no means of asserting them. To talk to those imps about justice and mercy, would have been as absurd as to reason with bears and tigers. Lead and steel are the only arguments that they understand.

After remaining in this life of misery and despair about a week, which, by the way, seemed a month, Master Thomas, very much to my surprise, and greatly to my relief, came to the prison, and took me out, for the purpose, as he said, of sending me to Alabama, with a friend of his, who would emancipate me at the end of eight years. I was glad enough to get out of prison; but I had no faith in the story that this friend of Capt. Auld would emancipate me, at the end of the time indicated. Besides, I never had heard of his having a friend in Alabama, and I took the announcement, simply as an easy and comfortable method of shipping me off to the far south. There was a little scandal, too, connected with the idea of one Christian selling another to the Georgia traders, while it was deemed every way proper for them to sell to others. I thought this friend in Alabama was an invention, to meet this difficulty, for Master Thomas was quite jealous of his Christian reputation, however unconcerned he might be about his real Christian character. In these remarks, however, it is possible that I do Master Thomas Auld injustice. He certainly did not exhaust his power upon me, in the case, but acted, upon the whole, very generously, considering the nature of my offense. He had the power and the provocation to send me, without reserve, into the very everglades of Florida, beyond the remotest hope of emancipation; and his refusal to exercise that power, must be set down to his credit.

After lingering about St. Michael's a few days, and no friend from Alabama making his appearance, to take me there, Master Thomas decided to send me back again to Baltimore, to live with his brother Hugh, with whom he was now at peace; possibly he became so by his profession of religion, at the camp-meeting in the Bay Side. Master Thomas told me that he wished me to go to Baltimore, and learn a trade; and that, if I behaved myself properly, he would emancipate me at twenty-five! Thanks for this one beam of hope in the future. The promise had but one fault; it seemed too good to be true.

FIVE

CRAZY HORSE

"I Have Spoken" (1877)

LAKOTA WARRIOR CRAZY HORSE WAS BLEEDING out when he provided this deathbed testimony. While Crazy Horse was attempting to escape detention at Fort Robinson, Nebraska, to visit his sick wife forty miles away, a private in the US military lethally stabbed him with a bayonet. It wasn't the first time Crazy Horse had fought back. *Tasunke Witco*, also known as Crazy Horse, was born a member of the Oglala Lakota circa 1840 and was a full-fledged warrior by the time he reached his teens. Throughout the 1860s and 1870s, he was known for forging coalitions to resist forced resettlement on reservations. In 1876, Crazy Horse led a successful attack against Custer's Seventh US Cavalry battalion in what has come to be known variously as the Battle of the Little Bighorn, Custer's Last Stand, and the Battle of the Greasy Grass.

"In the Spirit of Crazy Horse!" remains a rallying cry for those who continue to fight the legacies of settler colonialism, white supremacy, and prisons. Through his struggle—and all the struggles of First Nation peoples—we understand that sometimes the price of dignity and freedom is not just prison, but death.

MY FRIEND, I do not blame you for this. Had I listened to you this trouble would not have happened to me. I was not hostile to the white man. Sometimes my young men would attack the Indians who were their enemies and took their ponies. They did it in return.

We had buffalo for food, and their hides for clothing and our tepees. We preferred hunting to a life of idleness on the reservations, where we were driven against our will. At times we did not get enough to eat, and we were not allowed to leave the reservation to hunt.

We preferred our own way of living. We were no expense to the government then. All we wanted was peace and to be left alone. Soldiers were sent out in the winter, who destroyed our villages. [He referred to the winter before, when his village was destroyed by Colonel Reynolds, Third Cavalry.] Then Long Hair [Custer] came in the same way. They say we massacred him, but he would have done the same to us had we not defended ourselves and fought to the last. Our first impulse was to escape with our squaws[5] and papooses, but we were so hemmed in that we had to fight.

After that I went up on Tongue River with a few of my people and lived in peace. But the government would not let me alone. Finally, I came back to Red Cloud agency. Yet I was not allowed to remain quiet. I was tired of fighting. I went to Spotted Tail agency and asked that chief and his agent to let me live there in peace. I came here with the agent [Lee] to talk with the big white chief, but was not given a chance. They tried to confine me, I tried to escape, and a soldier ran his bayonet into me. I have spoken.

SIX

EUGENE DEBS

Prison Labor, Its Effect on Industry and Trade

(1899)

NAMED AFTER THE FRENCH AUTHORS EUGÈNE SUE and Victor Hugo, Eugene Victor "Gene" Debs was born on November 5, 1855, in Terre Haute, Indiana. The term "prison-industrial complex" did not exist in 1899 when he delivered this speech, but Debs, later to be known as Prisoner 9653, lays out a blistering critique of incarceration, the convict-leasing system, and the economic and social ramifications of the prison system in general. Debs emphasizes how prisons prey on the poor, fail to produce reform, and likely increase crime. Moreover, he claims prison enables a privileged few to profit from the crimes of others and often leaves people worse off after prison than they were before. Put simply, Debs argues that prison perpetuates slavery.

When he delivered this address, Debs had already been sent to prison once for his role in organizing the national railroad strike against the Pullman Palace Car Company. As with so many others before and since, the experience of incarceration further radicalized him and inspired him to become socialist. He went to prison again in 1918, this time for his opposition to our nation's role in World War I. He was sentenced to ten years, of which he served two before receiving a presidential pardon.

A prisoner with a poison pen, Debs remained a thorn in the side of the status quo as a worker, unionist, and enemy of the capitalist class. He ran for president five times on the Socialist ticket. His fifth and final run was managed from his prison cell. Alas, he did not go from prisoner to president, as

Nelson Mandela did decades later in South Africa, but he did get nearly a million votes.

Debs warned that capitalism would never release its hold on prison labor. This has proved to be true, even with the demise of the convict-leasing program. Prison labor, he told us, was a symptom indicating a sick system, and capitalism was the root of the problem. Debs died October 20, 1926, at the age of seventy.

IN MY early years I stood before the open door of a blazing furnace and piled in the fuel to create steam to speed a locomotive along the iron track of progress and civilization. In the costume of the craft, through the grime of mingled sweat and smoke and dust I was initiated into the great brotherhood of labor. The locomotive was my alma mater. I mastered the curriculum and graduated with the degree of D. D., not, as the lexicons interpret the letters, "Doctor of Divinity," but that better signification, "Do and Dare"—a higher degree than Aristotle conferred in his Lyceum or Plato thundered from his academy.

I am not in the habit of telling how little I know about Latin to those who have slaked their thirst for learning at the Pierian springs, but there is a proverb that has come down to us from the dim past which reads "Omnia vincit labor" and which has been adopted as the shibboleth of the American labor movement because, when reduced to English, it reads "Labor overcomes all things." In a certain sense this is true. Labor has built this great metropolis of the new world, built it as coral insects build the foundations of islands—build and die; build from the fathomless depth of the ocean until the mountain billows are dashed into spray as they beat against the fortifications beneath which the builders are forever entombed and forgotten.

Here in this proud city where wealth has built its monuments grander and more imposing than any of the seven wonders of the world named in classic lore, if you will excavate for facts you will find the remains, the bones of the toilers, buried and imbedded in their foundations. They lived, they wrought, they died. In their time they may have laughed and sung and danced to the music of their clanking chains. They married, propagated their species, and perpetuated conditions which, growing steadily worse, are today the foulest blots the imagination can conceive upon our much-vaunted civilization.

And from these conditions there flow a thousand streams of vice and crime which have broadened and deepened until they constitute a perpetual menace to the peace and security of society. Jails, workhouses, reformatories and penitentiaries have been crowded with victims, and the question how to control these institutions and their unfortunate inmates is challenging the most serious thought of the most advanced nations on the globe.

The particular phase of this grave and melancholy question which we are to consider this evening is embodied in the subject assigned the speakers: "Prison Labor, Its Effects on Industry and Trade."

I must confess that it would have suited my purpose better had the subject been transposed so as to read: "Industry and Trade, Their Effect on Labor," for, as a Socialist, I am convinced that the prison problem is rooted in the present system of industry and trade, carried forward, as it is, purely for private profit without the slightest regard to the effect upon those engaged in it, especially the men, women and children who perform the useful, productive labor which has created all wealth and all civilization.

Serious as is the problem presented in the subject of our discussion, it is yet insignificant when compared with the vastly greater question of the effect of our social and economic system upon industry and trade.

The pernicious effect of prison contract labor upon "free labor," so called, when brought into competition with it in the open market, is universally conceded, but it should not be overlooked that prison labor is itself an effect and not a cause, and that convict labor is recruited almost wholly from the propertyless, wage-working class and that the inhuman system which has reduced a comparative few from enforced idleness to crime, has sunk the whole mass of labor to the dead level of industrial servitude.

It is therefore with the economic system, which is responsible for, not only prison labor, but for the gradual enslavement and degradation of all labor, that we must deal before there can be any solution of the prison labor problem or any permanent relief from its demoralizing influences.

But we will briefly consider the effect of prison labor upon industry and then pass to the larger question of the cause of prison labor and its appalling increase, to which the discussion logically leads.

From the earliest ages there has been a prison problem. The ancients had their bastilles and their dungeons. Most of the pioneers of progress, the haters of oppression, the lovers of liberty, whose names now glorify the pantheon of the world, made such institutions a necessity in their day. But civilization advances, however slowly, and there has been some progress. It required five hundred years to travel from the inquisition to the injunction.

In the earlier days punishment was the sole purpose of imprisonment. Offenders against the ruling class must pay the penalty in [a] prison cell, which, not infrequently, was equipped with instruments of torture. With the civilizing process came the idea of the reformation of the culprit, and this idea prompts every investigation made of the latter-day problem. The inmates must be set to work for their own good, no less than for the good of the state.

It was at this point that the convict labor problem began and it has steadily expanded from that time to this, and while there have been some temporary modifications of the evil, it is still an unmitigated curse from which there can be no escape while an economic system endures in which labor, that is to say the laborer, man, woman and child, is sold to the lowest bidder in the markets of the world.

More than thirty years ago Professor E. C. Wines and Professor Theodore W. Dwight, then commissioners of the Prison Association of New York, made a report to the legislature of the state on prison industry in which they said:

> Upon the whole it is our settled conviction that the contract system of convict labor, added to the system of political appointments, which necessarily involves a low grade of official qualification and constant changes in the prison staff, renders nugatory, to a great extent, the whole theory of our penitentiary system. Inspection may correct isolated abuses; philanthropy may relieve isolated cases of distress; and religion may effect isolated moral cures; but genuine, radical, comprehensive, systematic improvement is impossible.

The lapse of thirty years has not affected the wisdom or logic of the conclusion. It is as true now as it was then. Considered in his most favorable light, the convict is a scourge to himself, a menace to society and a burden to industry, and whatever system of convict labor may be tried, it will ultimately fail of its purpose at reformation of the criminal or the relief of industry as long as thousands of "free laborers," who have committed no crime, are unable to get work and make an honest living. Not long ago I visited a penitentiary in which a convict expressed regret that his sentence was soon to expire. Where was he to go, and what was he to do? And how long before he would be sentenced to a longer term for a greater crime?

The commission which investigated the matter in Ohio in 1877 reported to the legislature as follows:

> The contract system interferes in an undue manner with the honest industry of the state. It has been the cause of crippling the business of many of our manufacturers; it has been the cause of driving many of them out of business; it has been the cause of a large percentage of reductions which have taken place in the wages of our mechanics; it has been the cause of pauperizing a large portion of our laborers and increasing crime in a corresponding degree; it has been no benefit to the state; as a reformatory measure it has been a complete, total and miserable failure; it has hardened more criminals than any other cause; it has made total wrecks morally of thousands and thousands who would have been reclaimed from the paths of vice and crime under a proper system of prison management, but who have resigned their fate to a life of hopeless degradation; it has not a single commendable feature. Its tendency is pernicious in the extreme. In short, it is an insurmountable barrier in the way of the reformation of the unfortunates who are compelled to live and labor under its evil influences; it enables a class of men to get rich out of the crimes committed by others; it leaves

> upon the fair escutcheon of the state a relic of the very worst form of human slavery; it is a bone of ceaseless contention between the state and its mechanical and industrial interests; it is abhorred by all and respected by none except those, perhaps, who make profit and gain out of it. It should be tolerated no longer but abolished at once.

And yet this same system is still in effect in many of the states of the Union. The most revolting outrages have been perpetrated upon prison laborers under this diabolical system. Read the official reports and stand aghast at the atrocities committed against these morally deformed and perverted human creatures, your brothers and my brothers, for the private profit of capitalistic exploiters and the advancement of Christian civilization.

What a commentary on the capitalist competitive system! First, men are forced into idleness. Gradually they are driven to the extremity of begging or stealing. Having still a spark of pride and self-respect they steal and are sent to jail. The first sentence seals their doom. The brand of Cain is upon them. They are identified with the criminal class. Society, whose victims they are, has exiled them forever, and with this curse ringing in their ears they proceed on their downward career, sounding every note in the scale of depravity until at last, having graduated in crime all the way from petit larceny to homicide, their last despairing sigh is wrung from them by the hangman's halter. From first to last these unfortunates, the victims of social malformation, are made the subjects of speculation and traffic. The barbed iron of the prison contractor is plunged into their quivering hearts that their torture may be coined into private profit for their exploiters.

In the investigation in South Carolina, where the convicts had been leased to railroad companies, the most shocking disclosure were made. Out of 285 prisoners employed by one company, 128, or more than 40 per cent, died as the result, largely, of brutal treatment.

It is popular to say that society must be protected against its criminals. I prefer to believe that criminals should be protected against society, at least while we live under a system that makes the commission of crime necessary to secure employment.

The Tennessee tragedy is still fresh in the public memory. Here, as elsewhere, the convicts, themselves brutally treated, were used as a means of dragging the whole mine-working class down to their crime-cursed condition. The Tennessee Coal and Iron Company leased the convicts for the express purpose of forcing the wages of miners down to the point of subsistence. Says the official report: "The miners were compelled to work in competition with low-priced convict labor, the presence of which was used by the company as a scourge to force free laborers to its terms." Then the miners, locked out, their families suffering, driven to desperation, appealed to force, and in a twinkling the laws of the state were trampled down, the authorities overpowered and defied, and almost five hundred convicts set at liberty.

Fortunately the system of leasing and contracting prison labor for private exploitation is being exposed and its frightful iniquities laid bare. Thanks to organized labor and to the spirit of prison reform, this horrifying phase of the evil is doomed to disappear before an enlightened public sentiment.

The public account system, though subject to serious criticism, is far less objectionable than either the lease or the contract or the piece-price system. At least the prisoner's infirmities cease to be the prey of speculative greed and conscienceless rapacity.

The system of manufacturing for the use of state, county and municipal institutions, adopted by the state of New York, is an improvement upon those hitherto in effect, but it is certain to develop serious objections in course of time. With the use of modern machinery the limited demand will soon be supplied, and then what? It may be in order to suggest that the prisoners could be employed in making shoes and clothes for the destitute poor and school books for their children and many other articles which the poor sorely need but are unable to buy.

Developing along this line it would be only a question of time until the state would he manufacturing all things for the use of the people, and then perhaps the inquiry would be pertinent: If the state can give men steady employment after they commit crime, and manufacturing can be carried forward successfully by their labor, why can it not give them employment before they are driven to that extremity, thereby preventing them from becoming criminals?

All useful labor is honest labor, even if performed in a prison. Only the labor of exploiters, such as speculators, stock gamblers, beef-embalmers[6] and their mercenary politicians, lawyers and other parasites—only such is dishonest labor. A thief making shoes in a penitentiary is engaged in more useful and therefore more honest labor than a "free" stonemason at work on a palace whose foundations are laid in thc skulls and bones, and cemented in the sweat and blood of ten thousand victims of capitalistic exploitation. In both cases the labor is compulsory. The stonemason would not work for the trust-magnate were he not compelled to.

In ancient times only slaves labored. And as a matter of fact only slaves labor now. The millions are made by the magic of manipulation. The coal miners of West Virginia, Pennsylvania, Ohio, Indiana and Illinois receive an average wage of less than seventy-five cents a day. They perform the most useful and necessary labor, without which your homes, if possible at all, would be cheerless as caves and the great heart of industry would cease to throb. Are they free men, or are they slaves? And what is the effect of their labor on trade and industry and upon themselves and their families? Dante would search the realms of inferno in vain for such pictures of horror and despair as are to be found in the mining regions of free America.

To the student of social science the haggard fact stands forth that under the competitive system of production and distribution the prison problem will never be solved—and its effect upon trade and industry will never be greatly modified. The fact will remain that whatever labor is performed by prison labor could and should be performed by free labor, and when in the march of economic progress the capitalist system of industry for private profit succumbs to the socialist system of industry for human happiness, when the factory, which is now a penitentiary crowded with life convicts, among whom children often constitute the majority—when this factory is transformed into a temple of science, and the machine, myriad-armed and tireless, is the only slave, there will be no prison labor and the problem will cease to vex the world, and to this it is coming in obedience to the economic law, as unerring in its operation as the law of gravitation.

That prison labor is demoralizing in its effect on trade and industry whenever and wherever brought into competition with it, especially under the various forms of the contract system, is of course conceded, but that it has been, or is at present, a great factor in such demoralization is not admitted. There is a tendency to exaggerate the blighting effects of prison labor for the purpose of obscuring the one overshadowing cause of demoralized trade and impoverished industry.

Prison labor did not reduce the miner to a walking hunger-pang, his wife to a tear-stained rag, and his home to a lair. Prison labor is not responsible for the squares of squalor and miles of misery in New York, Chicago and all other centers of population. Prison labor is not chargeable with the sweating dens in which the victims of capitalistic competition crouch in dread and fear until death comes to their rescue. Prison labor had no hand in Coeur d'Alene, Tennessee, Homestead, Hazelton, Virdin, Pana, that suburb of hell called Pullman and other ensanguined industrial battlefields where thousands of workingmen after being oppressed and robbed were imprisoned life felons, and shot down like vagabond dogs; where venal judges issued infamous injunctions and despotic orders at the behest of their masters, enforcing them with deputy marshals armed with pistols and clubs and supported by troops with gleaming bayonets and shotted guns to drain the veins of workingmen of blood, but for whose labor this continent would still be a wilderness. Only the tortures of hunger and nakedness provoked protest, and this was silenced by the bayonet and bullet; by the club and the blood that followed the blow.

Prison labor is not accountable for the appalling increase in insanity, in suicide, in murder, in prostitution and a thousand other forms of vice and crime which pollute every fountain and contaminate every stream designed to bless the world.

Prison labor did not create our army of unemployed, but has been recruited from its ranks, and both owe their existence to the same social and economic system.

Nor are the evil effects confined exclusively to the poor working class. There is an aspect of the case in which the rich are as unfortunate as the poor. The destiny of the capitalist class is irrevocably linked with the working class. Fichte, the great German philosopher, said, "Wickedness increases in proportion to the elevation of rank."

Prison labor is but one of the manifestations of our economic development and indicates its trend. The same cause that demoralized industry has crowded our prisons. Industry has not been impoverished by prison labor, but prison labor is the result of impoverished industry. The limited time at my command will not permit an analysis of the process.

The real question which confronts us is our industrial system and its effects upon labor. One of these effects is, as I have intimated, prison labor. What is its cause? What makes it necessary? The answer is, the competitive system, which creates wage-slavery, throws thousands out of employment and reduces the wages of thousands more to the point of bare subsistence.

Why is prison labor preferred to "free labor"? Simply because it is cheaper; it yields more profit to the man who buys, exploits and sells it. But this has its limitations. Capitalist competition that throngs the streets with idle workers, capitalist production that reduces human labor to a commodity and ultimately to crime—this system produces another kind of prison labor in the form of child labor which is being utilized more and more to complete the subjugation of the working class. There is this difference: The prison laborers are clothed and housed and fed. The child laborers whose wage is a dollar a week, or even less, must take care of themselves.

Prison labor is preferred because it is cheap. So with child labor. It is not a question of prison labor, or of child labor, but of cheap labor.

Tenement-house labor is another form of prison labor.

The effects of cheap labor on trade and industry must be the same, whether such labor is done by prisoners, tenement house slaves, children or starving "hoboes."

The prison laborer produces by machinery in abundance but does not consume. The child likewise produces, but owing to its small wages, does not consume. So with the vast army of workers whose wage grows smaller as the productive capacity of labor increases, and then society is afflicted with overproduction, the result of under-consumption. What follows? The panic. Factories close down, wage-workers are idle and suffer, middle-class business men are forced into bankruptcy, the army of tramps is increased, vice and crime are rampant and prisons and work-houses are filled to overflowing as are sewers when the streets of cities are deluged with floods.

Prison labor, like all cheap labor, is at first a source of profit to the capitalist, but finally it turns into a two-edged sword that cuts into and destroys the system that produced it.

First, the capitalist pocket is filled by the employment of cheap labor—and then the bottom drops out of it.

In the cheapening process, the pauperized mass have lost their consuming power.

The case may now be summed up as follows:

First. Prison labor is bad; it has a demoralizing effect on capitalist trade and industry.

Second. Child labor, tenement house and every other form of cheap labor is bad; it is destructive of trade and industry.

Third. Capitalist competition is bad; it creates a demand for cheap labor.

Fourth. Capitalist production is bad; it creates millionaires and mendicants, economic masters and slaves, thus intensifying the class struggle.

This indicates that the present capitalist system has outlived its usefulness, and that it is in the throes of dissolution. Capitalism is but a link in the chain of social and economic development. Just as feudalism developed capitalism and then disappeared, so capitalism is now developing socialism, and when the new social system has been completely evolved the last vestige of capitalism will fade into history.

The gigantic trust marks the change in production. It is no longer competitive but co-operative. The same mode of distribution, which must inevitably follow, will complete the process.

Co-operative labor will be the basis of the new social system, and this will be for use and not for profit. Labor will no longer be bought and sold. Industrial slavery will cease. For every man there will be the equal right to work with every other man, and each will receive the fruit of his labor. Then we shall have economic equality. Involuntary idleness will be a horror of the past. Poverty will relax its grasp.

The army of tramps will be disbanded because the prolific womb which now warms these unfortunates into life will become barren. Prisons will be depopulated, and the prison labor problem will be solved.

Each labor-saving machine will lighten the burden and decrease the hours of toil. The soul will no longer be subordinated to the stomach. Man will live a complete life, and the march will then begin to an ideal civilization.

There is a proverb which the Latin race sent ringing down the centuries which reads, "Omnia vincit amor," or "Love conquers all things." Love and labor in alliance, working together, have transforming, redeeming and emancipating power. Under their benign sway the world can be made better and brighter.

Isaiah saw in prophetic vision a time when nations should war no more—when swords should be transformed into plowshares and spears into pruning hooks. The fulfillment of the prophecy only awaits an era when love and labor, in holy alliance, shall solve the economic problem.

Here, on this occasion, in this great metropolis with its thousand spires pointing heavenward, where opulence riots in luxury which challenges hyperbole, and poverty rots in sweat shops which only a Shakespeare or a Victor Hugo could describe, and the transfer to canvas would palsy the hand of a Michael Angelo—here, where wealth and want and woe bear irrefutable testimony of deplorable conditions, I stand as a socialist, protesting against the wrongs perpetrated upon Les Miserables, and pleading as best I can for a higher civilization.

The army of begging Lazaruses, with the dogs licking their sores at the gates of palaces, where the rich are clothed in purple and fine linen with their tables groaning beneath the luxuries of all climes, make the palaces on the highland where fashion holds sway, and music lends its charms, a picture in the landscape which, in illustrating disparity, brings into bolder relief the hut and the hovel in the hollow where want, gaunt and haggard, sits at the door and where light and plenty, cheerfulness and hope are forever exiled by the despotic decree of conditions as cruel as when the Czar of Russia orders to his penal mines in Siberia the hapless subjects who dare whisper the sacred word liberty—as cruel as when this boasted land of freedom commands that a far-away, innocent people shall be shot down in jungle and lagoon, in their bamboo huts, because they dream of freedom and independence.

These conditions are as fruitful of danger to the opulent as they are of degradation to the poor. It is neither folly nor fanaticism to assert that the country cannot exist under such conditions. The higher law of righteousness, of love and labor will prevail. It is a law which commends itself to reasoning men, a primal law enacted long before Jehovah wrote the decalogue amidst the thunders and lightnings of Sinai. It is a law written upon the tablets of every man's heart and conscience. It is a law infinitely above the creeds and dogmas and tangled disquisitions of the churches—the one law which in its operations will level humanity upward until men, redeemed from greed and every debasing ambition, shall obey its mandates and glory in its triumph.

Love and labor will give us the Socialist Republic—the Industrial Democracy—the equal rights of all men and women, and the emancipation of all from the vicious and debasing thralldoms of past centuries.

SEVEN

GERONIMO

In Prison and On the WarPath (1905)

GERONIMO'S LAST WORDS ARE RUMORED TO BE this utterance of resistance and regret: "I should have never surrendered. I should have fought until I was the last man alive."[7] Whether or not he actually spoke these words we cannot know for certain. Born into the Chiricahua Apache community in the 1820s, he lived a warrior's life fighting colonial expansion on two fronts—the colonial Mexican army and the US Army—and lost the last twenty-three years of his life as a prisoner of war.

According to the National Archives, in 1874 US authorities forcibly removed approximately four thousand Apache people to barren land on a reservation in San Carlos, Arizona. Geronimo had led the Apache people on escapes from reservations, but was repeatedly captured by the US military. The largest of these breakouts occurred in May 1885, when Geronimo led a group of 35 men, 8 boys, and 101 women for ten months around the Arizona-Mexico border.[8] Overpowered, Geronimo and his band of warriors were at one point being pursued by five thousand US soldiers and an additional three thousand non-Native Mexican soldiers. Geronimo surrendered after being falsely promised he would be permitted to return to Apache territory. Instead, US authorities sent Geronimo and his fellow prisoners of war to hard labor at Fort Pickens, Florida, then Alabama, and then Fort Sill in Oklahoma Territory.[9] There were no prisons in Apache society prior to the ones imposed by the Anglo invasion. Writer and naturalist Henry David Thoreau, whose life span overlapped Geronimo's, once noted, "In an unjust society the only place for a just man is prison." Hunted, attacked, forcibly sequestered, and then exoticized as a manufactured symbol of a "savage" pre-colonial past, Geronimo is honored here for who he was: an Apache warrior who fought so that he, his family, and his sovereign community could live freely on their own terms.

IN PRISON AND ON THE WARPATH

SOON AFTER we arrived in New Mexico two companies of scouts were sent from San Carlos. When they came to Hot Springs they sent word for me and Victoria to come to town.[10] The messengers did not say what they wanted with us, but as they seemed friendly, we thought they wanted a council, and rode in to meet the officers. As soon as we arrived in town soldiers met us, disarmed us, and took us both to headquarters, where we were tried by court-martial. They asked us only a few questions, and then Victoria was released and I was sentenced to the guardhouse. Scouts conducted me to the guardhouse and put me in chains. When I asked them why they did this they said it was because I had left Apache Pass.

I do not think that I ever belonged to those soldiers at Apache Pass, or that I should have asked them where I might go. Our bands could no longer live in peace together, and so we had quietly withdrawn, expecting to live with Victoria's band, where we thought we would not be molested. They also sentenced seven other Apaches to chains in the guardhouse.

I do not know why this was done, for these Indians had simply followed me from Apache Pass to Hot Springs. If it was wrong—and I do not think it was wrong—for us to go to Hot Springs, I alone was to blame. They asked the soldiers in charge why they were imprisoned and chained, but received no answer.

I was kept a prisoner for four months, during which time I was transferred to San Carlos. Then I think I had another trial, although I was not present. In fact, I do not know that I had another trial, but I was told that I had, and at any rate I was released.

After this we had no more trouble with the soldiers, but I never felt at ease any longer at the Post. We were allowed to live above San Carlos at a place now called Geronimo. A man whom the Indians called "Nick Golee" was agent at this place. All went well here for a period of two years, but we were not satisfied.

In the summer of 1883 a rumor was current that the officers were again planning to imprison our leaders. This rumor served to revive the memory of all our past wrongs—the massacre in the tent at Apache Pass, the fate of Mangus-Colorado, and my own unjust imprisonment, which might easily have been death to me. Just at this time we were told that the officers wanted us to come up the river above Geronimo to a fort [Fort Thomas] to hold a council with them. We did not believe that any good could come of this conference, or that there was any need of it; so we held a council ourselves, and fearing treachery, decided to leave the reservation. We thought it more manly to die on the warpath than to be killed in prison.

There were in all about 250 Indians, chiefly the Bedonkohe and Nedni Apaches, led by myself and Whoa. We went through Apache Pass and just west of there had a fight with the United States troops. In this battle we killed three soldiers and lost none.

We went on toward Old Mexico, but on the second day after this, United States soldiers overtook us about three o'clock in the afternoon and we fought until dark. The ground where we were attacked was very rough, which was to our advantage, for the troops were compelled to dismount in order to fight us. I do not know how many soldiers we killed, but we lost only one warrior and three children. We had plenty of guns and ammunition at this time. Many of the guns and much ammunition we had accumulated while living in the reservation, and the remainder we had obtained from the White Mountain Apaches when we left the reservation.

Troops did not follow us any longer, so we went south almost to Casa Grande and camped in the Sierra de Sahuaripa Mountains. We ranged in the mountains of Old Mexico for about a year, then returned to San Carlos, taking with us a herd of cattle and horses.

Soon after we arrived at San Carlos the officer in charge, General Crook, took the horses and cattle away from us. I told him that these were not white men's cattle, but belonged to us, for we had taken them from the Mexicans during our wars. I also told him that we did not intend to kill these animals, but that we wished to keep them and raise stock on our range. He would not listen to me, but took the stock. I went up near Fort Apache and General Crook ordered officers, soldiers, and scouts to see that I was arrested; if I offered resistance they were instructed to kill me.

This information was brought to me by the Indians. When I learned of this proposed action I left for Old Mexico, and about four hundred Indians went with me. They were the Bedonkohe, Chokonen, and Nedni Apaches. At this time Whoa was dead, and Naiche was the only chief with me. We went south into Sonora and camped in the mountains. Troops followed us, but did not attack us until we were camped in the mountains west of Casa Grande. Here we were attacked by Government Indian scouts. One boy was killed and nearly all of our women and children were captured.[11]

After this battle we went south of Casa Grande and made a camp, but within a few days this camp was attacked by

Mexican soldiers. We skirmished with them all day, killing a few Mexicans, but sustaining no loss ourselves.

That night we went east into the foothills of the Sierra Madre Mountains and made another camp. Mexican troops trailed us, and after a few days attacked our camp again. This time the Mexicans had a very large army, and we avoided a general engagement. It is senseless to fight when you cannot hope to win.

That night we held a council of war; our scouts had reported bands of United States and Mexican troops at many points in the mountains. We estimated that about two thousand soldiers were ranging these mountains seeking to capture us.

General Crook had come down into Mexico with the United States troops. They were camped in the Sierra de Antunez Mountains. Scouts told me that General Crook wished to see me and I went to his camp. When I arrived General Crook said to me, "Why did you leave the reservation?" I said: "You told me that I might live in the reservation the same as white people lived. One year I raised a crop of corn, and gathered and stored it, and the next year I put in a crop of oats, and when the crop was almost ready to harvest, you told your soldiers to put me in prison, and if I resisted to kill me. If I had been let alone I would now have been in good circumstances, but instead of that you and the Mexicans are hunting me with soldiers." He said: "I never gave any such orders; the troops at Fort Apache, who spread this report, knew that it was untrue." Then I agreed to go back with him to San Carlos.

It was hard for me to believe him at that time. Now I know that what he said was untrue,[12] and I firmly believe that he did issue the orders for me to be put in prison, or to be killed in case I offered resistance.

EIGHT

MOTHER JONES

Early Years, The Haymarket Tragedy, and In Rockefeller's Prisons (1925)

MARY HARRIS "MOTHER" JONES WAS BORN IN Cork, Ireland, in 1830. Famine in her native Ireland chased her family to the shores of North America. She lost a husband and four children to the yellow fever epidemic, and, following that, a raging inferno claimed her business, home, and belongings in Chicago. Famine, plague, and fire thus molded the contours of her life, exposing and heightening the contradictions between the haves and have-nots, the workers and industrialists. Jones knew which side she was on, and these excerpts from her autobiography detail her coming to political consciousness and the arc that led her to become one of the most iconic labor organizers in US history. "Pray for the dead, and fight like hell for the living" was her war cry. Once considered the "most dangerous woman in America," Mother Jones, by her own account, didn't back down from the threat of jail, and, like so many union organizers, spent time locked up for her efforts. Mother Jones put her faith in the power of working people and their immense potential to stand up and fight. Indeed, she proves that the people are the makers of history. "All over the country she had roamed," Upton Sinclair wrote, "and wherever she went, the flame of protest had leaped up in the hearts of men; her story was a veritable Odyssey of revolt."

EARLY YEARS

I WAS born in the city of Cork, Ireland, in 1830. My people were poor. For generations they had fought for Ireland's freedom. Many of my folks have died in that struggle. My father, Richard Harris, came to America in 1835, and as soon as he had become an American citizen he sent for his family. His work as a laborer with railway construction crews took him to Toronto, Canada. Here I was brought up but always as the child of an American citizen. Of that citizenship I have ever been proud.

After finishing the common schools, I attended the Normal school with the intention of becoming a teacher. Dress-making too, I learned proficiently. My first position was teaching in a convent in Monroe, Michigan. Later, I came to Chicago and opened a dress-making establishment. I preferred sewing to bossing little children. However, I went back to teaching again, this time in Memphis, Tennessee. Here I was married in 1861. My husband was an iron moulder and a staunch member of the Iron Moulders' Union.

In 1867, a fever epidemic swept Memphis. Its victims were mainly among the poor and the workers. The rich and the well-to-do fled the city. Schools and churches were closed. People were not permitted to enter the house of a yellow fever victim without permits. The poor could not afford nurses. Across the street from me, ten persons lay dead from the plague. The dead surrounded us. They were buried at night quickly and without ceremony. All about my house I could hear weeping and the cries of delirium. One by one, my four little children sickened and died. I washed their little bodies and got them ready for burial. My husband caught the fever and died. I sat alone through nights of grief. No one came to me. No one could. Other homes were as stricken as was mine. All day long, all night long, I heard the grating of the wheels of the death cart.

After the union had buried my husband, I got a permit to nurse the sufferers. This I did until the plague was stamped out.

I returned to Chicago and went again into the dressmaking business with a partner. We were located on Washington Street near the lake. We worked for the aristocrats of Chicago, and I had ample opportunity to observe the luxury and extravagance of their lives. Often while sewing for the lords and barons who lived in magnificence on the Lake Shore Drive, I would look out of the plate glass windows and see the poor, shivering wretches, jobless and hungry, walking along the frozen lake front. The contrast of their condition with that of the tropical comfort of the people for whom I sewed was painful to me. My employers seemed neither to notice nor to care.

Summers, too, from the windows of the rich, I used to watch the mothers come from the west side slums, lugging babies and little children, hoping for a breath of cool, fresh air from the lake. At night, when the tenements were stifling hot, men, women and little children slept in the parks. But the rich, having donated to the charity ice fund, had, by the time it was hot in the city, gone to seaside and mountains.

In October, 1871, the great Chicago fire burned up our establishment and everything that we had. The fire made thousands homeless. We stayed all night and the next day without food on the lake front, often going into the lake to keep cool. Old St. Mary's church at Wabash Avenue and Peck Court was thrown open to the refugees and there I camped until I could find a place to go.

Nearby in an old, tumbled down, fire-scorched building the Knights of Labor held meetings. The Knights of Labor was the labor organization of those days. I used to spend my evenings at their meetings, listening to splendid speakers. Sundays we went out into the woods and held meetings.

Those were the days of sacrifice for the cause of labor. Those were the days when we had no halls, when there were no high-salaried officers, no feasting with the enemies of labor. Those were the days of the martyrs and the saints.

I became acquainted with the labor movement. I learned that in 1865, after the close of the Civil War, a group of men met in Louisville, Kentucky. They came from the North and from the South; they were the "blues" and the "greys" who a year or two before had been fighting each other over the question of chattel slavery. They decided that the time had come to formulate a program to fight another brutal form of slavery—industrial slavery. Out of this decision had come the Knights of Labor.

From the time of the Chicago fire I became more and more engrossed in the labor struggle and I decided to take an active part in the efforts of the working people to better the conditions under which they worked and lived. I became a member of the Knights of Labor.

One of the first strikes that I remember occurred in the Seventies. The Baltimore and Ohio Railroad employees went on strike and they sent for me to come help them. I went. The mayor of Pittsburgh swore in as deputy sheriffs a lawless, reckless bunch of fellows who had drifted into that city during the panic of 1873. They pillaged and burned and rioted and looted. Their acts were charged up to the striking workingmen. The governor sent the militia.

The Railroads had succeeded in getting a law passed that in case of a strike, the train-crew should bring in the locomotive to the round-house before striking. This law the strikers faithfully obeyed. Scores of locomotives were housed in Pittsburgh.

One night a riot occurred. Hundreds of box cars standing on the tracks were soaked with oil and set on fire and sent down the tracks to the roundhouse. The roundhouse caught fire. Over one hundred locomotives, belonging to the Pennsylvania Railroad Company were destroyed. It was a wild night. The flames lighted the sky and turned to fiery flames the steel bayonettes of the soldiers.

The strikers were charged with the crimes of arson and rioting, although it was common knowledge that it was not they who instigated the fire; that it was started by hoodlums backed by the businessmen of Pittsburgh who for a long time had felt that the Railroad Company discriminated against their city in the matter of rates.

I knew the strikers personally. I knew that it was they who had tried to enforce orderly law. I knew they disciplined their members when they did violence. I knew, as everybody knew, who really perpetrated the crime of burning the railroad's property. Then and there I learned in the early part of my career that labor must bear the cross for others' sins, must be the vicarious sufferer for the wrongs that others do.

These early years saw the beginning of America's industrial life. Hand [in] hand with the growth of factories and the expansion of railroads, with the accumulation of capital and the rise of banks, came anti-labor legislation. Came strikes. Came violence. Came the belief in the hearts and minds of the workers that legislatures but carry out the will of the industrialists.

THE HAYMARKET TRAGEDY

From 1880 on, I became wholly engrossed in the labor movement. In all the great industrial centers the working class was in rebellion. The enormous immigration from Europe crowded the slums, forced down wages and threatened to destroy the standard of living fought for by American working men. Throughout the country there was business depression and much unemployment. In the cities there was hunger and rags and despair.

Foreign agitators who had suffered under European despots preached various schemes of economic salvation to the workers. The workers asked only for bread and a shortening of the long hours of toil. The agitators gave them visions. The police gave them clubs.

Particularly the city of Chicago was the scene of strike after strike, followed by boycotts and riots. The years preceding 1886 had witnessed strikes of the lake seamen, of dock laborers and street railway workers. These strikes had been brutally suppressed by policemen's clubs and by hired gunmen. The grievance on the part of the workers was given no heed. John Bonfield, inspector of police, was particularly cruel in the suppression of meetings where men peacefully assembled to discuss matters of wages and of hours. Employers were defiant and open in the expression of their fears and hatreds. The Chicago Tribune, the organ of the employers, suggested ironically that the farmers of Illinois treat the tramps that poured out of the great industrial centers as they did other pests, by putting strychnine in the food.

The workers started an agitation for an eight-hour day. The trades unions and the Knights of Labor endorsed the movement but because many of the leaders of the agitation were foreigners, the movement itself was regarded as "foreign" and as "un-American." Then the anarchists of Chicago, a very small group, espoused the cause of the eight-hour day. From then on the people of Chicago seemed incapable of discussing a purely economic question without getting excited about anarchism.

The employers used the cry of anarchism to kill the movement. A person who believed in an eight-hour working day was, they said, an enemy to his country, a traitor, an anarchist. The foundations of government were being gnawed away by the anarchist rats. Feeling was bitter. The city was divided into two angry camps. The working people on one side—hungry, cold, jobless, fighting gunmen and police clubs with bare hands. On the other side the employers, knowing neither hunger nor cold, supported by the newspapers, by the police, by all the power of the great state itself.

The anarchists took advantage of the widespread discontent to preach their doctrines. Orators used to address huge crowds on the windy, barren shore of Lake Michigan. Although I never endorsed the philosophy of anarchism, I often attended the meetings on the lake shore, listening to what these teachers of a new order had to say to the workers.

Meanwhile the employers were meeting. They met in the mansion of George M. Pullman on Prairie Avenue or in the residence of Wirt Dexter, an able corporation lawyer. They discussed means of killing the eight-hour movement which was to be ushered in by a general strike. They discussed methods of dispersing the meetings of the anarchists.

A bitterly cold winter set in. Long unemployment resulted in terrible suffering. Bread lines increased. Soup kitchens could not handle the applicants. Thousands knew actual misery.

On Christmas day, hundreds of poverty-stricken people in rags and tatters, in thin clothes, in wretched shoes paraded on fashionable Prairie Avenue before the mansions of the rich, before their employers, carrying the black flag. I thought the parade an insane move on the part of the anarchists, as it only served to make feeling more bitter. As a matter of fact, it had no educational value whatever and only served to increase the employers' fear, to make the police more savage, and the public less sympathetic to the real distress of the workers

The first of May, which was to usher in the eight-hour day uprising, came. The newspapers had done everything to alarm the people. All over the city there were strikes and walkouts. Employers quaked in their boots. They saw revolution. The workers in the McCormick Harvester Works gathered outside the factory. Those inside who did not join the strikers were called scabs. Bricks were thrown. Windows were broken. The scabs were threatened. Someone turned in a riot call.

The police without warning charged down upon the workers, shooting into their midst, clubbing right and left. Many were trampled under horses' feet. Numbers were shot dead. Skulls were broken. Young men and young girls were clubbed to death.

The Pinkerton agency formed armed bands of ex-convicts and hoodlums and hired them to capitalists at eight dollars a day, to picket the factories and incite trouble.

On the evening of May 4th, the anarchists held a meeting in the shabby, dirty district known to later history as Haymarket Square. All about were railway tracks, dingy saloons and the dirty tenements of the poor. A half a block away was the Desplaines Street Police Station presided over by John Bonfield, a man without tact or discretion or sympathy, a most brutal believer in suppression as the method to settle industrial unrest.

Carter Harrison, the mayor of Chicago, attended the meeting of the anarchists and moved in and about the crowds in the square. After leaving, he went to the Chief of Police and instructed him to send no mounted police to the meeting, as it was being peacefully conducted and the presence of mounted police would only add fuel to fires already burning red in the workers' hearts. But orders perhaps came from other quarters, for disregarding the report of the mayor, the chief of police sent mounted policemen in large numbers to the meeting.

One of the anarchist speakers was addressing the crowd. A bomb was dropped from a window overlooking the square. A number of the police were killed in the explosion that followed.

The city went insane and the newspapers did everything to keep it like a madhouse. The workers' cry for justice was drowned in the shriek for revenge. Bombs were "found" every five minutes. Men went armed and gun stores kept open nights. Hundreds were arrested. Only those who had agitated for an eight-hour day, however, were brought to trial and a few months later hanged. But the man, Schnaubelt, who actually threw the bomb was never brought into the case, nor was his part in the terrible drama ever officially made clear.

The leaders in the eight-hour day movement were hanged Friday, November the 11th. That day Chicago's rich had chills and fever. Rope stretched in all directions from the jail. Police men were stationed along the ropes armed with riot rifles. Special patrols watched all approaches to the jail. The roofs about the grim stone building were black with police. The newspapers fed the public imagination with stories of uprisings and jail deliveries.[13]

But there were no uprisings, no jail deliveries, except that of Louis Lingg, the only real preacher of violence among all the condemned men. He outwitted the gallows by biting a percussion cap and blowing off his head.

The Sunday following the executions, the funerals were held. Thousands of workers marched behind the black hearses, not because they were anarchists but they felt that these men, whatever their theories, were martyrs to the workers' struggle. The procession wound through miles and miles of streets densely packed with silent people.

In the cemetery of Waldheim, the dead were buried. But with them was not buried their cause. The struggle for the eight-hour day, for more human conditions and relations between man and man lived on, and still lives on.

Seven years later, Governor Altgeld, after reading all the evidence in the case, pardoned the three anarchists who had escaped the gallows and were serving life sentences in jail. He said the verdict was unjustifiable, as had William Dean Howells and William Morris at the time of its execution. Governor Altgeld committed political suicide by his brave action but he is remembered by all those who love truth and those who have the courage to confess it.

IN ROCKEFELLER'S PRISONS

I was in Washington, D. C., at the time of the great coal strike against the Rockefeller holdings in southern Colorado. Ten years previous a strike against long endured exploitation and tyranny had been brutally suppressed with guns and by starvation. But the bitterness and despair of the workers smouldered and smouldered long after the fires of open rebellion had been extinguished. Finally after a decade of endurance the live coals in the hearts of the miners leaped into a roaring fire of revolt.

One day I read in the newspaper that Governor Ammons of Colorado said that Mother Jones was not to be allowed to go into the southern field where the strike was raging.

That night I took a train and went directly to Denver. I got a room in the hotel where I usually stayed. I then went up to Union headquarters of the miners, after which I went to the station and bought my ticket and sleeper to Trinidad in the southern field.

When I returned to the hotel, a man who had registered when I did, came up to me and said, "Are you going to Trinidad, Mother Jones?"

"Of course," said I.

"Mother, I want to tell you that the governor has detectives at the hotel and railway station watching you."

"Detectives don't bother me," I told him.

"There are two detectives in the lobby, one up in the gallery, and two or three at the station, watching the gates to see who board the trains south."

I thanked him for his information. That night I went an hour or so before the coaches were brought into the station way down into the railway yards where the coaches stood ready to be coupled to the train. I went to the section house. There was an old section hand there. He held up his lantern to see me.

"Oh, Mother Jones," he said, "and is it you that's walking the ties!"

"It's myself," said I, "but I'm not walking. I have a sleeper ticket for the south and I want to know if the trains are made up yet. I want to go aboard."

"Sit here," he said, "I'll go see. I don't know." I knew he understood without any explaining why I was there.

"I wish you would tell the porter to come back with you," said I.

He went off, his light bobbing at his side. Pretty soon he returned with the porter.

"What you want, Mother?" says he.

"I want to know if the berths are made up yet?"

"Do you want to get on now, Mother?"

"Yes."

"Then yours is made up."

I showed him my tickets and he led me across the tracks.

"Mother," he said, "I know you now but later I might find it convenienter not to have the acquaintance."

"I understand," said I. "Now here's two dollars to give to the conductor. Tell him to let Mother Jones off before we get to the Santa Fe crossing. That will be early in the morning."

"I sure will," said he.

I got on board the sleeper in the yards and was asleep when the coaches pulled into the Denver station for passengers south. I was still asleep when the train pulled out of the depot.

Early in the morning the porter awakened me. "Mother," he said, "the conductor is going to stop the train for you. Be ready to hop."

When the train slowed down before we got to the crossing, the conductor came to help me off.

"Are you doing business, Mother?" said he.

"I am indeed," said I. "And did you stop the train just for me?"

"I certainly did!"

He waved to me as the train pulled away. "Goodbye, Mother."

It was very early and I walked into the little town of Trinidad and got breakfast. Down at the station a company of military were watching to see if I came into town. But no Mother Jones got off at the depot, and the company marched back to headquarters, which was just across the street from the hotel where I was staying.

I was in Trinidad three hours before they knew I was there. They telephoned the governor. They telephoned General Chase in charge of the militia. "Mother Jones is in Trinidad!" they said.

"Impossible!" said the governor. "Impossible!" said the general.

"Nevertheless, she is here!"

"We have had her well watched, the hotels and the depots," they said.

"Nevertheless, she is here!"

My arrest was ordered.

A delegation of miners came to me. "Boys," I said, "they are going to arrest me but don't make any trouble. Just let them do it."

"Mother," said they, "we aren't going to let them arrest you!"

"Yes, you will. Let them carry on their game."

While we were sitting there talking, I heard footsteps tramping up the stairs.

"Here they come," said I and we sat quietly waiting.

The door opened. It was a company of militia.

"Did you come after me, boys?" said I. They looked embarrassed.

"Pack your valise and come," said the captain.

They marched me down stairs and put me in an automobile that was waiting at the door.

The miners had followed. One of them had tears rolling down his cheeks.

"Mother," he cried, "I wish I could go for you!"

We drove to the prison first, passing cavalry and infantry and gunmen, sent by the state to subdue the miners. Orders were given to drive me to the Sisters' Hospital, a portion of which had been turned into a military prison. They put me in a small room with white plastered walls, with a cot, a chair and a table, and for nine weeks I stayed in that one room, seeing no human beings but the silent military. One stood on either side of the cell door, two stood across the hall, one at the entrance to the hall, two at the elevator entrance on my floor, two on the ground floor elevator entrance.

Outside my window a guard walked up and down, up and down day and night, day and night, his bayonet flashing in the sun.

"Lads," said I to the two silent chaps at the door, "the great Standard Oil is certainly afraid of an old woman!"

They grinned.

My meals were sent to me by the sisters. They were not, of course, luxurious. In all those nine weeks I saw no one, received not a letter, a paper, a postal card. I saw only landscape and the bayonet flashing in the sun.

Finally, Mr. Hawkins, the attorney for the miners, was allowed to visit me. Then on Sunday, Colonel Davis came to me and said the governor wanted to see me in Denver.

The colonel and a subordinate came for me that night at nine o'clock. As we went down the hall, I noticed there was not a soldier in sight. There was none in the elevator. There was none in the entrance way. Everything was strangely silent. No one was about. A closed automobile waited us. We three got in.

"Drive the back way!" said the colonel to the chauffeur.

We drove through dark, lonely streets. The curtains of the machine were down. It was black outside and inside. It was the one time in my life that I thought my end had come; that I was to say farewell to the earth, but I made up my mind that I would put up a good fight before passing out of life!

When we reached the Santa Fe crossing I was put aboard the train. I felt great relief, for the strike had only begun and I had much to do. I went to bed and slept till we arrived in Denver. Here I was met by a monster, called General Chase, whose veins run with ice water. He started to take me to Brown Palace Hotel. I asked him if he would permit me to go to a less aristocratic hotel, to the one I usually stopped at. He consented, telling me he would escort me to the governor at nine o'clock.

I was taken before the governor that morning. The governor said to me, "I am going to turn you free but you must not go back to the strike zone!"

"Governor," I said, "I am going back."

"I think you ought to take my advice," he said, "and do what I think you ought to do."

"Governor," said I, "if Washington took instructions from such as you, we would be under King George's descendants yet! If Lincoln took instructions from you, Grant would never have gone to Gettysburg. I think I had better not take your orders."

I stayed on a week in Denver. Then I got a ticket and sleeper for Trinidad. Across the aisle from me was Reno, Rockefeller's detective. Very early in the morning, soldiers awakened me.

"Get up," they said, "and get off at the next stop!"

I got up, of course, and with the soldiers I got off at Walsenburg, fifty miles from Trinidad. The engineer and the fireman left their train when they saw the soldiers putting me off.

"What are you going to do with that old woman?" they said. "We won't run the train till we know!"

The soldiers did not reply.

"Boys," I said, "go back on your engine. Someday it will be all right."

Tears came trickling down their cheeks, and when they wiped them away, there were long, black streaks on their faces.

I was put in the cellar under the courthouse. It was a cold, terrible place, without heat, damp and dark. I slept in my clothes by day, and at night I fought great sewer rats with a beer bottle. "If I were out of this dungeon," thought I, "I would be fighting the human sewer rats anyway!"

For twenty-six days I was held a military prisoner in that black hole. I would not give in. I would not leave the state. At any time, if I would do so, I could have my freedom. General Chase and his bandits thought that by keeping me in that cold cellar, I would catch the flue or pneumonia, and that would settle for them what to do with "old Mother Jones."

Colonel Berdiker, in charge of me, said, "Mother, I have never been placed in a position as painful as this. Won't you go to Denver and leave the strike field?"

"No, Colonel, I will not," said I.

The hours dragged underground. Day was perpetual twilight and night was deep night. I watched people's feet from my cellar window; miners' feet in old shoes; soldiers' feet, well shod in government leather; the shoes of women with the heels run down; the dilapidated shoes of children; barefooted boys. The children would scrooch down and wave to me but the soldiers shooed them off.

One morning when my hard bread and sloppy coffee were brought to me, Colonel Berdiker said to me, "Mother, don't eat that stuff!" After that he sent my breakfast to me—good, plain food. He was a man with a heart, who perhaps imagined his own mother imprisoned in a cellar with the sewer rats' union.

The colonel came to me one day and told me that my lawyers had obtained a habeas corpus for me and that I was to be released; that the military would give me a ticket to any place I desired.

"Colonel," said I, "I can accept nothing from men whose business it is to shoot down my class whenever they strike for decent wages. I prefer to walk."

"All right, Mother," said he, "Goodbye!"

The operators were bringing in Mexicans to work as scabs in the mines. In this operation they were protected by the military all the way from the Mexican borders. They were brought in to the strike territory without knowing the conditions, promised enormous wages and easy work. They were packed in cattle cars, in charge of company gunmen, and if when arriving, they attempted to leave, they were shot. Hundreds of these poor fellows had been lured into the mines with promises of free land. When they got off the trains, they were driven like cattle into the mines by gunmen.

This was the method that broke the strike ten years previously. And now it was the scabs of a decade before who were striking—the docile, contract labor of Europe.

I was sent down to El Paso to give the facts of the Colorado strike to the Mexicans who were herded together for the mines in that city. I held meetings, I addressed Mexican gatherings, I got the story over the border. I did everything in my power to prevent strike breakers going into the Rockefeller mines.

In January, 1914, I returned to Colorado. When I got off the train at Trinidad, the militia met me and ordered me back on the train. Nevertheless, I got off. They marched me to the telegrapher's office, then they changed their minds, and took me to the hotel where they had their headquarters. I told them I wanted to get my breakfast. They escorted me to the dining room.

"Who is paying for my breakfast?" said I.

"The state," said they.

"Then as the guest of the state of Colorado I'll order a good breakfast." And I did—all the way from bacon to pie.

The train for Denver pulled in. The military put me aboard it. When we reached Walsenburg, a delegation of miners met the train, singing a miner's song. They sang at the top of their lungs till the silent, old mountains seemed to prick up their ears. They swarmed into the train.

"God bless you, Mother!"

"God bless you, my boys!"

"Mother, is your coat warm enough? It's freezing cold in the hills!"

"I'm all right, my lad." The chap had no overcoat—a cheap cotton suit, and a bit of woolen rag around his neck.

Outside in the station stood the militia. One of them was a fiend. He went about swinging his gun, hitting the miners, and trying to prod them into a fight, hurling vile oaths at them. But the boys kept cool and I could hear them singing above the shriek of the whistle as the train pulled out of the depot and wound away through the hills.

From January on until the final brutal outrage—the burning of the tent colony in Ludlow—my ears wearied with the stories of brutality and suffering. My eyes ached with the misery I witnessed. My brain sickened with the knowledge of man's inhumanity to man.

It was, "Oh, Mother, my daughter has been assaulted by the soldiers—such a little girl!"

"Oh, Mother, did you hear how the soldiers entered Mrs. Hall's house, how they terrified the little children, wrecked the home, and did worse—terrible things—and just because Mr. Hall, the undertaker, had buried two miners whom the militia had killed!"

And, "Oh Mother, did you hear how they are arresting miners for vagrancy, for loafing, and making them work in company ditches without pay, making them haul coal and clear snow up to the mines for nothing!"

"Mother, Mother, listen! A Polish fellow arrived as a strike breaker. He didn't know there was a strike. He was a big, strapping fellow. They gave him a star and a gun and told him to shoot strikers!"

"Oh, Mother, they've brought in a shipment of guns and machine guns—what's to happen to us!"

A frantic mother clutched me. "Mother Jones," she screamed, "Mother Jones, my little boy's all swollen up with the kicking and beating he got from a soldier because he said, 'Howdy, John D. feller!' 'Twas just a kid teasing, and now he's lying like dead!"

"Mother, 'tis an outrage for an adjutant general of the state to shake his fist and holler in the face of a grey-haired widow for singing a union song in her own kitchen while she washes the dishes!"

"It is all an outrage," said I. " 'Tis an outrage indeed that Rockefeller should own the coal that God put in the earth for all the people. 'Tis an outrage that gunmen and soldiers are here protecting mines against workmen who ask a bit more than a crust, a bit more than bondage! 'Tis an ocean of outrage!"

"Mother, did you hear of poor, old Colner? He was going to the post office and was arrested by the militia. They marched him down hill, making him carry a shovel and a pick on his back. They told him he was to die and he must dig his own grave. He stumbled and fell on the road. They kicked him and he staggered up. He begged to be allowed to go home and kiss his wife and children goodbye.

" 'We'll do the kissing,' laughed the soldiers.

"At the place they picked out for his grave, they measured him, and then they ordered him to dig—two feet deeper, they told him. Old Colner began digging while the soldiers stood around laughing and cursing and playing craps for his tin watch. Then Colner fell fainting into the grave. The soldiers left him there till he recovered by himself. There he was alone—and he staggered back to camp, Mother, and he isn't quite right in the head!"

I sat through long nights with sobbing widows, watching the candles about the corpse of the husband burn down to their sockets.

"Get out and fight," I told those women. "Fight like hell till you go to Heaven!" That was the only way I knew to comfort them.

I nursed men back to sanity who were driven to despair. I solicited clothes for the ragged children, for the desperate mothers. I laid out the dead, the martyrs of the strike. I kept the men away from the saloons, whose licenses as well as those of the brothels, were held by the Rockefeller interests.

The miners armed, armed as it is permitted every American citizen to do in defense of his home, his family; as he is permitted to do against invasion. The smoke of armed battle rose from the arroyos and ravines of the Rocky Mountains.

No one listened. No one cared. The tickers in the offices of 26 Broadway sounded louder than the sobs of women and children. Men in the steam-heated luxury of Broadway offices could not feel the stinging cold of Colorado hillsides where families lived in tents.

Then came Ludlow and the nation heard. Little children roasted alive make a front-page story. Dying by inches of starvation and exposure does not.

On the 19th of April, 1914, machine guns, used on the strikers in the Paint Creek strike, were placed in position above the tent colony of Ludlow. Major Pat Hamrock and Lieutenant K.E. Linderfelt were in charge of the militia, the majority of whom were company gunmen sworn in as soldiers.

Early in the morning soldiers approached the colony with a demand from headquarters that Louis Tikas, leader of the Greeks, surrender two Italians. Tikas demanded a warrant for their arrest. They had none. Tikas refused to surrender them. The soldiers returned to headquarters. A signal bomb was fired. Then another. Immediately the machine guns began spraying the flimsy tent colony, the only home the wretched families of the miners had, spraying it with bullets. Like iron rain, bullets fell upon men, women and children.

The women and children fled to the hills. Others tarried. The men defended their home with their guns. All day long the firing continued. Men fell dead, their faces to the ground. Women dropped. The little Snyder boy was shot through the head, trying to save his kitten. A child carrying water to his dying mother was killed.

By five o'clock in the afternoon, the miners had no more food, nor water, nor ammunition. They had to retreat with their wives and little ones into the hills. Louis Tikas was riddled with shots while he tried to lead women and children to safety. They perished with him.

Night came. A raw wind blew down the canyons where men, women and children shivered and wept. Then a blaze lighted the sky. The soldiers, drunk with blood and with the liquor they had looted from the saloon, set fire to the tents of Ludlow with oil-soaked torches. The tents, all the poor furnishings, the clothes and bedding of the miners' families burned. Coils of barbed wire were stuffed into the well, the miners' only water supply.

After it was over, the wretched people crept back to bury their dead. In a dugout under a burned tent, the charred bodies of eleven little children and two women were found—unrecognizable. Everything lay in ruins. The wires of bed springs writhed on the ground as if they, too, had tried to flee the horror. Oil and fire and guns had robbed men and women and children of their homes and slaughtered tiny babies and defenseless women. Done by order of Lieutenant Linderfelt, a savage, brutal executor of the will of the Colorado Fuel and Iron Company.

The strikers issued a general call to arms: every able-bodied man must shoulder a gun to protect himself and his family from assassins, from arson and plunder. From jungle days to our own so-named civilization, this is a man's inherent right.

To a man they armed, throughout the whole strike district. Ludlow went on burning in their hearts.

Everybody got busy. A delegation from Ludlow went to see President Wilson. Among them was Mrs. Petrucci whose three tiny babies were crisped to death in the black hole of Ludlow. She had something to say to her President.

Immediately he sent the United States cavalry to quell the gunmen. He studied the situation, and drew up proposals for a three-year truce, binding miner and operator. The operators scornfully refused.

A mass meeting was called in Denver. Judge Lindsay spoke. He demanded that the operators be made to respect the laws of Colorado. That something be done immediately. It was. The Denver Real Estate Exchange appointed a committee to spit on Judge Lindsey for his espousal of the cause of the miners.

Rockefeller got busy. Writers were hired to write pamphlets which were sent broadcast to every editor in the country, bulletins. In these leaflets, it was shown how perfectly happy was the life of the miner until the agitators came; how joyous he was with the company's saloon, the company's pigstys for homes, the company's teachers and preachers and coroners. How the miners hated the state law of an eight-hour working day, begging to be allowed to work ten, twelve. How they hated the state law that they should have their own check weighman to see that they were not cheated at the tipple.

And all the while the mothers of the children who died in Ludlow were mourning their dead.

NINE

NICOLA SACCO

Letter to His Son Dante (1927)

TWO DAYS BEFORE NICOLA SACCO WAS STRAPPED into an electric chair and executed in a Massachusetts prison, he wrote this letter to his fourteen-year-old son, Dante. Nicola Sacco and Bartolomeo Vanzetti, a shoemaker and a poor fish peddler, had been arrested, charged, and convicted of robbery and first-degree murder. The two working-class Italian immigrants met on a picket line, became comrades, and hoped to build a world with "no government, no police, no judges, no bosses, no authority." In order to avoid being drafted during World War I, the two hightailed it to Mexico in the summer of 1917. Several years later, their act of conscientious objection was held against them in court. During the trial, their radical politics took center stage, trumping lack of evidence, perjured witnesses, and judicial bias. Eyewitnesses to the crime said the assailants "looked Italian." At the time of his arrest, Sacco was found with a loaded gun and anarchist literature, but nothing that connected him to any crime. Possession of a firearm, a history of draft dodging, and radical politics, undoubtedly worked against him, a scary combination for the nativist and xenophobic American establishment. There has been no era in US history when this equation has not been perceived as a threat. Thus, Sacco and Vanzetti were guilty of being foreigners, anarchists, and armed with principles that guided them to refuse to fight in World War I.

Dante was a young kid when his father went to jail, and a teenager when his father was executed. Confronting death, Nicola's words to Dante exude love and solidarity as he implores him to be strong, and to "help the weak ones that cry for help . . . the persecuted and the victim." He assures him that by doing so, "in this struggle of life you will find more love and you will be loved." Confronting his own death, he maintains an abundance of faith in intergenerational struggle: "Yes, Dante, they can crucify our bodies today as they are doing, but they cannot destroy our ideas, that will remain for the youth of the future to come." His unwavering confidence in the future is remarkable. Perhaps he was heartened by the support of the leftist literati, academics, activists, and outraged workers, and the throngs of justice-loving people who took to the streets the world over to stand in solidarity with them. Despite this support and lack of evidence connecting them to the crime, Nicola Sacco and Bartolomeo Vanzetti were killed by our government.

August 18, 1927
My Dear Son and Companion:
Since the day I saw you last I had always the idea to write you this letter, but the length of my hunger strike and the thought I might not be able to explain myself, made me put it off all this time.

The other day, I ended my hunger strike and just as soon as I did that I thought of you to write to you, but I find that I did not have enough strength and I cannot finish it at one time. However, I want to get it down in any way before they take us again to the death-house, because it is my conviction that just as soon as the court refuses a new trial to us they will take us there. And between Friday and Monday, if nothing happens, they will electrocute us right after midnight, on August 22nd. Therefore, here I am, right with you with love and with open heart as ever I was yesterday.

I never thought that our inseparable life could be separated, but the thought of seven dolorous years makes it seem it did come, but then it has not changed really the unrest and the heart-beat of affection. That has remained as it was. More. I say that our ineffable affection reciprocal, is today more than any other time, of course. That is not only a great deal but it is grand because you can see the real brotherly love, not only in joy but also and more in the struggle of suffering. Remember this, Dante. We have demonstrated this, and modesty apart, we are proud of it.

Much we have suffered during this long Calvary. We protest today as we protested yesterday. We protest always for our freedom.

If I stopped hunger strike the other day, it was because there was no more sign of life in me. Because I protested with my hunger strike yesterday as today I protest for life and not for death.

I sacrificed because I wanted to come back to the embrace of your dear little sister Ines and your mother and all the beloved friends and comrades of life and not death. So Son, today life begins to revive slow and calm, but yet without horizon and always with sadness and visions of death.

Well, my dear boy, after your mother had talked to me so much and I had dreamed of you day and night, how joyful it was to see you at last. To have talked with you like we used to in the days—in those days. Much I told you on that visit and more I wanted to say, but I saw that you will remain the same affectionate boy, faithful to your mother who loves you so much, and I did not want to hurt your sensibilities any longer, because I am sure that you will continue to be the same boy and remember what I have told you. I knew that and what here I am going to tell you will touch your sensibilities, but don't cry Dante, because many tears have been wasted, as your mother's have been wasted for seven years, and never did any good. So, Son, instead of crying, be strong, so as to be able to comfort your mother, and when you want to distract your mother from the discouraging soulness, I will tell you what I used to do. To take her for a long walk in the quiet country, gathering wild flowers here and there, resting under the shade of trees, between the harmony of the vivid stream and the gentle tranquility of the mother nature, and I am sure that she will enjoy this very much, as you surely would be happy for it. But remember always, Dante, in the play of happiness, don't you use all for yourself only, but down yourself just one step, at your side and help the weak ones that cry for help, help the prosecuted and the victim, because [they] are your better friends; they are the comrades that fight and fall as your father and Bartolo fought and fell yesterday for the conquest of the joy of freedom for all and the poor workers. In this struggle of life you will find more love and you will be loved.

I am sure that from what your mother told me about what you said during these last terrible days when I was lying in the iniquitous death-house—that description gave me happiness because it showed you will be the beloved boy I had always dreamed.

Therefore, whatever should happen tomorrow, nobody knows, but if they should kill us, you must not forget to look at your friends and comrades with the smiling gaze of gratitude as you look at your beloved ones, because they love you as they love every one of the fallen persecuted comrades. I tell you, your father that is all the life to you, your father that loved you and saw them, and knows their noble faith (that is mine) their supreme sacrifice that they are still doing for our freedom, for I have fought with them, and they are the ones that still hold the last of our hope that today they can still save us from electrocution, it is the struggle and fight between the rich and the poor for safety and freedom, Son, which you will understand in the future of your years to come, of this unrest and struggle of life's death.

Much I thought of you when I was lying in the death-house—the singing, the kind tender voices of the children from the playground, where there was all the life and the joy of liberty—just one step from the wall which contains the buried agony of three buried souls. It would remind me so often of you and your sister Ines, and I wish I could see you every moment. But I feel better that you did not come to the death-house so that you could not see the horrible picture of three lying in agony waiting to be electrocuted, because I do not know what effect it would have on your young age. But then, in another way if you were not so sensitive it would be very useful to you tomorrow when you could use this horrible memory to hold up to the world the shame of the country in this cruel persecution and unjust death. Yes, Dante, they can crucify our bodies today as they are doing, but they cannot destroy our ideas, that will remain for the youth of the future to come.

Dante, when I said three human lives buried, I meant to say that with us there is another young man by the name of Celestino Maderios [*sic*] that is to be electrocuted at the same time with us. He has been twice before in that horrible death-house, that should be destroyed with the hammers of real progress—that horrible house that will shame forever the future of the citizens of Massachusetts. They should destroy that house and put up a factory or school, to teach many of the hundreds of the poor orphan boys of the world.

Dante, I say once more to love and be nearest to your mother and the beloved ones in these sad days, and I am sure that with your brave heart and kind goodness they will feel less discomfort. And you will also not forget to love me a little for I do—O, Sonny! thinking so much and so often of you.

Best fraternal greetings to all the beloved ones, love and kisses to your little Ines and mother. Most hearty affectionate embrace.

Your Father and Companion

P.S. Bartolo send[s] you the most affectionate greetings. I hope that your mother will help you to understand this letter because I could have written much better and more simple, if I was feeling good. But I am so weak.

TEN

ANGELO HERNDON

You Cannot Kill the Working Class (1937)

BORN IN 1913 IN OHIO, JUST FORTY-EIGHT YEARS after the abolition of slavery, Herndon was a labor organizer, Communist Party member, civil rights activist, and the first Black political prisoner to publish an autobiography. As a thirteen-year-old laborer in a coal mine, his experience of poor working conditions influenced his decision to join the Young Communist League USA in 1930. In July 1932 he was arrested for organizing a march to Georgia's state capitol to petition for unemployment insurance. Convicted of the crime of "inciting an insurrection," based on a rarely invoked 1861 Georgia state law intended to prevent slave revolts, Herndon was sentenced to eighteen to twenty years in a chain gang. His case highlights the racial and political injustice faced by Americans of color in the Jim Crow South. This testimony, first published as a five-cent pamphlet in 1937 by the International Labor Defense and the League of Struggle for Negro Rights, was used to educate readers about the struggle for workers' rights in the South. Herndon positions the exploitation Black workers experienced in the labor movement as a direct inheritance from the violence and traumas of slavery. When workers organized across racial lines against the interests of the property class, the response was a reign of terror in the form of intimidation, violence, prison, and death. Herndon emphasized interracial solidarity because he recognized its potential power in his own life. Most of all, his account shows us what a group of committed, mobilized, and organized people who understand the circumstances of their oppression can do. They can unify to transcend social protocol, custom, and law. They can empower the multitudes to stand up to bullying and fear. They can overcome violence and intimidation. They can win better wages and better working conditions, and, significantly, they can free people from their prison cells and save them from state-sanctioned death. While written in black ink, Herndon teaches us that US history is stained with Black blood. May we never forget his lessons.

YOU CANNOT KILL THE WORKING CLASS

MY GREAT-GRANDMOTHER was ever such a tiny girl when some white plantation owners rode up to the Big House and arranged to carry her off. They bargained for a bit and then came down to the Negro quarters and grabbed her away from her mother. They could do that because my great-grandmother's folks were slaves in Virginia.

My great-grandmother lived to be very old. She often told me about those times.

There is one story of hers that keeps coming back to me. She was still a young girl, and mighty pretty, and some rich young white men decided they wanted her. She resisted, so they threw her down on the floor of the barn, and tied her up with ropes, and beat her until the blood ran. Then they sent to the house for pepper and salt to rub in the wounds.

Her daughter—my grandmother—couldn't remember much about slave days. While she was still a child, the Civil War was fought out and chattel slavery was ended. One childhood scene, though, was scarred on her mind. It was during the Civil War. Some white men burst into her cabin. They seized her sister and strung her to a tree, and riddled her body with bullets. My grandmother herself stayed hidden, and managed to get away alive.

I remember these stories, not because they were so different from life in my own day, but for the opposite reason. They were exactly like some of the things that happened to me when I went South.

My father, Paul Herndon, and my mother, Hattie Herndon, lived for many years in Birmingham, and then came North. They settled down in Wyoming, Ohio, a little steel and mining town just outside of Cincinnati.

I Am Born into a Miner's Family

I was born there on May 6, 1913. My name was put down in the big family Bible as Eugene Angelo Braxton Herndon.

They say that once a miner, always a miner. I don't know if that's so, but I do know that my father never followed any other trade. His sons never doubted that they would go down into the mines as soon as they got old enough. The wail of the mine whistle morning and night, and the sight of my father coming home with his lunch-pail, grimy from the day's coating of coal-dust, seemed a natural and eternal part of our lives.

Almost every working-class family, especially in those days, nursed the idea that one of its members, anyway, would get out of the factory and wear clean clothes all the time and sit at a desk. My family was no exception. They hoped that I would be the one to leave the working-class. They were ready to make almost any sacrifices to send me through high-school and college. They were sure that if a fellow worked hard and had intelligence and grit, he wouldn't have to be a worker all his life.

I haven't seen my mother or most of my family for a long time—but I wonder what they think of that idea now!

My father died of miner's pneumonia when I was very small, and left my mother with a big family to care for.

Besides myself, there were six other boys and two girls. We all did what we could. Mother went out to do housework for rich white folks. An older brother got a job in the steel mills. I did odd jobs, working in stores, running errands, for $2 and $3 a week. They still had the idea they could scrimp and save and send me through college. But when I was 13, we saw it wouldn't work.

I Go To Work

So one fine morning in 1926, my brother Leo and I started off for Lexington, Ky. It was just across the border, and it had mines, and we were miner's kids.

A few miles outside of Lexington, we were taken on at a small mine owned by the powerful DeBardeleben Coal Corporation. There didn't seem to be any question in anyone's mind about a kid of 13 going to work, and I was given a job helping to load coal.

We worked under the contracting system. One worker contracts to get a certain amount of work done, and a number of workers are put under him. The contractor's pay depends on how much the men under him load. It's a clever way of getting one worker to speed the others up. It divides the workers against each other, and saves a good deal of management expenses for the operators.

On my job we were paired off in twos, shoveling coal into the cars. We got about $35 per estimate. An estimate is two weeks. Remember, that was in 1926, before the crash, and we averaged 10 or 11 hours a day, and sometimes worked 14. Besides this, we had to walk three or four miles from the surface of the mine to our work, for there was no mantrip. We didn't get any pay for this time.

They deducted about $10 or $15 every estimate for bath, school, doctor, hospital, insurance, and supplies. We had to buy all our mining supplies, like carbide, lamps, dynamite, fuses, picks and so on, at the company store. The company store soaked us.

They weighed our coal and charged us for the slate in it. They cheated awfully on the slate. Then after they skinned us that way, they skinned us again on the weight. The check-weighman had been hired by the company. He had the scales all fixed beforehand, and the cars just slid over the scales. Everybody could see it was a gyp, but we weren't organized and though we grumbled we couldn't get any satisfaction.

The Company Town

We lived in the company town. It was pretty bad. The houses were just shacks on unpaved streets. We seldom had anything to eat that was right. We had to buy everything from the company store, or we'd have lost our jobs. They kept our pay low and paid only every two weeks, so we had to have credit between times. We got advances in the form of clackers, which could be used only in the company store. Their prices were very high. I remember paying 30 cents a pound for pork-chops in the company store and then noticing that the butcher in town was selling them for 20 cents. The company store prices were just robbery without a pistol.

The safety conditions in the mine were rotten. The escapeways were far from where we worked, and there was never enough timbering to keep the rocks from falling. There were some bad accidents while I was there. I took all the skin off my right hand pushing a car up into the facing. The cars didn't have enough grease and there were no cross-ties just behind me to brace my feet against. That was a bit of the company's economy. The car slipped, the track turned over, and the next thing I knew I had lost all the skin and a lot of the flesh off my right hand. The scars are there to this day.

This DeBardeleben mine in Lexington was where the Jim-Crow system first hit me. The Negroes and whites very seldom came in contact with each other. Of course there were separate company patches for living quarters. But even in the mine the Negroes and the whites worked in different places. The Negroes worked on the North side of the mine and the whites on the South.

The Negroes never got a look-in on most of the better-paying jobs. They couldn't be section foremen, or electricians, or surveyors, or head bank boss, or check weighman, or steel sharpeners, or engineers. They could only load the coal, run the motors, be mule-boys, pick the coal, muck the rock. In other words, they were only allowed to do the muscle work.

Besides that, the Negro miners got the worst places to work. We worked in the low coal, only 3 or 4 feet high. We had to wear knee pads, and work stretched flat on our bellies most of the time.

A Slashing Pay-Cut

One day the company put up a notice that due to large overhead expenses, they would have to cut our pay from 42 to 31 cents a ton. We were sore as hell. But there wasn't any union in the mine, and practically none of us had had any experience at organization, and though we grumbled plenty we didn't take any action. We were disgusted, and some of us quit. Whites and Negroes both.

I was one of those who quit. My contact with unions, and with organization, and the Communist Party, and unity between black and white miners—all that was still in the future. The pay-cut and the rotten conditions got my goat, and I walked off, because as yet I didn't know of anything else to do.

Well, my brother Leo and I set out for Birmingham, where there were relatives—and plenty more mines. I was out of work for a long time. Finally I went to an employment agency and paid down $3 for a job. They signed a lot of us on to work putting up the plant of the Goodyear Rubber Company at Gadsden, Ala. They carried us up there on trucks, promising us we would get $3 a day. When we got there they told us we would get only $1.75 a day. We started work with the concrete mixer, preparing the foundations for the place. We worked night and day, often two shifts one right after the other. We worked like dogs and slept in stifling tents and ate rotten food.

At the end of the first week we lined up to get our pay. Around the pay-office stood dozens of uniformed policemen and company guards. The foreman came out and told us that we had no pay coming, because everything we'd earned had been eaten up by transportation and flops and food.

We were wild with anger. We kept swarming up to the pay-office, but as quick as a group formed there the cops and guards drove us away. The Goodyear Company wouldn't even agree to send us back to Birmingham.

I still didn't have any idea what to do about things like this. I didn't figure we men could get together and organize and make the company come across.

Leo and I hitch-hiked back to Birmingham, and made the round of the mines. I finally got work at the Docena mine of the Tennessee Coal, Iron and Railroad Co.

The Lords of Alabama

I want to talk a little about that. When I sat in jail this spring and read that the workers of the Tennessee Coal and Iron Company had come out on strike, I knew that a new day had come in the South. The T.C.I. just about owns Alabama. It owns steel mills and coal-mines and a railroad and all sorts of subsidiary plants. It owns company patches and houses. It certainly owns most of the Alabama officials. It dictates the political life of the state. It has made Jim-Crowism a fine art. It has stool-pigeons in every corner. The T.C.I. is like some great, greedy brute that holds a whip over the whole state. Its shadow is everywhere—on factories, schools, judges' benches, even the pulpits of churches.

The Tennessee Coal and Iron Company has always been in the forefront of the fight against unions, in the South. They had—and still have—a company-union scheme, which they make a great deal out of, but which doesn't fool any of the workers. I noticed that whatever checkweighman the company put up, would always be elected.

I started surface work at the Docena mine, helping to build transformation lines, cutting the right of way for wires. I was supposed to get $2.78 a day, but there were lots of deductions.

The Power of Organization

It was while I was on this job that I first got a hint of an idea that workers could get things by organizing and sticking together.

It happened this way: one of my buddies on the job was killed by a trolley wire. The shielding on that wire had been down two weeks, and the foreman had seen it down, but hadn't bothered with it. All of us surface men quit work for the day, when we saw our buddy lying, burnt and still, tangled up in that wire.

The next week we were called before the superintendent to explain the accident. Of course we were expected to whitewash the foreman and the company, so they wouldn't have to pay any insurance to the dead man's family. Something got into me, and I spoke up and said that the foreman and the whole company was to blame. The men backed me up. One of the foremen nudged me and told me to hush. He said: "Boy, you're talking too damn much." But I kept on. The foreman was removed and the dead man's family got some compensation from the T.C.I.

That was my first lesson in organization.

By this time the crisis had hit the United States. Mines and factories closed their doors, and businesses crashed, and workers who had never been out of jobs before began to tramp the streets. Those of us who still had jobs found our wages going down, down. The miners got one cut after another. Often, when we got our pay-envelopes, we'd find a blank strip. That meant that the company had taken all our wages for supplies and food advances.

I Begin to Question

The Jim-Crow system was in full force in the mines of the Tennessee Coal and Iron Company, and all over Birmingham. It had always burnt me up, but I didn't know how to set about fighting it. My parents and grand-parents were hard-boiled Republicans, and told me very often that Lincoln had freed the slaves, and that we'd have to look to the Republican Party for everything good. I began to wonder about that. Here I was, being Jim-Crowed and cheated. Every couple of weeks I read about a lynching somewhere in the South. Yet there sat a Republican government up in Washington, and they weren't doing a thing about it.

My people told me to have faith in God, and he would make everything come right. I read a lot of religious tracts, but I got so I didn't believe them. I figured that there was no use for a Negro to go to heaven, because if he went there it would only be to shine some white man's shoes.

I wish I could remember the exact date when I first attended a meeting of the Unemployment Council, and met up with a couple of members of the Communist Party. That date means a lot more to me than my birthday, or any other day in my life.

The workers in the South, mostly deprived of reading-matter, have developed a wonderful grapevine system for transmitting news. It was over this grapevine that we first heard that there were "Reds" in town.

The foremen—when they talked about it—and the newspapers, and the big-shot Negroes in Birmingham, said that the Reds were foreigners, and Yankees, and believed in killing people, and would get us in a lot of trouble. But out of all the talk I got a few ideas clear about the Reds. They believed in organizing and sticking together. They believed that we didn't have to have bosses on our backs. They believed that Negroes ought to have equal rights with whites. It all sounded O.K. to me. But I didn't meet any of the Reds for a long time.

I Find the Working-Class Movement

One day in June, 1930, walking home from work, I came across some handbills put out by the Unemployment Council in Birmingham. They said: "Would you rather fight—or starve?" They called on the workers to come to a mass meeting at 3 o'clock.

Somehow I never thought of missing that meeting. I said to myself over and over: "It's war! It's war! And I might as well get into it right now!" I got to the meeting while a white fellow was speaking. I didn't get everything he said, but this much hit me and stuck with me: that the workers could only get things by fighting for them, and that the Negro and white workers had to stick together to get results. The speaker described the conditions of the Negroes in Birmingham, and I kept saying to myself: "That's it." Then a Negro spoke from the same platform, and somehow I knew that this was what I'd been looking for all my life.

At the end of the meeting I went up and gave my name. From that day to this, every minute of my life has been tied up with the workers' movement.

I joined the Unemployment Council, and some weeks later the Communist Party. I read all the literature of the movement that I could get my hands on, and began to see my way more clearly.

I had some mighty funny ideas at first, but I guess that was only natural. For instance, I thought that we ought to start by getting all the big Negro leaders like [Oscar] DePriest and [W. E. B.] Du Bois and Walter White into the Communist Party, and then we would have all the support we needed. I didn't know then that DePriest and the rest of the leaders of that type are on the side of the bosses, and fight as hard as they can against the workers. They don't believe in fighting against the system that produces Jim-Crowism. They stand up for that system, and try to preserve it, and so they are really on the side of Jim-Crowism and inequality. I got rid of all these ideas after I heard Oscar Adams and others like him speak in Birmingham.

Misleaders in Action

That happened this way: Birmingham had just put on a Community Chest drive. The whites gave and the Negroes gave. Some gave willingly, thinking it was really going to help feed the unemployed, and the rest had it taken out of their wages. There was mighty little relief handed out to the workers, even when they did get on the rolls. The Negroes only got about half what the whites got. Some of the workers waiting at the relief station made up a take-off on an old prison song. I remember that the first two lines of it went:

I've counted the beans, babe,
I've counted the greens...

The Unemployment Council opened a fight for cash relief, and aid for single men, and equal relief for Negro and white. They called for a meeting in Capitol Park, and we gathered about the Confederate Monument, about 500 of us, white and Negro, and then we marched on the Community Chest headquarters. There were about 100 cops there. The officials of the Community Chest spoke, and said that the best thing for the Negroes to do was to go back to the farms. They tried very hard to give the white workers there the idea that if the Negroes went back to the farms, the whites would get a lot more relief.

Of course our leaders pointed out that the small farmers and share-croppers and tenants on the cotton-lands around Birmingham were starving, and losing their land and stock, and hundreds were drifting into the city in the hope of getting work.

Then Oscar Adams spoke up. He was the editor of the *Birmingham Reporter*, a Negro paper. What he said opened my eyes—but not in the way he expected. He said we shouldn't be misled by the leaders of the Unemployment Council, that we should go politely to the white bosses and officials and ask them for what they wanted, and do as they said.

Adams said: "We Negroes don't want social equality." I was furious. I said inside of myself: "Oscar Adams, we Negroes want social and every other kind of equality. There's no reason on God's green earth why we should be satisfied with anything less."

Traitors in the Ranks

That was the end of any ideas I had that the big-shots among the recognised Negro leaders would fight for us, or really put up any struggle for equal rights. I knew that Oscar Adams and the people like him were among our worst enemies, especially dangerous because they work from inside our ranks and a lot of us get the idea that they are with us and of us.

I look back over what I've written about those days since I picked up the leaflet of the Unemployment Council, and wonder if I've really said what I mean. I don't know if I can get across to you the feeling that came over me whenever I went to a meeting of the Council, or of the Communist Party, and heard their speakers and read their leaflets. All my life I'd been sweated and stepped on and Jim-Crowed. I lay on my belly in the mines for a few dollars a week, and saw my pay stolen and slashed, and my buddies killed. I lived in the worst section of town, and rode behind the "Colored" signs on streetcars, as though there was something disgusting about me. I heard myself called "nigger" and "darky," and I had to say "Yes, sir" to every white man, whether he had my respect or not.

I had always detested it, but I had never known that anything could be done about it. And here, all of a sudden, I had found organizations in which Negroes and whites sat together, and worked together, and knew no difference of race or color. Here were organizations that weren't scared to come out for equality for the Negro people, and for the rights of the workers. The Jim-Crow system, the wage-slave system, weren't everlasting after all! It was like all of a sudden turning a corner on a dirty, old street and finding yourself facing a broad, shining highway.

The bosses, and the Negro misleaders like Oscar Adams, told us that these Reds were "foreigners" and "strangers" and that the Communist program wasn't acceptable to the workers in the South. I couldn't see that at all. The leaders of the Communist Party and the Unemployment Council seemed people very much like the ones I'd always been used to. They were workers, and they talked our language. Their talk sure sounded better to me than the talk of Oscar Adams, or the President of the Tennessee Coal, Iron and Railroad Co. who addressed us every once in a while. As for the program not being acceptable to us—I felt then, and I know now, that the Communist program is the only program that the Southern workers—whites and Negroes both—can possibly accept in the long run. It's the only program that does justice to the Southern worker's ideas that everybody ought to have an equal chance, and that every man has rights that must be respected.

Work Against Odds

The Communist Party and the Unemployment Council had to work under the most difficult conditions. We tried to have a little headquarters, but it was raided and closed by the police. We collected money for leaflets, penny by penny, and mimeographed them on an old, rickety hand-machine we kept in a private home. We worked very quietly, behind drawn shades, and were always on the look-out for spies and police. We put the leaflets out at night, from door-step to door-step. Some of our members who worked in factories sneaked them in there.

Sometimes we would distribute leaflets in a neighborhood, calling for a meeting in half an hour on a certain corner. We would put up just one speaker, he would give his message in the fewest possible words, we would pass out pamphlets and leaflets, and the meeting would break up before the cops could get on the scene.

The bosses got scared, and the Ku Klux Klan got busy. The Klan would parade up and down the streets, especially in the Negro neighborhoods, in full regalia, warning the Negroes to keep away from the Communists. They passed out leaflets saying: "Communism Must Be Wiped Out. Alabama Is a Good Place for Good Negroes, but a Bad Place for Negroes Who Want Social Equality."

In June, 1930, I was elected a delegate to the National Unemployment Convention in Chicago. Up to this point I had been staying with relatives in Birmingham. They were under the influence of the Negro misleaders and preachers, and they told me that if I went to the convention I need never come to their house again. The very morning I was to leave, I found a leaflet on my doorstep, put there by the Ku Klux Klan.

I went to Chicago, riding the rods to get there.

A World Movement

In Chicago, I got my first broad view of the revolutionary workers' movement. I met workers from almost every state in the union, and I heard about the work of the same kind of organizations in other countries, and it first dawned on me how strong and powerful the working-class was. There wasn't only me and a few others in Birmingham. There were hundreds, thousands, millions of us!

My family had told me not to come back. What did I care? My real family was the organization. I'd found that I had brothers and sisters in every corner of the world, I knew that we were all fighting for one thing and that they'd stick by me. I never lost that feeling, in all the hard days to come, in Fulton Tower Prison with the threat of the electric chair and the chain-gang looming over me.

I went back to Birmingham and put every ounce of my strength into the work of organization. I built groups among the miners. I read and I studied. I worked in the Young Communist League under the direction of Harry Simms, the young white boy who was later, during the strike of the Kentucky miners, to give his life for the working-class.

I helped organize an Anti-Lynching Conference in Chattanooga. This conference selected delegates to the first convention of the League of Struggle for Negro Rights, held in St. Louis in 1930.

Death Penalty to the Lynchers

I myself was not a delegate to the St. Louis Conference—but the decisions of the conference impressed me. All the Negro organizations before this, and all the white liberal groups, had pussy-footed and hesitated and hemmed and hawed on the burning issue of lynching. When I read the slogan of the League of Struggle for Negro Rights—"Death Penalty to Lynchers!"—the words seemed blazed right across the page. The St. Louis Conference called for a determined struggle for equality for the Negro people.

I had a number of experiences about this time, that taught me a great deal. I went into the Black Belt, and talked with the Negro and white share-croppers and tenants. The price of cotton had crashed, and the burden was being put on the croppers and tenants, so the landlords might go on living in style. There was practically nothing to eat in the cabins. The croppers had applied for government loans, but when the loans came the landlords, with the help of the rural postmasters, stole the money. There was as yet no Share Croppers Union, which was later to challenge the landlords' system of debt-slavery.

A Negro preacher with whom I had made contact notified a Negro secret service-man that I was about, and together they tried to terrorize me. The preacher said: "I don't know anything about the conditions of the people here. I only know that I myself am happy and comfortable." Well, the upshot of it was that the preacher called the sheriff, and [a] lynch-mob began to form, and I escaped by grabbing the first train out of town. My escape was a matter of minutes. It was a white sharecropper who supplied me with the funds to get away.

Scottsboro

It was while I was in New Orleans for a few weeks as representative of the Trade Union Unity League, that I first saw the name Scottsboro. I want to go into that a bit, because the Scottsboro case marked a new stage in the life of the Negro people—and the white workers too—in the United States.

One morning I picked up a capitalist paper and saw that "nine black brutes had raped two little white girls." That was the way the paper put it. There was a dock strike on at the time in New Orleans, and the bosses would have been glad to see this issue, the Scottsboro case, used as a method of whipping up hatred of white and Negro longshoremen against each other.

I knew the South well enough to know at once that here was a vicious frame-up. I got to work right away organizing committees among the workers of New Orleans. We visited clubs, unions, churches to get support for the Scottsboro boys.

On May 31, 1931, I went as a delegate to the first All-Southern Scottsboro Conference, held in Chattanooga.

The hall where the conference was to be held was surrounded by gunmen and police, but we went through with the meeting just the same. The bosses and dicks were boiling mad because we had white and Negro meeting together—and saying plainly that the whole Scottsboro case was a rotten frame-up. I spoke at that conference.

While I was in Chattanooga that trip, I went to a meeting in a Negro church addressed by William Pickens, field secretary of the National Association for the Advancement of Colored People. Pickens made an attack on the International Labor Defense. He said we shouldn't get the governor and the courts mad. We should try to be polite to them. He said: "You people don't know how to fight. Give your money to me and to lawyers and we'll take care of this." Then he attacked the mothers of the Scottsboro boys as being a lot of ignorant fools.

Well, I was so mad I hardly knew what I was doing. I spoke up and said that the Scottsboro boys would never get out of prison until all the workers got together and brought terrific pressure on the lynchers. I said: "We've been polite to the lynchers entirely too long. As long as we O.K. what they do, as long as we crawl to them and assure them we have no wish to change their way of doing things—just so long we'll be slaves."

What Scottsboro Means

Later, while I lay in jail in Atlanta, I followed the Scottsboro case as best I could. Every time I got a paper—and that wasn't too often—I looked eagerly for news of the Scottsboro boys. I was uplifted, brimming over with joy because of the splendid fight we made at the new trial in Decatur. I could hardly contain myself when I saw how the workers were making the Scottsboro case a battering-ram against Jim-Crowism and oppression. I watched the protests in the Scottsboro case swelling to a roar that echoed from one end of the world to the other. And I'd pace that cell, aching to get out and throw myself into the fight.

If you know the South as I do, you know what the Scottsboro case means. Here were the landlords in their fine plantation homes, and the big white bosses in their city mansions, and the whole brutal force of dicks and police who do their bidding. There they sat, smug and self-satisfied, and oh, so sure that nothing could ever interfere with them and their ways. For all time they would be able to sweat and cheat the Negro people, and jail and frame and lynch and shoot them, as they pleased.

And all of a sudden someone laid a hand on their arm and said: "STOP." It was a great big hand, a powerful hand, the hand of the workers. The bosses were shocked and horrified and scared. I know that. And I know also that after the fight began for the Scottsboro boys, every Negro worker in mill or mine, every Negro cropper on the Black Belt plantations, breathed a little easier and held his head a little higher.

I'm ahead of my story now, because I got carried away by the thought of Scottsboro.

I settled down for work in Birmingham, especially among the miners. Conditions in the mines had become worse than horrible. The company had gunmen patrolling the highways, watching the miners. I was arrested several times during this period, and quizzed and bullied.

During one of these arrests the police demanded that I tell them where the white organizers lived. They said: "Where's that guy Tom? We'd like to lay our hands on the son-of-a-bitch."

I said: "I haven't seen Tom for days."

All of a sudden one of the policemen struck me across the mouth. "Mr. Tom to you, you bastard!" he roared.

The Willie Peterson Frame-Up

But it was during the Willie Peterson frame-up that I first got a real taste of police brutality.

There was frame-up in the air for weeks before the Peterson case started. The miners were organizing against wage-cuts; the white and Negro workers were beginning to get together and demand relief and jobs and the human rights that had been taken from them. If bosses could engineer a frame-up against some Negro, a lot of white workers would begin to think about that instead of about bread and jobs. If they could be made to think of the Negroes they worked with as rapists and murderers, they wouldn't be so anxious to organize with them in unions and Unemployment Councils. Also, such frame-ups are always the excuse for terrorizing the Negroes.

On August 3, in Birmingham, two white girls were killed. More than 70 Negroes were lynched in the fury that was whipped up around this case! One of the papers said that the man who shot these girls was a Negro, and that he had made a "Communist speech" to them before the murder.

A dragnet was thrown out, and I was one of the first to be caught.

I was lying in bed when a large white man came to our window and put a gun in my face. At the same moment there was a crash, and some other men broke in the door. My roommate and I were forced out of bed and handcuffed. We didn't know what it was all about.

I was locked up. About an hour later, police came to my cell and dragged me down the stairs and into a car. I was carried to the woods, about 20 miles out of town. On the way one of the gun-thugs kept pointing out places where he had killed "niggers."

The car stopped and we all got out. They asked me: "Who shot Nell Williams?" I said I didn't know.

Third Degree

Two of the men pulled their coats off and slipped a rubber hose from their trousers. I was still handcuffed. They began to beat me over the head. When one man got tired, another would take the hose from him and go on with the beating. They said they knew that I had shot Nell Williams. They demanded that I point out some of the white comrades. I shut my lips tight over my teeth, and said nothing.

Next morning I couldn't get my hat on my swollen head. My ears were great raw lumps of flesh.

Willie Peterson, an unemployed coal-miner, a veteran of the World War, was framed for that murder. He is as innocent as I was.

By now I was known to every stool-pigeon and policeman in Birmingham, and my work became extremely difficult. It was decided to send me to Atlanta.

I want to describe the conditions of the Atlanta workers, because that will give some idea of why the Georgia bosses find it necessary to sentence workers' organizers to the chain-gang. I couldn't say how many workers were unemployed—the officials keep this information carefully hidden. It was admitted that 25,000 families, out of 150,000 population, were on relief. Hundreds who were jobless were kept off the relief rolls.

In the factories, the wages were little higher than the amount of relief doled out to the unemployed. The conditions of the Southern textile workers is known to be extremely bad, but Atlanta has mills that even the Southern papers talk about as "sore spots." The Fulton Bag Company was one of these. There, and in the Piedmont and other textile plants, young girls worked for $6 and even less a week, slaving long hours in ancient, unsanitary buildings.

In the spring of 1930, six organizers of the workers—two white women, two white men and two Negro men—were arrested and indicted for "inciting to insurrection." The state was demanding that they be sent to the electric chair.

Splitting the Workers

The Black Shirts—a fascist organization—held parades quite often, demanding that all jobs be taken away from Negroes and given to whites. They said that all the Negroes should go back to Africa. I smiled the first time I heard this—it amused me to see how exactly the program of Marcus Garvey fitted in with the program of the Klan.

Of course the demand of the Black Shirts to give all the jobs to the whites was an attempt to split the white workers from the Negroes and put an end to joint struggles for relief. As organizer for the Unemployment Council, I had to fight mighty hard against this poison.

From the cradle onward, the Southern white boy and girl are told that they are better than Negroes. Their birth certificates are tagged "white"; they sit in white schools, play in white parks and live on white streets. They pray in white churches, and when they die they are buried in white cemeteries. Everywhere before them are signs: "For White." "For Colored." They are taught that Negroes are thieves, and murderers, and rapists.

I remember especially one white worker, a carpenter, who was one of the first people I talked to in Atlanta. He was very friendly to me. He came to me one day and said that he agreed with the program, but something was holding him back from joining the Unemployment Council.

"What's that, Jim?" I asked. Really, though, I didn't have to ask. I knew the South, and I could guess.

"Well, I just don't figure that white folks and Negroes should mix together," he said. "It won't never do to organize them in one body."

I said: "Look here, Jim. You know that the carpenters and all the other workers get a darn sight less pay for the same work in the South than they do in other parts. Did you ever figure out why?"

He hadn't.

The Price of Division

"Well," I said, "I'll tell you why. It's because the bosses have got us all split up down here. We Southern workers are as good fighters as there are anywhere, and yet we haven't been able to get equal wages with the workers in other places, and we haven't got any rights to speak of. That's because we've been divided. When the whites go out on strike, the bosses call in the Negroes to scab. When the Negroes strike, the bosses call in the whites to scab.

"Did you ever figure out why the unions here are so weak? It's because the whites don't want to organize with the Negroes, and the Negroes don't trust the whites.

"We haven't got the simplest human rights down here. We're not allowed to organize and we're not allowed to hold our meetings except in secret. We can't vote—most of us—because the bosses are so anxious to keep the Negroes from voting that they make laws that take this right away from the white workers too.

"We Southern workers are like a house that's divided against itself. We're like an army that goes out to fight the enemy and stops on the way because its men are all fighting each other.

"Take this relief business, now," I said. "The commissioners tell the whites that they can't give them any more relief because they have to feed so many Negroes, and the Negroes ought to be chased back to the farms. Then they turn around and tell the Negroes that white people have to come first on the relief, so there's nothing doing for colored folks. That way they put us off, and get us scrapping with each other.

"Now suppose the white unemployed, and the Negro unemployed, all go to the commissioners together and say: 'We're all starving. We're all in need. We've decided to get together into one strong, powerful organization to make you come across with relief.'

"Don't you think that'll bring results, Jim?" I asked him. "Don't you see how foolish it is to go into the fight with half an army when we could have a whole one? Don't you think that an empty belly is a pretty punk exchange for the honor of being called a 'superior' race? And can't you realize that as long as one foot is chained to the ground the other can't travel very far?"

What Happened to Jim

Jim didn't say anything more that day. I guess he went home and thought it over. He came back about a week later and invited me to his house. It was the first time he'd ever had a Negro in the house as a friend and equal. When I got there I found two other Negro workers that Jim had brought into the Unemployment Council.

About a month later Jim beat up a rent collector who was boarding up the house of an evicted Negro worker. Then he went to work and organized a committee of whites and Negroes to see the mayor about the case. "Today it's the black worker across town; tomorrow it'll be me," Jim told the mayor.

There are a lot of Jims today, all over the South.

We organized a number of block committees of the Unemployment Councils, and got rent and relief for a large number of families. We agitated endlessly for unemployment insurance.

In the middle of June, 1932, the state closed down all the relief stations. A drive was organized to send all the jobless to the farms.

We gave out leaflets calling for a mass demonstration at the courthouse to demand that the relief be continued. About

1,000 workers came, 600 of them white. We told the commissioners we didn't intend to starve. We reminded them that $800,000 had been collected in the Community Chest drive. The commissioners said there wasn't a cent to be had.

But the very next day the commission voted $6,000 for relief to the jobless!

On the night of July 11, I went to the Post Office to get my mail. I felt myself grabbed from behind and turned to see a police officer.

I was placed in a cell, and was shown a large electric chair, and told to spill everything I knew about the movement. I refused to talk, and was held incommunicado for eleven days. Finally I smuggled out a letter through another prisoner, and the International Labor Defense got on the job.

The Insurrection Law

Assistant Solicitor John Hudson rigged up the charge against me. It was the charge of "inciting to insurrection." It was based on an old statute passed in 1861, when the Negro people were still chattel slaves, and the white masters needed a law to crush slave insurrection and kill those found giving aid to the slaves. The statute read:

> *If any person be in any manner instrumental in bringing, introducing or circulating within the state any printed or written paper, pamphlet, or circular for the purpose of exciting insurrection, revolt, conspiracy or resistance on the part of slaves, Negroes or free persons of color in this state he shall be guilty of high misdemeanor which is punishable by death.*

Since the days of the Civil War that law had lain, unused and almost forgotten. Now the slaves of the new order—the white and black slaves of capitalism—were organizing. In the eyes of the Georgia masters, it was a crime punishable by death.

The trial was set for January 16, 1933. The state of Georgia displayed the literature that had been taken from my room, and read passages of it to the jury. They questioned me in great detail. Did I believe that the bosses and government ought to pay insurance to unemployed workers? That Negroes should have complete equality with white people? Did I believe in the demand for the self-determination of the Black Belt—that the Negro people should be allowed to rule the Black Belt territory, kicking out the white landlords and government officials? Did I feel that the working-class could run the mills and mines and government? That it wasn't necessary to have bosses at all?

The Unseen Jury

I told them I believed all of that—and more.

The courtroom was packed to suffocation. The I.L.D. attorneys, Benjamin J. Davis, Jr., and John H. Geer, two young Negroes—and I myself—fought every step of the way. We were not really talking to that judge, nor to those prosecutors, whose questions we were answering. Over their heads we talked to the white and Negro workers who sat on the benches, watching, listening, learning. And beyond them we talked to the thousands and millions of workers all over the world to whom this case was a challenge.

We demanded that Negroes be placed on jury rolls. We demanded that the insulting terms, "nigger" and "darky," be dropped in that court. We asserted the right of the workers to organize, to strike, to make their demands, to nominate candidates of their choice. We asserted the right of the Negro people to have complete equality in every field.

The state held that my membership in the Communist Party, my possession of Communist literature, was enough to send me to the electric chair. They said to the jury: "Stamp this damnable thing out now with a conviction that will automatically carry with it a penalty of electrocution."

And the hand-picked lily-white jury responded: "We, the jury, find the defendant guilty as charged, but recommend that mercy be shown and fix his sentence at from 18 to 20 years."

I had organized starving workers to demand bread, and I was sentenced to live out my years on the chain-gang for it. But I knew that the movement itself would not stop. I spoke to the court and said: "They can hold this Angelo Herndon and hundreds of others, but it will never stop these demonstrations on the part of Negro and white workers who demand a decent place to live in and proper food for their kids to eat."

I said: "You may do what you will with Angelo Herndon. You may indict him. You may put him in jail. But there will come thousands of Angelo Herndons. If you really want to do anything about the case, you must go out and indict the social system. But this you will not do; for your role is to defend the system under which the toiling masses are robbed and oppressed.

"You may succeed in killing one, two, even a score of working-class organizers. But you cannot kill the working class."

Fulton Tower Prison

Now began the long months in Fulton Tower Prison. How can I describe those days? I was starved. I was ill, I was denied the sight of friends, denied the literature of the class struggle, which meant more than food and drink to me. I was tortured by the jailers, who taunted me, and threatened me, and searched feverishly for a thousand and one ways to make the days of a jailed man a living hell.

But worse than anything was the way time dragged, dragged, till each separate minute became an eternity of torture. Time became my personal enemy—an enemy I had to fight with all my strength. The first hours became a day, and the first days became weeks, and then began the long succession of months—six of them, a year of them, seventeen, eighteen, nineteen. I lay on my filthy bunk, and studied the patterns on walls and ceilings, and learned to know every spot and crack. I watched the shadows of the jail bars on the floor shorten and lengthen again. I saw men come and go, and now and again return. Prisoners arrived with horrible stories of torture and brutality on the chain-gang for which I was headed. I said good-bye to ten men as they left the cell to go to the death-chair.

Meanwhile, beyond the walls, the working-class movement was fighting on. Sometimes I got a newspaper, torn and dirty, and lay on the floor piecing it together. Sometimes—very rarely—a friend was allowed to see me for a moment. In this way I learned what was going on.

The crisis got worse, and the New Deal came in. The workers learned that it meant more hunger and misery, and strikes broke out. The map of the United States was dotted with strikes. The workers in the very hell-holes I had once slaved in, downed tools and fought to better their conditions. The farmers massed to stop the sale of their land. The Scottsboro fight went on ceaselessly, was carried across the world, piled up new mountains of strength.

In Germany, Hitler took over power, poured a sea of blood over the country, and yet could not drown the organizations, the fighting spirit of the working-class. The Chinese Soviets tore a fifth of China from the grip of the foreign and the native exploiters.

In the Soviet Union, the workers, all power in their hands, built vast new dams and power-stations, laid new railways, fired new blast furnaces, planted great farms and built, stone upon stone, the structure of a new society of peace and plenty.

The war danger flared and died down and flared again—the workers watching constantly to stamp out the spark.

"The Workers Will Set Me Free"

I wanted to be out in the struggle, taking my part in it, doing my share. But not for one minute did I doubt that the workers would make me free. Even the news that the Georgia Supreme Court had denied me a new trial did not dishearten me. From the letters I received, I knew that the workers everywhere were fighting for me. I wrote letters—never knowing if they would leave the jail or not—and I read what papers and books I had, and I waited.

The day I heard that the International Labor Defense had had a bail set for me, I packed up my belongings and got ready to go. The jailers laughed at me. "Bail set ain't bail raised," they said. But I knew I'd go. And I went.

One morning Joe Brodsky, the lawyer who'd also fought for the Scottsboro boys, came to my cell and said: "We're going, Angelo."

The working-class had determined on my release, and I was free. They had raised, penny by penny, the enormous sum of $15,000 to get a class brother out of jail.

I took the train for the North. All along the way I was greeted by my comrades. In Washington, in Baltimore, in Philadelphia and Newark, workers stood on the platform to watch the train come by, and they cheered me, and I cheered their spirit and their determination. I stepped out of the train at Pennsylvania Station, into the arms of 7,000 of my white and Negro class-brothers and class-sisters.

I am happy to be out. Now, for a time at least, I can take my place once more in the ranks of the working-class. Now I am back in the fight.

ELEVEN

ETHEL AND JULIUS ROSENBERG

Selected Letters (1951-1953)

ETHEL AND JULIUS ROSENBERG, MEMBERS OF THE Communist Party during the height of McCarthyism, were arrested, convicted, and electrocuted after spending two years trying to prove their innocence in the Death House at Sing Sing. Ethel Greenglass was born in the state of New York in 1915, and Julius Rosenberg was born three years later, also in New York. They were married in 1939 and arrested in 1950. The two were executed by the state after being accused of selling military secrets about the atomic bomb to the Soviet Union vice-consul, and we are left to contemplate the legacy of their example. The following excerpts from their letters indicate the bleakness of incarceration, along with their deep love and fidelity to each other, their family, and their values. Like so many prisoners, they were relegated to epistolary communication. Prisoners, denied other means of connection, write letters, thus prison letters constitute a corpus of literature all its own. Husband and wife wrote many letters over the course of the bewildering years they spent in prison. They wrote to each other, their lawyer, the president, family, friends, and, compellingly, to their two young children. Can you imagine sitting down to write one final letter to your children, realizing they would grow into adulthood without the treasure of parental love and protection? A knock on the door interrupted their family life, and Julius was arrested. Two weeks later, Ethel went to court to answer questions but never returned. Despite shoddy evidence, despite false testimony, and despite the international movement that rose in their defense, they were executed on their fourteenth wedding anniversary. If they were not safe from a knock on the door, who among us is? Are our rights different from theirs? People today, including political enemies of the state, are still subjected to state-sanctioned murder, often under the guise of "death by incarceration," aka life in prison with no possibility of parole. In their final, futile appeal to President Eisenhower they declared and forewarned: "We now again solemnly declare our innocence. The guilt in this case, if we die, will be America's. The shame, if we die, will dishonor this generation, and pervade history until future Americans recapture the heritage of truth, justice and equality before the law." And also, this: "The present mirrors the future." Their legacy remains a chilling reminder of the reach of the state and the lengths our government goes to in order to silence insurgent consciousness.

Sept. 23, 1951
Dearest Sweetheart,
In spite of the gloom and terrible lament, which I share with you, your powerful words exude courage and understanding. This is all the more admirable because at the time when the cold endless torment of this incarceration engulfs you, you take heart and see clearly as a socially conscious person, that our fight is part and parcel of mankinds [sic] seeking and striving against the tyrants. Even though I take heart from your encouraging words my heart aches for you, my love. Your lot is such a difficult one and I can only send you by way of this paper some little comfort. If I could only be with you, it would be so much easier for us to pass the coming hurdles together. Keep in mind that there will be a happy ending to our present predicament and together we will once more move along paths of decency, honor and love.

Our legal consultation was excellent but all too short. The manner in which Manny presented this one point for our appeal, its thoroughness both morally and legally proves once again that he's tops as a lawyer. I have all the confidence in the world that the appeal brief will be a masterpiece. It is gratifying to me to see that he has his whole heart in it. The Guardian articles are swell but are only a small beginning as I feel that a greater effort is needed and more means have to be found to make public the facts in our case to counteract the adverse distortions that have been foisted on the public. I hope to hear that within a month's time some definite organizational steps will have be [sic] made to coordinate this campaign and start the avalanche of truth. Believe me honey I feel a lot better with every bit of progress and every positive step made in our behalf. We must keep in mind that a tremendous and long drawn out effort is necessary as the despoilers of truth are well entrenched and their political motives blindly drives [sic] them to perpetuate this frameup. I have faith in the people and their will will force the justice department to honor the law of the land and set us free.

It is true that not enough discussion was had on the crucial situation at home but it is my opinion that the next few weeks will bring some positive results on this problem also. We'll have to ease up on pressing Manny at least until his appeal brief is completed. My glorious woman we were so busy I could only look at you but for moments when all the time I wanted to look at you and to devour you with my eyes. I join you in our eternal longing and vigil always wanting to be in your arms. My lovely one I send you all my heart—

Your Julius

Jan 15. 1953
My Darling,
The press is gripped with a frenzy for they are trying to offset the mountainous support we are getting by increasing the lines of newsprint used against us to greater proportions. The Journal American feature writer Bob Considine began a series of articles this last Sunday about us. Wednesday the World Telegram started a series. The rest of the papers chimmed [sic] in with Editorials and special articles. Always additional & newer stories are invented to take the place of the weak and unconvincing record that there is in this case. Ethel I read at least seven papers daily and I can truthfully say that they are showing signs of desperation. They are actually pleading with us to save them from complete exposure of this horrible miscarriage of justice. It is they who have pulled off this foul political frameup and now they will feel the full fury of the storm that they helped unleash.

It takes a great deal of strength sitting here facing our doom while such powerful forces are in combat deciding our fate. However, our faith in the good people everywhere is more than justified because they have shown by their actions that they will not let this happen here. Every word and line I read I begin to formulate answers immediately but as yet this week I haven't put anything on paper. I think I'll save my say for Manny's next visit.

Another thing I've noticed is that my longing for you is increasing. I never though [sic] it possible to miss you so much. The pain is very severe. My love for you is overwhelmingly powerful and I continue to draw on it for new strength & continued encouragement. Dearest wife there is no greater hurt than being falsely accused and forced to suffer separation from loved ones when all mind and body cries out against this ghastly wrong. It staggers the imagination to think that we could possibly endure such dire hardships which are greatly aggravated because we are completely innocent. Our determination to prove as you've so aptly stated before "the indestructibility of the human being" and to show the power of the dignity of the individual cables us to hold fast to our principles and withstand the mounting pressure. Bunny girl I embrace you with all the love of my heart and adore you with all the love of my mind and although we're apart the emotional and mutal [sic] satisfaction you've given me in these difficult hours never fails to inspire me and satisfies my greatest need and assuages a great deal of my agony. No man can ask for more from another person even though she be his wife. I do hope we can once again take up our life together because there is so much that is beautiful in our relationship and no matter what happens to us I am happy for the sweet life we've lived together. I never asked for much but I was very lucky to have you and the children and I always got most out of life depending on how much I contributed to advancing the common good. Always devoted to you.

Your own Julie

Mr. Emanuel H. Bloch
7 W. 16th Street
New York, New York
June 19, 1953

Dear Manny,
The following letter is to be delivered to my children:

Dearest Sweethearts, my most precious children,

Only this morning it looked like we might be together again after all. Now that this cannot be I want so much for you to know all that I have come to know. Unfortunately I may write only a few simple words; the rest your own lives must teach you, even as mine taught me.

At first, of course, you will grieve bitterly for us, but you will not grieve alone. That is our consolation and it must eventually be yours.

Eventually, too, you must come to believe that life is worth the living. Be comforted that even now, with the end of ours slowly approaching that we know this with a conviction that defeats the executioner!

Your lives must teach you, too, that good cannot really flourish in the midst of evil; that freedom and all the things that go to make up a truly satisfying and worthwhile life, must sometimes be purchased very dearly. Be comforted, then, that we were serene and understood with the deepest kind of understanding, that civilization had not as yet progressed to the point where life did not have to be lost for the sake of life; and that we were comforted in the sure knowledge that others would carry on after us.

We wish we might have had the tremendous joy and gratification of living our lives out with you. Your Daddy who is with me in these last momentous hours sends his heart and all the love that is in it for his dearest boys. Always remember that we were innocent and could not wrong our conscience.

We press you close and kiss you with all our strength.

Lovingly,
Daddy and Mommy—
Julie and Ethel

P.S.—to Manny:—The Ten Commandments religious medal and chain—and my wedding ring. I wish you to present to our children as a token of our undying love—

P.S.— to Manny: Please be certain to give my best wishes to Saul Miller. Tell him I love and honor him with all my heart—Tell him I want him to know that I feel he shares my triumph—For I have no fear and no regrets—Only that the release from the trap was not completely effectuated and the qualities I possessed could not expand to their fullest capacities—I want him to have the pleasure of knowing how much he meant to me, how much he did to help me grow up—All my love to all our dear ones.

Love you so much
Ethel
Death House
Sing Sing Prison
Ossining, New York

June 16, 1953
The President of The United States

We, JULIUS ROSENBERG and ETHEL ROSENBERG, husband and wife, are now confined in the Death House in Sing Sing Prison, awaiting electrocution on June 18, our fourteenth wedding anniversary. We address this petition to you for the exercise of your supreme power to prevent—"a crime worse than murder"—our unjust deaths.

We appealed to you once before. Our sentences, we declared there, violated truth and the instincts of civilized mankind.

We told you the truth: we are innocent.

The truth does not change.

We now again solemnly declare our innocence.

The guilt in this case, if we die, will be America's. The shame, if we die, will dishonor this generation, and pervade history until future Americans recapture the heritage of truth, justice and equality before the law. Our case has made new precedents in the law of this land—evil precedents, unjust, inhuman and with not even that concern for human life shown the protection of the rights of property.

The highest court of the United States—its Supreme Court enshrined in pure white marble halls—has just denied us a stay of our executions, although with death so close, it closed its doors to us to seek its review of weighty questions going to the heart of the justice of our convictions and sentences. And yet, unheard of in the annals of our law, four judges—four of the most distinguished members of that bench—had voted to let us live, at least long enough to vindicate our rights before them. Thus, the opportunity we struggled to achieve is now denied.

Instead our accusers torture us, in the face of death, with the guarantee of life for the price of a confession of guilt. Close upon the execution date—as though to draw upon the last full measure of dread of death and love of life—their high negotiator came bearing this tainted proffer of life. We refuse this iniquitous bargain, even as perhaps the last few days of our young lives are slipping away. We cannot besmirch our names by bearing false witness to save ourselves. Do not dishonor America, Mr. President, by considering as a condition of our right to survive, the delivery of a confession of guilt of a crime we did not commit.

You may not believe us, but the shamefulness of our convictions has already bitten deeply into the consciences of reasoning men. Justices Black and Douglas (and perhaps Frankfurter, as well) of the United States Supreme Court, have noted their unwillingness to leave history to ponder the justice of death sentences responsive to a verdict, procured by prosecution conduct which a reviewing court held could not be "too severely condemned," so "wholly reprehensible" and productive of prejudice to us so beyond recall that "a new trial... should have been granted."

You may not believe us, because there is in the court record an undisturbed verdict of guilt. But we defended our innocence on that very record. Printed unabridged in the tens of thousands, the record itself, according to the Government the strength of its case, has convinced untold numbers of our innocence and instilled, in more, grave doubts of the correctness of the verdict.

The world-wide sense of disbelief in our guilt is epitomized by the considered conclusion, from the record, of Dr. Harold C. Urey, our foremost nuclear physicist whose scientific labors represent a major contribution to the defense of our country.

"The case against the ROSENBERGS," he declared, "outrages logic and justice... it depends on patently perjured testimony."

You may not believe us, but the passage of even the few short months, since last we appealed to you, is confirming our prediction that, in the inexorable operation of time and conscience, the truth of our innocence would emerge.

Evidence recently discovered, reveals proof positive, short of recantations by the Greenglasses, the prosecution witnesses-in-chief—the one, imprisoned, under the aegis of the Government; the other, free, under the constant threat of indictment for her admitted capital crime—that a case was constructed against us on a pyramid of lies. The new evidence should, at the very least, persuade you that doubt of our guilt is not so aggravated that good conscience demands that we live.

We submitted proof to the courts that Greenglass was said by his own wife, to have a "tendency to hysteria" and, from her knowledge of him since he was ten years old, to "say things were so even if they were not."

We submitted documentary evidence to show that David Greenglass, trapped by his own misdeeds, hysterical with fear for his own life and that of Ruth, his wife, fell back on his life-long habit of lying, exploited by his shrewd-minded and equally guilty wife, to fabricate, bit by bit, a monstrous tale that has sent us, his own flesh and blood, down and [sic] long and terrible path toward death.

We submitted proof to show that David Greenglass stole uranium from Los Alamos, in a venture concededly unconnected with us. This fact both he and Ruth concealed at the trial, to avoid destruction of their claim that they were pawns in our hands and to cloak their independent motivation to bargain with the Government for the "cooperation" which inculpated us and saved them.

In fact, who knows the real crime of the Greenglasses that moved David to the dreadful penance of sending his own sister to her death. For on his apprehension, we showed, he admitted he lied to the authorities about the "espionage" material he gave to Gold.

But that his trial testimony against us resulted from the later fabrications of his animal desire to preserve himself and his wife, the mother of his children, is evident from our new proof that at first, he incriminated neither of us, or mentioned that the crime committed was "the crime worse than murder": the theft of the "secret" of the atom bomb.

We submitted actual physical evidence (the missing console table), never produced in court against us, to show the Greenglasses and the Government collaborated to bring into the trial false testimony that we had in our home an expensive console table, given to us by the "Russians" and equipped for micro filming purposes. The table itself belies the Greenglass testimony. It is not a specially constructed table, but one bought by us at R.M. Macy's for about $21.00, as we testified at our trial.

We submitted documentary evidence to show the unconscionable quid pro quo, for the Greenglass' testimony implicating us. Here, where we face death, the Government offered first that neither of the Greenglasses should even be charged with crime. The brazenness of the "deal" was transparent. The proposal changed in form but not in substance, Ruth, the wife, would go free and David, although to be named as a defendant, would receive no penalty. Finally, only after the suspicions of our attorney that this filthy bargain was in the making were revealed in open court, did the Government, to save face, first propose that David Greenglass might be required to serve some prison term. The sordid "deal," all know, has been fulfilled: Ruth is free; David may soon be; we are in the Death House.

We asked the courts to overturn the scandalous convictions, conceived in fraud and consummated in perjury. But the disposition we received was summary. Our right to an open trial of our proof was frustrated. We were foreclosed from the opportunity to expose the fraud and perjury. We were prevented from exhausting our appellate remedies. We were accorded only the trappings, but not the substance of justice.

Can our deaths, hastened by the assumed blindness of those who refuse to see the travesty, exonerate American justice where history will resurrect the unburied doubts?

The present mirrors the future. Never before have more people in all lands and in all walks of life been so shaken as by our imminent fate. Our inhuman sentences of death have already produced a traumatic shock to the moral sense of the world.

If you will not hear our voices, hear the voices of the world.

Hear the Pope: who spoke three times in the name of Christian compassion. Hear his Cardinal in France who "is passionately hoping" that our lives be spared in the name of "charity and peace." Listen to the pleas of 5,000 of our Protestant ministers beseeching in the name of God; the Rabbis of France, "in the very name of our common ideal of justice and generosity."

Hear the great and the humble: from Einstein, whose name is legend, to the tyros in the laboratories of Manchester; from struggling students at Grenoble to Oxford professors; from the world-famous movie directors of Rome to the bit players of London; from the dock workers at Liege to cotton spinners of India; from the peasants of Italy to the philosophers of Israel; from Mauriac, the Nobel literatteur, to reports in Mexico City; from the stenographers of Rotterdam to the transport workers of England; from the auto workers of Detroit to the auto workers of Paris; from Nexo of Denmark to Sequeiros [sic] of Mexico to Seghers of Germany to Duhamel of France; from Australia to Argentina; from Uruguay to Sweden; from Cuba to Canada to New Zealand.

Read the tons of petitions, letters, post-cards, stacked high in your filing rooms, from the plain and gentle-folk of our land. They marched before your door in such numbers as never before, as have their brothers and sisters in London, Paris, Melbourne, Buenos Aires, Ottawa, Rome. They ask you not to orphan our two young boys. They ask you in the name of the conscience of the world, in the name of humanity, brotherhood and peace to spare our lives.

Hear the great and the humble for the sake of America.

Do not hear only our accusers in the Department of Justice whom the law makes advisers to you on our right to clemency. Does not their self-interest to secure the challenged verdict, by our deaths, tarnish their advice? Does not their conceded concealment from you of most persuasive pleas on our behalf, impair the integrity of their counsel?

Let us recall John de Stogumbur, the English chaplain of Shaw's "St. Joan," who had been one of the most bloodthirsty advocates of Joan's proposed burning, as he came rushing in from this "glorious" spectacle, overcome with remorse and sobbing like one demented:

"You don't know; you haven't seen; it is so easy to talk when you don't know. You madden yourself with words: you damn yourself because it feels grand to throw oil on the flaming hell of your own temper. But when it is brought home to you; when you see the thing you have done; when it's blinding your eyes, stifling your nostrils, tearing your heart—then, then—Oh, God, take away this sight from me—Oh, Christ! deliver me from this fire that is consuming me—she cried to thee in the midst of it: Jesus! Jesus! she is in thy bosom; and I am in hell for ever more."

We ask you, Mr. President, the civilized head of a civilized nation to judge our plea with reason and humanity. And remember, we are a father and a mother.

Ethel Rosenberg
Julius Rosenberg

TWELVE

MARTIN LUTHER KING JR.

Letter from Birmingham City Jail (1963)

THE SON AND GRANDSON OF BAPTIST PASTORS, Michael King Jr. was born in segregated Atlanta, Georgia, in 1929. When King Sr. traveled to Germany and became inspired by the sixteenth-century Protestant Reformation, he changed his own name and his son's to Martin Luther. A precocious student, Martin Luther King Jr. graduated from high school at age fifteen and earned a PhD in systemic theology from Boston University by the age of twenty-six. Dr. King entered the civil rights struggles of the era and was elected president of the Southern Christian Leadership Conference in 1957. He traveled and spoke out against injustice tirelessly, leading strikes, boycotts, marches, and picket lines. He was named *Time* magazine's "Man of the Year" and at age thirty-five became the youngest recipient of the Nobel Peace Prize. King was arrested for acts of nonviolent civil disobedience more than two dozen times. He was assassinated in 1968 in Memphis, Tennessee, where he had traveled to stand in solidarity with striking garbage workers.

Written "alone in a narrow jail cell" over an eleven-day stretch, King's renowned jail letter weaves biblical references, historical examples, philosophy, and moral arguments to justify breaking unjust laws "openly and lovingly." His argument shifts from the question "Is it legal or illegal?" to "Is it ethical or unethical?" In his moral landscape, the oppressed lead, and sincere allies take direction from them. King heralds those "willingly going to jail for conscience's sake" as righteous heroes, establishing civil rights as a historical certainty and civil disobedience as a moral imperative. Multitudes of courageous protesters, including those who participated in the famed lunch-counter sit-ins in North Carolina three years earlier, were already confronting unjust segregation laws in public spaces around the nation when King wrote this letter. His elevation of nonviolent civil disobedience, coupled with moral certitude, has deeply transformed protest movements around the world, bringing clarity, courage, and inspiration to those willing to go to jail to bend "the arc of the moral universe" toward justice.

LETTER FROM BIRMINGHAM CITY JAIL

WHILE CONFINED here in the Birmingham city jail, I came across your recent statement calling our present activities "unwise and untimely." Seldom, if ever, do I pause to answer criticism of my work and ideas. If I sought to answer all of the criticisms that cross my desk, my secretaries would be engaged in little else in the course of the day, and I would have no time for constructive work. But since I feel that you are men of genuine good will and your criticisms are sincerely set forth, I would like to answer your statement in what I hope will be patient and reasonable terms.

I think I should give the reason for my being in Birmingham, since you have been influenced by the argument of "outsiders coming in." I have the honor of serving as president of the Southern Christian Leadership Conference, an organization operating in every Southern state, with headquarters in Atlanta, Georgia. We have some eighty-five affiliate organizations all across the South, one being the Alabama Christian Movement for Human Rights. Whenever necessary and possible, we share staff, educational and financial resources with our affiliates. Several months ago our local affiliate here in Birmingham invited us to be on call to engage in a nonviolent direct-action program if such were deemed necessary. We readily consented, and when the hour came we lived up to our promises. So I am here, along with several members of my staff, because we were invited here. I am here because I have basic organizational ties here.

Beyond this, I am in Birmingham because injustice is here. Just as the eighth-century prophets left their little villages and carried their "thus saith the Lord" far beyond the boundaries of their hometowns; and just as the Apostle Paul left his little village of Tarsus and carried the gospel of Jesus Christ to practically every hamlet and city of the Greco-Roman world, I too am compelled to carry the gospel of freedom beyond my particular hometown. Like Paul, I must constantly respond to the Macedonian call for aid.

Moreover, I am cognizant of the interrelatedness of all communities and states. I cannot sit idly by in Atlanta and not be concerned about what happens in Birmingham. Injustice anywhere is a threat to justice everywhere. We are caught in an inescapable network of mutuality, tied in a single garment of destiny. Whatever affects one directly affects all indirectly. Never again can we afford to live with the narrow, provincial "outside agitator" idea. Anyone who lives inside the United States can never be considered an outsider.

You deplore the demonstrations that are presently taking place in Birmingham. But I am sorry that your statement did not express a similar concern for the conditions that brought the demonstrations into being. I am sure that each of you would want to go beyond the superficial social analyst who looks merely at effects and does not grapple with underlying causes. I would not hesitate to say that it is unfortunate that so-called demonstrations are taking place in Birmingham at this time, but I would say in more emphatic terms that it is even more unfortunate that the white power structure of this city left the Negro community with no other alternative.

In any nonviolent campaign there are four basic steps: collection of the facts to determine whether injustices are alive, negotiation, self-purification, and direct action. We have gone through all of these steps in Birmingham. There can be no gainsaying of the fact that racial injustice engulfs this community. Birmingham is probably the most thoroughly segregated city in the United States. Its ugly record of police brutality is known in every section of this country. Its unjust treatment of Negroes in the courts is a notorious reality. There have been more unsolved bombings of Negro homes and churches in Birmingham than in any other city in this nation. These are the hard, brutal, and unbelievable facts. On the basis of them, Negro leaders sought to negotiate with the city fathers. But the political leaders consistently refused to engage in good-faith negotiation.

Then came the opportunity last September to talk with some of the leaders of the economic community. In these negotiating sessions certain promises were made by the merchants, such as the promise to remove the humiliating racial signs from the stores. On the basis of these promises, Reverend Shuttlesworth and the leaders of the Alabama Christian Movement for Human Rights agreed to call a moratorium on any type of demonstration. As the weeks and months unfolded, we realized that we were the victims of a broken promise. The signs remained. As in so many experiences of the past, we were confronted with blasted hopes, and the dark shadow of a deep disappointment settled upon us. So we had no alternative except that of preparing for direct action, whereby we would present our very bodies as a means of laying our case before the conscience of the local and national community. We were not unmindful of the difficulties involved. So we decided to go through a process of self-purification. We started having workshops on nonviolence and repeatedly asked ourselves the questions, "Are you able to accept blows without retaliating?" and "Are you able to endure the ordeals of jail?" We decided to set our direct-action program around the Easter season, realizing that, with exception of Christmas, this was the largest shopping period of the year. Knowing that a strong economic withdrawal program would be the by-product of direct action, we felt that this was the best time to bring pressure on the merchants for the needed changes. Then it occurred to us that the March election was ahead, and so we speedily decided to postpone action until after election day. When we discovered that Mr. Conner was in the runoff, we decided again to postpone action so that the demonstration could not be used to cloud the issues. At this time we agreed to begin our nonviolent witness the day after the runoff.

This reveals that we did not move irresponsibly into direct action. We, too, wanted to see Mr. Conner defeated, so we went through postponement after postponement to aid in this community need. After this we felt that direct action could be delayed no longer.

You may well ask, "Why direct action, why sit-ins, marches, and so forth? Isn't negotiation a better path?" You are exactly right in your call for negotiation. Indeed, this is the purpose of direct action. Nonviolent direct action seeks to create such a crisis and establish such creative tension that a community that has consistently refused to negotiate is forced to confront the issue. It seeks so to dramatize the issue that it can no longer be ignored. I just referred to the creation of tension as a part of the work of the nonviolent resister. This may sound rather shocking. But I must confess that I am not afraid of the word "tension." I have earnestly worked and preached against violent tension, but there is a type of constructive nonviolent tension that is necessary for growth. Just as Socrates felt that it was necessary to create a tension in the mind so that individuals could rise from the bondage of myths and half-truths to the unfettered realm of creative analysis and objective appraisal, we must see the need of having nonviolent gadflies to create the kind of tension in society that will help men to rise from the dark depths of prejudice and racism to the majestic heights of understanding and brotherhood. So, the purpose of direct action is to create a situation so crisis-packed that it will inevitably open the door to negotiation. We therefore concur with you in your call for negotiation. Too long has our beloved Southland been bogged down in the tragic attempt to live in monologue rather than dialogue.

One of the basic points in your statement is that our acts are untimely. Some have asked, "Why didn't you give the new administration time to act?" The only answer that I can give to this inquiry is that the new administration must be prodded about as much as the outgoing one before it acts. We will be sadly mistaken if we feel that the election of Mr. Boutwell will bring the millennium to Birmingham. While Mr. Boutwell is much more articulate and gentle than Mr. Conner, they are both segregationists, dedicated to the task of maintaining the status quo. The hope I see in Mr. Boutwell is that he will be reasonable enough to see the futility of massive resistance to desegregation. But he will not see this without pressure from the devotees of civil rights. My friends, I must say to you that we have not made a single gain in civil rights without determined legal and nonviolent pressure. History is the long and tragic story of the fact that privileged groups seldom give up their privileges voluntarily. Individuals may see the moral light and voluntarily give up their unjust posture;

but, as Reinhold Niebuhr has reminded us, groups are more immoral than individuals.

We know through painful experience that freedom is never voluntarily given by the oppressor; it must be demanded by the oppressed. Frankly, I have never yet engaged in a direct-action movement that was "well timed" according to the timetable of those who have not suffered unduly from the disease of segregation. For years now I have heard the word "wait." It rings in the ear of every Negro with a piercing familiarity. This "wait" has almost always meant "never." It has been a tranquilizing thalidomide, relieving the emotional stress for a moment, only to give birth to an ill-formed infant of frustration. We must come to see with the distinguished jurist of yesterday that "justice too long delayed is justice denied." We have waited for more than three hundred and forty years for our God-given and constitutional rights. The nations of Asia and Africa are moving with jetlike speed toward the goal of political independence, and we still creep at horse-and-buggy pace toward the gaining of a cup of coffee at a lunch counter. I guess it is easy for those who have never felt the stinging darts of segregation to say "wait." But when you have seen vicious mobs lynch your mothers and fathers at will and drown your sisters and brothers at whim; when you have seen hate-filled policemen curse, kick, brutalize, and even kill your black brothers and sisters with impunity; when you see the vast majority of your twenty million Negro brothers smothering in an airtight cage of poverty in the midst of an affluent society; when you suddenly find your tongue twisted and your speech stammering as you seek to explain to your six-year-old daughter why she cannot go to the public amusement park that has just been advertised on television, and see tears welling up in her little eyes when she is told that Funtown is closed to colored children, and see the depressing clouds of inferiority begin to form in her little mental sky, and see her begin to distort her little personality by unconsciously developing a bitterness toward white people; when you have to concoct an answer for a five-year-old son asking in agonizing pathos, "Daddy, why do white people treat colored people so mean?"; when you take a cross-country drive and find it necessary to sleep night after night in the uncomfortable corners of your automobile because no motel will accept you; when you are humiliated day in and day out by nagging signs reading "white" and "colored"; when your first name becomes "nigger" and your middle name becomes "boy" (however old you are) and your last name becomes "John," and when your wife and mother are never given the respected title "Mrs."; when you are harried by day and haunted by night by the fact that you are a Negro, living constantly at tiptoe stance, never knowing what to expect next, and plagued with inner fears and outer resentments; when you are forever fighting a degenerating sense of "nobodyness"—then you will understand why we find it difficult to wait. There comes a time when the cup of endurance runs over and men are no longer willing to be plunged into an abyss of injustice where they experience the bleakness of corroding despair. I hope, sirs, you can understand our legitimate and unavoidable impatience.

You express a great deal of anxiety over our willingness to break laws. This is certainly a legitimate concern. Since we so diligently urge people to obey the Supreme Court's decision of 1954 outlawing segregation in the public schools, it is rather strange and paradoxical to find us consciously breaking laws. One may well ask, "How can you advocate breaking some laws and obeying others?" The answer is found in the fact that there are two types of laws: there are just laws, and there are unjust laws. I would agree with St. Augustine that "An unjust law is no law at all."

Now, what is the difference between the two? How does one determine when a law is just or unjust? A just law is a man-made code that squares with the moral law, or the law of God. An unjust law is a code that is out of harmony with the moral law. To put it in the terms of St. Thomas Aquinas, an unjust law is a human law that is not rooted in eternal and natural law. Any law that uplifts human personality is just. Any law that degrades human personality is unjust. All segregation statutes are unjust because segregation distorts the soul and damages the personality. It gives the segregator a false sense of superiority and the segregated a false sense of inferiority. To use the words of Martin Buber, the great Jewish philosopher, segregation substitutes an "I–it" relationship for the "I–thou" relationship and ends up relegating persons to the status of things. So segregation is not only politically, economically, and sociologically unsound, but it is morally wrong and sinful. Paul Tillich has said that sin is separation. Isn't segregation an existential expression of man's tragic separation, an expression of his awful estrangement, his terrible sinfulness? So I can urge men to obey the 1954 decision of the Supreme Court because it is morally right, and I can urge them to disobey segregation ordinances because they are morally wrong.

Let us turn to a more concrete example of just and unjust laws. An unjust law is a code that a majority inflicts on a minority that is not binding on itself. This is difference made legal. On the other hand, a just law is a code that a majority compels a minority to follow, and that it is willing to follow itself. This is sameness made legal.

Let me give another explanation. An unjust law is a code inflicted upon a minority which that minority had no part in enacting or creating because it did not have the unhampered right to vote. Who can say that the legislature of Alabama which set up the segregation laws was democratically elected? Throughout the state of Alabama all types of conniving methods are used to prevent Negroes from becoming registered voters, and there are some counties without a single Negro registered to vote, despite the fact that the Negroes constitute a majority of the population. Can any law set up in such a state be considered democratically structured?

These are just a few examples of unjust and just laws. There are some instances when a law is just on its face and unjust in its application. For instance, I was arrested Friday on a charge of parading without a permit. Now, there is nothing wrong with an ordinance which requires a permit for a parade, but when the ordinance is used to preserve segregation and to deny citizens the First Amendment privilege of peaceful assembly and peaceful protest, then it becomes unjust.

Of course, there is nothing new about this kind of civil disobedience. It was seen sublimely in the refusal of Shadrach, Meshach, and Abednego to obey the laws of Nebuchadnezzar because a higher moral law was involved. It was practiced superbly by the early Christians, who were willing to face hungry lions and the excruciating pain of chopping blocks before submitting to certain unjust laws of the Roman Empire. To a degree, academic freedom is a reality today because Socrates practiced civil disobedience.

We can never forget that everything Hitler did in Germany was "legal" and everything the Hungarian freedom fighters did in Hungary was "illegal." It was "illegal" to aid and comfort a Jew in Hitler's Germany. But I am sure that if I had lived in Germany during that time, I would have aided and comforted my Jewish brothers even though it was illegal. If I lived in a Communist country today where certain principles dear to the Christian faith are suppressed, I believe I would openly advocate disobeying these anti-religious laws.

I must make two honest confessions to you, my Christian and Jewish brothers. First, I must confess that over the last few years I have been gravely disappointed with the white moderate. I have almost reached the regrettable conclusion that the Negro's great stumbling block in the stride toward freedom is not the White Citizens Councillor or the Ku Klux Klanner but the white moderate who is more devoted to order than to justice; who prefers a negative peace which is the absence of tension to a positive peace which is the presence of justice; who constantly says, "I agree with you in the goal you seek, but I can't agree with your methods of direct action"; who paternalistically feels that he can set the timetable for another man's freedom; who lives by the myth of time; and who constantly advises the Negro to wait until a "more convenient season." Shallow understanding from people of good will is more frustrating than absolute misunderstanding from people of ill will. Lukewarm acceptance is much more bewildering than outright rejection.

In your statement you asserted that our actions, even though peaceful, must be condemned because they precipitate violence. But can this assertion be logically made? Isn't this like condemning the robbed man because his possession of money precipitated the evil act of robbery? Isn't this like condemning Socrates because his unswerving commitment to truth and his philosophical delvings precipitated the misguided popular mind to make him drink the hemlock? Isn't this like condemning Jesus because His unique God-consciousness and never-ceasing devotion to His will precipitated the evil act of crucifixion? We must come to see, as federal courts have consistently affirmed, that it is immoral to urge an individual to withdraw his efforts to gain his basic constitutional rights because the quest precipitates violence. Society must protect the robbed and punish the robber.

I had also hoped that the white moderate would reject the myth of time. I received a letter this morning from a white brother in Texas which said, "All Christians know that the colored people will receive equal rights eventually, but is it possible that you are in too great of a religious hurry? It has taken Christianity almost 2000 years to accomplish what it has. The teachings of Christ take time to come to earth." All that is said here grows out of a tragic misconception of time. It is the strangely irrational notion that there is something in the very flow of time that will inevitably cure all ills. Actually, time is neutral. It can be used either destructively or constructively. I am coming to feel that the people of ill will have used time much more effectively than the people of good will. We will have to repent in this generation not merely for the vitriolic words and actions of the bad people but for the appalling silence of the good people. We must come to see that human progress never rolls in on wheels of inevitability. It comes through the tireless efforts and persistent work of men willing to be co-workers with God, and without this hard work time itself becomes an ally of the forces of social stagnation.

You spoke of our activity in Birmingham as extreme. At first I was rather disappointed that fellow clergymen would see my nonviolent efforts as those of an extremist. I started thinking about the fact that I stand in the middle of two opposing forces in the Negro community. One is a force of complacency made up of Negroes who, as a result of long years of oppression, have been so completely drained of self-respect and a sense of "somebodiness" that they have adjusted to segregation, and, on the other hand, of a few Negroes in the middle class who, because of a degree of academic and economic security and because at points they profit by segregation, have unconsciously become insensitive to the problems of the masses. The other force is one of bitterness and hatred and comes perilously close to advocating violence. It is expressed in the various black nationalist groups that are springing up over the nation, the largest and best known being Elijah Muhammad's Muslim movement. This movement is nourished by the contemporary frustration over the continued existence of racial discrimination. It is made up of people who have lost faith in America, who have absolutely repudiated Christianity, and who have concluded that the white man is an incurable devil. I have tried to stand between these two forces, saying that we need not follow the do-nothingism of the complacent or the hatred and despair of the black nationalist. There is a more excellent way, of love and nonviolent protest. I'm grateful to God that, through the Negro church, the dimension of nonviolence entered our struggle. If this philosophy had not emerged, I am convinced that by now many streets of the South would be flowing with floods of blood. And I am further convinced that if our white brothers dismiss as "rabble-rousers" and "outside agitators" those of us who are working through the channels of nonviolent direct action and refuse to support our nonviolent efforts, millions of Negroes, out of frustration and despair, will seek solace and security in black nationalist ideologies, a development that will lead inevitably to a frightening racial nightmare.

Oppressed people cannot remain oppressed forever. The urge for freedom will eventually come. This is what has happened to the American Negro. Something within has reminded him of his birthright of freedom; something without has reminded him that he can gain it. Consciously and unconsciously, he has been swept in by what the Germans call the Zeitgeist, and with his black brothers of Africa and his brown and yellow brothers of Asia, South America, and the Caribbean, he is moving with a sense of cosmic urgency toward the promised land of racial justice. Recognizing this vital urge that has engulfed the Negro community, one should readily understand public demonstrations. The Negro has many pent-up resentments and latent frustrations. He has to get them out. So let him march sometime; let him have his prayer pilgrimages to the city hall; understand why he must have sit-ins and freedom rides. If his repressed emotions do not come out in these nonviolent ways, they will come out in ominous expressions of violence. This is not a threat; it is a fact of history. So I have not said to my people, "Get rid of your discontent." But I have tried to say that this normal and healthy discontent can be channeled through the creative outlet of nonviolent direct action. Now this approach is being dismissed as extremist. I must admit that I was initially disappointed in being so categorized.

But as I continued to think about the matter, I gradually gained a bit of satisfaction from being considered an extremist. Was not Jesus an extremist in love?—"Love your enemies, bless them that curse you, pray for them that despitefully use you." Was not Amos an extremist for justice?—"Let justice roll down like waters and righteousness like a mighty stream." Was not Paul an extremist for the gospel of Jesus Christ?—"I bear in my body the marks of the Lord Jesus." Was not Martin Luther an extremist?—"Here I stand; I can do no other so help me God." Was not John Bunyan an extremist?—"I will stay in jail to the end of my days before I make a mockery of my conscience." Was not Abraham Lincoln an extremist?—"This nation cannot survive half slave and half free." Was not Thomas Jefferson an extremist?—"We hold these truths to be self-evident, that all men are created equal." So the question is not whether we will be extremist, but what kind of extremists we will be. Will we be extremists for hate, or will we be extremists for love? Will we be extremists for the preservation of injustice, or will we be extremists for the cause of justice?

I had hoped that the white moderate would see this. Maybe I was too optimistic. Maybe I expected too much. I guess I should have realized that few members of a race that has oppressed another race can understand or appreciate the deep groans and passionate yearnings of those that have been oppressed, and still fewer have the vision to see that injustice must be rooted out by strong, persistent, and determined action. I am thankful, however, that some of our white brothers have grasped the meaning of this social revolution and committed themselves to it. They are still all too small in quantity, but they are big in quality. Some, like Ralph McGill, Lillian Smith, Harry Golden, and James Dabbs, have written about our struggle in eloquent, prophetic, and understanding terms. Others have marched with us down nameless streets of the South. They sat in with us at lunch counters and rode in with us on the freedom rides. They have languished in filthy roach-infested jails, suffering the abuse and brutality of angry policemen who see them as "dirty nigger lovers." They, unlike many of their moderate brothers, have recognized the urgency of the moment and sensed the need for powerful "action" antidotes to combat the disease of segregation.

Let me rush on to mention my other disappointment. I have been disappointed with the white church and its leadership. Of course, there are some notable exceptions. I am not unmindful of the fact that each of you has taken some significant stands on this issue. I commend you, Reverend Stallings, for your Christian stand this past Sunday in welcoming Negroes to your Baptist Church worship service on a nonsegregated basis. I commend the Catholic leaders of this state for integrating Springhill College several years ago.

But despite these notable exceptions, I must honestly reiterate that I have been disappointed with the church. I do not say that as one of those negative critics who can always find something wrong with the church. I say it as a minister of the gospel who loves the church, who was nurtured in its bosom, who has been sustained by its Spiritual blessings, and who will remain true to it as long as the cord of life shall lengthen.

I had the strange feeling when I was suddenly catapulted into the leadership of the bus protest in Montgomery several years ago that we would have the support of the white church. I felt that the white ministers, priests, and rabbis of the South would be some of our strongest allies. Instead, some few have been outright opponents, refusing to understand the freedom movement and misrepresenting its leaders; all too many others have been more cautious than courageous and have remained silent behind the anesthetizing security of stained-glass windows.

In spite of my shattered dreams of the past, I came to Birmingham with the hope that the white religious leadership of this community would see the justice of our cause and with deep moral concern serve as the channel through which our just grievances could get to the power structure. I had hoped that each of you would understand. But again I have been disappointed.

I have heard numerous religious leaders of the South call upon their worshipers to comply with a desegregation decision because it is the law, but I have longed to hear white ministers say, follow this decree because integration is morally right and the Negro is your brother. In the midst of blatant injustices inflicted upon the Negro, I have watched white churches stand on the sidelines and merely mouth pious irrelevancies and sanctimonious trivialities. In the midst of a mighty struggle to rid our nation of racial and economic injustice, I have heard so many ministers say, "Those are social issues which the gospel has nothing to do with," and I have watched so many churches commit themselves to a completely otherworldly religion which made a strange distinction between bodies and souls, the sacred and the secular.

There was a time when the church was very powerful. It was during that period that the early Christians rejoiced when they were deemed worthy to suffer for what they believed. In those days the church was not merely a thermometer that recorded the ideas and principles of popular opinion; it was the thermostat that transformed the mores of society. Wherever the early Christians entered a town the power structure got disturbed and immediately sought to convict them for being "disturbers of the peace" and "outside agitators." But they went on with the conviction that they were "a colony of heaven" and had to obey God rather than man. They were small in number but big in commitment. They were too God-intoxicated to be "astronomically intimidated." They brought an end to such ancient evils as infanticide and gladiatorial contest.

Things are different now. The contemporary church is so often a weak, ineffectual voice with an uncertain sound. It is so often the arch supporter of the status quo. Far from being disturbed by the presence of the church, the power structure of the average community is consoled by the church's often vocal sanction of things as they are.

But the judgment of God is upon the church as never before. If the church of today does not recapture the sacrificial spirit of the early church, it will lose its authentic ring, forfeit the loyalty of millions, and be dismissed as an irrelevant social club with no meaning for the twentieth century. I meet young people every day whose disappointment with the church has risen to outright disgust.

I hope the church as a whole will meet the challenge of this decisive hour. But even if the church does not come to the aid of justice, I have no despair about the future. I have no fear about the outcome of our struggle in Birmingham, even if our motives are presently misunderstood. We will reach the goal of freedom in Birmingham and all over the nation, because the goal of America is freedom. Abused and scorned though we may be, our destiny is tied up with the destiny of America. Before the Pilgrims landed at Plymouth, we were here. Before the pen of Jefferson scratched across the pages of history the majestic word of the Declaration of Independence, we were here. For more than two centuries our foreparents labored here without wages; they made cotton king; and they built the homes of their masters in the midst of brutal injustice and shameful humiliation—and yet out of a bottomless vitality our people continue to thrive and develop. If the inexpressible cruelties of slavery could not stop us, the opposition we now face will surely fail. We will win our freedom because the sacred heritage of our nation and the eternal will of God are embodied in our echoing demands.

I must close now. But before closing I am impelled to mention one other point in your statement that troubled me profoundly. You warmly commended the Birmingham police force for keeping "order" and "preventing violence." I don't believe you would have so warmly commended the police force if you had seen its angry violent dogs literally biting six unarmed, nonviolent Negroes. I don't believe you would so quickly commend the policemen if you would observe their ugly and inhuman treatment of Negroes here in the city jail; if you would watch them push and curse old Negro women and young Negro girls; if you would see them slap and kick old Negro men and young boys, if you would observe them, as they did on two occasions, refusing to give us food because we wanted to sing our grace together. I'm sorry that I can't join you in your praise for the police department. It is true that they have been rather disciplined in their public handling of the demonstrators. In this sense they have been publicly "nonviolent." But for what purpose? To preserve the evil system of segregation. Over the last few years I have consistently preached that nonviolence demands that the means we use must be as pure as the ends we seek. So I have tried to make it clear that it is wrong to use immoral means to attain moral ends. But now I must affirm that it is just as wrong, or even more, to use moral means to preserve immoral ends.

I wish you had commended the Negro demonstrators of Birmingham for their sublime courage, their willingness to suffer, and their amazing discipline in the midst of the most inhuman provocation. One day the South will recognize its real heroes. They will be the James Merediths, courageously and with a majestic sense of purpose facing jeering and hostile mobs and the agonizing loneliness that characterizes the life of the pioneer. They will be old, oppressed, battered Negro women, symbolized in a seventy-two-year-old woman of Montgomery, Alabama, who rose up with a sense of dignity and with her people decided not to ride the segregated buses, and responded to one who inquired about her tiredness with ungrammatical profundity, "My feets is tired, but my soul is rested." They will be young high school and college students, young ministers of the gospel and a host of their elders courageously and nonviolently sitting in at lunch counters and willingly going to jail for conscience's sake. One day the South will know that when these disinherited children of God sat down at lunch counters they were in reality standing up for the best in the American dream and the most sacred values in our Judeo-Christian heritage.

Never before have I written a letter this long—or should I say a book? I'm afraid that it is much too long to take your precious time. I can assure you that it would have been much shorter if I had been writing from a comfortable desk, but what else is there to do when you are alone for days in the dull monotony of a narrow jail cell other than write long letters, think strange thoughts, and pray long prayers?

If I have said anything in this letter that is an understatement of the truth and is indicative of an unreasonable impatience, I beg you to forgive me. If I have said anything in this letter that is an overstatement of the truth and is indicative of my having a patience that makes me patient with anything less than brotherhood, I beg God to forgive me.

Yours for the cause of Peace and Brotherhood,
Martin Luther King, Jr.

THIRTEEN

MALCOLM X

Saved

MALCOLM LITTLE WAS BORN MAY 19, 1925, IN OMAHA, Nebraska. Following a jailhouse conversion to Islam, he changed his name to Malcolm X to free himself of "the White slavemaster name of 'Little.'" A remarkable orator, he dedicated his life to analyzing history, organizing, preaching, confronting white supremacy, and advancing Black power. In this excerpt from his autobiography, he presents the quintessential prison transformation story. Like Frederick Douglass, Malcolm X emphasizes the central role literacy plays in liberation. His spiritual emancipation, which preceded his physical freedom, illustrates what rehabilitation can look like. Studying the dictionary, learning world history, and honing his oratory skills changed his life and the lives of countless others living beneath the mountain, and has changed our world. Decades later, after mass incarceration has stolen millions of lives and created swelling prison populations, this text remains an intergenerational gift, still relevant in the twenty-first century. The formula of mental emancipation remains powerful: when imprisoned people become politicized and utilize tools to develop an analysis of their oppression, a power greater than any other is unlocked. A father of six girls, Malcolm X was thirty-nine years old when he was assassinated on February 19, 1965, at the Audubon Ballroom in Washington Heights, New York. Ossie Davis delivered the eulogy at his funeral in Harlem, saying, "If you knew him you would know why we must honor him.... And, in honoring him, we honor the best in ourselves."

I DID write to Elijah Muhammad. He lived in Chicago at that time, at 6116 South Michigan Avenue. At least twenty-five times I must have written that first one-page letter to him, over and over. I was trying to make it both legible and understandable. I practically couldn't read my handwriting myself; it shames even to remember it. My spelling and my grammar were as bad, if not worse. Anyway, as well as I could express it, I said I had been told about him by my brothers and sisters, and I apologized for my poor letter.

Mr. Muhammad sent me a typed reply. It had an all but electrical effect upon me to see the signature of the "Messenger of Allah." After he welcomed me into the "true knowledge," he gave me something to think about. The black prisoner, he said, symbolized white society's crime of keeping black men oppressed and deprived and ignorant, and unable to get decent jobs, turning them into criminals.

He told me to have courage. He even enclosed some money for me, a five-dollar bill. Mr. Muhammad sends money all over the country to prison inmates who write to him, probably to this day.

Regularly my family wrote to me, "Turn to Allah . . . pray to the East."

The hardest test I ever faced in my life was praying. You understand. My comprehending, my believing the teachings of Mr. Muhammad had only required my mind's saying to me, "That's right!" or "I never thought of that."

But bending my knees to pray that act—well, that took me a week. You know what my life had been. Picking a lock to rob someone's house was the only way my knees had ever been bent before.

I had to force myself to bend my knees. And waves of shame and embarrassment would force me back up.

For evil to bend its knees, admitting its guilt, to implore the forgiveness of God, is the hardest thing in the world. It's easy for me to see and to say that now. But then, when I was the personification of evil, I was going through it. Again, again, I would force myself back down into the praying-to-Allah posture. When finally I was able to make myself stay down—I didn't know what to say to Allah.

For the next years, I was the nearest thing to a hermit in the Norfolk Prison Colony. I never have been more busy in my life. I still marvel at how swiftly my previous life's thinking pattern slid away from me, like snow off a roof. It is as though someone else I knew of had lived by hustling and crime. I would be startled to catch myself thinking in a remote way of my earlier self as another person.

The things I felt, I was pitifully unable to express in the one-page letter that went every day to Mr. Elijah Muhammad. And I wrote at least one more daily letter, replying to one of my brothers and sisters. Every letter I received from them added something to my knowledge of the teachings of Mr. Muhammad. I would sit for long periods and study his photographs.

I've never been one for inaction. Everything I've ever felt strongly about, I've done something about. I guess that's why, unable to do anything else, I soon began writing to people I had known in the hustling world, such as Sammy the Pimp, John Hughes, the gambling-house owner, the thief Jumpsteady, and several dope peddlers. I wrote them all about Allah and Islam and Mr. Elijah Muhammad. I had no idea where most of them lived. I addressed their letters in care of the Harlem or Roxbury bars and clubs where I'd known them.

I never got a single reply. The average hustler and criminal was too uneducated to write a letter. I have known many slick, sharp-looking hustlers, who would have you think they had an interest in Wall Street; privately, they would get someone else to read a letter if they received one. Besides, neither would I have replied to anyone writing me something as wild as "the white man is the devil."

What certainly went on the Harlem and Roxbury wires was that Detroit Red was going crazy in stir, or else he was trying some hype to shake up the warden's office.

During the years that I stayed in the Norfolk Prison Colony, never did any official directly say anything to me about those letters, although, of course, they all passed through the prison censorship. I'm sure, however, they monitored what I wrote to add to the files which every state and federal prison keeps on the conversion of Negro inmates by the teachings of Mr. Elijah Muhammad.

But at that time, I felt that the real reason was that the white man knew that he was the devil.

Later on, I even wrote to the Mayor of Boston, to the Governor of Massachusetts, and to Harry S Truman. They never answered; they probably never even saw my letters. I hand-scratched to them how the white man's society was responsible for the black man's condition in this wilderness of North America.

It was because of my letters that I happened to stumble upon starting to acquire some kind of a homemade education.

I became increasingly frustrated at not being able to express what I wanted to convey in letters that I wrote, especially those to Mr. Elijah Muhammad. In the street, I had been the most articulate hustler out there—I had commanded attention when I said something. But now, trying to write simple English, I not only wasn't articulate, I wasn't even functional. How would I sound writing in slang, the way I would say it, something such as, "Look, daddy, let me pull your coat about a cat, Elijah Muhammad."

Many who today hear me somewhere in person, or on television, or those who read something I've said, will think I went to school far beyond the eighth grade. This impression is due entirely to my prison studies.

It had really begun back in the Charlestown Prison, when Bimbi first made me feel envy of his stock of knowledge. Bimbi had always taken charge of any conversation he was in, and I had tried to emulate him. But every book I picked up had few sentences which didn't contain anywhere from one to nearly all of the words that might as well have been in Chinese. When I just skipped those words, of course, I really ended up with little idea of what the book said. So I had come to the Norfolk Prison Colony still going through only book-reading motions. Pretty soon, I would have quit even these motions, unless I had received the motivation that I did.

I saw that the best thing I could do was get hold of a dictionary—to study, to learn some words. I was lucky enough to reason also that I should try to improve my penmanship. It was sad. I couldn't even write in a straight line. It was both ideas together that moved me to request a dictionary along with some tablets and pencils from the Norfolk Prison Colony school.

I spent two days just riffling uncertainly through the dictionary's pages. I'd never realized so many words existed! I didn't know which words I needed to learn. Finally, just to start some kind of action, I began copying.

In my slow, painstaking, ragged handwriting, I copied into my tablet everything printed on that first page, down to the punctuation marks.

I believe it took me a day. Then, aloud, I read back, to myself, everything I'd written on the tablet. Over and over, aloud, to myself, I read my own handwriting.

I woke up the next morning, thinking about those words—immensely proud to realize that not only had I written so much at one time, but I'd written words that I never knew were in the world. Moreover, with a little effort, I also could remember what many of these words meant. I reviewed the words whose meanings I didn't remember. Funny thing, from the dictionary first page right now, that "aardvark" springs to my mind. The dictionary had a picture of it, a long-tailed, long-eared, burrowing African mammal, which lives off termites caught by sticking out its tongue as an anteater does for ants.

I was so fascinated that I went on—I copied the dictionary's next page. And the same experience came when I studied that. With every succeeding page, I also learned of people and places and events from history. Actually the dictionary is like a miniature encyclopedia. Finally the dictionary's A section had filled a whole tablet—and I went on into the B's. That was the way I started copying what eventually became the entire dictionary. It went a lot faster after so much practice helped me to pick up handwriting speed. Between what I wrote in my tablet, and writing letters, during the rest of my time in prison I would guess I wrote a million words.

I suppose it was inevitable that as my word-base broadened, I could for the first time pick up a book and read and now begin to understand what the book was saying. Anyone who has read a great deal can imagine the new world that opened. Let me tell you something: from then until I left that prison, in every free moment I had, if I was not reading in the library, I was reading on my bunk. You couldn't have gotten me out of books with a wedge. Between Mr. Muhammad's teachings, my correspondence, my visitors—usually Ella and Reginald—and my reading of books, months passed without my even thinking about being imprisoned. In fact, up to then, I never had been so truly free in my life.

The Norfolk Prison Colony's library was in the school building. A variety of classes was taught there by instructors who came from such places as Harvard and Boston universities. The weekly debates between inmate teams were also held in the school building. You would be astonished to know how worked up convict debaters and audiences would get over subjects like "Should Babies Be Fed Milk?"

Available on the prison library's shelves were books on just about every general subject. Much of the big private collection that Parkhurst had willed to the prison was still in crates and boxes in the back of the library—thousands of old books. Some of them looked ancient: covers faded, old-time parchment-looking binding. Parkhurst, I've mentioned, seemed to have been principally interested in history and religion. He had the money and the special interest to have a lot of books that you wouldn't have in general circulation. Any college library would have been lucky to get that collection.

As you can imagine, especially in a prison where there was heavy emphasis on rehabilitation, an inmate was smiled upon if he demonstrated an unusually intense interest in books. There was a sizable number of well-read inmates, especially the popular debaters. Some were said by many to be practically walking encyclopedias. They were almost celebrities. No university would ask any student to devour literature as I did when this new world opened to me, of being able to read and understand.

I read more in my room than in the library itself. An inmate who was known to read a lot could check out more than the permitted maximum number of books. I preferred reading in the total isolation of my own room.

When I had progressed to really serious reading, every night at about ten P. M. I would be outraged with the "lights out." It always seemed to catch me right in the middle of something engrossing.

Fortunately, right outside my door was a corridor light that cast a glow into my room. The glow was enough to read by, once my eyes adjusted to it. So when "lights out" came, I would sit on the floor where I could continue reading in that glow.

At one-hour intervals the night guards paced past every room. Each time I heard the approaching footsteps, I jumped into bed and feigned sleep. And as soon as the guard passed, I got back out of bed onto the floor area of that light-glow, where I would read for another fifty-eight minutes—until the guard approached again. That went on until three or four every morning. Three or four hours of sleep a night was enough for me. Often in the years in the streets I had slept less than that.

The teachings of Mr. Muhammad stressed how history had been "whitened"—when white men had written history books, the black man simply had been left out. Mr. Muhammad couldn't have said anything that would have struck me much harder. I had never forgotten how when my class, me and all of those whites, had studied seventh-grade United States history back in Mason, the history of the Negro had been covered in one paragraph, and the teacher had gotten a big laugh with his joke, "Negroes' feet are so big that when they walk, they leave a hole in the ground."

This is one reason why Mr. Muhammad's teachings spread so swiftly all over the United States, among all Negroes, whether or not they became followers of Mr. Muhammad. The teachings ring true—to every Negro. You can hardly show me a black adult in America—or a white one, for that matter—who knows from the history books anything like the truth about the black man's role. In my own case, once I heard of the "glorious history of the black man," I took special pains to hunt in the library for books that would inform me on details about black history.

I can remember accurately the very first set of books that really impressed me. I have since bought that set of books and have it at home for my children to read as they grow up. It's called *Wonders of the World*. It's full of pictures of archaeological finds, statues that depict, usually, non-European people.

I found books like Will Durant's *Story of Civilization*. I read H. G. Wells' *Outline of History*. *Souls Of Black Folk* by W. E. B. Du Bois gave me a glimpse into the black people's history before they came to this country. Carter G. Woodson's *Negro History* opened my eyes about black empires before the black slave was brought to the United States, and the early Negro struggles for freedom.

J. A. Rogers' three volumes of *Sex and Race* told about race-mixing before Christ's time; about Aesop being a black man who told fables; about Egypt's Pharaohs; about the great Coptic Christian Empires; about Ethiopia, the earth's oldest continuous black civilization, as China is the oldest continuous civilization. Mr. Muhammad's teaching about how the white man had been created led me to *Findings in Genetics* by Gregor Mendel. (The dictionary's G section was where I had learned what "genetics" meant.) I really studied this book by the Austrian monk. Reading it over and over, especially certain sections, helped me to understand that if you started with a black man, a white man could be produced; but starting with a white man, you never could produce a black man because the white gene is recessive. And since no one disputes that there was but one Original Man, the conclusion is clear.

During the last year or so, in the *New York Times*, Arnold Toynbee used the word "bleached" in describing the white man. (His words were: "White (i.e. bleached) human beings of North European origin...") Toynbee also referred to the European geographic area as only a peninsula of Asia. He said there is no such thing as Europe. And if you look at the globe, you will see for yourself that America is only an extension of Asia. (But at the same time Toynbee is among those who have helped to bleach history. He has written that Africa was the only continent that produced no history. He won't write that again. Every day now, the truth is coming to light.)

I never will forget how shocked I was when I began reading about slavery's total horror. It made such an impact upon me that it later became one of my favorite subjects when I became a minister of Mr. Muhammad's. The world's most monstrous crime, the sin and the blood on the white man's hands, are almost impossible to believe. Books like the one by Frederick Olmstead opened my eyes to the horrors suffered when the slave was landed in the United States. The European woman, Fannie Kimball, who had married a Southern white slaveowner, described how human beings were degraded. Of course I read *Uncle Tom's Cabin*. In fact, I believe that's the only novel I have ever read since I started serious reading.

Parkhurst's collection also contained some bound pamphlets of the Abolitionist Anti-Slavery Society of New England. I read descriptions of atrocities, saw those illustrations of black slave women tied up and flogged with whips; of black mothers watching their babies being dragged off, never to be seen by their mothers again; of dogs after slaves, and of the fugitive slave catchers, evil white men with whips and clubs and chains and guns. I read about the slave preacher Nat Turner, who put the fear of God into the white slavemaster.

Nat Turner wasn't going around preaching pie-in-the-sky and "non-violent" freedom for the black man. There in Virginia one night in 1831, Nat and seven other slaves started out at his master's home and through the night they went from one plantation "big house" to the next, killing, until by the next morning 57 white people were dead and Nat had about 70 slaves following him. White people, terrified for their lives, fled from their homes, locked themselves up in public buildings, hid in the woods, and some even left the state. A small army of soldiers took two months to catch and hang Nat Turner. Somewhere I have read where Nat Turner's example is said to have inspired John Brown to invade Virginia and attack Harper's Ferry nearly thirty years later, with thirteen white men and five Negroes.

I read Herodotus, "the father of History," or, rather, I read about him. And I read the histories of various nations, which opened my eyes gradually, then wider and wider, to how the whole world's white men had indeed acted like devils, pillaging and raping and bleeding and draining the whole world's non-white people. I remember, for instance, books such as Will Durant's story of Oriental civilization, and Mahatma Gandhi's accounts of the struggle to drive the British out of India.

Book after book showed me how the white man had brought upon the world's black, brown, red, and yellow peoples every variety of the sufferings of exploitation. I saw how since the sixteenth century, the so-called "Christian trader" white man began to ply the seas in his lust for Asian and African empires, and plunder, and power. I read, I saw, how the white man never has gone among the non-white peoples bearing the Cross in the true manner and spirit of Christ's teachings—meek, humble, and Christ-like.

I perceived, as I read, how the collective white man had been actually nothing but a piratical opportunist who used

Faustian machinations to make his own Christianity his initial wedge in criminal conquests. First, always "religiously," he branded "heathen" and "pagan" labels upon ancient non-white cultures and civilizations. The stage thus set, he then turned upon his nonwhite victims his weapons of war.

I read how, entering India—half a billion deeply religious brown people—the British white man, by 1759, through promises, trickery and manipulations, controlled much of India through Great Britain's East India Company. The parasitical British administration kept tentacling out to half of the subcontinent. In 1857, some of the desperate people of India finally mutinied—and, excepting the African slave trade, nowhere has history recorded any more unnecessary bestial and ruthless human carnage than the British suppression of the non-white Indian people.

Over 115 million African blacks—close to the 1930's population of the United States—were murdered or enslaved during the slave trade. And I read how when the slave market was glutted, the cannibalistic white powers of Europe next carved up, as their colonies, the richest areas of the black continent. And Europe's chancelleries for the next century played a chess game of naked exploitation and power from Cape Horn to Cairo.

Ten guards and the warden couldn't have torn me out of those books. Not even Elijah Muhammad could have been more eloquent than those books were in providing indisputable proof that the collective white man had acted like a devil in virtually every contact he had with the world's collective non-white man. I listen today to the radio, and watch television, and read the headlines about the collective white man's fear and tension concerning China. When the white man professes ignorance about why the Chinese hate him so, my mind can't help flashing back to what I read, there in prison, about how the blood forebears of this same white man raped China at a time when China was trusting and helpless. Those original white "Christian traders" sent into China millions of pounds of opium. By 1839, so many of the Chinese were addicts that China's desperate government destroyed twenty thousand chests of opium. The first Opium War was promptly declared by the white man. Imagine! Declaring war upon someone who objects to being narcotized! The Chinese were severely beaten, with Chinese-invented gunpowder. The Treaty of Nanking made China pay the British white man for the destroyed opium; forced open China's major ports to British trade; forced China to abandon Hong Kong; fixed China's import tariffs so low that cheap British articles soon flooded in, maiming China's industrial development.

After a second Opium War, the Tientsin Treaties legalized the ravaging opium trade, legalized a British-French-American control of China's customs. China tried delaying that Treaty's ratification; Peking was looted and burned.

"Kill the foreign white devils!" was the 1901 Chinese war cry in the Boxer Rebellion. Losing again, this time the Chinese were driven from Peking's choicest areas. The vicious, arrogant white man put up the famous signs, "Chinese and dogs not allowed."

Red China after World War II closed its doors to the Western white world. Massive Chinese agricultural, scientific, and industrial efforts are described in a book that *Life* magazine recently published. Some observers inside Red China have reported that the world never has known such a hate-white campaign as is now going on in this non-white country where, present birth-rates continuing, in fifty more years Chinese will be half the earth's population. And it seems that some Chinese chickens will soon come home to roost, with China's recent successful nuclear tests.

Let us face reality. We can see in the United Nations a new world order being shaped, along color lines—an alliance among the non-white nations. America's U.N. Ambassador Adlai Stevenson complained not long ago that in the United Nations "a skin game" was being played. He was right. He was facing reality. A "skin game" is being played. But Ambassador Stevenson sounded like Jesse James accusing the marshal of carrying a gun. Because who in the world's history ever has played a worse "skin game" than the white man?

Mr. Muhammad, to whom I was writing daily, had no idea of what a new world had opened up to me through my efforts to document his teachings in books.

When I discovered philosophy, I tried to touch all the landmarks of philosophical development. Gradually, I read most of the old philosophers, Occidental and Oriental. The Oriental philosophers were the ones I came to prefer; finally, my impression was that most Occidental philosophy had largely been borrowed from the Oriental thinkers. Socrates, for instance, traveled in Egypt. Some sources even say that Socrates was initiated into some of the Egyptian mysteries. Obviously Socrates got some of his wisdom among the East's wise men.

I have often reflected upon the new vistas that reading opened to me. I knew right there in prison that reading had changed forever the course of my life. As I see it today, the ability to read awoke inside me some long dormant craving to be mentally alive. I certainly wasn't seeking any degree, the way a college confers a status symbol upon its students. My homemade education gave me, with every additional book that I read, a little bit more sensitivity to the deafness, dumbness, and blindness that was afflicting the black race in America. Not long ago, an English writer telephoned me from London, asking questions. One was, "What's your alma mater?" I told him, "Books." You will never catch me with a free fifteen minutes in which I'm not studying something I feel might be able to help the black man.

Yesterday I spoke in London, and both ways on the plane across the Atlantic I was studying a document about how the United Nations proposes to insure the human rights of the oppressed minorities of the world. The American black man is the world's most shameful case of minority oppression. What makes the black man think of himself as only an internal United States issue is just a catch-phrase, two words, "civil rights." How is the black man going to get "civil rights" before first he wins his human rights? If the American black man will start thinking about his human rights, and then start thinking of himself as part of one of the world's great peoples, he will see he has a case for the United Nations.

I can't think of a better case! Four hundred years of black blood and sweat invested here in America, and the white man still has the black man begging for what every immigrant fresh off the ship can take for granted the minute he walks down the gangplank.

But I'm digressing. I told the Englishman that my alma mater was books, a good library. Every time I catch a plane, I have with me a book that I want to read—and that's a lot of books these days. If I weren't out here every day battling the white man, I could spend the rest of my life reading, just satisfying my curiosity—because you can hardly mention anything I'm not curious about. I don't think anybody ever got more out of going to prison than I did. In fact, prison enabled me to study far more intensively than I would have if my life had gone differently and I had attended some college. I imagine that one of the biggest troubles with colleges is there are too many distractions, too much panty-raiding, fraternities, and boola-boola and all of that. Where else but in a prison could I have attacked my ignorance by being able to study intensely sometimes as much as fifteen hours a day?

Schopenhauer, Kant, Nietzsche, naturally, I read all of those. I don't respect them; I am just trying to remember some of those whose theories I soaked up in those years. These three, it's said, laid the groundwork on which the Fascist and Nazi philosophy was built. I don't respect them because it seems to me that most of their time was spent arguing about things that are not really important. They remind me of so many of the Negro "intellectuals," so-called, with whom I have come in contact—they are always arguing about something useless.

Spinoza impressed me for a while when I found out that he was black. A black Spanish Jew. The Jews excommunicated him because he advocated a pantheistic doctrine, something like the "allness of God," or "God in everything." The Jews read their burial services for Spinoza, meaning that he was dead as far as they were concerned; his family was run out of Spain, they ended up in Holland, I think.

I'll tell you something. The whole stream of Western philosophy has now wound up in a cul-de-sac. The white man has perpetrated upon himself, as well as upon the black man, so gigantic a fraud that he has put himself into a crack. He did it through his elaborate, neurotic necessity to hide the black man's true role in history.

And today the white man is faced head on with what is happening on the Black Continent, Africa. Look at the artifacts being discovered there, that are proving over and over again, how the black man had great, fine, sensitive civilizations before the white man was out of the caves. Below the Sahara, in the places where most of America's Negroes' foreparents were kidnapped, there is being unearthed some of the finest craftsmanship, sculpture and other objects, that has ever been seen by modern man. Some of these things now are on view in such places as New York City's Metropolitan Museum of Art. Gold work of such fine tolerance and workmanship that it has no rival. Ancient objects produced by black hands...refined by those black hands with results that no human hand today can equal.

History has been so "whitened" by the white man that even the black professors have known little more than the most ignorant black man about the talents and rich civilizations and cultures of the black man of millenniums ago. I have lectured in Negro colleges and some of these brainwashed black Ph.D.'s, with their suspenders dragging the ground with degrees, have run to the white man's newspapers calling me a "black fanatic." Why, a lot of them are fifty years behind the times. If I were president of one of these black colleges, I'd hock the campus if I had to, to send a bunch of black students off digging in Africa for more, more and more proof of the black race's historical greatness. The white man now is in Africa digging and searching. An African elephant can't stumble without falling on some white man with a shovel. Practically every week, we read about some great new find from Africa's lost civilizations. All that's new is white science's attitude. The ancient civilizations of the black man have been buried on the Black Continent all the time.

Here is an example: a British anthropologist named Dr. Louis S. B. Leakey is displaying some fossil bones—a foot, part of a hand, some jaws, and skull fragments. On the basis of these, Dr. Leakey has said it's time to rewrite completely the history of man's origin.

This species of man lived 1,818,036 years before Christ. And these bones were found in Tanganyika. In the Black Continent.

It's a crime, the lie that has been told to generations of black men and white men both. Little innocent black children, born of parents who believed that their race had no history. Little black children seeing, before they could talk, that their parents considered themselves inferior. Innocent black children growing up, living out their lives, dying of old age—and all of their lives ashamed of being black. But the truth is pouring out of the bag now.

Two other areas of experience which have been extremely formative in my life since prison were first opened to me in the Norfolk Prison Colony. For one thing, I had my first experiences in opening the eyes of my brainwashed black brethren to some truths about the black race. And, the other: when I had read enough to know something, I began to enter the Prison Colony's weekly debating program—my baptism into public speaking.

I have to admit a sad, shameful fact. I had so loved being around the white man that in prison I really disliked how Negro convicts stuck together so much. But when Mr. Muhammad's teachings reversed my attitude toward my black brothers, in my guilt and shame I began to catch every chance I could to recruit for Mr. Muhammad.

You have to be careful, very careful, introducing the truth to the black man who has never previously heard the truth about himself, his own kind, and the white man. My brother Reginald had told me that all Muslims experienced this in their recruiting for Mr. Muhammad. The black brother is so brainwashed that he may even be repelled when he first hears the truth. Reginald advised that the truth had to be dropped only a little bit at a time. And you had to wait a while to let it sink in before advancing the next step.

I began first telling my black brother inmates about the glorious history of the black man—things they never had dreamed. I told them the horrible slavery-trade truths that they never knew.

I would watch their faces when I told them about that, because the white man had completely erased the slaves' past, a Negro in America can never know his true family name, or even what tribe he was descended from: the Mandingos, the Wolof, the Serer, the Fula, the Fanti, the Ashanti, or others. I told them that some slaves brought from Africa spoke Arabic, and were Islamic in their religion. A lot of these black convicts still wouldn't believe it unless they could see that a white man had said it. So, often, I would read to these brothers selected passages from white men's books. I'd explain to them that the real truth was known to some white men, the scholars; but there had been a conspiracy down through the generations to keep the truth from black men.

I would keep close watch on how each one reacted. I always had to be careful. I never knew when some brainwashed black imp, some dyed-in-the-wool Uncle Tom, would nod at me and then go running to tell the white man. When one was ripe—and I could tell—then away from the rest, I'd drop it on him, what Mr. Muhammad taught: "The white man is the devil."

That would shock many of them—until they started thinking about it.

This is probably as big a single worry as the American prison system has today—the way the Muslim teachings, circulated among all Negroes in the country, are converting new Muslims among black men in prison, and black men are in prison in far greater numbers than their proportion in the population.

The reason is that among all Negroes the black convict is the most perfectly preconditioned to hear the words, "the white man is the devil."

You tell that to any Negro. Except for those relatively few "integration"-mad so-called "intellectuals," and those black men who are otherwise fat, happy, and deaf, dumb, and blinded, with their crumbs from the white man's rich table, you have struck a nerve center in the American black man. He may take a day to react, a month, a year; he may never respond, openly; but of one thing you can be sure—when he thinks about his own life, he is going to see where, to him, personally, the white man sure has acted like a devil.

And, as I say, above all Negroes, the black prisoner. Here is a black man caged behind bars, probably for years, put there by the white man. Usually the convict comes from among those bottom-of-the-pile Negroes, the Negroes who through their entire lives have been kicked about, treated like children—Negroes who never have met one white man who didn't either take something from them or do something to them.

You let this caged-up black man start thinking, the same way I did when I first heard Elijah Muhammad's teachings: let him start thinking how, with better breaks when he was young and ambitious he might have been a lawyer, a doctor, a scientist, anything. You let this caged-up black man start realizing, as I did, how from the first landing of the first slave ship, the millions of black men in America have been like sheep in a den of wolves. That's why black prisoners become Muslims so fast when Elijah Muhammad's teachings filter into their cages by way of other Muslim convicts. "The white man is the devil" is a perfect echo of that black convict's lifelong experience.

I've told how debating was a weekly event there at the Norfolk Prison Colony. My reading had my mind like steam under pressure. Some way, I had to start telling the white man about himself to his face. I decided I could do this by putting my name down to debate.

Standing up and speaking before an audience was a thing that throughout my previous life never would have crossed my mind. Out there in the streets, hustling, pushing dope, and robbing, I could have had the dreams from a pound of hashish and I'd never have dreamed anything so wild as that one day I would speak in coliseums and arenas, at the greatest American universities, and on radio and television programs, not to mention speaking all over Egypt and Africa and in England.

But I will tell you that, right there, in the prison, debating, speaking to a crowd, was as exhilarating to me as the discovery of knowledge through reading had been. Standing up there, the faces looking up at me, things in my head coming out of my mouth, while my brain searched for the next best thing to follow what I was saying, and if I could sway them to my side by handling it right, then I had won the debate—once my feet got wet, I was gone on debating. Whichever side of the selected subject was assigned to me, I'd track down and study everything I could find on it. I'd put myself in my opponent's place and decide how I'd try to win if I had the other side; and then I'd figure a way to knock down those points. And if there was any way in the world, I'd work into my speech the devilishness of the white man.

"Compulsory Military Training—Or None?" That's one good chance I got unexpectedly, I remember. My opponent flailed the air about the Ethiopians throwing rocks and spears at Italian airplanes, "proving" that compulsory military training was needed. I said the Ethiopians' black flesh had been spattered against trees by bombs the Pope in Rome had blessed, and the Ethiopians would have thrown even their bare bodies at the airplanes because they had seen that they were fighting the devil incarnate.

They yelled "foul," that I'd made the subject a race issue. I said it wasn't race, it was a historical fact, that they ought to go and read Pierre van Paassen's *Days of Our Years*, and something not surprising to me, that book, right after the debate, disappeared from the prison library. It was right there in prison that I made up my mind to devote the rest of my life to telling the white man about himself—or die. In a debate about whether or not Homer had ever existed, I threw into those white faces the theory that Homer only symbolized how white Europeans kidnapped black Africans, then blinded them so that they could never get back to their own people. (Homer and Omar and *Moor*, you see, are related terms; it's like saying Peter, Pedro, and *petra*, all three of which mean rock.) These blinded Moors the Europeans taught to sing about the Europeans' glorious accomplishments. I made it clear that was the devilish white man's idea of kicks. Aesop's *Fables*—another case in point. "Aesop" was only the Greek name for an Ethiopian.

Another hot debate I remember I was in had to do with the identity of Shakespeare. No color was involved there; I just got intrigued over the Shakespearean dilemma. The King James translation of the Bible is considered the greatest piece of literature in English. Its language supposedly represents the ultimate in using the King's English. Well, Shakespeare's language and the Bible's language are one and the same. They say that from 1604 to 1611, King James got poets to translate, to write the Bible. Well, if Shakespeare existed, he was then the top poet around. But Shakespeare is nowhere reported connected with the Bible. If he existed, why didn't King James use him? And if he did use him, why is it one of the world's best kept secrets?

I know that many say that Francis Bacon was Shakespeare. If that is true, why would Bacon have kept it secret? Bacon wasn't royalty, when royalty sometimes used the nom de plume because it was "improper" for royalty to be artistic or theatrical. What would Bacon have had to lose? Bacon, in fact, would have had everything to gain.

In the prison debates I argued for the theory that King James himself was the real poet who used the nom de plume Shakespeare. King James was brilliant. He was the greatest king who ever sat on the British throne. Who else among royalty, in his time, would have had the giant talent to write Shakespeare's works? It was he who poetically "fixed" the Bible—which in itself and its present King James version has enslaved the world.

When my brother Reginald visited, I would talk to him about new evidence I found to document the Muslim teachings. In either volume 43 or 44 of The Harvard Classics, I read Milton's *Paradise Lost*. The devil, kicked out of Paradise, was trying to regain possession. He was using the forces of Europe, personified by the Popes, Charlemagne, Richard the Lionhearted, and other knights. I interpreted this to show that the Europeans were motivated and led by the devil, or the personification of the devil. So Milton and Mr. Elijah Muhammad were actually saying the same thing.

I couldn't believe it when Reginald began to speak ill of Elijah Muhammad. I can't specify the exact things he said. They were more in the nature of implications against Mr. Muhammad—the pitch of Reginald's voice, or the way that Reginald looked, rather than what he said.

It caught me totally unprepared. It threw me into a state of confusion. My blood brother, Reginald, in whom I had so much confidence, for whom I had so much respect, the one who had introduced me to the Nation of Islam. I couldn't believe it! And now Islam meant more to me than anything I ever had known in my life. Islam and Mr. Elijah Muhammad had changed my whole world.

Reginald, I learned, had been suspended from the Nation of Islam by Elijah Muhammad. He had not practiced moral restraint. After he had learned the truth, and had accepted the truth, and the Muslim laws, Reginald was still carrying on improper relations with the then secretary of the New York Temple. Some other Muslim who learned of it had made charges against Reginald to Mr. Muhammad in Chicago, and Mr. Muhammad had suspended Reginald.

When Reginald left, I was in torment. That night, finally, I wrote to Mr. Muhammad, trying to defend my brother, appealing for him. I told him what Reginald was to me, what my brother meant to me.

I put the letter into the box for the prison censor. Then all the rest of that night, I prayed to Allah. I don't think anyone ever prayed more sincerely to Allah. I prayed for some kind of relief from my confusion.

It was the next night, as I lay on my bed, I suddenly, with a start, became aware of a man sitting beside me in my chair. He had on a dark suit, I remember. I could see him as plainly as I see anyone I look at. He wasn't black, and he wasn't white. He was light-brown-skinned, an Asiatic cast of countenance, and he had oily black hair.

I looked right into his face.

I didn't get frightened. I knew I wasn't dreaming. I couldn't move, I didn't speak, and he didn't. I couldn't place him racially—other than that I knew he was a non-European. I had no idea whatsoever who he was. He just sat there. Then, suddenly as he had come, he was gone.

Soon, Mr. Muhammad sent me a reply about Reginald. He wrote, "If you once believed in the truth, and now you are beginning to doubt the truth, you didn't believe the truth in the first place. What could make you doubt the truth other than your own weak self?"

That struck me. Reginald was not leading the disciplined life of a Muslim. And I knew that Elijah Muhammad was right, and my blood brother was wrong. Because right is right, and wrong is wrong. Little did I then realize the day would come when Elijah Muhammad would be accused by his own sons as being guilty of the same acts of immorality that he judged Reginald and so many others for.

But at that time, all of the doubt and confusion in my mind was removed. All of the influence that my brother had wielded over me was broken. From that day on, as far as I am concerned, everything that my brother Reginald has done is wrong.

But Reginald kept visiting me. When he had been a Muslim, he had been immaculate in his attire. But now, he wore things like a T-shirt, shabby-looking trousers, and sneakers. I could see him on the way down. When he spoke, I heard him coldly. But I would listen. He was my blood brother. Gradually, I saw the chastisement of Allah—what Christians would call "the curse"—come upon Reginald. Elijah Muhammad said that Allah was chastising Reginald—and that anyone who challenged Elijah Muhammad would be chastened by Allah. In Islam we were taught that as long as one didn't know the truth, he lived in darkness. But once the truth was accepted, and recognized, he lived in light, and whoever would then go against it would be punished by Allah.

Mr. Muhammad taught that the five-pointed star stands for justice, and also for the five senses of man. We were taught that Allah executes justice by working upon the five senses of those who rebel against His Messenger, or against His truth. We were taught that this was Allah's way of letting

Muslims know His sufficiency to defend His Messenger against any and all opposition, as long as the Messenger himself didn't deviate from the path of truth. We were taught that Allah turned the minds of any defectors into a turmoil. I thought truly that it was Allah doing this to my brother.

One letter, I think from my brother Philbert, told me that Reginald was with them in Detroit. I heard no more about Reginald until one day, weeks later, Ella visited me; she told me that Reginald was at her home in Roxbury, sleeping. Ella said she had heard a knock, she had gone to the door, and there was Reginald, looking terrible. Ella said she had asked, "Where did you come from?" And Reginald had told her he came from Detroit. She said she asked him, "How did you get here?" And he had told her, "I walked."

I believed he had walked. I believed in Elijah Muhammad, and he had convinced us that Allah's chastisement upon Reginald's mind had taken away Reginald's ability to gauge distance and time. There is a dimension of time with which we are not familiar here in the West. Elijah Muhammad said that under Allah's chastisement, the five senses of a man can be so deranged by those whose mental powers are greater than his that in five minutes his hair can turn snow white. Or he will walk nine hundred miles as he might walk five blocks.

In prison, since I had become a Muslim, I had grown a beard. When Reginald visited me, he nervously moved about in his chair; he told me that each hair on my beard was a snake. Everywhere, he saw snakes.

He next began to believe that he was the "Messenger of Allah." Reginald went around in the streets of Roxbury, Ella reported to me, telling people that he had some divine power. He graduated from this to saying that he was Allah.

He finally began saying he was greater than Allah.

Authorities picked up Reginald, and he was put into an institution. They couldn't find what was wrong. They had no way to understand Allah's chastisement. Reginald was released. Then he was picked up again, and was put into another institution.

Reginald is in an institution now. I know where, but I won't say. I would not want to cause him any more trouble than he has already had.

I believe, today, that it was written, it was meant, for Reginald to be used for one purpose only: as a bait, as a minnow to reach into the ocean of blackness where I was, to save me.

I cannot understand it any other way.

After Elijah Muhammad himself was later accused as a very immoral man, I came to believe that it wasn't a divine chastisement upon Reginald, but the pain he felt when his own family totally rejected him for Elijah Muhammad, and this hurt made Reginald turn insanely upon Elijah Muhammad.

It's impossible to dream, or to see, or to have a vision of someone whom you never have seen before—and to see him exactly as he is. To see someone, and to see him exactly as he looks, is to have a pre-vision.

I would later come to believe that my pre-vision was of Master W. D. Fard, the Messiah, the one whom Elijah Muhammad said had appointed him—Elijah Muhammad—as His Last Messenger to the black people of North America.

My last year in prison was spent back in the Charlestown Prison. Even among the white inmates, the word had filtered around. Some of those brainwashed black convicts talked too much. And I know that the censors had reported on my mail. The Norfolk Prison Colony officials had become upset. They used as a reason for my transfer that I refused to take some kind of shots, an inoculation or something.

The only thing that worried me was that I hadn't much time left before I would be eligible for parole-board consideration. But I reasoned that they might look at my representing and spreading Islam in another way: instead of keeping me in they might want to get me out.

I had come to prison with 20/20 vision. But when I got sent back to Charlestown, I had read so much by the lights-out glow in my room at the Norfolk Prison Colony that I had astigmatism and the first pair of the eyeglasses that I have worn ever since.

I had less maneuverability back in the much stricter Charlestown Prison. But I found that a lot of Negroes attended a Bible class, and I went there.

Conducting the class was a tall, blond, blue-eyed (a perfect "devil") Harvard Seminary student. He lectured, and then he started in a question-and-answer session. I don't know which of us had read the Bible more, he or I, but I had to give him credit; he really was heavy on his religion. I puzzled and puzzled for a way to upset him, and to give those Negroes present something to think and talk about and circulate.

Finally, I put up my hand; he nodded. He had talked about Paul.

I stood up and asked, "What color was Paul?" And I kept talking, with pauses, "He had to be black... because he was a Hebrew... and the original Hebrews were black... weren't they?"

He had started flushing red. You know the way white people do. He said "Yes."

I wasn't through yet. "What color was Jesus... he was Hebrew, too... wasn't he?"

Both the Negro and the white convicts had sat bolt upright. I don't care how tough the convict, be he brainwashed black Christian, or a "devil" white Christian, neither of them is ready to hear anybody saying Jesus wasn't white. The instructor walked around. He shouldn't have felt bad. In all of the years since, I never have met any intelligent white man who would try to insist that Jesus was white. How could they? He said, "Jesus was brown."

I let him get away with that compromise.

Exactly as I had known it would, almost overnight the Charlestown convicts, black and white, began buzzing with the story. Wherever I went, I could feel the nodding. And anytime I got a chance to exchange words with a black brother in stripes, I'd say, "My man! You ever heard about somebody named Mr. Elijah Muhammad?"

FOURTEEN

ELIJAH MUHAMMAD

Message to the Blackman in America (1965)

ELIJAH MUHAMMAD SPENT FOUR YEARS IN PRISON (1942–1946), convicted of sedition after calling on Black men to dodge the draft. His experience in prison convinced him that investing in incarcerated people was worthwhile. Malcolm X's jailhouse transformation, for instance, began with the attention and encouragement of Elijah Muhammad, who wrote him letters, inspired him to read and study history, and even sent money to ease his circumstances of imprisonment, although they later had a falling-out. Muhammad was born Elijah Poole in 1897, in Sandersville, Georgia. Situated at the intersection of two Native American trails, Sandersville is a small town that was established due to the Georgia land lottery of 1805, which doled out land to white settlers. Poole changed his name to Muhammad in 1931 when he converted to Islam. He had been named after the slave-owning, land-owning patrician Middleton Pool Jr. (the "e" was added later). At the time of his death in 1861, Pool Jr. legally owned and enslaved twenty-two humans, including a boy who would grow up to be Muhammad's father. Muhammad's early life was marked by economic deprivation, sharecropping, hard physical labor, limited educational opportunities, and racial violence, including witnessing a lynching. These experiences, combined with his exposure to the teachings of Wallace D. Fard, the founder of the Nation of Islam, shaped Muhammad's views. He espoused the virtues of Islam, specifically pitched to the circumstances of Black Americans, preaching the values of Black separatism, Black economic development, knowledge of history, and the importance of confronting the deleterious impact of white supremacy. Religion wielded against the oppressed serves many purposes, including placating and rationalizing their circumstances. In contrast, he did not pledge fealty or deference to the religion introduced by slave masters and their descendants, and he did not guarantee nonviolence. In his book *Message to the Blackman in America* he addresses the impact of internalized inferiority and the hypocrisy of whiteness, American values, and Christianity.

By the time he died in 1975, although forsaken by some, Elijah Muhammad's influence on Black Americans as leader of the Nation of Islam was undeniable. The presence of the Nation of Islam remains a powerful current in contemporary prison culture, with adherents at the forefront of organizing and agitating for dignity and rights.

FIRST, LOVE YOURSELF

One of the greatest handicaps among the so-called Negroes is that there is no love for self, nor love for his or her own kind. This not having love for self is the root cause of hate (dislike), disunity, disagreement, quarreling, betraying, stool pigeons and fighting and killing one another. How can you be loved, if you have not love for self and your own nation and dislike being a member of your own? Then what nation will trust your love and membership?

You say of yourself, "I love everybody." This cannot be true. Love for self comes first. The Bible, the book that you claim to believe says, "Love the brotherhood" (I Peter 2:17). "Love one another" (John 15:17). Love of self comes first. The one who loves everybody is the one who does not love anyone. This is the false teaching of the Christians for the Christians war against Christians. They have the Bible so twisted by adding in and taking out of the truth that it takes only God or one whom God has given the knowledge of the Book to understand it.

The Bible puts more stress upon the "love for thy neighbor" than the "love for the brother." When asked "Who is my neighbor?" the answer was contrary and incorrect. Jesus' answer was that of two men who were on a journey. They were not from the same place. One was from Jerusalem, the other one was a Samaritan. The Samaritan came to where the man from Jerusalem lay wounded by the robbers who had stripped him of his possessions. The Samaritan showed sympathy for the fellow traveler. (He was not a neighbor in the sense of the word. A neighbor can be an enemy.) Many enemies live in the same neighborhood of a good neighbor. But, the answer that Jesus gave was a futile one which can could be classified as a parable of the so-called Negroes and their slave-masters.

The so-called Negroes fell into the hands of the slave-masters, who have robbed, spoiled, wounded and killed them. The Good Samaritan here would be the Mahdi (Allah)—God in Person, as He is often referred to by the Christians as the "the second coming of Jesus, or the Son of Man to judge man." This one will befriend the poor (the so-called Negroes) and heal their wounds by pouring into their heads knowledge of self and others and free them of the yoke of slavery and kill the slave-masters, as Jehovah did in the case of Pharaoh and his people to free Israel from bondage and the false religion and gods of Pharaoh.

There were many other proofs in the Bible which agree with the above answer.

Love yourself and your kind. Let us refrain from doing evil to each other, and let us love each other as brothers, as we are the same flesh and blood. In this way, you and I will not have any trouble in uniting. It is a fool who does not love himself and his people. Your black skin is the best, and never try changing its color. Stay away from intermixing with your slave-master's children. Love yourself and your kind.

BLACKMAN, ACCEPT YOUR OWN

It is an act of intelligence and love for us to accept our own.

One will say, What is our own? No. 1, our own people—our own earth, God and His Religion, Islam (the religion of peace) and our own place in the sun. This Divine call to us to accept our own makes sense. Everything of life will accept its kind as its own.

Why the so-called [Negro] (members of the Great Asiatic Nation of the Tribe of Shabazz) refuses to accept his own is because of being made blind, deaf and dumb to the knowledge of self and kind by the devils when they were babies under slavery.

Today, they cling to this same enemy of their fathers and the enemies of all Black people upon the face of the earth because they cannot see any hope for a future for themselves in their own kind and self, due to the lack of knowledge of self.

They beg the enemy even for friendship, which is like the frog pleading to the snake not to swallow him after the snake has gotten him in his mouth.

The Black people of America have been swallowed by the slave-masters, who are a race of devils, says all-wise God, Allah, and now refuse to let us go free without hindrance and hold us as a prey against the will of Allah in the person of Master Fard Muhammad, who now seeks our deliverance, since our people love the enemy more than God.

For God to fulfill His promises to deliver us from our enemies, He must go to war against the enemy and break the enemy's power of resistance to free us. War is inevitable. The so-called Negroes must come to the knowledge of Truth, that they have no future in their enemies who are the enemies of Almighty God, Allah. God must come to put an end to war and, that is to say, destroy those who love to make war and delight in making mischief.

The American white people delight in mistreating us, their former slaves.

There is no justice for us among such people, the devils in person. They hate us if we try being good; they have turned upon us, who have turned to Allah and have accepted His true religion, Islam, and are persecuting and killing some of us just because we are Muslims and they fear the teachings of Islam and the history and knowledge of the devils and that All of our people will believe in Allah, and His true religion, Islam.

They hate unity among the so-called Negroes. A continued war is made upon us by the white devils of America.

Why shouldn't we accept our own and return to our own? There is no future in this people for us. They have hundreds and thousands of my followers in jails and state and government penitentiaries and are falsely accusing many more and putting them under unjust heavy penalties and long terms of imprisonment just because they want to be Muslims.

The refusal of the Supreme Court to hear the unjust judges' decisions against my followers (the Muslims) in Louisiana and the killing and the wicked unjust plan that the Los Angeles Court seeks to place against the poor innocent Muslims that Allah saved from the police guns last April 27, 1962, is enough for the unintelligent animal world to shudder and weep.

Shouldn't Allah destroy such an unjust people as our slave-masters' children? The day of visitation has come. She shall reap what she has sown.

X

The doom of America approaches, and there are many people who do not really know why. There are also many who would not like to know. As I have always said, truth hurts—especially the guilty. It is the expressed purpose of the coming of God, whose proper name is Allah, to make manifest the sins of a people who He would destroy, justifying His destruction of that people.

America represents herself as a Christian nation. This means that they are followers of Jesus, whom they call the Christ and say that they are crystallized into him and God and have become one. As they say, God the Father, Jesus the Son and the Holy Ghost.

They profess to be a friend and defenders of all peace-loving and freedom-loving people. The only people we really see that they want to be friends of are themselves and their kind. They are really sincere when they say that they are freedom-loving people. Above all, the White man the world over wants to be free to rule and dominate the aboriginal people.

Today America's doom is set like a die. She cannot escape; it is impossible. For her to escape would classify the prophets of God and God Himself as predicting lies. When God appeared to me in the person of Master Fard Muhammad, to whom praises are due forever, in 1931 in Detroit, He said that America was His number one enemy on His list for destruction.

While he mentioned other European Whites as getting a little extension of time, He singled America and Germany out as being the two worst vicious, evil, destructive trouble-makers of the entire nation earth. And that America had mistreated us (the so-called Negroes) so much that she cannot be equally paid back for the evils she has done to the poor Black slaves.

There are thousands and tens of thousands of American so-called Negroes and in those tens of thousand are such professional and educated class of people as preachers, ministers of the white man's Christianity, even scientists, scholars of many kinds and technicians of all kinds who have become submerged into the love and worship of the White race because of advantages.

Today they preach the gospel of being an American citizen and worship equally their intermarriage with White Americans who used the Black women from the time they were brought here 400 years ago until this very day, as they would their stock and cattle.

It is a perfect shame and disgrace to see men of the Black nation professing themselves to be spiritual guides of God and His people, endorsing and backing the rule of enemies who have spoiled and exploited them to the extent that they are not recognized even among their own kind outside America. These ignorant Black people will oppose anyone who preaches freedom, justice and equality and some of this earth that we can call our own.

They are the first to go to the policemen and F.B.I. seeking persecution for those who stand for freedom, justice and equality and independence for the Black man of America by their admired and worshiped enemy (the White race). They will accuse them of trying to overthrow the government or even of causing trouble.

The White man has looked into their faces many times as into their children's faces and cursed them and called them Black Negroes and told us to our faces that they hate us and should kill us.

All of my life I have heard this, and all of their lives they have heard the same from the mouths of these people. But today they wish to save their skin by sacrificing their poor, blind, deaf and dumb people to the destroyer for their own selfish gains.

I have begged and begged for many years for just a conference with them, but they will not come near. But they will go to the White man and beg him to drive Elijah and his followers out and even kill them. This is the enemy, but Elijah Muhammad is laid as a stumbling stone. That stone that has been rejected by the builders. Whosoever falls on that stone will be broken to pieces, and whosoever the stone falls upon will be ground into powder.

No wonder the Bible says, woe, woe unto such professional class that stand in the way of those who would enter the Kingdom of Heaven. They refuse to go in themselves and seek to prevent those who are trying to enter.

I am sorry for my poor people who should be helping in the right way to get a permanent future of freedom, justice and equality and who now, due to fear, are doing everything to oppose it. They are dumb enough to the knowledge of the scripture of what God has prophesied he would do in this day and time, and they make mockery even of the Messenger of God because God did not choose one of them or one of their proud politicians. They make mockery of him as being too ignorant to lead them.

But let them tell you what type of an Apostle or prophet God promised them. Was it a man from some of the enemy colleges and universities with an arm full of degrees coming from these institutions of learning of the enemy?

Let them read their scriptures and see what type of man God promised to choose for a last messenger. How many of the prophets in the past were educated men of the civilization in which they were born before the call of God?

The sins of America are terrible. She has risen up in this part of the earth which was wilderness forsaken by all our people for thousands and thousands of years and was used for a kind of exile continent. The White man came out of Europe in desperation seeking a place to expand and began to kill the aboriginals of this continent (the Red Indian) and take their homes. This was one of her great sins.

The White man has left a remnant of that people for the sake of mockery and for his children to see the people their fathers conquered in taking this land of the Indians for their own land (as they call it today). God never intended that the people of the earth go about killing each other to rob each other of their homes. It was never done by anyone but the White race.

He was not satisfied in killing all the aboriginals here to take their homes but went back into the old world of Africa and Asia and deceived and brought our fathers here for no other purpose than to make them slaves and to experiment on them.

They have never been a friend to us, nor do they ever intend to be. They cannot be a friend because they were not created in any such nature to be a true friend to anyone, not even to themselves. Today she is being upset with wars, little scrimmages breaking out here and there over the earth keeping her busy running from one fire to the other trying to prevent the fire from spreading into a national or international fire.

She must get a taste of what she has put upon other people. Therefore, Almighty God Himself is stirring up the nations of the earth against her. And, as it is written, they shall come against her as she has gone against other people and taken away their wealth and brought it and poured it into her treasuries, so shall it be done to her.

FIFTEEN

GEORGE JACKSON

Selected Prison Letters (1970) and "Toward the United Front" (1972)

SOME OF THE MOST IMPORTANT LETTERS EVER written begin with "Dear Mama." The salutation often heads George Jackson's jailhouse missives to his mother, where he unpacks his analysis of the world and reckons with the toll the rigged system played in compromising their lives. Spanning the course of six years he wrote frequent letters to family, friends, and associates, a selection of which comprise his first book, *Soledad Brother: The Prison Letters of George Jackson*. You'll read a small selection of those letters here, along with a chapter from his second book, *Blood in My Eye*, which was published shortly after his suspicious death in San Quentin, shot dead before the age of thirty by prison guards who claimed he was trying to escape. This was an end he seemed prepared for: "Dear Mama..." he laments, "I have surrendered all hope of happiness for myself in this life to the prospect of effecting some improvement in our circumstances as a whole. I have a plan, I will give, and give, and give of myself until it proves our making or my end."

Give he did, though he did not live long enough to see the unfurling of his influence in the world. Highlighting the systemic and institutionalized oppression faced by Black Americans, Jackson's insurgent words leave a legacy many consider the foundation of contemporary abolitionist thought and continue to inspire those seeking to understand and connect their life circumstances to the conditions that created them. In "Toward the United Front," Jackson emphasizes unity among oppressed groups, critiques capitalism and imperialism, notes the centrality of violence in revolution, underlines the importance of education and consciousness-raising, and states the need for political autonomy and self-determination for oppressed groups.

Jackson's life story has led to a greater understanding of the harm caused by the carceral system. Accused of stealing $70 from a gas station, he went to prison instead of university, but the ninety-nine books found in his cell, along with the two he wrote, constitute an abolitionist curriculum, one developed in "Prison University." "Dear Mama... You have not failed. You have been failed, by history and events, and people over whom you had no control." He gave and gave and gave, and his generational impact has been immense. "Dear Mama" is also the title of Tupac Shakur's 1995 song that celebrates his mother for doing the best she could while falling short, in part, due to the stacked system. Tupac was born just two months before Jackson was killed. His mother, a Black Panther and political prisoner, imprisoned when he was in utero, was acquitted one month before he was born. It was not until Shakur's second stint in jail, when he was already famous, that he was introduced to George Jackson's writings and found them meaningful. Our lives and life stories intersect in ways seen and unseen. Important lessons are always handed down from one generation to the next.

LETTERS

March 12, 1965

Dear Mama,

The things you speak of are uppermost in my mind and my heart. I am not too manly or sophisticated to say that I love you and all the rest with a devotion and dedication that will continue to grow until I pass from this existence. Anything that will please you, and that falls within human accomplishment, I will carry out. I say this with confidence because of my certainty that you would never ask me to please you by surrendering my mental liberty and self-respect; I wouldn't want to live were these, my last two real possessions, to be lost.

Any confidence you put in me, Mama, will be well placed. This is not mere talk, my ego is nowhere involved. If we are to surmount these barriers standing between us, and finally work things around to our advantage, on a few points we must be agreed. You must listen to me. I've been trying to say something. Stop closing my voice off from your mind! My hair has started to turn gray and I'm beginning to look like an old man. My best efforts up to now have all fallen far short of their intended goals. I know, however, just as sure as day follows night that I will win the last round. That is the one I always win, the important one.

I feel that you understand the situation better than most who live on your level. From your last letter, I know you are intelligent enough to understand. I have it before me now and I glean much to indicate that this is so. But there is much that has escaped your understanding, and it is quite reasonable that this be true. You have no way of learning and bettering. However, if you will honor my humble voice, I would very much like to pass on to you just a thought or two I have had. All that I ask is that you hear me, and think about what I say. Do not just read over the lines. Think of what I say in relation to things past, and the vague possibility that is our future. I'm not just another convict or "Negro." I'm one who really loves you and who has been observing with a practiced eye and an almost photographic memory. But first let me clear up one other incidental thing. Robert[14] has never said anything unattractive or belittling about you. Each of his letters expresses almost total grief for the condition of your health. He blames me even, then himself, but never the right people. He feels he has failed you, me, and all the others, and he keeps trying to learn if I also blame him. Of course I do not blame him or you, or myself. I place the blame for the social ills that have caused us discomfort and unhappiness squarely upon the shoulders of those responsible: the people in control!!

It is mainly on this subject that I am going to speak now. To get it across I am going to write two letters, this one and another sheet also tonight. This should be read first for the idea to follow in logical order.[15]

I am going to do exactly as you say concerning the show of good conduct here. I have never raised my hand against any man, since I've been an adult that is, except in self defense, but there has been an element of aggressiveness in the way that I have handled these incidents. I'll have to always defend my person, but I promise you that unless there is a direct threat to my existence I will never have another bit of trouble here. Understand though that you do not live in the real rip-and-tear world. You have escaped it by surrendering your self-determination and freedom of thought in a tranquilizing conformity to the wishes of whoever may hold the strings. Consequently you do not know how hard it is to live in peace even for a short period with people who deify violence, and vilify peace and harmony.

George

March 12, 1965

Dear Mama

I will try what you advised. I know it to be the best way at this point in the little game. But should I fail you are not to say, "George is no good." You must try to understand that now, just as in the past, there are other considerations and influences that enter into the course of events that turn our lives one way or the other.

Have you ever wondered how you and I and all our kind lost their identity so fast? The last blacks were brought into this country only 75 to 80 years ago, three generations at most. This is too short a time for us to have lost as much as we have. No other people have completely been divorced from their own as we have in such a short period. I don't even know my name. Have you ever wondered about this? The answer is found in the fact that we lost control of the circumstances surrounding our lives. We were alienated from our sources, isolated, and remolded to fit in certain forms, to fill a specific purpose. No consideration was or has ever been given to our being anything other than what we were originally intended to be (I ask for electronics or drafting and I'm told to be practical). You must realize, understand fully, that we have little or no control over our lives. You must then stop giving yourself pain by feeling that you failed somewhere. You have not failed. You have been failed, by history and events, and people over whom you had no control. Only after you understand this can you then go on to make the necessary alterations that will bring some purpose and value to your life; you must gain some control! I have said this to Robert a hundred times but it makes no impression at all. He writes back in the same vein as he did the time before I said anything. He just doesn't have the mental equipment. Will you look deeper and think on the matter and then explain to him? I was born knowing exactly nothing. I had no one, no one, to teach me the things of real value. The school systems are gauged to teach youth what to think, not how to think. Robert never had the time to say even hello, and neither of you really knew anything to give me anyway, because your parents knew nothing. Do you see where the cycle brings us, to the real source of the trouble, the alienation and the abandonment, the pressure from without, the system and its supporters? I didn't know either. So we must look to the people whose responsibility it is to see to it that the benefits of society pass down to all concerned for an answer. If a good god exists then they are the ones who must make an appeal to him for forgiveness: forgiveness for relinquishment and dereliction of duty! I don't need god, religion, belief, etc. I need control, control of the determining factors relating to the unquestioning support and loyalty of my mother, father, brothers, sisters. You need Robert and I need him and he needs you. We all need each other. The standards and emotions we have used in the past to regulate our relations defy all nature and run contrary to all known precedent. When did blood cease to be thicker than and more binding than all else? We must look to each other and destroy the barriers placed between us with trust, and love. I am committed and I will do all that I have to. I am equal to anything that is required. Help me when you can, the only way you can, by trying to understand.

I don't want a package this year; save the money; save all you can. I am living very badly now and just to stay alive is an ordeal, but I see something better. It is vague, and is a possibility at best, but I know a place, a refuge where people love and live.

George

June 9, 1965
Dear Father,
We can spend twenty-five dollars a month here at the canteen for toilet articles, a few dry goods, and food. But we can spend any amount through the mail on such things as books, typewriters, correspondence courses in all the liberal arts. I spend what you have sent me on books. Many that are

of interest and value to me cannot be obtained here in the library.

Anything that you send me in the way of finances is a good investment, the returns will be forthcoming after the successful conclusion of the wars.

Mao Tse-tung, leader of the Chinese Communist party, has written many works on politics and war. Please ascertain the exact titles of his works and who they are published by and how much each costs. Also the price of the *Encyclopedia Africana* by William Du Bois. How many volumes are there in the set? Who publishes them? It is very important that I have the publisher's name and address, because if I come by the money to purchase these books I need the exact titles and publishers. To read and study the major works of these two authors would be the climax of my education, an education in itself. Du Bois was a mere fool in his earlier days; but right at the close of his eventful life he gave up this life of toil, deprivation, and tears to join his own kind. He left the United States, went to Ghana, and wrote the *Encyclopedia Africana*.

It is difficult, very difficult to get any facts concerning our history and our way of life. The lies, half-truths, and propaganda have won total sway over the facts. We have no knowledge of our heritage. Our economic status has reduced our minds to a state of complete oblivion. The young black who comes out of college or the university is as ignorant and unlearned as the white laborer. For all practical purposes he is worse off than when he went in, for he has learned only the attitudes and ways of the snake, and a few well-worded lies. The ruling culture refuses to let us know how much we did to advance civilization in our lands long ago. It refuses to recognize and appreciate our craft and strength and allow us some of the fruits of our labor. All this has left an emptiness in our lives, a void, a vacuum that must soon be filled by hostilities.

I am most certainly committed, until the day I'm sent to the warrior's rest. By the ruling culture's acts of greed and barbarism the uncommitted will soon learn that compromise with such an enemy is impossible. Our two fortunes move along a collision course. I'm prepared in every aspect, I have nothing, I can lose nothing!

George

June, 1965

Dear Father,

One of those tall ultrabright electrical fixtures used to illuminate the walls and surrounding area at night casts a direct beam of light in my cell at night. (I moved to a different cell last week). Consequently I have enough light, even after the usual twelve o'clock lights-out, to read or study by. I don't really have to sleep now if I choose not to. The early hours of morning are the only time of the day that one can find any respite from the pandemonium caused by these the most uncultured of San Quentin inmates. I don't let the noise bother me even in the evenings when it rises to maddening intensity, because I try to understand my surroundings. I've asked myself, as I do about all the other aspects of life, why—why do white cons act and react as if they were animals of a lower order than we black men (some blacks get foolish also but we don't refer to them as "men")? Why just because they look like shaved monkeys must they also act like them? It's frayed nerves, caused by the harsh terms that defeat brought when they went against the system, the same system that runs this place. I must ask myself why did they go against the system and why are the terms so harsh? Could it be that a man will most always pursue his interests, system or no? But why should so many people's interests lie outside the system? Why doesn't the system encompass the needs and requirements of all or, to be realistic, the majority. We now come to the part of the question around which the whole contention pivots: Why are the terms so harsh, the price of defeat so high? What is it that causes a man to become power-mad, to deify exploitation and mendacity and vilify the compatible, harmonious things of nature, how many times have you heard that "everyone should help fight the evils of communism," etc.?

George

July, 1965

Dear Father,

I am perplexed and hard pressed in finding a solution or reason that will adequately explain why we are so eager to follow Charlie. Why we are so impressed with his apparent know-how. A glance at his history shows that it has been one long continuous war. At no time in European history has there been a period of peace and harmony. Every moment of his past has been spent in the breakdown of civilization by causing war, disruption, disease, and artificial famine. You send me a date from the moment he emerged from his cave-dwelling days and I'll tell you which of his tribes were at war, either on us or on themselves. The whole of the Western European's existence here in the U.S. has been the same one long war with different peoples. This is the only thing they understand, the only thing they respect—the only thing they can do with any dexterity. Do you accept this miscreant as the architect of the patterns that must guide your future life! If so, we must part company, and it is best we do so now, before the trouble begins. But please stop and think so that you can turn yourself around in time, so that the developments to come won't shock you so badly. I have not wasted my time these last three or four years. I speak with some authority and people are listening. People like me are going to be shaping your tomorrows. So just sit back, open your mind, and watch, since you can't marshal the fundamentals to help me.

Yes, my friend, I remember everything, the reason that Delora and I had to spend that summer and winter in Harrisburg is known and remembered by me. I remember the garbage right under the side and back of our place on Racine. Mama having to wash and wring clothes by hand, carrying Penny and Jon while some fat redheaded mama sat on her behind. I remember how strange people looked to me when I finally had to be sent to Skinner School. You never knew why I was almost killed the first day I went, but I do. I remember how the rent and clothes for us children kept you broke and ragged. All of us hungry, if not for food—the other things that make life bearable. After you and Mama settled down you had no recreational outlets whatever. And everyone on Warren Blvd. knows how you would beat me all the way home from our baseball games in the alley. Robert, can you see how absurd you sound to me when you speak on "the good life," or something about being a free adult? I know you have never been free. I know that few blacks over here have ever been free. The forms of slavery merely changed at the signing of the Emancipation Proclamation from chattel slavery to economic slavery. If you could see and talk to some of the blacks I meet in here you would immediately understand what I mean, and see that I'm right. They are all average, all with the same backgrounds, and in for the same thing, some form of food getting. About 70 to 80 percent of all crime in the U.S. is perpetrated by blacks, "the sole reason for this is that 98 percent of our number live below the poverty level in bitter and abject misery"! You must take off your rose-colored glasses and stop pretending. We have suffered an unmitigated wrong! How do you think I felt when I saw you come home each day a little more depressed than the day before? How do you think I felt when I looked in your face and saw the clouds forming, when I saw you look around and see your best efforts go for nothing—nothing. I can count the times on my hands that you managed to work up a smile.

George

July, 1965

Dear Father,

Well I guess you know that I'm aware that this is not the best of all possible lives. You also know that I thank you for trying to cushion the shocks and strains that history has made it our lot to have to endure. But the make-believe game has ended now. I don't think it necessary for me to burden myself with listing strains we've endured. You are intelligent enough to know. At each phase of this long train of tyrannies, we have conducted ourselves in a very meek and civilized manner, with only polite please [sic] for justice and moderation, all to no avail. We have shown a noble indisposition to react with the passion that each new oppression engenders. But any fool should be able to see that this cannot be allowed to continue. Any fool should be able to see that nature allows no such imbalances as this to exist for long. We have petitioned for judicial redress. We have remonstrated, supplicated, demonstrated, and prostrated ourselves before the feet of our self-appointed administrators. We have done all that we can do to circumvent the eruption that now comes on apace. The point of no return in our relationship has long been passed. I know what must and will take place so I follow my ends through to their most glorious conclusion. Don't make me waste my time and energy winning you to a position that you should already support with all your sympathies. The same forces that have made your life miserable, the same forces that have made your life senseless and unrewarding, threaten me and all our posterity. I know the way out. If you cannot help, sit back and listen, watch. You are charged with the responsibility of acknowledging the truth, my friend, and supporting it with whatever means, no matter how humble, are in your power. I am charged to right the wrong, lift the burden from the backs of future generations. I will not shrink from my duties. I will never falter or waver before the task, but we will go forward—to resolve this conflict once and forever. Of all the twenty thousand known years of advanced civilization, the years that are now coming on will be the most momentous.

George

March 3, 1966,
Dear Mama,
Always good to hear from you, though it makes me sad to know that you are not well. Just hold on though and circumstances will take a definite turn for the better, no ifs or ands about this. The way lies open for us. I'm not just talking or hoping. I know there is a better life for us. I know what there is to be had and of all there is to be had I plan to claim for us the lion's share.

You are right of course in what you contend. The black woman has in the past few hundred years been the only force holding us together and holding us up. She has absorbed the biggest part of the many shocks and strains of existence under a slave order. The men can think of nothing more effective than pimping, gambling, or petty theft. I've heard men brag about being pimps of black women and taking money from black women who are on relief. Things like this I find odious, disgusting—you are right, the black men have proven themselves to be utterly detestable and repulsive in the past. Before I would succumb to such subterfuge I would scratch my living from the ground on hands and knees, or die in a hail of bullets! My hat goes off to every one of you, you have my profoundest respect. I have surrendered all hope of happiness for myself in this life to the prospect of effecting some improvement in our circumstances as a whole. I have a plan, I will give, and give, and give of myself until it proves our making or my end. The men of our group have developed as a result of living under a ruthless system a set of mannerisms that numb the soul. We have been made the floor mat of the world, but the world has yet to see what can be done by men of our nature, by men who have walked the path of disparity, of regression, of abortion, and yet come out whole. There will be a special page in the book of life for the men who have crawled back from the grave. This page will tell of utter defeat, ruin, passivity, and subjection in one breath, and in the next, overwhelming victory and fulfillment.

So take care of yourself, and hold on.

Love,

George

March 20, 1966

Dear Mama,

We have to order books from a bookstore owned by one of the staff here. It is contrary to institution policy for someone to send us books from outside. This is the rule, the law, so I guess it cannot be helped. Situations of this type are what this country is built on, the wonderful system that made it great.

I've read as much St. Augustine as I could stomach. If you don't know about him and Jerome, Leibniz, and the rest of that lunatic fringe yet, my love, you are hurting. Why do you say things like that to me? You know how I feel about those people. You know that I am completely aware of all of them.

I can never be deceived again by them. I know their awesome capacity for evil, I'm victim of it now. That Pope Pius XII, the guy you let us pray for, gave Mussolini his blessing as he was about to embark upon his misadventure in Ethiopia. I could give you thousands of examples of this type. I have explained my feeling to you many, many times, so I won't go any further with this. If children being blown out of this existence while attending church services, men being lynched for a gesture, colonialism, the inquisition, and H-bombs haven't affected you, nothing I say here can help you. If you could live my life one week and see the things I see, feel the pain I feel, and die a little bit each day as I do, all your illusions and apparitions would vanish. You talk to me like I was born yesterday, like I was still a little boy. All my life now you have told me about European gods and European Christians who were supposed to be knowledgeable. When do you plan to say something that will help me? You may not know any better. If not, I am wrong in saying what I have, but I find it hard to admit that my mother could be so insensitive to the truth! You disrespect me, Mama, when you talk to me like that. It's like you saying to me, "George, you're a fool. You do not have eyes to see, ears to hear, and a brain to interpret, so I'll tell you any kind of outrageous story." Ordinary people, the mediocre, need to feel or believe in something greater than themselves. It gives them false security and it makes them feel that help may be forthcoming. This is self-delusion in the extreme. I cannot partake in any foolishness. Do you want me to be mediocre like the rest of the herd? When I need strength, Mama, I reach down within myself. I draw out of the reserves I've built—the necessary endurance to face down my opposition. I call on myself, I have faith in myself. This is where it must always come from in the end—yourself. I place no one and nothing above myself. What any man has done before me I can do. If there is a god, Mama, he hates me and I'll have to resist what he or it is doing to us. All my life, Mama, I've had to work things out for myself. I've had help from no quarter. I've been alone now for a long time. This is why I've had so much pain and trouble. Robert gave me nothing. You gave me god and that horrible church. Even god managed to take something away from me. I have nothing left but myself.

Love,
George

March, 1967
Dear Mama,
Papa[16] has had the "true release, and at last the clasp of peace." For him to have received this at such a great age and without violence is no small consolation. I loved him dearly and thought of him as one of our most practical and level-headed kin. You probably don't remember the long walks and talks Papa and I used to take, or the long visits when he lived on Lake Street and we lived on Warren. But I remember. He used to say things, probably just thinking aloud, sure that I wasn't listening or would not comprehend. But I did, and I think I knew him better than most. Do you remember how I used to answer "What" to every question put to me, and how Papa would deride me for this? He later in the course of our exchanges taught me to answer questions with "Why" instead of "What."

Another of our games helped me greatly with my powers of observation. When we would walk, he told me to always look at the large signboards as deeply as possible and after we had passed one, he would make me recite all that was on it. I would never remember as much detail as he, but I did win a kind word or two on occasion. We played this same game at his house with pictures and objects spread out on the table or bed.

I wish he could have survived to see and enjoy the new world we plan to create from this chaos. If I could have gotten out of here last year he would never have gone out on sardines and crackers. I don't know how anyone else views the matter and don't care, but now for me his is one more voice added to the already thunderous chorus that cries from unmarked and unhallowed graves for vindication.

Don't wait for me to change or modify my attitudes in the least. I *cannot understand,* as you put it, or as you would have me understand. I am a man, you are a woman. Being a woman, you may expect to be and enjoy being tyrannized. Perhaps you actually like walking at the heel of another, or otherwise placing yourself beneath another, but for me this is despicable. I refuse to even attempt to *understand* why I should debase myself or concede or compromise any part, the smallest part, of anything on earth to anyone who is not of my kind in thought and form. I love you, Mama, but I must be frank. Why did Papa die alone and hungry? Why did you think me insane for wanting a new bicycle instead of the old one I stole piece by piece and put together? Why did you allow us to worship at a White altar? Why even now, following tragedy after tragedy, crisis after crisis, do you still send Jon to that school where he is taught to feel inferior, and why do you continue to send me Easter cards? This is the height of disrespect you show me. You never wanted me to be a Man nor Jon either. You don't want us to resist and defeat our Enemies. What is wrong with you, Mama? No other mama in history has acted the way you act under stress situations.

I won't be a good *boy* ever.

Love,
George

TOWARD THE UNITED FRONT

A new unitarian and progressive current has sprung up in the movement centering on political prisoners. How can this unitarian conduct be developed further in the face of determined resistance from the establishment? How can it be used to isolate reactionary elements?

Unitary conduct implies a "search" for those elements in our present situation which can become the basis for joint action. It involves a conscious reaching for the relevant, the entente, and especially, in our case, the reconcilable. Throughout the centralizing authoritarian process of Amerikan history, the ruling classes have found it necessary to discourage and punish any genuine opposition to hierarchy. But there have always been individuals and groups who rejected the ideal of two unequal societies, existing one on top of the other.

The men who placed themselves above the rest of society through guile, fortuitous outcome of circumstance and sheer brutality have developed two principal institutions to deal with any and all serious disobedience—the prison and institutionalized racism. There are more prisons of all categories in the United States than in all other countries of the world combined. At all times there are two-thirds of a million people or more confined to these prisons. Hundreds are destined to be legally executed, thousands more quasi-legally. Other thousands will never again have any freedom of movement barring a revolutionary change in all the institutions that combine to make up the order of things. One third of a million people may not seem like a great number compared with the total population of two hundred million. However, compared with the one million who are responsible for all the affairs of men within the extended state, it constitutes a striking contrast. What I want to explore now are a few of the subtle elements that I have observed to be standing in the path of a much-needed united front (nonsectarian) to effectively reverse this legitimatized rip-off.

Prisons were not institutionalized on such a massive scale by the people. Most people realize that crime is simply the result of a grossly disproportionate distribution of wealth and privilege, a reflection of the present state of property relations. There are no wealthy men on death row, and so few in the general prison population that we can discount them altogether. Imprisonment is an aspect of class struggle from the outset. It is the creation of a closed society which attempts to isolate those individuals who disregard the structures of a hypocritical establishment as well as those who attempt to challenge it on a mass basis. Throughout its history, the United States has used its prisons to suppress any organized efforts to challenge its legitimacy—from its attempts to break up the early Working Men's Benevolent Association to the banning of the Communist Party during what I regard as the fascist takeover of this country, to the attempts to destroy the Black Panther Party.

The hypocrisy of Amerikan fascism forces it to conceal its attack on political offenders by the legal fiction of conspiracy laws and highly sophisticated frame-ups. The masses must be taught to understand the true function of prisons. Why do they exist in such numbers? What is the real underlying economic motive of crime and the official definition of types of offenders or victims? The people must learn that when one "offends" the totalitarian state it is patently not an offense against the people of that state, but an assault upon the privilege of the privileged few.

Could anything be more ridiculous than the language of blatantly political indictments: "The People of the State...vs. Angela Davis and Ruchell Magee" or "The People of the State...vs. Bobby Seale and Ericka Huggins." What people? Clearly the hierarchy, the armed minority.

We must educate the people in the real causes of economic crimes. They must be made to realize that even crimes of passion are the psycho-social effects of an economic order that was decadent a hundred years ago. All crime can be traced to objective socioeconomic conditions—socially productive or counterproductive activity. In all cases, it is determined by the economic system, the method of economic organization. "The People of the State...vs. John Doe" is as tenuous as the clearly political frame-ups. It's like stating "The People vs. The People." Man against himself. Official definitions of crime are simply attempts by the establishment to suppress the forces of progress.

Prisoners must be reached and made to understand that they are victims of social injustice. This is my task working from within (while I'm here, my persuasion is that the war goes on no matter where one may find himself on bourgeois-dominated soil). The sheer numbers of the prisoner class and the terms of their existence make them a mighty reservoir of revolutionary potential. Working alone and from within a steel-enclosed society, there is very little that people like myself can do to awake the restrained potential revolutionary outside the walls. That is part of the task of the "Prison Movement."

The "Prison Movement," the August 7th movement and all similar efforts educate the people in the illegitimacy of establishment power and hint at the ultimate goal of revolutionary consciousness at every level of struggle. The goal is always the same: the creation of an infrastructure capable of fielding a people's army.

Each of us should understand that revolution is aggressive. The manipulators of the system cannot or will not meet our legitimate demands. Eventually this will move us all into a violent encounter with the system. These are the terminal years of capitalism, and as we move into more and more basic challenges to its rule, history clearly forewarns us that when the prestige of power fails a violent episode precedes its transformation.

We can attempt to limit the scope and range of violence in revolution by mobilizing as many partisans as possible at every level of socio-economic life. But given the hold that the ruling class has on this country, and its history of violence, nothing could be more certain than civil disorders, perhaps even civil war. I don't dread either. There are no good aspects of monopoly capital, so no reservations need be recognized in its destruction. Monopoly capital is the enemy. It crushes the life force of all of the people. It must be completely destroyed, as quickly as possible, utterly, totally, ruthlessly, relentlessly destroyed.

With this as a common major goal, it would seem that anti-establishment forces would find little difficulty in developing common initiatives and methods consistent with the goals of mass society. Regretfully, this has not been the case. Only the prison movement has shown any promise of cutting across the ideological, racial and cultural barricades that have blocked the natural coalition of left-wing forces at all times in the past. So this movement must be used to provide an example for the partisans engaged at other levels of struggle. The issues involved and the dialectic which flows from an understanding of the clear objective existence of overt oppression could be the springboard for our entry into the tide of increasing world-wide socialist consciousness.

In order to create a united left, whose aim is the defense of political prisoners and prisoners in general, we must renounce the idea that all participants must be of one mind, and should work at the problem from a single party line or with a single party line or with a single method. The reverse of this is actually desirable. "From all according to ability." Each partisan, outside the vanguard elements, should work at radicalizing in the area of their natural environment, the places where they pursue their normal lives when not attending the rallies and demonstrations. The vanguard elements (organized party workers of all ideological persuasions) should go among the people concentrated at the rallying point with consciousness-raising strategy, promoting commitment and providing concrete, clearly defined activity. The vanguard elements must search out people who can and will contribute to the building of the commune, the infrastructure, with pen and clipboard in hand. For those who aren't ready to take that step, a "packet" of pamphlets should be provided for their education.

All of this, of course, means that we are moving, and on a mass level: Not all in our separate directions—but firmly under the disciplined and principled leadership of the Vanguard Black Panther Communist Party. "One simply cannot act without a head." Democratic centralism is the only way to deal effectively with the Amerikan ordeal. The central committee of the people's vanguard party must make its presence felt throughout the various levels of the overall movement.

With the example of unity in the prison movement, we can begin to break the old behavioral patterns that have repeatedly allowed bourgeois capitalism, its imperialism and fascism, to triumph over the last several decades. We tap a massive potential reservoir of partisans for cadre work. We make it possible to begin to address one of the most complex psycho-social by-products that economic man with his private enterprise has manufactured—Racism.

I've saved this most critical barrier to our needs of unity for last. Racism is a matter of ingrained traditional attitudes conditioned through institutions. For some, it is as natural a reflex as breathing. The psycho-social effects of segregated environments compounded by bitter class repression have served in the past to render the progressive movement almost totally impotent.

The major obstacle to a united left in this country is white racism. There are three categories of white racists: the overt, self-satisfied racist who doesn't attempt to hide his antipathy; the self-interdicting racist who harbors and nurtures racism in spite of his best efforts; and the unconscious racist, who has no awareness of his racist preconceptions.

I deny the existence of black racism outright, by fiat I deny it. Too much black blood has flowed between the chasm that separates the races. It's fundamentally unfair to expect the black man to differentiate at a glance between the various kinds of white racists. What the apologists term black racism is either a healthy defense reflex on the part of the sincere black partisan who is attempting to deal with the realistic problems of survival and elevation, or the racism of the government stooge organs.

As black partisans, we must recognize and allow for the existence of all three types of racists. We must understand their presence as an effect of the system. It is the system that must be crushed, for it continues to manufacture new and deeper contradictions of both class and race. Once it is destroyed, we may be able to address the problems of racism at an even more basic level. But we must also combat racism while we are in the process of destroying the system. The self-interdicting racist, no matter what his acquired conviction or ideology, will seldom be able to contribute with his actions in any really concrete way. His role in revolution, barring a change of basic character, will be minimal throughout. Whether the basic character of a man can be changed at all is still a question. But . . . we have in the immediacy of the "Issues in Question" the perfect opportunity to test the validity of materialist philosophy again, because we don't have to guess, we have the means of proof.

The need for unitarian conduct goes much deeper than the liberation of Angela, Bobby, Ericka, Magee, Los Siete, Tijerina, white draft-resisters, and now the indomitable and faithful James Carr.[17] We have fundamental strategy to be proved—tested and proved. The activity surrounding the protection and liberation of people who fight for us is an important aspect of the struggle. But it is important only if it provides new initiatives that redirect and advance the revolution under new progressive methods. There must be a collective redirection of the old guard—the factory and union agitator—with the campus activist who can counter the ill-effects of fascism at its training site, and with the lumpenproletariat intellectuals who possess revolutionary scientific-socialist attitudes to deal with the masses of street people already living outside the system. They must work toward developing the unity of the pamphlet and the silenced pistol. Black, brown and white are all victims together. At the end of this massive collective struggle, we will uncover our new man, the unpredictable culmination of the revolutionary process. He will be better equipped to wage the real struggle, the permanent struggle after the revolution—the one for new relationships between men.

SIXTEEN

ANGELA DAVIS

Jail Letter and "Beneath the Mountain" Victory Speech

IMAGINE A WORLD WITH ANGELA DAVIS NOT FREE. Imagine her convicted of the three capital felonies that she was charged with after being captured in 1970, and rather than spending her life among us, speaking, writing, organizing, teaching, and developing the ideas that have contributed to our collective radical evolution, spending the rest of her lifetime caged in prison. Imagine her isolated from the communities that sustain her, permitted two short visits and a few monitored calls a week. Imagine every letter sent in, or that she sent out, subjected to censors. Working for pennies an hour, and with no access to anything beyond a woefully inadequate prison library, how much research and writing would she be able to produce? Mercifully, we don't have to confront this scenario. After sixteen months, amid an international groundswell of revolutionary solidarity, she beat the charges when three "not guilty" verdicts were delivered to a courtroom filled with joyous supporters. And she did not come out cowed and cowering. Instead, Davis emerged from prison victorious—Afro huge, fist pumping. Ever since, she has used her experience of incarceration to transmit societal truths about human liberation and the counter-emancipatory forces of capitalism, racism, militarism, and the penal system. Almost all of Angela's work has recognized that unfree people often lead the way to liberation because their experiences and knowledge point to the best pathways for abolishing systems of oppression. She attests that solidarity is the strongest antidote to isolation and terror imposed by prisons. But how many Angela

Davises remain in prison today? How many remain silenced and isolated, every interaction surveilled by the state? We remain bereft of their profound contributions. Her letter from Marin County Jail—published here for the first time—gives a glimpse of some of her earliest anti-prison iterations. "People are beginning to talk not only about reforming the prisons," she wrote, "but about abolishing them altogether." By the time she and the Free Angela movement won her case in June 1972, that vision had evolved into a revolutionary pledge. "For our vow will be fulfilled," she said in her first public speech after winning her freedom, "only when we, or our children, or our grandchildren will have succeeded in seizing the reins of history, in determining the destiny of mankind and creating a society where prisons are unheard-of because the racism and the exploitative economic arrangement that reproduces want for the many and wealth for the few will have become relics of a past era." That era has not yet come. Until it does, millions of men and women will continue to endure the nightmare of private, state, and federal prisons, as well as county jails, military stockades, and immigration detention centers, buried deep beneath the mountain.

JAIL LETTER
1971

Sisters and Brothers,
During the past year, scores of letters from men and women chained to America's military apparatus have been brought to my cell. Although I have attempted to answer as many as circumstances permit, I have not been able to reach all those people who have reached out to me. Those of you who have written should know that your messages of support and solidarity have provided me with an endless source of strength.

Because of you and many other sisters and brothers, the almost total isolation which the jailors have imposed upon me has hardly done its job of eroding and breaking my spirit.

Over the past few years, movements against all forms of racism, economic misery, and war have found themselves the target of harsh repressive measures. Government terror and intimidation have frightened some people away from the front lines of struggle. One would think that those struggles, located in the most perilous regions of the government machine, would be the first to collapse. But sisters and brothers whose commitment necessarily carries the greatest risks, who are surrounded by terror and intimidation, often have been most persistent in ensuring the continued life and vitality of our struggle. In America's military structure, and in the dungeons of her penal system, enclaves of resistance continue to grow stronger. Wherever there is an American military base, wherever there is a prison, the will to fight oppression is fiercely asserting itself. In both places there is aggressive and growing resistance to the war being waged against people of color and poor working people.

Both the military and prison systems—together with the police and court structure—play critical roles in maintaining a political and economic balance that favors the wealthy who rule this country. They are the life-nerve of the American government's oppressive power. In their own ways, both the prisons and the military touch almost every section of the people in this country who are not among the powerful. Black people, Chicanos, Puerto Ricans, Native Americans, working people and the poor. As a consequence, both the military and the prisons reflect many of the ills which afflict American society as a whole.

In recent years, the people in this country have learned a great deal from prisoners and from men and women in the military. The long-concealed brutalities woven into the normal routine of prison life have been laid bare. People are beginning to talk not only about reforming the prisons—but about abolishing them altogether.

From those who have experienced it firsthand, people have learned the military is used to maim and kill people in Indochina who are trying to seize control over their destinies—who are trying to be free. And at the same time, that monstrous machine oppresses those whom it forces to fight its battles.

Prisoners have realized this; sisters and brothers in the military have realized this. Indeed, the great achievement of these two movements has been to expose the ugly face not just on the prisons and the military, but on the entire fabric of American society.

And so, because sisters and brothers in these movements have sought and discovered creative and demonstrative ways of conveying new levels of understanding to the people of this country, the repression has grown more intense. George Jackson has been murdered; the Soledad Brothers and the San Quentin 6 are being assaulted under the guise of legal justice. The case against Billy Smith is an example of the kind frame-up which attempts to intimidate others in the military who might be drawn into the struggle.[18]

Prisons are full of beautiful, committed, strong, struggling people. Their beauty, commitment, and strength are a threat to the rich, to racism, and to the wars which sacrifice human life for profit and power.

Repression will not turn us away from our struggle. What we must begin to do now is create more effective lines of communication and more mutually supportive activities for those of us who are fighting it out in the prisons and those fighting it out in the military. We need to intensify our efforts to reach our sisters in the ghettos, the barrios, the factories, and on unemployment lines, and brothers out there in the streets of this country, all of us joining together in a common struggle.

This is the way we can put freedom on the agenda.

BENEATH THE MOUNTAIN

Victory Speech
Delivered at Embassy Auditorium
Los Angeles, California
June 9, 1972

It's really a wonderful feeling to be back among the people. To be back among all of you who fought so long and so hard, among all of you who actually achieved my freedom. And I really wish you could have been there in the courtroom at the moment when those three "not guilty" verdicts were pronounced, because that victory was just as much yours as it was mine. And as we laughed and cried, these were expressions of our joy as we witnessed what was a real people's victory, and in spirit you were all there at that moment.

Over the last few days, I've been literally overwhelmed with congratulations and expressions of solidarity, whether it's been in meetings or on the streets or in restaurants; in the black and brown communities in northern California, wherever I've gone I've been greeted with hugs and kisses and it's really been beautiful. Even in a city like San Jose, among the white population, many many people have come out and have congratulated me and have told me that actually, they were behind us all the time. And during these last days I have sensed a real feeling of unity and togetherness and a kind of collective enthusiasm which I have rarely experienced on such a massive scale.

And in the midst of all of this it's sort of difficult for me to grasp that I am the person around whom all of this enthusiasm has emerged. Yet because of it I feel that I have a special responsibility—a special responsibility to you who have stood with me in struggle. But sometimes I have to admit when I'm off by myself and I reflect on everything that has happened over the last two years, I really wonder whether or not I will be able to meet the role which history has cut out for me, which you have cut out for me, but I promise I am going to try. That, I promise.

When it all started—and I'm speaking of myself—when I experienced the first stirrings of a commitment to the cause of freedom, the last thing I envisioned at that time were ambitions to become a figure known to great numbers of people. At that time I was simply aspiring to do everything I could to give my meager talents and energies to the cause of my people; to the cause of black people and brown people; and to all racially oppressed, and economically oppressed people in this country and throughout the globe. But history doesn't always conform to our own personal desires. It doesn't always conform to the blueprints we set up for our lives.

My life, and the lives of my family, my mother, my comrades, my friends, has really been drastically transformed over the last two years. For what happened was that as our movement—and particularly our movement right here in Los Angeles, our movement to free political prisoners, our movement to free all oppressed people—as that movement began to grow and become stronger and develop in breadth, it just so happened that I was the one who—one of the ones who was singled out by the government's finger of repression. It just so happened that I was destined to become yet another symbol of what the government intends to do—what the government in this state would do to every person who refuses to be its passive, submissive subjects.

But then, but then came the surge of a massive popular resistance, then came thousands and thousands and hundreds of thousands of people who were rising up to save me as we had tried to rise up and save the Soledad Brothers and other political prisoners. And what happened was that the government's plan, the government's project of repression fell apart; it backfired. The government could not, through me, terrorize people who would openly demonstrate their opposition to racism, to war, to poverty, to repression.

And on the contrary, people let it be known that they would not be manipulated by terror. They would stand behind all their sisters and brothers who had been caught in the government's web of repression. I was one of those who was entrapped in that web. And the thousands and millions of people throughout the world came together in struggle and saved me from the fate the government had planned as an example to all of you who were disposed to resist. You intervened and saved my life, and now I am back among you, and as I was wrested away from you in struggle, so likewise I return in struggle. I return in struggle with a very simple message, a very simple message: We've just begun our fight. We've just begun.

And while we celebrate the victory of my own acquittal, and also of the release on appeal of a very beautiful brother from a Texas prison—I don't know if you know him, his name is Leotis Johnson. He was a SNCC, SCLC organizer in Texas and was framed up on a marijuana charge. He was released just a few days ago after having spent four years, four years in a Texas prison. We have to celebrate that victory, too, but as we celebrate these victories, we must also be about the business of transforming our joy, our enthusiasm into an even deeper commitment to all our sisters and brothers who do not yet have cause to celebrate.

And as I say this, I remember very, very vividly the hundreds of women who were with me in the New York Women's House of Detention, most of them black and brown women, all of them from the poorest strata of this society. I remember the women in the sterile cells of Marin County Jail, and the women in the dimly lit, windowless cells in Santa Clara County. There is still the savage inhumanity of Soledad Prison. One Soledad brother, our brother George, has been murdered. The two who survived were recently acquitted, but hundreds more are awaiting our aid and solidarity.

There are hundreds and thousands of Soledad Brothers, or San Quentin Brothers, or Folsom Brothers, or CIW sisters,[19] all of whom are prisoners of an insanely criminal social order. So let us celebrate, but let us celebrate in the only way that is compatible with all the pain and suffering that so many of our sisters and brothers must face each morning as they awake to the oppressive sight of impenetrable concrete and steel. As they awake to the harsh banging of heavy iron doors opening and closing at the push of a button. As they awake each morning to the inevitable jangling of the keepers' keys—keys which are a constant reminder that freedom is so near, yet so far away. Millenniums and millenniums away.

So let us celebrate in the only way that is fitting. Let the joy of victory be the foundation of an undying vow; a renewed commitment to the cause of freedom. For we know now that victories are possible, though the struggles they demand are long and arduous. So let our elation merge with a pledge to carry on this fight until a time when all the antiquated ugliness and brutality of jails and prisons linger on only as a mere, a mere memory of a nightmare. For our vow will be fulfilled only when we, or our children, or our grandchildren will have succeeded in seizing the reins of history, in determining the destiny of mankind and creating a society where prisons are unheard-of because the racism and the exploitative economic arrangement which reproduces want for the many and wealth for the few will have become relics of a past era.

It has been said many times that one can learn a great deal about a society by looking towards its prisons. Look towards its dungeons and there you will see in concentrated and microcosmic form the sickness of the entire system. And today in the United States of America in 1972 there is something that is particularly revealing about the analogy between the prison and the larger society of which it is a reflection. For in a painfully real sense, we are all prisoners of a society whose bombastic proclamations of freedom and justice for all are nothing but meaningless rhetoric.

For this society's accumulated wealth, its scientific achievements are swallowed up by the avarice of a few capitalists and by insane projects of war and other irrational ventures. We are imprisoned in a society where there is so much wealth and so many sophisticated scientific and technological skills that anyone with just a little bit of common sense can see the insanity of a continued existence of ghettos and barrios and the poverty which is there.

For when we see the rockets taking off towards the moon, and the B-52s raining destruction and death on the people of Vietnam, we know that something is wrong. We know that all we have to do is to redirect that wealth and that energy and channel it into food for the hungry, and to clothes for the needy; into schools, hospitals, housing, and all the material things that are necessary, all the material things that are necessary in order for human beings to lead decent, comfortable lives—in order to lead lives which are devoid of all the pressures of racism, and yes, male supremacist attitudes and institutions and all the other means with which the rulers manipulate the people. For only then can freedom take on a truly human meaning. Only then can we be free to live and to love and be creative human beings.

In this society, in the United States of America today, we are surrounded by the very wealth and the scientific achievements which hold forth a promise of freedom. Freedom is so near, yet at the same time it is so far away. And this thought invokes in me the same sensation I felt as I reflected on my own condition in a jail in New York City. For from my cell, I could look down upon the crowded streets of Greenwich Village, almost tasting the freedom of movement and the freedom of space which had been taken from me and all my sisters in captivity.

It was so near but at the same time so far away because somebody was holding the keys that would open the gates to freedom. Our condition here and now—the condition of all of us who are brown and black and working women and men—bears a very striking similarity to the condition of the prisoner. The wealth and the technology around us tells us that a free, humane, harmonious society lies very near. But at the same time it is so far away because someone is holding the keys and that someone refuses to open the gates to freedom. Like the prisoner, we are locked up with the ugliness of racism and poverty and war and all the attendant mental frustrations and manipulations.

We're also locked up with our dreams and visions of freedom, and with the knowledge that if we only had the keys—if we could only seize them from the keepers, from the Standard Oils, the General Motors, and all the giant corporations, and of course from their protectors, the government—if we could only get our hands on those keys we could transform these visions and these dreams into reality. Our situation bears a very excruciating similarity to the situation of the prisoner, and we must never forget this. For if we do, we will lose our desire for freedom and our will to struggle for liberation.

As black people, as brown people, as people of color, as working men and women in general, we know and we experience the agony of the struggle for existence each day. We are locked into that struggle. The parallels between our lives and the lives of our sisters and brothers behind bars are very clear. Yet there is a terrifying difference in degree between life on this side of the bars and life on the other side. And just as we must learn from the similarities and acquire an awareness of all the forces which oppress us out here, it is equally important that we understand that the plight of the prisoner unfolds in the rock-bottom realms of human existence.

Our sisters and brothers down there need our help, and our solidarity in their collective strivings and struggles in the same elemental way that we all need fresh air, and nourishment and shelter. And when I say this, I mean it to be taken quite literally, because I recall too well that in the bleak silence and solitude of a Marin County isolation cell, you, the people, were my only hope, my only promise of life.

Martin Luther King told us what he saw when he went to the mountaintop. He told us of visions of a new world of freedom and harmony, told us of the sisterhood and brotherhood of humankind. Dr. King described it far more eloquently than I could ever attempt to do. But there's also the foot of the mountain, and there are also the regions beneath the surface. And I am returning from a descent, together with thousands and thousands of our sisters and brothers, into the ugly depths of society. I want to try to tell you a little something about those regions. I want to attempt to persuade you to join in the struggle to give life and breath to those who live sealed away from everything that resembles human decency.

Listen for a moment to George Jackson's description of life in Soledad Prison's O-Wing:

> This place destroys the logical processes of the mind. A man's thoughts become completely disorganized. The noise, madness streaming from every throat, frustrated sounds from the bars, metallic sounds from the walls, the steel trays, the iron beds bolted to the wall, the hollow sounds from a cast iron sink, a toilet, the smells, the human waste thrown at us, unwashed bodies, the rotten food. One can understand the depression felt by an inmate on max row. He's fallen as far as he can get into the social trap. Relief is so distant that it is very easy for him to lose his hopes. It's worse than Vietnam. And the guards with the carbines, and their sticks and tear gas are there to preserve this terror, to preserve it at any cost.

This in fact is what they told us at the trial in San Jose. I'd like to read a passage from our cross examination of one Sgt. Murphy, who was being questioned about San Quentin's policy about preventing escapes:

> Question: "And to be certain I understand the significance of that policy, sir, does that policy mean that if people are attempting to escape, and if they have hostages, and if the guards are able at all to prevent that escape, that they are to prevent that escape even if it means that every hostage is killed?"
>
> Answer: "That is correct."
>
> Question: "And that means whether they're holding one judge or five judges, or one woman or twenty women, or one child or twenty children, that the policy

> of San Quentin guards is that at all costs they must prevent the escape. Is that right?"
>
> Answer: "That also includes the officers that work in the institution, sir."
>
> Question: "Alright. Even if they are holding other officers who work in the institution, that should not deter the San Quentin correctional officers from preventing an escape at all costs. Is that right?"
>
> Answer: "That is correct."
>
> Question: "In other words, it is more important to prevent the escape than to save human life. Is that correct?"
>
> Answer: "Yes, sir."

You can find this in the official court records of the trial. This Sgt. Murphy told us that day why San Quentin guards were so eager to pump their bullets into the bodies of Jonathan Jackson, William Christmas, James McClain, and Ruchell Magee, even if it meant that a judge, a D.A., and women jurors might also be felled by their bullets. The terror of life in prison, its awesome presence in the society at large, could not be disturbed. Murphy called the prison by its rightful name. He captured the essence of the sociopolitical function of prisons today, for he was talking about a self-perpetuating system of terror. For prisons are political weapons; they function as means of containing elements in this society which threaten the stability of the larger system.

In prisons, people who are actually or potentially disruptive of the status quo are confined, contained, punished, and in some cases, forced to undergo psychological treatment by mind-altering drugs. This is happening in the state of California. The prison system is a weapon of repression. The government views young black and brown people as actually and potentially the most rebellious elements of this society. And thus the jails and prisons of this society are overflowing with young people of color. Anyone who has seen the streets of ghettos and barrios can already understand how easily a sister or a brother can fall victim to the police who are always there en masse.

Depending on the area, this country's prison population contains from 45 percent to 85 percent people of color. Nationally, 60 percent of all women prisoners are black. And tens of thousands of prisoners in city and county jails have never been convicted of any crime; they're simply there, victims—they're there under the control of insensitive, incompetent, and often blatantly racist public defenders who insist that they plead guilty even though they know that their client is just as innocent as they are. And for those who have committed a crime, we have to seek out the root cause. And we seek this cause not in them as individuals, but in the capitalist system that produces the need for crime in the first place.

As one student of the prisons system has said, "Thus, the materially hungry must steal to survive, and the spiritually hungry commit anti-social acts because their human needs cannot be met in a property-oriented state. It is a fair estimate," he goes on to say, "that somewhere around 90 percent of the crimes committed would not be considered crimes or would not occur in a people-oriented society." In October 1970 a prisoner who had taken part in The Tombs Rebellion in New York gave the following answers to questions put to him by a newsman.

> Question: "What is your name?"
> Answer: "I am a revolutionary."
> Question: "What are you charged with?"

Answer: "I was born black."
Question: "How long have you been in?"
Answer: "I've had trouble since the day I was born."

Once our sisters and brothers are entrapped inside these massive medieval fortresses and dungeons, whether for nothing at all or whether for frame-up political charges, whether for trying to escape their misery through a petty property crime, through narcotics or prostitution, they are caught in a vicious circle.

For if on the other side of the walls they try to continue or to begin to be men and women, the brutality they face, the brutality they must face, increases with mounting speed. I remember very well the women in the house of detention in New York who vowed to leave the heroin alone which was beginning to destroy their lives. Women who vowed to stand up and fight a system which had driven them to illusory escape through drugs. Women who began to outwardly exhibit their new commitment and their new transformation. And these were the women whom the worst of the matrons sought out, to punish them, and to put them in the hole.

George Jackson was murdered by mindless, carbine-toting San Quentin guards because he refused, he resisted, and he helped to teach his fellow prisoners that there was hope through struggle. And now in San Quentin—in San Quentin's Adjustment Center, which is a euphemistic term for the worst of the worst in prison—there are six more brothers who are facing charges of murder stemming from that day when George was killed. There was Fleeta Drumgo, who as a Soledad Brother was recently acquitted from similar frame-up charges. There are Hugo Pinell, Larry Spain, Luis Talamantez, David Johnson, and Willie Tate.

As I was saved and freed by the people so we must save and free these beautiful, struggling brothers. We must save them. And we must also save and free Ruchell Magee. And Wesley Robert Wells, who has spent over forty years of his life in California's prison system because he refused to submit, because he was a man. We must save, right here in southern California, Gary Lawton. And Geronimo Ortega, and Ricardo Chavez. And all of our sisters and brothers who must live with and struggle together against the terrible realities of captivity.

My freedom was achieved as the outcome of a massive, a massive people's struggle. Young people and older people, black, brown, Asian, Native American and white people, students and workers. The people seized the keys which opened the gates to freedom. And we've just begun. The momentum of this movement must be sustained, and it must be increased. Let us try to seize more keys and open more gates and bring out more sisters and brothers so that they can join the ranks of our struggle out here.

In building a prison movement, we must not forget our brothers who are suffering in military prisons and the stockades on bases throughout the country and across the globe. Let us not forget Billy Dean Smith. Billy Dean Smith, one of our black brothers who is now awaiting court-martial in Fort Ord, California. In Vietnam, this courageous brother from this city—from Watts, in fact, I think—would not follow orders. For he refused, he refused to murder the Vietnamese whom he knew as his comrades in the struggle for liberation. He would not follow orders.

And, of course, in the eyes of his superiors, he was a very, very dangerous example to the other GIs. He had to be eliminated. So he was falsely accused with killing two white officers in Vietnam. In Biên Hòa, Vietnam. We must free Billy

Dean Smith. We must free Billy Dean Smith and all his brothers and comrades who are imprisoned in the military.

We must be about the business of building a movement so strong and so powerful that it will not only free individuals like me—like the Soledad Brothers, the San Quentin Six, Billy Dean Smith—but one which will begin to attack the very foundations of the prison system itself.

And in doing this, the prison movement must be integrated into our struggles for black and brown liberation, and to our struggles for an end to material want and need. A very long struggle awaits us. And we know that it would be very romantic and idealistic to entertain immediate goals of tearing down all the walls of all the jails and prisons throughout this country. We should take on the task of freeing as many of our sisters and brothers as possible. And at the same time we must demand the ultimate abolition of the prison system along with the revolutionary transformation of this society. [*applause*] However, however, within the context of fighting for fundamental changes, there is something else we must do.

We must try to alter the very fabric of life behind walls as much as is possible through struggle, and there are a thousand concrete issues around which we can build this movement: uncensored and unlimited mail privileges, visits of the prisoners' choice, minimum wage levels in prison, adequate medical care—and for women this is particularly important when you consider that in some prisons a woman, a pregnant woman has to fight just to get one glass of milk per day. I saw this in New York. There are other issues. Literature must be uncensored. Prisoners must have the right to school themselves as they see fit. If they wish to learn about Marxism, Leninism, and about socialist revolution, then they should have the right to do it.

This is their right and they should have the full flexibility to do so. There should be no more "kangaroo courts" behind prison walls. There should be no more kangaroo courts wherein one can be charged with a simple violation of prison regulations and end up spending the rest of one's life there simply because the parole board would have it that way. And there must be an end, there must be an end to the tormenting, indeterminate sentence policy with which a prisoner like George Jackson could be sentenced from one year to life after having been convicted of stealing a mere seventy-five dollars.

For if you talk to any prisoner in the state of California and in other states where the indeterminate sentence law prevails, they will inevitably say that this is the most grueling aspect of life in prison. Going before a board of ex-cops, ex-narcotics agents, ex–FBI agents, and ex–prison guards and year after year after year after year being told to wait it out until next time.

These are just a few of the issues that we are going to have to deal with. And all of them, every single one of them, is the kind of issue which any decent human being should be able to understand.

The need, the very urgent need to join our sisters and brothers behind bars in their struggle was brought home during the rebellion and the massacre at Attica last year.

And I would like to close by reading a brief passage from a set of reflections I wrote in Marin County Jail upon hearing of the Attica revolt and massacre:

> The damage has been done, scores of men—some yet nameless—are dead. Unknown numbers are wounded. By now it would seem more people should realize that such explosions of repression are not isolated aberrations in a society not terribly disturbing. For we have witnessed Birmingham and Orangeburg, Jackson State, Kent State, My Lai, and San Quentin August 21. The list is unending.

None of these explosions emerged out of nothing. Rather, they all crystallized and attested to profound and extensive social infirmities.

But Attica was different from these other episodes in one very important respect. For this time the authorities were indicted by the very events themselves; they were caught red-handed in their lies. They were publicly exposed when to justify that massacre—a massacre which was led by Governor Rockefeller and agreed to by President Nixon—when they hastened to falsify what had occurred.

Perhaps this in itself has pulled greater numbers of people from their socially-inflicted slumber. Many have already expressed outrage, but outrage is not enough. Governments and prison bureaucracies must be subjected to fears and unqualified criticism for their harsh and murderous repression. But even this is not enough, for this is not yet the root of the matter. People must take a forthright stand in active support of prisoners and their grievances. They must try to comprehend the eminently human content of prisoners' stirrings and struggles. For it is justice that we seek, and many of us can already envision a world unblemished by poverty and alienation, one where the prison would be but a vague memory, a relic of the past.

But we also have immediate demands for justice right now, for fairness, and for room to think and live and act.

Thank you.

SEVENTEEN

MARTIN SOSTRE

The New Prisoner (1972)

MARTIN SOSTRE SURVIVED TWO SEPARATE PRISON sentences, totaling twenty years, too many of which were spent in the torturous isolation of solitary confinement. And what happened? He became a revolutionary. The conditions designed to break him seemed instead to whet his commitment, refine his intellect, broaden his understanding of how prisons impose hierarchy, and deepen his desire to expose the contradictions of the system. Following a prison conversion to Islam, the self-proclaimed "street dude" and "hustler" who was schooled in "the methods of the streets" began reading voraciously. While he didn't remain a lifelong adherent to Islam, his commitment to education transformed him into a public intellectual and a jailhouse lawyer. Following the completion of his first prison sentence he became a powerful community organizer and the proprietor of Afro Asian Books, a radical bookstore in Buffalo, New York. Devoted to the notion that incarcerated people should be respected as the human beings they are, Sostre organized for the right to practice religion and exercise full political expression. He also fought against prison slave labor, the use of solitary confinement as retaliation, and invasive strip searches. Intimidation from prison officials and unabashed bias against him in court could neither deter him nor stop him. Through his writing we see he remained fueled with revolutionary optimism that people can change the world. Sostre attempted to bridge a divide between those who struggled on the "ghetto streets" and those on the prison block. He emphasized solidarity, the unifying power of a vanguard prisoner underclass, and believed that the circumstances of oppression were what provided incentive for the masses to unite. Human rights will never be bestowed by those in power; rather, they are seized by those brave enough and willing to organize, struggle, and fight for them. In full faith he assures: "Revolutionary spirit overcomes all obstacles."

THE NEW PRISONER

"LISTEN, PIG, are you really that naive to believe you can fool and pacify us with nightly bribes of ten-cent candy bars and cookie snacks while caging us like animals in your inhuman steel cages; by removing the wire screen from the visiting room but replacing it with the three foot wide table thrust between our mothers, wives, children and loved ones to maintain your inhuman separation; by changing the color of our uniforms from gray to green (and those of our jailers), while exploiting our slave labor for pennies a day; by establishing a phony furlough program which is programmed to exclude from eligibility 1,690 prisoners out of 1,700;[20] by passing a token equalization bill? After Attica?! Well dream on, pig, until the next rude awakening overtakes you.

"Your widely-publicized prison reform programs—a smoke screen not only to cover up the greatest domestic massacre in a century, but also to conceal your current repressive pacification program consisting of the post-Attica multi-million-dollar appropriation for guns, gas, chemical sprays, for training killers on their effective use, construction of additional gun towers and assault tunnels within your prison camps from which to shoot us down, building and reinforcing special treatment housing or maxi-maxi units (euphemisms for solitary confinement torture chambers), etc.—will have the same success as your Vietnamization Program in Vietnam upon which they are patterned. Indeed, as in Vietnam, your repressive prison pacification program, sub nom prison reform, has already proven counter-productive in that it has set in motion dynamic revolutionary forces that will effect the overthrow of your racist-capitalist system.

"Are you so spiritually dead and blind that you fail to perceive the cause, effect and consequences of your repressive acts? Are you so hung up on the repressive-genocidal aspect of your racist-oriented technology that, despite your resounding defeat by the heroic Vietnamese people who, bare-footed and bamboo-housed, neutralized your advanced technology with resolute human spirit and revolutionary warfare, you still refuse to believe that your perverse technology cannot prevail over human spirit?

"If Attica fell to us in a matter of hours despite it being your most secure maximum security prison-fortress equipped with your latest repressive technology, so shall fall all your fortresses, inside and out. Revolutionary spirit conquers all obstacles.

"Every one of your prison camps has now become a revolutionary training camp feeding trained revolutionary cadres to each revolutionary foco in the ghetto. The recruits are the thousands of Black militants and revolutionaries framed and kidnapped from the ghettos in your desperate effort to put down the spreading Black Rebellion. While on the surface it appears you've cooled the ghettos, all you've done was remove the dynamic elements, dumped us in your prison camps where our diverse ideologies and experiences cross-fertilized, hardened and embittered us in your dehumanizing cages by abuse, breaking up our families, etc., to then return us to the ghettos as fully-hardened revolutionary cadres. Your oppressive mentality blinds you to these clear facts.

"Do you not see that we've converted your prison camps into revolutionary training camps for cadres of the Black liberation struggle? More important, your prisons have become ideological crucibles and battle grounds. Soon you shall reap the harvest."

The above capsulizes the ideology of thousands of Black revolutionaries being repressed in your prison camps. Although expressed in many ways—rhetorically and organizationally through the many militant and revolutionary prisoners' groups formed in every prison in the u.s.—the basic ideology is the same: using our time in prison to get it together for our return to the ghetto. While I speak only for prison camps in New York State—and I've been tortured in the major ones: Sing Sing, Clinton, Attica, Green Haven, Wallkill, and Auburn—I have compared notes with many out-of-state prisoners serving time in New York prison camps and found that the identical ideological situation exists in out-of-state prisons.

We are all political prisoners regardless of the crimes invoked by white racist oppressors to legitimize their kidnapping us from the ghettos and torturing us in their cages. You don't believe it? Well, what crimes did our forebears commit when they were kidnapped from Africa, imprisoned aboard slave ships and brought to America where their labor was exploited for 350 years? Didn't you legalize these crimes against Black people and codify them in your slave codes? Didn't you legitimize your genocidal slaughter of the American Indians and theft of their land by legislating Indian laws and the Homestead Act? Were not these crimes politically motivated and [did they not form] the very foundation of United States capitalism? And are you not now the benefactor of this loot and enjoying a standard of living many times higher than your kin in Europe, South Africa and Australia?

Yet, after our forebears were forced to build for you the richest country in the world with their blood and slave labor, the descendants of the white racist kidnappers, murderers and robbers who inherited the bloodstained loot have deluded themselves in the belief that they are the guardians of "law and order," that their victims must recognize them as such, acquiesce in their oppression, and relinquish all claims to their stolen heritage!

The consequences of this self-delusion shall soon bear bitter fruit, as surely as the invasion of Vietnam effected the present ignoble defeat at the hands of the heroic Vietnamese people. The delusion of the oppressor will be submerged by the reality of the struggle waged by the oppressed.

So continue pursuing your Eichmann-like repressive policies which your sadistic racist pig torturers are seeking to enforce. Never will they succeed in breaking our spirit to resist injustices; or convince us that they are the lawful authority—nay, their very outlaw acts remove all doubt (if it ever existed) that they are the outlaws, since they violate not only the laws of humanity but also the constitutional and statutory laws they are duty-bound to uphold.

Indeed, they are much more than outlaws, they are mass murderers. No prisoner in the history of New York State—possibly of the United States—has ever borne the stigma of being the mass-murderer of 43 persons. Yet the mass murderers of 43 persons will not be indicted. They continue in office enjoying political largess and passing themselves off as upholders of law and order.

The "people" who put them in office uphold and praise them for their savagery at Attica. They defend the deliberate premeditated murder at Attica, just as Eichmann defended his mass murders at his trial by pleading that he was an innocent concentration camp administrator caught in the middle and "following orders." But the Israeli Court, following precedents of the Nuremberg Tribunal, rejected this defense on grounds that each individual is a free agent bearing responsibility for his or her individual acts.

The people support and acquiesce in the continuance in office of these mass murderers. They raise no outraged cry against them. They make no demand for their impeachment; no demand that the mass murderers be arrested, charged with murder and indicted. The message therefore is very clear: the white racist people of this oppressive racist society are our enemies who go along with every injustice perpetrated against us by their elected representatives. Their support of bestial, genocidal acts against us reflects their consciousness.

The McKay Report whitewashing the Attica Massacre is a case in point.[21] Its statement, in regard to the taking of hostages, that "the holding of human lives for ransom is wrong and only leads to more violence and to a backlash that makes change more difficult," evokes sardonic smiles when read by us, the real hostages whose human lives are being held for exploitative ransom—as were the human lives of our forebears—solely because we are Black. Or does the dictum that holding hostages leads to more violence, apply only when Blacks hold White hostages and not when Black hostages are held by Whites?

But if your dictum has universal validity, does it not then follow that the rising tide of Black rebellion in America by your 25 million Black hostages is the natural legacy of the "wrong" which you state "only leads to more violence"? Keep on tripping, pig, for reality will trip you up.

Despite your self-delusion that you can pervert reality with lies, the fact is that "when everything has failed" (as it already has, since we cannot get justice from our oppressors)—"when a person is pressed to the wall" (as we already are)—"the taking of hostages may be the only way of reaching the outside world"—as Bill Kunstler correctly observed. The reality is that we politically aware prisoners, whom you cannot deceive into believing the lie that you murderous outlaws are the guardians and dispensers of law and justice, shall continue to employ all means necessary to free ourselves from your genocidal white racist oppression.

Hostage-taking is to us as legitimate a means of struggle as was your seizure of agents of the Crown during the American Revolutionary War, and the seizure of British tea during the Boston Tea Party. We, and not our oppressors, are the sole deciders of what means to employ in our liberation struggle.

The Attica Rebellion not only was the direct consequence of your systematic denial of our basic human rights, but of your adamant refusal to accord us the civilized treatment ordered by Federal Courts in *Sostre v. McGinnis*, *Sostre v. Rockefeller*, *Sostre v. Otis*, and in many other decisions.

Despite this fact being common knowledge to thousands of lawyers, judges, legislators, administrators and ordinary "people" familiar with the sweeping prison reforms ordered by Federal Courts in the *Sostre v. Rockefeller* and *Sostre v. Otis* decisions, and the millions of words written on the causes of Attica, why hasn't this fact—the obdurate refusal of outlaw State officials to obey Federal Court orders—been exposed? It is due to the white racist conspiracy of silence inherent in oppressive-racist America when the victims of white atrocities are Black.

When the 28 Attica Reform Demands presented to and accepted by Commissioner Russell Oswald on September 12, 1971, are viewed against the background of *Sostre v. Rockefeller*, *Sostre v. Otis* and other directives, it becomes clear that your refusal to comply with the directives of the Courts and implement the reforms resulted in the Attica Rebellion fifteen months later. The following facts represent irrefutable evidence that, had the provisions of the Federal Court mandates been complied with, and had other legitimate grievances brought to your attention by us prior to September 1971 been redressed, not one person would have died or been injured on September 9–13, 1971.

The first three of the 28 Attica Reform Demands dealt solely with procedures to be adopted after the anticipated agreement between the State officials and rebelling prisoners, and the return of prisoners to their cells. These three demands seek the provision of food, water and shelter (necessities of life which even animals in the zoo receive as a matter of course), an Observers Committee to monitor this operation, complete administrative and legal amnesty for the rebels.

Reform Demand no. 4 sought "the application of the New York State Minimum Wage Law Standards to all work done by inmates. Every effort will be made to make the records of payment available to inmates." This grievance (and many others) was brought to the attention of your prison officials on at least four occasions. Each time it was rebuffed and repressed usually with force.

The first time it was presented was in July 1970 when slaves in the Attica Metal Shop presented their demand for a minimum wage. You responded out of your usual "gorilla" bag by throwing into solitary confinement the representatives presenting the grievance. Having no outlet for this legitimate grievance, and having it compounded by your additional injustice of punishing our representatives, we responded with a work strike in the Metal Shop. Warden Mancusi and Commissioner Oswald reacted by confining to solitary confinement all the leaders. In July and August 1970 the strike leaders were transferred to Auburn and other prison camps throughout the state.

Seeking to pacify with crumbs the spreading prisoner discontent with the five to thirty cents per day slave wage of New York State prisons, you then raised prison wages to twenty-five cents for the lowest job category, and up to one dollar per day for the highest. But you immediately raised the already outrageously high commissary prices—e.g., we are forced to pay 40¢ for a two-pound box of sugar while outside you pay 59¢ for a five-pound bag—and cancelled out the few pennies raise in our slave wages.

The second time this grievance was brought to your attention was on November 4, 1970, during the Black Solidarity Day rebellion in Auburn Prison. In fact, it was the same militant leaders of the Attica Metal Shop strike that were transferred to Auburn Prison who led the Solidarity Day rebellion at Auburn.

The third time the unredressed slave labor grievance was presented to you was in July 1971 when the Attica Liberation Faction sent Oswald a list of grievances including the demand for higher wages. As usual, they were rebuffed.

The fourth time this labor grievance was brought to Oswald's attention was in July 1971 when prisoners in Green Haven presented to Warden Zelker and Oswald their list of grievances in the form of 13 Prisoners' Demands, headed by the demand for a Prisoners' Labor Union. The following is a copy of the Prisoners' Demands:

PRISONERS' DEMANDS

Attention:
We the inmates of Green Haven Prison demand . . .

That there be set up an Inmate Labor Union free from the creation of, and the control by, the State or any correctional agency thereof, that administers to the prisoners. But instead however, a private organization whose main concern is the welfare of the prisoners. To be headed by dedicated lawyers, whom we will choose, to act as President, Vice President, Treasurer, and people from organizations in our communities to serve on the Board of Directors of such a Union.

1. We demand that when a person is released on Conditional Release, all institutional holds be resolved. Conditional Release is time earned by inmates, therefore, he should not be held as if on parole. The present guidelines of Conditional Release are illegal and a form of chattel or indentured servitude.
2. We demand that there be a review board set up to bring about the release of those adults who have served ten (10) and more years for a crime that has been long atoned for.
3. We demand a complete revision of the New York State sentencing statutes—everyone sentenced under the old Penal Law (pre-1967) be recalled before court for re-sentencing under the new law.
4. We demand that there be an "Inmate Law Office" where we can set up inmate lawyers to study, prepare and review each inmate's case, who so wishes, and perfect appeals, legal briefs and all forms of writs and petitions in order to present our grievances and other important issues before the courts and other municipal bodies.
5. We demand that all inmates be allowed to correspond with whomever wishes to write him. The correspondent should be left up to the corresponding parties—not the institutional administrators. We further demand that we be allowed to order and receive any periodicals, books, newspapers, magazines or literature that we would normally be able to read if we were free men.

6. We demand that all inmates have religious and political freedom...that any religious and political books published in the u.s.a. be allowed to enter the prisons, so that prisoners can learn and get about to up-lift their wretched souls.
7. We demand a well-balanced, wholesome and nutritious diet. That the f.d.a. inspect all penal institutions to enforce cleanliness and diets.
8. We demand proper medical attention both by the prison hospital and dental department. We demand that the dental department use and administer novocaine for all filling of teeth.
9. We demand an immediate end to cruel and inhuman treatment and brutality by prison officials.
10. We demand that we be able to obtain personal typewriters, to be kept in our cells, in order to help us prepare ourselves for society and in order to prepare legal material for the courts in our legal efforts.
11. We demand that Deputy Superintendent H. Sawner and his Gestapo agents be removed from their positions and jobs because of the use of cruel and inhuman treatment issued out to prisoners.
12. Last, we demand to be treated like men..."

On August 18, 1971, Earl Smoake, one of the militant representatives of Green Haven, wrote to Zelker and Oswald asking to discuss with them the Prisoners' Labor Union and the other twelve grievances set forth above. He received no reply.

However, when on August 23, 1971, Earl Smoake discussed the organization of the Labor Union in a meeting with his fellow prisoners in the prison yard, he was thrown into solitary confinement.

Thus Oswald was presented with the labor grievance on at least four occasions prior to the Attica Rebellion. He ignored them and used force to repress our legitimate desire to receive some of the fruits of our labor and end the inhuman and unconstitutional treatment of prisoners in the prison-fortress of New York State.

Reform demand no. 6 of the Attica rebels demanded that the State "allow all New York State prisoners to be politically active without intimidation or reprisal." Why should it have been necessary to demand the right to exercise constitutionally protected political rights without intimidation or reprisal when the Federal Court thirteen months earlier in *Sostre v. Rockefeller,* had already enjoined the Commissioner of Correction and Warden Mancusi of Attica "from punishing Sostre for having in his possession political literature and for setting forth his political views orally or in writing?" The answer is clear: your outlaw prison officials disregarded the Court's mandate and continued to punish us for exercising our political beliefs.

The same applies to Reform Demand no. 7 which seeks the allowance of "true religious freedom." Were not prison officials ordered by the Federal Courts in *Sostre v. McGinnis,* to permit the exercise of the First Amendment right to worship? Why then should prisoners still have to demand the exercise of this "preferred-right" seven years later? Is it not obvious that your State prison officials are nothing but outlaws and criminals who use the U.S. Constitution and Court orders for toilet paper? Is it not obvious also that your State and Federal Courts, members of the same oppressive political structure to which your prison officials belong, are co-conspirators in the conspiracy against prisoners to deny us our Constitutional and human rights?

The pleadings of the case prove that *Sostre v. McGinnis* was the result of a six-year spiritual, physical and legal struggle led by three determined prisoners. The struggle commenced in Clinton Prison during 1958 when we first sued in Plattsburgh Supreme Court via writ of mandamus seeking the exercise of religious freedom.

The spiritual and physical aspect of the struggle involved years of torture in solitary confinement, beatings, tear gassings while locked in cages, bread and water diets, and many other barbarities inflicted by the State to break our spirit, health and resoluteness, and coerce other prisoners from joining our ranks. But far from breaking our spirit in the solitary confinement dungeons of Clinton and Attica Prisons, these dungeons became the "foco" of rebellion which spread to every prison in the State and involved hundreds of prisoners. The story of the spread of the struggle, how the problem became so serious that the State Attorney General was forced to set up a special bureau to handle the scores of Muslim complaints flooding the courts, and how the Muslim struggle evolved into the revolutionary struggle which led to the Attica Rebellion, is detailed in my forthcoming book.

It took six years of suffering and litigation to get the *Sostre v. McGinnis* ruling in 1964. I personally spent five years in solitary confinement struggling, and had my sentence not expired in September 1964, while in Attica solitary confinement, I probably would have spent many more years under torture. The 1964 ruling of the 2d Circuit Court (*Sostre v. McGinnis*) remanded the case to State Court where it was stalled through *Bryant v. Wilkins, SaMarion v. McGinnis,* to demand no. 7 of the Attica Rebellion to "allow true religious freedom"—seven more years! Thus the struggle to exercise a First Amendment "preferred" right took from 1958 till 1971, thirteen years of torture, suffering and death at the hands of racist outlaw savages who recognize no law except that of force, violence and murder.

Demands T. 8, 9, 17 and 25 of the Attica rebels seeking the end of arbitrary censorship of literature and correspondence, the employment of Black and Spanish-speaking officers, and the end of unlimited punishment in solitary confinement were already ordered by the U.S. District Court (Constance Baker Motley, J.) sixteen months earlier in *Sostre v. Rockefeller*.

The depraved savagery of your outlaw prison officials and your judicial co-conspirators is reflected in the rest of the reform demands. The very fact we have to demand "rehabilitation" from those whose primary function is the rehabilitation of prisoners, and food and medical treatment—basic necessities of life recognized by all civilized beings—makes manifest the type of individuals into whose care the "People of the State of New York" have thrown us.

Our claim that your prison officials are the real outlaws and we prisoners the victims, is supported by the holding of the U.S. District Court in *Sostre v. Rockefeller*, supra, where the Court stated at page 863 that:

> It is not the function of our prison system to make prisoners conform in their political thought and belief to ideas acceptable to their jailers. On the other hand, one function is to try to rehabilitate the lawbreaker by convincing him of the validity of our legal system. There is little chance that such an objective will be achieved if prisoners are entrusted to those who likewise break the law by denying prisoners their basic constitutional rights. This Court holds that Sostre's confinement to punitive segregation for the letters he wrote and for refusal to answer questions about a political organization, and his subsequent punishment for mere possession of political

> literature, were unreasonable punishments and violated his First Amendment right to freedom of political expression.

The Attica Rebellion was the result of recognition, after decades of painful exhaustion of all peaceful means of obtaining redress, of the impossibility of obtaining justice within the "legal" framework of an oppressive racist society which was founded on the most heinous injustices: murder, robbery, slavery. The ghetto rebellions were the result of a reaching of the same conclusion by the oppressed masses after centuries of civil rights struggle and court litigations, such as the 1954 Brown school integration decision, which after a twenty-year struggle for implementation was nullified by anti-busing legislation. The rising tide of revolutionary guerrilla struggle throughout the world is likewise due to the failure of all other means to redress injustices heaped on the oppressed.

Attica defrocked the vicious outlaw murderers who were passing themselves off as lawful authorities. It is now a historical fact that the upholders of "law and order" are the mass murderers of 43 persons in the Attica Massacre. These are the murderers and torturers who are in charge of New York State and its prison camps.

The reality of what must be done has been made manifest through the process of elimination of "legal" remedies. No longer shall we waste time and suffer prolonged needless punishment and injustices litigating civil rights cases in your oppressive courts as we did in the 1950s and '60s. Gone forever is our naivete of the 1960s which deceived us into regarding as militant the "we want" programs we followed, which in reality were the product of 400 years of slave mentality, in which the foolish slaves begged their master to grant them freedom, justice, equality, fertile land, etc. We've been saying "we want" this and "we want" that for 400 years, but the truth of the matter is that those who have been robbed of their freedom and heritage obtain justice only by using all means necessary in the struggle against their oppressor.

Little did you imagine that the very dungeons used to torture us, where you forced us to sleep naked on the cold concrete floor with windows opened to give us pneumonia, on bread and water diet, and with a five-gallon paint bucket for a toilet, would become the crucibles from which evolved the new hardened prisoner and the Vanguard revolutionary ideology which has now spread throughout New York State prison and into the ghettos.

The Vanguard revolutionary ideology formulated by the survivors of your torture dungeons is reflected in the following program:

PROGRAM OF BLACK VANGUARD FOR LIBERATION

WHY WE FIGHT, OUR AIMS AND OBJECTIVES

1. Since our heritage of 350 years of Black slave labor was stolen and invested in the development of this continent of North America by our oppressors, our aim is to recover this stolen heritage by liberating, through revolutionary armed struggle and all means necessary, a portion of this developed land from our oppressor's control. We shall establish our Black independent nation on this liberated territory which is ours by right of our labor invested in its development, our blood shed in its behalf, and by right of birth and history.
2. Our armed struggle for liberation, like that in Africa, Asia and South America, is a just struggle. We seek not to steal someone else's land and property, but to recover our stolen heritage: the product of 350 years of Black slave labor

stolen from our ancestors and employed by our oppressors to make the U.S. the richest country in the world.

3. We fight for the liberation of Black people held captive in ghetto colonies inside the United States by the white racist oppressor. By liberation we mean complete freedom from the physical, political, social and economic control of the white racist U.S. government, and the establishment of our own independent Black nation.
4. Since our struggle for liberation in America is a part of the world revolutionary struggle for liberation against the common U.S. enemy and its allies, we will use the same means employed by all oppressed peoples to liberate ourselves: guerrilla warfare, first and foremost.
5. As a first step towards nationhood, we must obtain revolutionary bases from which to operate. We must seize areas in urban and rural Black communities from the control of the oppressor. From these liberated and expanding areas we will wage our war of liberation.
6. Our independent Black nation will be a Socialist nation based on the principle that people, and not property, are the most precious of all possessions. Having freed ourselves from 400 years of genocidal white racist capitalism, we are not about to imitate our white oppressors by establishing a Black capitalist nation.

Does the Vanguard program differ from the "we want" programs like day does from night? Don't you wish we had remained mentally dead and in the "we want" trick bag while believing all the while we had the "key" to the problem of our oppression? It's too late now, for once mental chains are broken there is no return to the status quo ante.

We, the new politically aware prisoner, will soon galvanize the revolutionary struggle in America to its new phase that will hasten the overthrow of your exploitative racist society, recover the product of our stolen slave labor which you now enjoy, and obtain revolutionary justice for all oppressed people.

EIGHTEEN

ASSATA SHAKUR

Women in Prison: How It Is with Us and Two Poems

INSURGENT HEROINE AND QUEEN MOTHER ASSATA Shakur, a self-proclaimed "20th-century escaped slave," was born JoAnne Byron in 1947 in Jamaica, Queens. Engaged in the Black freedom movements of the era, Shakur joined the Black Panthers and later the Black Liberation Army. She was ambushed by police on the New Jersey Turnpike in 1973 and, despite lack of evidence, was convicted and sentenced to life in prison for the murder of a state trooper. In 1979, Assata orchestrated her own jailbreak with the help of comrades in the Black Liberation Army. She made her way to the sympathetic nation of Cuba, which granted her amnesty despite US requests for extradition. While hers is a fabled story of victory and self-emancipation, the text included here was written beneath the mountain during an opaque and uncertain moment. Assata describes the anguish, alienation, terror, discomfort, infantilization, and victimization that defined her everyday existence in a women's prison. Her words offer invaluable insights into the relationships between guards and prisoners, the criminogenic effects of capitalism, and the connections between slavery and incarceration. Assata's analysis suggests that the key to prison abolition is the politicization of incarcerated populations, in this case, women. Effective insurgency is contingent upon an understanding of one's condition and the ability to articulate a liberation-oriented analysis. Only prisoners who develop a sense of revolutionary literacy can manifest the political agency necessary for solidarity, collective action, and liberation. This episode of Assata Shakur's life story, published one year before her glorious escape, reminds us that revolutionary action, when informed by political consciousness, can, against all odds, lead to deliverance. The rousing power of this message echoes in the lines of the following stanza which have been affectionately dubbed "The Assata Chant." Voiced by large crowds in call-and-response fashion at rallies and demonstrations, it galvanizes and encourages new generations of activists.

It is our duty to fight for our freedom
It is our duty to win
We must love each other and support each other
We have nothing to lose but our chains

WOMEN IN PRISON
HOW IT IS WITH US

Clinton Correctional Facility for Women
1978

WE SIT in the bull pen. We are all black. All restless. And we are all freezing. When we ask, the matron tells us that the heating system cannot be adjusted. All of us, with the exception of a woman, tall and gaunt, who looks naked and ravished, have refused the bologna sandwiches. The rest of us sit drinking bitter, syrupy tea. The tall, fortyish woman, with sloping shoulders, moves her head back and forth to the beat of a private tune while she takes small, tentative bites out of a bologna sandwich. Someone asks her what she's in for. Matter-of-factly, she says, "They say I killed some nigga. But how could I have when I'm buried down in South Carolina?" Everybody's face gets busy exchanging looks. A short, stout young woman wearing men's pants and men's shoes says,

"Buried in South Carolina?" "Yeah," says the tall woman. "South Carolina, that's where I'm buried. You don't know that? You don't know shit, do you? This ain't me. This ain't me." She kept repeating, "This ain't me" until she had eaten all the bologna sandwiches. Then she brushed off the crumbs and withdrew, head moving again, back into that world where only she could hear her private tune.

Lucille comes to my tier to ask me how much time a "C" felony conviction carries. I know, but i cannot say the words. I tell her i will look it up and bring the sentence charts for her to see. I know that she has just been convicted of manslaughter in the second degree. I also know that she can be sentenced up to fifteen years. I knew from what she had told me before that the District Attorney was willing to plea bargain: Five years probation in exchange for a guilty plea [on] a lesser charge.

Her lawyer felt that she had a case: specifically, medical records which would prove that she had suffered repeated physical injuries as the result of beatings by the deceased and, as a result of those beatings, on the night of her arrest her arm was mutilated (she must still wear a brace on it) and one of her ears was partially severed in addition to other substantial injuries. Her lawyer felt that her testimony, when she took the stand in her own defense, would establish the fact that not only had she been repeatedly beaten by the deceased, but that on the night in question he told her he would kill her, viciously beat her and mauled her with a knife. But there is no self-defense in the state of New York.

The District Attorney made a big deal of the fact that she drank. And the jury, affected by t.v. racism, "law and order," petrified by crime and unimpressed with Lucille as a "responsible citizen," convicted her. And i was the one who had to tell her that she was facing fifteen years in prison while we both silently wondered what would happen to the four teen-age children that she had raised almost single-handedly.

Spikey has short time, and it is evident, the day before she is to be released, that she does not want to go home. She comes to the Bing (Administrative Segregation) because she has received an infraction for fighting. Sitting in front of her cage and talking to her i realize that the fight was a desperate, last-ditch effort in hope that the prison would take away her "good days." She is in her late thirties. Her hands are swollen. Enormous. There are huge, open sores on her legs. She has about ten teeth left. And her entire body is scarred and ashen. She has been on drugs about twenty years. Her veins have collapsed. She has fibrosis epilepsy and edema. She has not seen her three children in about eight years. She is ashamed to contact home because she robbed and abused her mother so many times.

When we talk it is around the Christmas holidays and she tells me about her bad luck. She tells me that she has spent the last four Christmases in jail and tells me how happy she is to be going home. But i know that she has nowhere to go and that the only "friends" she has in the world are here in jail. She tells me that the only regret she has about leaving is that she won't be singing in the choir at Christmas. As i talk to her i wonder if she will be back. I tell her good bye and wish her luck. Six days later, through the prison grapevine, i hear that she is back. Just in time for the Christmas show.

We are at sick call. We are waiting on wooden benches in a beige and orange room to see the doctor. Two young women who look only mildly battered by life sit wearing pastel dresses and pointy-toed state shoes. (Wearing "state" is often a sign that the wearer probably cannot afford to buy sneakers in commissary.) The two are talking about how well they were doing on the street. Eavesdropping, i find out that they both have fine "old men" that love the mess out of them. I find out that their men dress fly and wear some baad clothes and so do they. One has 40 pairs of shoes while the other has 100 skirts. One has 2 suede and 5 leather coats. The other has 7 suedes and 3 leathers. One has 3 mink coats, a silver fox and a leopard. The other has 2 minks, a fox jacket, a floor length fox and a chinchilla. One has 4 diamond rings and the other has 5. One lives in a duplex with a sunken tub and a sunken living room with a water fall. The other describes a mansion with a revolving living room. I'm relieved when my name is called. I had been sitting there feeling very, very sad.

There are no criminals here at Riker's Island Correctional Institution for Women (New York), only victims. Most of the women (over 95 percent) are black and Puerto Rican. Many were abused children. Most have been abused by men and all have been abused by "the system."

There are no big-time gangsters here, no premeditated mass murderers, no godmothers. There are no big-time dope dealers, no kidnappers, no Watergate women. There are virtually no women here charged with white collar crimes like embezzling or fraud. Most of the women have drug related cases. Many are charged as accessories to crimes committed by men. The major crimes that women here are charged with are prostitution, pick-pocketing, shop lifting, robbery and drugs. Women who have prostitution cases or who are doing "fine" time make up a substantial part of the short-term population. The women see stealing or hustling as necessary for the survival of themselves or their children because jobs are scarce and welfare is impossible to live on. One thing is clear: amerikan capitalism is in no way threatened by the women in prison on Riker's Island.

One gets the impression when first coming to Riker's Island that the architects conceived of it as a prison modelled after a juvenile center. In the areas where visitors usually pass there is plenty of glass and plenty of plants and flowers. The cell blocks consist of two long corridors with cells on each side connected by a watch room where the guards are stationed, called a bubble. Each corridor has a day room with a t.v., tables, multi-colored chairs, a stove that doesn't work and a refrigerator. There's a utility room with a sink and a washer and dryer that do not work.

Instead of bars the cells have doors which are painted bright, optimistic colors with slim glass observation panels. The doors are controlled electronically by the guards in the bubble. The cells are called rooms by everybody. They are furnished with a cot, a closet, a desk, a chair, a plastic upholstered headboard that opens for storage, a small book case, a mirror, a sink and a toilet. The prison distributes brightly colored bedspreads and throw rugs for a homey effect. There is a school area, a gym, a carpeted auditorium, two inmate cafeterias and outside recreation areas that are used during the summer months only.

The guards have successfully convinced most of the women that Riker's Island is a country club. They say that it is a playhouse compared to some other prisons (especially male): a statement whose partial veracity is not predicated upon the humanity of correction officials at Riker's Island, but, rather, by contrast to the unbelievably barbaric conditions of other prisons. Many women are convinced that they are, somehow, "getting over." Some go so far as to reason that because they are not doing hard time, they are [not] really in prison.

This image is further reinforced the pseudo-motherly attitude many of the guards; a deception which all too often successfully reverts women children. The guards call the women inmates by their first names. The women address the guards either as Officer, Miss—or by nicknames (Teddy Bear, Spanky,

Aunt Louise, Squeeze, Sarge, Black Beauty, Nutty Mahogany, etc.). Frequently, when a woman returns to Riker's she will make the rounds, gleefully embracing her favorite guard: the prodigal daughter returns.

If two women are having a debate about any given topic the argument will often be resolved by "asking the officer." The guards are forever telling the women to "grow up," to "act like ladies," to "behave" and to be "good girls." If an inmate is breaking some minor rule like coming to say "hi" to her friend on another floor or locking in a few minutes late, a guard will say, jokingly, "don't let me have to come down there and beat your butt." It is not unusual to hear a guard tell a woman, "what you need is a good spanking." The tone is often motherly, "didn't I tell you, young lady, to...," or, "you know better than that," or, "that's a good girl." And the women respond accordingly. Some guards and inmates "play" together. One officer's favorite "game" is taking off her belt and chasing her "girls" down the hall with it, smacking them on the butt.

But beneath the motherly veneer, the reality of guard life is ever present. Most of the guards are black, usually from working class, upward bound, civil service–oriented backgrounds. They identify with the middle class, have middle class values and are extremely materialistic. They are not the most intelligent women in the world and many are extremely limited.

Most are aware that there is no justice in the amerikan judicial system and that blacks and Puerto Ricans are discriminated against in every facet of amerikan life. But, at the same time, they are convinced that the system is somehow "lenient." To them, the women in prison are "losers" who don't have enough sense to stay out of jail. Most believe in the boot strap theory—anybody can "make it" if they try hard enough. They congratulate themselves on their great accomplishments. In contrast to themselves they see the inmate as ignorant, uncultured, self-destructive, weak-minded and stupid. They ignore the fact that their dubious accomplishments are not based on superior intelligence or effort, but only on chance and a civil service list.

Many guards hate and feel trapped by their jobs. The guard is exposed to a certain amount of abuse from co-workers, from the brass as well as from inmates, ass kissing, robotizing and mandatory overtime. (It is common practice for guards to work a double shift at least once a week.) But no matter how much they hate the military structure, the infighting, the ugliness of their tasks, they are very aware of how close they are to the welfare lines. If they were not working as guards most would be underpaid or unemployed. Many would miss the feeling of superiority and power as much as they would miss the money, especially the cruel, sadistic ones.

The guards are usually defensive about their jobs and indicate by their behavior that they are not at all free from guilt. They repeatedly, compulsively say, as if to convince themselves, "This is a job just like any other job." The more they say it the more preposterous it seems.

The major topic of conversation here is drugs. Eighty percent of inmates have used drugs when they were in the street. Getting high is usually the first thing a woman says she's going to do when she gets out. In prison, as on the streets, an escapist culture prevails. At least 50 percent of the prison population take some form of psychotropic drug. Elaborate schemes to obtain contraband drugs are always in the works.

Days are spent in pleasant distractions: soap operas, prison love affairs, card playing and game playing. A tiny minority are seriously involved in academic pursuits or the learning of skills. An even smaller minority attempt to study available law books. There are no jail house lawyers and most of the women lack knowledge of even the most rudimentary legal procedures. When asked what happened in court, or, what their lawyers said, they either don't know or don't remember. Feeling totally helpless and totally railroaded a woman will curse out her lawyer or the judge with little knowledge of what is being done or of what should be done. Most plead guilty, whether they are guilty or not. The few who do go to trial usually have lawyers appointed by the state and usually are convicted.

Here, the word "lesbian" seldom, if ever, is mentioned. Most, if not all, of the homosexual relationships here involve role-playing. The majority of relationships are either asexual or semi-sexual. The absence of sexual consummation is only partially explained by prison prohibition against any kind of sexual behavior. Basically, the women are not looking for sex. They are looking for love, for concern and companionship. For relief from the overwhelming sense of isolation and solitude that pervades each of us.

Women who are "aggressive" or who play the masculine roles are referred to as butches, bulldaggers or stud broads. They are always in demand because they are always in the minority. Women who are "passive," or who play feminine roles are referred to as fems. The butch-fem relationships are often oppressive, resembling the most oppressive, exploitative aspect of a sexist society. It is typical to hear butches threatening fems with physical violence and it is not uncommon for butches to actually beat their "women." Some butches consider themselves pimps and go with the women who have the most commissary, the most contraband or the best outside connections. They feel they are a class above ordinary women which entitles them to "respect." They dictate to fems what they are to do and many insist the fems wash, iron, sew and clean their cells for them. A butch will refer to another butch as "man." A butch who is well liked is known as "one of the fellas" by her peers.

Once in prison changes in roles are common. Many women who are strictly heterosexual in the street become butch in prison. "Fems" often create butches by convincing an inmate that she would make a "cute butch." About 80 percent of the prison population engage in some form of homosexual relationship. Almost all follow negative, stereotypic male/female role models.

There is no connection between the women's movement and lesbianism. Most of the women at Riker's Island have no idea what feminism is, let alone lesbianism. Feminism, the women's liberation movement and the gay liberation movement are worlds away from women at Riker's.

The black liberation struggle is equally removed from the lives of women at Riker's. While they verbalize acute recognition that amerika is a racist country where the poor are treated like dirt they, nevertheless, feel responsible for the filth of their lives. The air at Riker's is permeated with self-hatred. Many women bear marks on their arms, legs and wrists from suicide attempts or self-mutilation. They speak about themselves in self-deprecating terms. They consider themselves failures.

While most women contend that whitey is responsible for their oppression, they do not examine the cause or source of that oppression. There is no sense of class struggle. They have no sense of communism, no definition of it, but they consider it a bad thing. They do not want to destroy Rockefella. They want to be like him. Nicky Barnes, a major dope seller, is discussed with reverence. When he was convicted practically everyone was sad. Many gave speeches about how kind, smart and generous he was; no one spoke about the sale of drugs to our children.

Politicians are considered liars and crooks. The police are hated. Yet, during cop and robber movies, some cheer loudly for the cops. One woman pasted photographs of Farrah Fawcett Majors all over her cell because she "is a baad police bitch." Kojak and Barretta get their share of admiration.

A striking difference between women and men prisoners at Riker's Island is the absence of revolutionary rhetoric among the women. We have no study groups. We have no revolutionary literature around. There are no groups of militants attempting to "get their heads together." The women at Riker's seem vaguely aware of what a revolution is but generally regard it as an impossible dream. Not at all practical.

While men in prison struggle to maintain their manhood there is no comparable struggle by women to preserve their womanhood. One frequently hears women say, "Put a bunch of bitches together and you've got nothin but trouble"; and, "Women don't stick together, that's why we don't have nothin." Men prisoners constantly refer to each other as brother. Women prisoners rarely refer to each other as sister. Instead, "bitch" and "whore" are the common terms of reference. Women, however, are much kinder to each other than men, and any form of violence other than a fist fight is virtually unknown. Rape, murder and stabbings at the women's prison are non-existent.

For many, prison is not that much different from the street. It is, for some, a place to rest and recuperate. For the prostitute prison is a vacation from turning tricks in the rain and snow. A vacation from brutal pimps. Prison for the addict is a place to get clean, get medical work done and gain weight. Often, when the habit becomes too expensive, the addict gets herself busted (usually subconsciously) so she can get back in shape, leave with a clean system ready to start all over again. One woman claims that for a month or two every year she either goes [to] jail or to the crazy house to get away from her husband.

For many the cells are not much different from the tenements, the shooting galleries and the welfare hotels they live in on the street. Sick call is no different from the clinic or the hospital emergency room. The fights are the same except they are less dangerous. The police are the same. The poverty is the same. The alienation is the same. The racism is the same. The sexism is the same. The drugs are the same and the system is the same. Riker's [Island] is just another institution. In childhood school was their prison, or youth houses or reform schools or children shelters or foster homes or mental hospitals or drug programs and they see all institutions as indifferent to their needs, yet necessary to their survival.

The women at Riker's Island come there from places like Harlem, Brownsville, Bedford-Stuyvesant, South Bronx and South Jamaica. They come from places where dreams have been abandoned like the buildings. Where there is no more sense of community. Where neighborhoods are transient. Where isolated people run from one fire trap to another. The cities have removed us from our strengths, from our roots, from our traditions. They have taken away our gardens and our sweet potato pies and given us McDonald's. They have become our prisons, locking us into the futility and decay of pissy hallways that lead nowhere. They have alienated us from each other and made us fear each other. They have given us dope and television as a culture.

There are no politicians to trust. No roads to follow. No popular progressive culture to relate to. There are no new deals, no more promises of golden streets and no place else to migrate. My sisters in the streets, like my sisters at Riker's

Island, see no way out. "Where can I go?," said a woman on the day she was going home. "If there's nothing to believe in," she said, "I can't do nothin except try to find cloud nine."

What of our Past? What of our History? What of our Future?

I can imagine the pain and the strength of my great great grandmothers who were slaves and my great great grandmothers who were Cherokee Indians trapped on reservations. I remembered my great grandmother who walked everywhere rather than sit in the back of the bus. I think about North Carolina and my home town and i remember the women of my grandmother's generation: strong, fierce women who could stop you with a look out the corners of their eyes. Women who walked with majesty; who could wring a chicken's neck and scale a fish. Who could pick cotton, plant a garden and sew without a pattern. Women who boiled clothes white in big black cauldrons and who hummed work songs and lullabys. Women who visited the elderly, made soup for the sick and shortnin bread for the babies.

Women who delivered babies, searched for healing roots and brewed medicines. Women who darned sox and chopped wood and layed bricks. Women who could swim rivers and shoot the head off a snake. Women who took passionate responsibility for their children and for their neighbors' children too.

The women in my grandmother's generation made giving an art form. "Here, gal, take this pot of collards to Sister Sue"; "Take this bag of pecans to school for the teacher"; "Stay here while I go tend Mister Johnson's leg." Every child in the neighborhood ate in their kitchens. They called each other sister because of feeling rather than as the result of a movement. They supported each other through the lean times, sharing the little they had.

The women of my grandmother's generation in my home town trained their daughters for womanhood. They taught them to give respect and to demand respect. They taught their daughters how to churn butter; how to use elbow grease. They taught their daughters to respect the strength of their bodies, to lift boulders and how to kill a hog; what to do for colic, how to break a fever and how to make a poultice, patchwork quilts, plait hair and how to hum and sing. They taught their daughters to take care, to take charge, and to take responsibility. They would not tolerate a "lazy heifer" or a "gal with her head in the clouds." Their daughters had to learn how to get their lessons, how to survive, how to be strong. The women of my grandmother's generation were the glue that held family and the community together. They were the backbone of the church. And of the school. They regarded outside institutions with dislike and distrust. They were determined that their children should survive and they were committed to a better future.

I think about my sisters in the movement. I remember the days when, draped in African garb, we rejected our foremothers and ourselves as castrators. We did penance for robbing the brother of his manhood, as if we were the oppressor. I remember the days of the Panther Party when we were "moderately liberated." When we were allowed to wear pants and expected to pick up the gun. The days when we gave doe-eyed looks to our leaders. The days when we worked like dogs and struggled desperately for the respect which they struggled desperately not to give us. I remember the black history classes that did mention women and the posters of our "leaders" where women were conspicuously absent. We visited our sisters who bore the complete responsibility of the children while the Brotha was doing his thing. Or had moved on to bigger and better things.

Most of us rejected the white women's movement. Miss ann was still Miss ann to us whether she burned her bras or not. We could not muster sympathy for the fact that she was trapped in her mansion and oppressed by her husband. We were, and still are, in a much more terrible jail. We knew that our experiences as black women were completely different from those of our sisters in the white women's movement. And we had no desire to sit in some consciousness-raising group with white women and bare our souls.

Women can never be free in a country that is not free. We can never be liberated in a country where the institutions that control our lives are oppressive. We can never be free while our men are oppressed. Or while the amerikan government and amerikan capitalism remain intact.

But it is imperative to our struggle that we build a strong black women's movement. It is imperative that we, as black women, talk about the experiences that shaped us; that we assess our strengths and weaknesses and define our own history. It is imperative that we discuss positive ways to teach and socialize our children.

The poison and pollution of capitalist cities is choking us. We need the strong medicine of our foremothers to make us well again. We need their medicines to give us strength to fight and the drive to win. Under the guidance of Harriet Tubman and Fannie Lou Hamer and all of our foremothers, let us rebuild a sense of community. Let us rebuild the culture of giving and carry on the tradition of fierce determination to move on closer to freedom.

AFFIRMATION

I believe in living.
I believe in the spectrum
of Beta days and Gamma people.
I believe in sunshine.
In windmills and waterfalls,
tricycles and rocking chairs.
And i believe that seeds grow into sprouts.
And sprouts grow into trees.
I believe in the magic of the hands.
And in the wisdom of the eyes.
I believe in rain and tears.
And in the blood of infinity.

I believe in life.
And i have seen the death parade
march through the torso of the earth,
sculpting mud bodies in its path.
I have seen the destruction of the daylight,
and seen bloodthirsty maggots
prayed to and saluted.

I have seen the kind become the blind
and the blind become the bind
in one easy lesson.
I have walked on cut glass.
I have eaten crow and blunder bread
and breathed the stench of indifference.

I have been locked by the lawless.
Handcuffed by the haters.
Gagged by the greedy.

And, if i know any thing at all,
it's that a wall is just a wall
and nothing more at all.
It can be broken down.

I believe in living.
I believe in birth.
I believe in the sweat of love
and in the fire of truth.

And i believe that a lost ship,
steered by tired, seasick sailors,
can still be guided home
to port.

LEFTOVERS—WHAT IS LEFT?

After the bears and the gates
and the degradation,
What is left?

After the lock ins and the lock outs
and the lock ups,
What is left?

I mean, after the chains that get entangled
in the gray of one's matter,
After the bars that get stuck
in the hearts of men and women,
What is left?

After the tears and disappointments,
After the lonely isolation,
After the cut wrists and the heavy noose,
What is left?

I mean, like, after the commissary kisses
and the get-your-shit-off blues,
After the hustler has been hustled,
What is left?

After the murderburgers and the goon squads
and the tear gas,
After the bulls and the bull pens
and the bull shit,
What is left?

Like after you know that god
can't be trusted,
After you know that the shrink
is a pusher
and the word is a whip
and the badge is a bullet,
What is left?

After you know that the dead
are still walking,
After you realize that silence
is talking,
that outside and inside
are just an illusions,
What is left?

I mean, like, where is the sun?
Where are her arms and
where are her kisses?
There are lip-prints on my pillow—
i am searching.
What is left?

I mean, like, nothing is standstill
and nothing is abstract.
The wing of a butterfly
can't take flight.
The foot on my neck is part
of a body.
The song that i sing is part
of an echo.
What is left?

I mean, like, love is specific.
Is my mind a machine gun?
Is my heart a hacksaw?
Can i make freedom real? Yeah!
What is left?

I am at the top and bottom
of a lower-archy.
I am an earth lover
from way back.
I am in love with
losers and laughter.
I am in love with
freedom and children.

Love is my sword
and truth is my compass.
What is left?

NINETEEN

RITA BO BROWN

Court Statement (1978)

RITA DARLING BROWN, POPULARLY KNOWN AS BO Brown, was a dedicated anti-prison advocate and working-class lesbian. When she robbed banks on behalf of the George Jackson Brigade, she was armed with more than just a gun. She was also armed with a revolutionary's critique of the prison system, an unwavering anti-capitalist worldview, and a rock-solid sense of solidarity with other oppressed people. We see here, in her pre-sentencing court statement, an ability to speak from multiple vantage points of marginalization which unite in the language of anti-prison ideology. The George Jackson Brigade, an urban guerrilla group named in honor of the assassinated revolutionary, was composed primarily of racially diverse, working-class, gay adherents. Operating out of Seattle from 1975 to 1978, it was one of several militant anti-capitalist formations based in the US at that time. Brown joined the brigade after her first stint in prison, embracing George Jackson's belief that the anti-prison movement had the power to unify the underclass and transform global social structures. Brown survived eight years beneath the mountain and continued to focus on abolition work after being released from prison. Her life and legacy are rich with lessons about community, loyalty, and the risks inherent in revolutionary praxis. "Struggle is good and change is good," said Brown. "They are not easy, but isn't that what life is? Is life really about making it easy so you can sit on your ass all the time and not do a motherfucking thing? I don't think so—I think life is living. I want to be struggling the day I die, cause then I will know I'm alive."

I STAND before this mockery of justice court to be condemned as its enemy—and I am its enemy! I am a member of the George Jackson Brigade and I know the answer to Bertolt Brecht's question: "Which is the biggest crime, to rob a bank or to found one?"

It is to my sisters and brothers of the working class that I am accountable—NOT to this court that harasses and searches my peers before they can enter what is supposed to be their courtroom. NOT to this or any court whose hidden purpose is to punish the poor and non-white in the name of the US government. A government which perpetuates the crimes of war and repression has NO right to prescribe punishment for those who resist the continuation of worldwide death and misery. This government didn't ask its citizens what we thought about CIA intervention in Chile or current US big business holdings in South Africa.

I am a native fighting on her homeground! I was born and raised right here. All my life has been spent in Oregon and Washington. My parents are working people. My father a mill worker for 32 years, my mother an unskilled laborer at the county nursing home. We always had to count every penny and do without some thing or another to make it from payday to payday. I have pumped gas, been a clerk, a mechanic, and a printer and a variety of other things. That makes me a common working person as is most of the population of this world. We have nothing to survive by except labor—our sweat. We are slaves! Forced to give our labor and our lives to maintain an economic system designed to serve only the rich—almost always white male corporate owners. This ruling class has no respect for human life. Its only concerns are private property and personal power. They manipulate us as puppets on their stage of greed.

I am a woman who is greatly concerned that the biggest areas of neglect in the so-called justice system are rape, wife battering, and child abuse. The womyn of today suffers every day from the oppression of sexism. Everywhere she looks she sees sexist stereotypes that scream: you are a sex object—you can't control your own body—men need to beat you sometimes—there is no such thing as rape, you must have asked for it. And if she can't cope with this insanity the male-dominated medical profession pronounces her crazy. Ninety percent of patients in mental hospitals are wimmin.

I am a lesbian—a womyn who totally loves wimmin. A womyn who loves herself and her sisters. A womyn who is proud to say that loving wimmin is a very beautiful and positive aspect of my life. When any womyn or man decides to be openly gay—to "come out"—we risk social disapproval, police harassment, and the very real possibility of being beaten in the streets. We are denied jobs, thrown out of public places, refused housing, our children can be stolen from us, and most shrinks still think we suffer from some incurable sexual illness. This blatant discrimination is the systematic denial of our democratic and human rights. It should never be a crime for any person to love and care about another person. The freedom to be what we are is what we all fight for! Wimmin loving wimmin and men loving men is nothing new. Since the beginning of humanity, we have loved, free and proud. Our culture, though sparsely documented due to the great efforts to suppress our herstory/ history, does exist. During the time of Sappho and Isle of Lesbos, our sexuality was open and accepted. Then the self-appointed rulers—the profiteers—marched across the earth and for boots they wore suppression. Suppression to crush all those who wouldn't conform to their ideas or recognize their right to destroy our various ways of life. We have been mighty warriors in many wars—Amazons and Romans. Not even Hitler, who killed us in one of his first experiments in annihilation, could destroy us. Joe McCarthy hunted us too. Today, the fear of homosexuality promoted by the "masters of unreason" encourages Anita Bryant–types of fascist campaigns based on hysteria and ignorance. This kind of institutionalized fear is repeatedly used to keep us from building strong resistance. It will work less and less as we learn to understand the tactics of psychological warfare used by the rich to keep all of us in our places. But, we must remain alert to the very real threat of fascism and destroy it before we find ourselves surrounded.

I love children. To me children are the most beautiful, honest, sincere, and creative of human beings. It is for their future as well as my own that I fight. My heart full of love for all people. My heart full of rage at the capitalist/imperialist system that traps and destroys us from birth. I am the anger of the people like the thunder that comes before the rain that will heal the earth.

I am an anti-authoritarian lesbian feminist anarcho-communist! I am an urban guerrilla committed to give my white life if necessary! As our comrade brother George Jackson said—and it's just as true today as it was almost 10 years ago when he said it—"We must come together, understand the reality of our situation, understand that fascism is already here, that people are already dying who could be saved, that generations will die or live butchered half-lives if we fail to act."

TWENTY

SAFIYA ASYA BUKHARI

Coming of Age: A Black Revolutionary (1979)

BORN IN BRONX, NEW YORK, IN 1950, SAFIYAH Bukhari experienced state brutality that moved her from the mentality of social worker to that of a revolutionary, dedicated to serving the needs of her community and strengthening community relations. Named Bernice Jones at birth, she hailed from a large family that deeply valued education as the means by which they could secure a solid place in American society. Bukhari was enrolled in a pre-med program at Brooklyn College when she made a lifelong commitment to work for social justice. What began with volunteering with the Black Panthers' Free Breakfast for Children program transitioned to her joining the Panthers and later the Black Liberation Army. Ambushed in a Virginia grocery store in 1975 on her way to Mississippi, she faced charges of armed robbery. Following a one-day trial, she was sentenced to forty years in prison. The following year, she escaped and spent two months eluding authorities until she was recaptured and forced to serve nearly nine years before securing parole and release. Severe health problems, for which she received inadequate care, plagued her throughout her duration in prison.

Being a Black woman in the United States radicalized Bukhari, heightening her awareness of the multiple ways race, class, and gender are wielded by those in power to deceive, evict, criminalize, and brutalize. She recognized that, though constrained, Black women are also formidable agents of change. In her analysis, women are central to the liberation of society as a whole. She argues that women, despite being oppressed, are the well from which we all draw strength, and that solidarity and truth are among the revolutionary's most potent weapons. That she, a prisoner at the time of writing this, teaches us lessons from her jail cell, demonstrates her agency. Is it possible that the most marginalized among us are the ones imbued with the power to point the way toward our collective liberation? We remember Safiya Bukhari while contemplating this question. Before her untimely death in 2003, Bukhari co-founded the Jericho Movement for US Political Prisoners and the Free Mumia Abu-Jamal Coalition in New York City. She advocated for others, stood up for political prisoners, used her experiences to raise the alarm about women's health issues in prison, and worked indefatigably for the common good.

GREEK MYTHOLOGY tells the story of Minos, ruler of the city of Knossos. Minos had a great labyrinth (maze) in which he kept the Minotaur, a monster that was half man and half bull, whose victims were boys and girls who would make it to the center of the maze only to be killed when they came face to face with the Minotaur. If an intended victim chanced to survive the encounter with the Minotaur, the person perished trying to find a way out of the many intricate passages. Finally, Theseus of Athens, with the help of Ariadne, Minos's daughter, entered the labyrinth, slayed the beast, and found his way out by following the thread he had unwound as he entered.

The maturation process is full of obstacles and entanglements for anyone, but for a Black woman in America it has all the markings of the Minotaur's maze. I had to say that, even though nothing as spectacular takes place in the maturation process of the average Black woman. But the day-to-day struggle for survival and growth reaps the same reward in the end in ten thousand different ways. The trick is to learn from each defeat and become stronger and more determined, to think and begin to develop the necessary strategies to ensure the annihilation of the beast....

I am one of a family of ten children. My parents were strict and religious, but proud and independent. One of the strongest influences of my childhood was my mother constantly telling us to hold our heads up and be proud because we were just as good or better than anyone else, and to stand up and fight for what we believe to be right.

There was a lot of competition in my family. You had to be competitive with ten children (all two years apart) growing up, each trying to live up to the other or be better. We were determined not to be caught up in the rut of the ghetto. We were going to get out, so each of us worked on our separate goals, ten *individuals*, one family, in our separate world.

We believed that with the right education we could "make it"; so that is the route we took searching for the "American Dream." I was going to be a doctor. In my second year of college, I pledged a sorority; it was here that the rose-colored glasses were cracked and rays of reality were allowed to filter in.

The sorority had decided to help "disadvantaged" children as one of our projects for the year and we were trying to decide what country to work with when one of the Sisters suggested that we work in the ghettos of New York. Personally, I had never even thought of people in the United States being disadvantaged, but only too lazy to work and "make it." I was in for one of the biggest rude awakenings of my life.

A few of us were sent to Harlem to investigate the situation. We talked to people on the street, in the welfare centers, from door to door, and watched them work and play, loiter on the corners and in the bars. What we came away with was a story of humiliation, degradation, deprivation, and waste that started in infancy and lasted until death—in too many cases, at an early age.

Even at this point, I did not see this as affecting me personally, but only as a sorority project. I was sort of a tourist who takes pity on the less fortunate.

The sorority decided to do what we could to help the children. The Black Panther Party was already running a Free Breakfast Program to feed the children. I had a daughter of my own at this point and decided that I would put my energies into this.

I could not get into the politics of the Black Panther Party, but I could volunteer to feed some hungry children; you see, children deserve a good start and you have to feed them for them to live to learn. It is difficult to think of reading and arithmetic when your stomach is growling. I am not trying to explain the logic of the Free Breakfast for Children Program, only showing how I had to be slowly awakened to the reality of life and shown the interconnection of things.

At five a.m. every morning, my daughter and I would get ready and go to the center where I was working on the Breakfast Program. It entailed cooking and serving breakfast, sometimes talking to the children about problems they were encountering, or helping them with their homework. Everything was going along smoothly until the number of children coming began to fall off. Finally, I began to question the children and found that the police had been telling the parents in the neighborhood not to send their children to the program because we were "feeding them poisoned food."

It is one thing to hear about the underhanded things the police do—you can choose to ignore it—but it is totally different to experience it for yourself. You must either lie to yourself or face it. I chose to face it and find out why the police felt it was so important to keep Black children from being fed that they told lies. I went back to the Black Panther Party and started attending some of their community political education classes.

First Encounter with the Police

Not long after that, I was forced to make a decision about the direction I was going in politically. I was on 42nd Street with a friend when we noticed a crowd gathered on the corner. In the center of the crowd was a Panther with some newspapers under his arm. Two police officers were also there. I listened in. The police were telling the Panther he could not sell newspapers on the corner and he was insisting that he could. Without a thought, I told the police that the Brother had a *constitutional right* to disseminate political literature anywhere, at which point the police asked for my identification and arrested the Sister and myself, along with the Brother who was selling the papers.

I had never been arrested before and I was naive enough to believe that all you had to do was be honest and everything would work out all right. I was wrong again. As soon as the police got us into the backseat of their car and pulled away from the crowd, the bestiality began to show. My friend went to say something and one of the police officers threatened to ram his nightstick up her if she opened her mouth again, and then ran on in a monologue about Black people. I listened and got angry.

At the Fourteenth Precinct, they separated us to search us. They made us strip. After the policewoman searched me, one of the male officers told her to make sure she washed her hand so she would not catch anything.

That night, I went to see my mother and explained to her about the bust and about a decision I had made. Momma and Daddy were in the kitchen when I got there. Daddy was sitting at the table and Momma was cooking. After I told them about the bust, they said nothing. Then I told them about how the police had acted, and they still said nothing. I said I could not sit still and allow the police to get away with that. I had to stand up for my rights as a human being. I remember my mother saying, "If you think it's right, then do it." I went back to Harlem and joined the Black Panther Party.

I spent the next year working with welfare mothers, in Liberation Schools, talking to students, learning the reality of life in the ghettos of America, and reevaluating many of the things I had been taught about the "land of the free and the home of the brave." About this time, I quit school and looked for a full-time job. I had education and skills, but there was always something wrong. What it was only became clear after I went to International Telephone and Telegraph to apply for a job as a receptionist-clerk. They told me I was *overqualified*. I ended up working in my friend's mother's beauty parlor and spent all my spare time with the Party.

By the summer of 1970, I was a full-time Party member and my daughter was staying with my mother. I was teaching some of the political education classes at the Party office and had established a liberation school in my section of the community. By listening to the elderly, I learned how they could not survive off their miserly social security checks—not pay the rent and eat, too—so they would pay their rent and eat from the dog food section of the supermarket or the garbage cans. I had listened to the middle-aged mother as she told of being evicted from her home and how she was sleeping on a subway with her children. She did so because welfare refused to help her unless she signed over all her property; out of desperation, she fraudulently received welfare. I watched a mother prostitute her body to put food in the mouth of her child, while another mother, mentally broken under the pressure, prostituted her eight-year-old child. I had seen enough of the ravages of dope, alcohol, and despair to know that a change was needed to make the world a better place in which my child could live. My mother had successfully kept me ignorant of the plight of Black people in America. Now I had learned it for myself, but I was still to learn a harsher lesson: the plight of the slave who dares to rebel.

Turbulent Times

The year 1971 saw many turbulent times in the Black Panther Party and changes in my life. I met and worked with many people who were to teach and guide me: Michael Cetewayo Tabor of the Panther 21; Albert Nuh Washington; and "Lost One" Robert Webb, who was responsible for my initial political education. Cet taught me to deal in a principled fashion, Nuh taught me compassion, and Robert taught me to be firm in my convictions.

When the split took place in the Black Panther Party, I was left in the position of communications and information officer of the East Coast Black Panther Party. Much later, I was to discover the vulnerability of that position. Many Party members went underground to work with the Black Liberation Army (BLA). I was among those elected to remain aboveground and supply necessary support. The police murders of youths such as Clifford Glover, Tyrone Guyton, etc., and the BLA's retaliation with the assassinations of police officers Piagentini and Jones and Laurie [and Foster] made the powers-that-be frantic. They pulled out all the stops in their campaign to rid the streets of rebellious slaves. By spring 1973, Comrades Assata Shakur and Sundiata Acoli were captured, along with Nuh and Jalil (Anthony Bottom); Twymon Myers was on the FBI's Ten Most Wanted List, and I was still traveling back and forth across the country trying to build necessary support mechanisms.

In 1972, I had recognized the need to depend on something other than myself. In less than two years, I had come to realize that nothing is permanent or secure in a world in which it is who you know and what you have that counts. I had seen friends and loved ones killed or thrown into prison; associates who I believed would never go back turned state's evidence or melted into the woodwork. Nuh introduced me to Islam, which gave me a new security, sense of purpose, and dignity.

By 1973, I was receiving a great deal of flak from the police because of what they "suspected" I might be doing. Mostly, it was because I did not have a record, they could not catch me doing anything, and I had gained the community's support. All the while, I actively and vocally supported BLA members.

Capture

On January 25, 1975, some other members of the Amistad Collective of the BLA and I went into the country in Virginia to practice night firing. We were to leave Virginia that night on our way to Jackson, Mississippi, because I wanted to be there on Sunday to see someone. Before returning to the crib where we were staying, we decided to stop at a store to pick up cold cuts for sandwiches to avoid stopping at roadside restaurants on the way down. We drove around looking for an open store. When we came to one, I told the Brothers to wait in the car and I would go in and be right back.

I entered the store, went past the registers, down an aisle to the meat counter and started checking for all-beef products. I heard the door open, saw two of the Brothers coming in, and did not give it a thought. I went back to what I was doing, but out of the corner of my left eye, I saw the manager's hand with a rifle pointed toward the door. I quickly got into an aisle just as the firing started. Up to this point, no words had been spoken. With the first lull in shooting,

Kombozi [Amistad] (one of my bodyguards and a member of the Amistad Collective) came down the aisle toward me. He was wearing a full-length army coat. It was completely buttoned. As he approached, he told me he had been shot. I did not believe him at first, because I saw no blood and his weapon was not drawn. He insisted, so I told him to lie down on the floor and I would take care of it.

Masai [Ehehosi] (my codefendant) apparently had made it out the door when the firing started because he reappeared at the door, trying to draw the fire so we could get out. I saw him get shot in the face and stumble backward out the door. I looked for a way out and realized there was none. I elected to play it low key to try to get help for Kombozi as soon as possible. That effort was wasted. The manager of the store and his son, Paul Green Sr. and Jr., stomped Kombozi to death in front of my eyes. Later, when I attempted to press countercharges of murder against them, the Commonwealth attorney called it "justifiable" homicide. Five minutes after the shoot-out, the FBI was on the scene. The next morning, they held a press conference in which they said I was notorious, dangerous, etc., and known to law enforcement agencies nationwide. My bail was set at one million dollars for each of the five counts against me.

Trial and Imprisonment

On April 16, 1975, after a trial that lasted one day, I was sentenced to forty years for armed robbery; that night, I arrived here at the Virginia Correctional Center for Women in Goochland. Directly following my arrival, I was placed in the maximum-security building. There I stayed until the threat of court action led them to release me into the general population. The day after my release into the general population,

I was told that the first iota of trouble I caused would land me back in the maximum-security building and there I would stay.

My emphasis then and for the next two years was on getting medical care as well as educational programs and activities for myself and the other women, with the priority being on medical care for myself. Inside the prison, I was denied care. The general feeling was that they could not chance hospitalization for fear I would escape; as such, they preferred to take a chance on my life. The courts said they saw no evidence of inadequate medical care, but rather a difference of opinion on treatment between the prison doctor and me.

The quality of "medical treatment" for women prisoners in Virginia must be at an all-time low. Their lives are in the hands of a "doctor" who examines a woman whose right ovary has been removed and tells her there is tenderness in the missing ovary. This "doctor" examines a woman who has been in prison for six months and tells her that she is six weeks pregnant and there is nothing wrong with her. She later finds her baby has died and mortified inside of her. Alternatively, he tells you that you are not pregnant and three months later, you give birth to a seven-pound baby boy. The list includes prescribing Maalox for a sore throat and diagnosing a sore throat that turns out to be cancer.

In December 1976, I started hemorrhaging and went to the clinic for help. No help of any consequence was given, so I escaped. Two months later, I was recaptured. While on escape a doctor had told me that I could endure the situation, take painkillers, or have surgery. I decided to use the lack of medical care as my defense for the escape to accomplish two things: (1) expose the level of medical care at the prison and (2) put pressure on them to give me the care I needed.

I finally got to the hospital in June 1978. By then, it was too late. I was so messed up inside that everything but one ovary had to go. Because of the negligence of the "doctor" and the lack of feeling on the part of the prison officials, I was forced to have a hysterectomy. When they brought me back to this prison in March 1977, because of the escape, they placed me in cell 5 on the segregation end of the maximum-security building—the same room they had placed me in on April 16, 1975. Today I remain in that cell, allegedly because of my escape, but in actuality because of my politics.

How do I know? Since I was returned to this institution on March 24, 1977, other women have escaped, been brought back, and been released to general population. Yesterday, after twenty-two months, my codefendant on the escape charge was okayed for release to general population. I was denied.

Despite my emotional and physical setbacks, I have learned a great deal. I have watched the oppressor play a centuries-old game on Black people—divide and conquer. Black women break under pressure and sell their men down the river. Then the oppressor separates the women from their children. In two strokes, the state does more damage than thirty years in prison could have done if the women had supported the men.

Now, more than ever before, Black women (New Afrikan women) have developed a mercenary outlook on life. No longer are they about family, community, and us as a people. They are about looking good, having fun, and "making it." Women's liberation is what they are talking about. Genuine women's liberation for Black women, however, will only come about with the liberation of Black people as a whole; that is, when for the first time since our forefathers were snatched from the African continent and brought to America as slave labor, we can be a family, and from that family build a community and a nation.

The powers that be were disconcerted when Black mothers, wives, and daughters and Black women in general stood by and, in many cases, fought beside their men when they were captured, shot, or victimized by the police and other agents of the government. They were frightened of the potential of Black women to wreak havoc when these women began to enter the prisons and jails in efforts to liberate their men. They were spurred into action when they were confronted with the fact that Black women were educating their children from the cradle up about the real enemies of Black people and about what must be done to eliminate this ever-present threat to the lives of Black people.

During the last four years of my incarceration, I watched and refrained from speaking because I did not want to alienate the "Left." Black men and women have fooled themselves into believing we were "making progress" because Patricia Harris, a Black woman, joined the president's cabinet and Andrew Young became ambassador to the United Nations. They failed to realize that it is simply politics, American style. There is no real progress being made. Indeed, one of Jimmy Carter's best friends, Vernon Jordan, head of the Urban League, had to concede in his annual economic review, *The State of Black America, 1979*, that the "income gap between Blacks and whites is actually widening."[22]

The sacrifices made by Black women in search of Black womanhood, like those made by the people of Knossos in attempting to slay the Minotaur, have been many, harsh, and cruel. We, too, can slay the beast (in our case American racism, capitalism, and sexism) and out of the ashes build a true and independent Black Nation in which we can take our rightful place as women, wives, and mothers, knowing that our children will live to be men and women, and our men will be allowed to recognize their manhood—to support and defend their families with dignity. Together building a future for ourselves! Build to win!

TWENTY-ONE

EVE GOLDBERG AND LINDA EVANS

The Prison Industrial Complex and the Global Economy (1998)

LINDA EVANS WAS A POLITICAL PRISONER SERVING a forty-year sentence when she and Eve Goldberg, a writer and filmmaker, collaborated on the following article. When this essay was published in 1998, they were writing to the pulse of the moment, spelling out the relationships between economy, public policy, law, the war on drugs, and skyrocketing prison rates, all captured in what was then a newly coined term: "the prison industrial complex." This phrasing built on the concept of a "military industrial complex"—lexicon forged during the previous anti-war era. Born in Iowa in 1947, Evans joined the ranks of the Weatherman-SDS as a politicized college student attending Michigan State University and was further politicized by a trip to Vietnam as part of a peace delegation in 1969. Goldberg, born in 1954, was raised in California, where she became a politically active high school student and continued her activism throughout years of study and work. She and Evans met in 1996 while doing support work for political prisoners. Convicted for several crimes, including "conspiracy to overthrow the U.S. government using force and violence," Linda Evans served sixteen years in federal prison before being pardoned by Bill Clinton in 2001 on his last day in office. When they co-wrote this article, the business of prisons was expanding here and around the world. They note, "Like any industry, the prison economy needs raw materials. In this case the raw materials are prisoners." Their message was pressing in 1998, and it remains so today. Goldberg and

Evans suggest that "the only alternative that will match the power of global capital is an internationalization of human solidarity." Prison issues—and prisoners themselves—are integral to this process and cannot be left out of the equation.

THE PRISON INDUSTRIAL COMPLEX AND THE GLOBAL ECONOMY

OVER 1.8 million people are currently behind bars in the United States. This represents the highest per capita incarceration rate in the history of the world. In 1995 alone, 150 new U.S. prisons were built and filled.

This monumental commitment to lock up a sizeable percentage of the population is an integral part of the globalization of capital. Several strands converged at the end of the Cold War, changing relations between labor and capital on an international scale: domestic economic decline, racism, the US role as policeman of the world, and growth of the international drug economy in creating a booming prison/industrial complex. And the prison/industrial complex is rapidly becoming an essential component of the US economy.

Prisons Are Big Business

Like the military/industrial complex, the prison/industrial complex is an interweaving of private business and government interests. Its twofold purpose is profit and social control. Its public rationale is the fight against crime.

Not so long ago, communism was "the enemy" and communists were demonized as a way of justifying gargantuan military expenditures. Now, fear of crime and the demonization of criminals serve a similar ideological purpose: to justify the use of tax dollars for the repression and incarceration of a growing percentage of our population. The omnipresent media blitz about serial killers, missing children, and "random violence" feeds our fear. In reality, however, most of the "criminals" we lock up are poor people who commit nonviolent crimes out of economic need. Violence occurs in less than 14 percent of all reported crime, and injuries occur in just 3 percent. In California, the top three charges for those entering prison are: possession of a controlled substance, possession of a controlled substance for sale, and robbery. Violent crimes like murder, rape, manslaughter and kidnaping don't even make the top ten.

Like fear of communism during the Cold War, fear of crime is a great selling tool for a dubious product.

As with the building and maintenance of weapons and armies, the building and maintenance of prisons are big business. Investment houses, construction companies, architects, and support services such as food, medical, transportation and furniture, all stand to profit by prison expansion. A burgeoning "specialty item" industry sells fencing, handcuffs, drug detectors, protective vests, and other security devices to prisons.

As the Cold War winds down and the Crime War heats up, defense industry giants like Westinghouse are re-tooling and lobbying Washington for their share of the domestic law enforcement market. "Night Enforcer" goggles used in the Gulf War, electronic "Hot Wire" fencing ("so hot NATO chose it for high-risk installations"), and other equipment once used by the military, are now being marketed to the criminal justice system.

Communication companies like AT&T, Sprint, and MCI are getting into the act as well, gouging prisoners with exorbitant phone calling rates, often six times the normal long-distance charge. Smaller firms like Correctional Communications Corp., dedicated solely to the prison phone business, provide computerized prison phone systems, fully equipped for systematic surveillance. They win government contracts by offering to "kick back" some of the profits to the government agency awarding the contract. These companies are reaping huge profits at the expense of prisoners and their families; prisoners are often effectively cut off from communication due to the excessive cost of phone calls.

One of the fastest-growing sectors of the prison industrial complex is private corrections companies. Investment firm Smith Barney is a part owner of a prison in Florida. American Express and General Electric have invested in private prison construction in Oklahoma and Tennessee. The Corrections Corporation of America, one of the largest private prison owners, already operates internationally, with more than 48 facilities in 11 states, Puerto Rico, the United Kingdom, and Australia. Under contract by governments to run jails and prisons, and paid a fixed sum per prisoner, the profit motive mandates that these firms operate as cheaply and efficiently as possible. This means lower wages for staff, no unions, and fewer services for prisoners. Private contracts also mean less public scrutiny. Prison owners are raking in billions by cutting corners which harm prisoners. Substandard diets, extreme overcrowding, and abuses by poorly trained personnel have all been documented and can be expected in these institutions which are unabashedly about making money.

Prisons are also a leading rural growth industry. With traditional agriculture being pushed aside by agribusiness, many rural American communities are facing hard times. Economically depressed areas are falling over each other to secure a prison facility of their own. Prisons are seen as a source of jobs in construction, local vendors and prison staff, as well as a source of tax revenues. An average prison has a staff of several hundred employees and an annual payroll of several million dollars.

Like any industry, the prison economy needs raw materials. In this case the raw materials are prisoners. The prison industrial complex can grow only if more and more people are incarcerated even if crime rates drop. "Three Strikes" and mandatory minimums (harsh, fixed sentences without parole) are two examples of the legal superstructure quickly being put in place to guarantee that the prison population will grow and grow and grow.

Labor and the Flight of Capital

The growth of the prison industrial complex is inextricably tied to the fortunes of labor. Ever since the onset of the Reagan-Bush years in 1980, workers in the United States have been under siege. Aggressive union busting, corporate deregulation, and especially the flight of capital in search of cheaper labor markets, have been crucial factors in the downward plight of American workers.

One wave of capital flight occurred in the 1970s. Manufacturing such as textiles in the Northeast moved south to South Carolina, Tennessee, Alabama, non-union states where wages were low. During the 1980s, many more industries (steel, auto, etc.) closed up shop, moving on to the "more competitive atmospheres" of Mexico, Brazil, or Taiwan where wages were a mere fraction of those in the US, and environmental, health and safety standards were much lower. Most seriously hurt by these plant closures and layoffs were African Americans and other semiskilled workers in urban centers who lost their decent-paying industrial jobs.

Into the gaping economic hole left by the exodus of jobs from US cities has rushed another economy: the drug economy.

The War on Drugs

The "War on Drugs," launched by President Reagan in the mid-1980s, has been fought on interlocking international and domestic fronts.

At the international level, the war on drugs has been both a cynical cover-up of US government involvement in the drug trade, as well as justification for US military intervention and control in the Third World.

Over the last 50 years, the primary goal of US foreign policy (and the military industrial complex) has been to fight communism and protect corporate interests. To this end, the US government has, with regularity, formed strategic alliances with drug dealers throughout the world. At the conclusion of World War II, the OSS (precursor to the CIA) allied itself with heroin traders on the docks of Marseille in an effort to wrest power away from communist dock workers. During the Vietnam War, the CIA aided the heroin-producing Hmong tribesmen in the Golden Triangle area. In return for cooperation with the US government's war against the Vietcong and other national liberation forces, the CIA flew local heroin out of Southeast Asia and into America. It's no accident that heroin addiction in the US rose exponentially in the 1960s.

Nor is it an accident that cocaine began to proliferate in the United States during the 1980s. Central America is the strategic halfway point for air travel between Colombia and the United States. The Contra War against Sandinista Nicaragua, as well as the war against the national liberation forces in El Salvador, was largely about control of this critical area. When Congress cut off support for the Contras, Oliver North and friends found other ways to fund the Contra re-supply operations, in part through drug dealing. Planes loaded with arms for the Contras took off from the southern United

States, offloaded their weapons on private landing strips in Honduras, then loaded up with cocaine for the return trip.

A 1996 exposé by the *San Jose Mercury News* documented CIA involvement in a Nicaraguan drug ring which poured thousands of kilos of cocaine into Los Angeles' African-American neighborhoods in the 1980s. Drug boss Danilo Blandon, now an informant for the DEA, acknowledged under oath the drugs-for-weapons deals with the CIA-sponsored Contras.

US military presence in Central and Latin America has not stopped drug traffic. But it has influenced aspects of the drug trade, and is a powerful force of social control in the region. US military intervention whether in propping up dictators or squashing peasant uprisings now operates under cover of the righteous war against drugs and "narco-terrorism."

[In] Mexico, for example, US military aid supposedly earmarked for the drug war is being used to arm Mexican troops in the southern part of the country. The drug trade, however (production, transfer, and distribution points) is all in the north. The "drug war money" is being used primarily to fight against the Zapatista rebels in the southern state of Chiapas who are demanding land reform and economic policy changes which are diametrically opposed to the transnational corporate agenda.

In the Colombian jungles of Cartagena de Chairá, coca has become the only viable commercial crop. In 1996, 30,000 farmers blocked roads and airstrips to prevent crop spraying from aircraft. The Revolutionary Armed Forces of Colombia (FARC) one of the oldest guerrilla organizations in Latin America, held 60 government soldiers hostage for nine months, demanding that the military leave the jungle, that social services be increased, and that alternative crops be made available to farmers. And given the notorious involvement of

Colombia's highest officials with the powerful drug cartels, it is not surprising that most US "drug war" military aid actually goes to fighting the guerrillas.

One result of the international war on drugs has been the internationalization of the US prison population. For the most part, it is the low-level "mules" carrying drugs into this country who are captured and incarcerated in ever-increasing numbers. At least 25 percent of inmates in the federal prison system today will be subject to deportation when their sentences are completed.

Here at home, the war on drugs has been a war on poor people. Particularly poor, urban, African American men and women. It's well documented that police enforcement of the new, harsh drug laws have been focused on low-level dealers in communities of color. Arrests of African-Americans have been about five times higher than arrests of whites, although whites and African-Americans use drugs at about the same rate. And, African-Americans have been imprisoned in numbers even more disproportionate than their relative arrest rates. It is estimated that in 1994, on any given day, one out of every 128 US adults was incarcerated, while one out of every 17 African-American adult males was incarcerated.

The differential in sentencing for powder and crack cocaine is one glaring example of institutionalized racism. About 90 percent of crack arrests are of African Americans, while 75 percent of powder cocaine arrests are of whites. Under federal law, it takes only five grams of crack cocaine to trigger a five-year mandatory minimum sentence. But it takes 500 grams of powder cocaine, 100 times as much, to trigger this same sentence. This flagrant injustice was highlighted by a 1996 nationwide federal prison rebellion when Congress refused to enact changes in sentencing laws that would equalize penalties.

Statistics show that police repression and mass incarceration are not curbing the drug trade. Dealers are forced to move, turf is reshuffled, already vulnerable families are broken up. But the demand for drugs still exists, as do huge profits for high-level dealers in this fifty-billion-dollar national industry.

From one point of view, the war on drugs can actually be seen as a pre-emptive strike. The state's repressive apparatus working overtime. Put poor people away before they get angry. Incarcerate those at the bottom, the helpless, the hopeless, before they demand change. What drugs don't damage (in terms of intact communities, the ability to take action, to organize) the war on drugs and mass imprisonment will surely destroy.

The crackdown on drugs has not stopped drug use. But it has taken thousands of unemployed (and potentially angry and rebellious) young men and women off the streets. And it has created a mushrooming prison population.

Prison Labor

An American worker who once upon a time made $8/hour, loses his job when the company relocates to Thailand where workers are paid only $2/day. Unemployed, and alienated from a society indifferent to his needs, he becomes involved in the drug economy or some other outlawed means of survival. He is arrested, put in prison, and put to work. His new salary: 22 cents/hour.

From worker, to unemployed, to criminal, to convict laborer, the cycle has come full circle. And the only victor is big business.

For private business, prison labor is like a pot of gold. No strikes. No union organizing. No unemployment insurance or workers' compensation to pay. No language problem, as in a foreign country. New leviathan prisons are being built with thousands of eerie acres of factories inside the walls. Prisoners do data entry for Chevron, make telephone reservations for TWA, raise hogs, shovel manure, make circuit boards, limousines, waterbeds, and lingerie for Victoria's Secret. All at a fraction of the cost of "free labor."

Prisoners can be forced to work for pennies because they have no rights. Even the 14th Amendment to the Constitution which abolished slavery, excludes prisoners from its protections.

And, more and more, prisons are charging inmates for basic necessities from medical care, to toilet paper, to use of the law library. Many states are now charging "room and board." Berks County Jail in Pennsylvania is charging inmates $10 per day to be there. California has similar legislation pending. So, while government cannot (yet) actually require inmates to work at private industry jobs for less than minimum wage, they are forced to by necessity.

Some prison enterprises are state-run. Inmates working at UNICOR (the federal prison industry corporation) make recycled furniture and work 40 hours a week for about $40 per month. The Oregon Prison Industries produces a line of "Prison Blues" blue jeans. An ad in their catalogue shows a handsome prison inmate saying, "I say we should make bell-bottoms. They say I've been in here too long." Bizarre, but true. The promotional tags on the clothes themselves actually tout their operation as rehabilitation and job training for prisoners, who of course would never be able to find work in the garment industry upon release.

Prison industries are often directly competing with private industry. Small furniture manufacturers around the country complain that they are being driven out of business by UNICOR which pays 23 cents/hour and has the inside track on government contracts. In another case, US Technologies sold its electronics plant in Austin, Texas, leaving its 150 workers unemployed. Six weeks later, the electronics plant reopened in a nearby prison.

Welcome to the New World Order

The proliferation of prisons in the United States is one piece of a puzzle called the globalization of capital.

Since the end of the Cold War, capitalism has gone on an international business offensive. No longer impeded by an alternative socialist economy or the threat of national liberation movements supported by the Soviet Union or China, transnational corporations see the world as their oyster. Agencies such as the World Trade Organization, World Bank, and the International Monetary Fund, bolstered by agreements like NAFTA and GATT, are putting more and more power into the hands of transnational corporations by putting the squeeze on national governments. The primary mechanism of control is debt. For decades, developing countries have depended on foreign loans, resulting in increasing vulnerability to the transnational corporate strategy for the global economy. Access to international credit and aid is given only if governments agree to certain conditions known as "structural adjustment."

In a nutshell, structural adjustment requires cuts in social services, privatization of state-run industry, repeal of agreements with labor about working conditions and minimum wage, conversion of multi-use farm lands into cash crop agriculture for export, and the dismantling of trade laws which protect local economies. Under structural adjustment, police and military expenditures are the only government spending that is encouraged. The sovereignty of nations is compromised when, as in the case of Vietnam, trade sanctions are threatened unless the government allows Camel cigarettes to litter the countryside with billboards, or promises to spend millions in the US-orchestrated crackdown on drugs.

The basic transnational corporate philosophy is this: the world is a single market; natural resources are to be exploited; people are consumers; anything which hinders profit is to be routed out and destroyed. The results of this philosophy in action are that while economies are growing, so is poverty, so is ecological destruction, so are sweatshops and child labor. Across the globe, wages are plummeting, indigenous people are being forced off their lands, rivers are becoming industrial dumping grounds, and forests are being obliterated. Massive regional starvation and "World Bank riots" are becoming more frequent throughout the Third World.

All over the world, more and more people are being forced into illegal activity for their own survival as traditional cultures and social structures are destroyed. Inevitably, crime and imprisonment rates are on the rise. And the United States law enforcement establishment is in the forefront, domestically and internationally, in providing state-of-the-art repression.

Within the United States, structural adjustment (sometimes known as the Contract With America) takes the form of welfare and social service cuts, continued massive military spending, and skyrocketing prison spending. Walk through any poor urban neighborhood: school systems are crumbling, after-school programs, libraries, parks and drug treatment centers are closed. But you will see more police stations and more cops. Often, the only "social service" available to poor young people is jail.

The dismantling of social programs, and the growing dominance of the right-wing agenda in US politics has been made possible, at least in part, by the successful repression of the civil rights and liberation movements of the 1960s and '70s. Many of the leaders—Martin Luther King Jr., Malcolm X, Fred Hampton, and many others—were assassinated. Others, like Geronimo ji Jaga Pratt, Leonard Peltier, and Mumia Abu-Jamal, have been locked up. Over 150 political leaders from the black liberation struggle, the Puerto Rican independence movement, and other resistance efforts are still in prison. Many are serving sentences ranging from 40 to 90 years. Oppressed communities have been robbed of radical political leadership which might have led an opposition movement. We are reaping the results.

The number of people in US prisons has more than tripled in the past 17 years from 500,000 in 1980 to 1.8 million in 1997. Today, more than five million people are behind bars, on parole, probation, or under other supervision by the criminal justice system. The state of California now spends more on prisons than on higher education, and over the past decade has built 19 prisons and only one branch university.

Add to this, the fact that increasing numbers of women are being locked up. Between 1980 and 1994, the number of women in prison increased five-fold, and women now make up the fastest growing segment of the prison population. Most of these women are mothers leaving future generations growing up in foster homes or on the streets.

Welcome to the New World Order.

What Is to Be Done?

Prisons are not reducing crime. But they are fracturing already vulnerable families and communities.

Poor people of color are being locked up in grossly disproportionate numbers, primarily for non-violent crimes. But Americans are not feeling safer. As "criminals" become scapegoats for our floundering economy and our deteriorating social structure, even the guise of rehabilitation is quickly disappearing from our penal philosophy. After all: rehabilitate for what? To go back into an economy which has no jobs? To go back into a community which has no hope? As education and other prison programs are cut back, or in most cases eliminated altogether, prisons are becoming vast, over-crowded, holding tanks. Or worse: factories behind bars.

And, prison labor is undercutting wages, something which hurts all working and poor Americans. It's a situation which can only occur because organized labor is divided and weak and has not kept step with organized capital.

While capital has globalized, labor has not. While the transnationals truly are fashioning our planet into a global village, there is still little communication or cooperation between workers around the world. Only an internationally linked labor movement can effectively challenge the power of the transnational corporations.

There have been some wonderful, shining instances of international worker solidarity. In the early 1980s, 3M workers in South Africa walked out in support of striking 3M workers in New Jersey. Recently, longshore workers in Denmark, Spain, Sweden and several other countries closed down ports around the world in solidarity with striking Liverpool dockers. The company was forced to negotiate. When Renault closed its plant in Belgium, 100,000 demonstrated in Brussels, pressuring the French and Belgium governments to condemn the plant closure and compel its reopening.

Here in the US, there is a glimmer of hope as the AFL-CIO has voted in some new, more progressive leadership. We'll see how that shapes up, and whether the last 50 years of anticommunist, bread-and-butter American unionism is really a thing of the past.

What is certain is that resistance to the transnational corporate agenda is growing around the globe:

In 1996, the people of Bougainville, a small New Guinea island, organized a secessionist rebellion, protesting the dislocations and ecological destruction caused by corporate mining on the island. When the government hired mercenaries from South Africa to train local troops in counterinsurgency warfare, the army rebelled, threw out the mercenaries, and deposed the Prime Minister.

A one-day General Strike shut down Haiti in January 1997. Strikers demanded the suspension of negotiations between the Prime Minister and the International Monetary Fund/World Bank. They protested the austerity measures imposed by the IMF and WB which would mean laying off 7,000 government workers and the privatization of the electric and telephone companies.

In Nigeria, the Ogoni people conducted a protracted eight-year struggle against Shell Oil. Acid rain, and hundreds of oil spills and gas flares were turning the once fertile countryside into a near wasteland. Their peaceful demonstrations, election boycotts, and pleas for international solidarity were met with violent government repression and the eventual execution of Ogoni writer-leader Ken Saro Wiwa.

In France, a month-long General Strike united millions of workers who protested privatization, a government worker pay freeze, and cutbacks in social services. Telephone, airline, power, postal, education, health care and metal workers all joined together, bringing business to a standstill. The right-wing Chirac government was forced to make minor concessions before being voted out for a new "socialist" administration.

At the Oak Park Heights Correctional Facility in Minnesota, 150 prisoners went on strike in March 1997, demanding to be paid the minimum wage. Although they lost a litigation battle to attain this right, their strike gained attention and support from several local labor unions.

Just as the prison industrial complex is becoming increasingly central to the growth of the US economy, prisoners are a crucial part of building effective opposition to the transnational corporate agenda. Because of their enforced invisibility, powerlessness, and isolation, it's far too common for prisoners to be left out of the equation of international solidarity. Yet, opposing the expansion of the prison/industrial complex, and supporting the rights and basic humanity of prisoners, may be the only way we can stave off the consolidation of a police state that represses us all, where you or a friend or family member may yourself end up behind bars.

Clearly, the only alternative that will match the power of global capitalism is an internationalization of human solidarity. Because, truly, we are all in this together.

TWENTY-TWO

MUMIA ABU-JAMAL

An Uncivil Action (1998)

PENNSYLVANIA GOVERNOR TOM RIDGE, IN POWER from 1995 to 2001, once bragged that he "had his pencil sharpened" to signal how eager he was to sign a death warrant for Mumia Abu-Jamal, one of the most famous political prisoners in US history. In fact, Ridge signed two, the first in 1995 and another in 1999. In the following essay—written in the days following the 1995 death warrant—Abu-Jamal relays what occurred when, with less than sixty days to live, in June 1995 he was subjected to another curtailment of liberty: a punishment for the misconduct of writing, "operating a business or profession of journalism." This additional infringement was set to deny him phone calls, visits, commissary purchases, and TV and radio access for thirty of his allotted fifty-nine days left on Earth. Following this tumultuous shock, Abu-Jamal says, "we went to work," meaning he, his lawyers, and the movements of people around the world that supported him, straightened their backs, swallowed their fear, and fought back. They did this through legal maneuvers, mobilizing, marching, and protesting.

It wasn't the first time Mumia Abu-Jamal pushed back against the tyranny of a racist system designed to silence him. Growing up in the projects of Philadelphia, Abu Jamal, named Wesley Cook when he was born in 1954, joined student movements to pressure the school system to change the curriculum to reflect African history and Black American achievements. At age fourteen, he was beaten so savagely by Philadelphia police officers while protesting a speech by presidential hopeful and renowned segregationist George Wallace, that his own mother walked past him in the hospital without recognizing him. Undeterred, Abu-Jamal continued standing up to tyranny when, later that year, he helped found a chapter of the Black Panther Party for Self Defense. There he learned to write from an advocacy perspective and began championing people's movements against racism, poverty, incarceration, repression, and police brutality. Over and over again, in the face of goliaths who aspired to kill him, Abu-Jamal refused to stay quiet, even though it cost him his liberty and nearly his life.

In this essay, Mumia exposes the circus of petty carceral retaliations and how the law, often in collusion with prison administration and court bureaucrats, is weaponized against the vulnerable. Law is revealed as a flimsy and porous concept interpreted at the expediency of state power and the caprice of deputized cowards positioned to bully, intimidate, and terrorize captives. He shows us that the law is a tool. It can be just or unjust. It can condemn, or it can liberate.

As he serves a life sentence for a crime he did not commit, Abu-Jamal's life story is a testament to how corrosive an unjust legal system can be, but it also illustrates the power of how love, not fear, arms us to triumph against state terror. Argentinean insurgent Che Guevara, executed in 1967 by a Bolivian soldier at the behest of CIA agents, famously wrote that a true revolutionary is "guided by a great feeling of love." Abu-Jamal's work and unconquered spirit—his incredible empathy, humanity, courage, and writing, which cannot be contained by prison bars—are testament to that truth. Mumia loves the people, and the people love him in return. It is a sentiment that has reached all corners of the earth.

Due to an international uproar on his behalf, prisoner AM-8335 was not put to death by Ridge's sharpened pencil. He currently resides in SCI Mahanoy in eastern Pennsylvania, where he continues to engage in the profession of journalism and organize revolutionary transformation. Author of thirteen books and thousands of broadcast essays, all produced under the eye of the state, Abu-Jamal is also co-editor of *Beneath the Mountain*. The fact that you are reading this book is proof that where there is repression, there will also be resistance. And who better to tell these stories of resistance than those who have lived them?

AN UNCIVIL ACTION

> *We are under a constitution, but the constitution is what the judges say it is.*
>
> —U.S. SUPREME COURT CHIEF JUSTICE CHARLES EVANS HUGHES (1862–1948)

FOR MOST PEOPLE in the nation who wear the label of Americans, the courts of the land are like memorial sites in the heart of a city; many, perhaps most, folks know they are there, but very few people actually go to see them. In an age when the national town meeting is more apt to be experienced while sitting on one's sofa than actually going out of the house into the public, what happens in the nation's courts depends upon what the media reports happens.

Popular reporting of such events depends upon the objectives, biases, and expertise of the reporter and the interests of the publisher/editor/owner.

Every civil trial is, at base, a conflict, a contest, or a war of words. The arbiter of that conflict is also engaged in a struggle, for although we like to think judges are Olympians who rule over courts with Delphic equanimity, they are but mortals driven and sometimes riven by the same passions as other men and women.

The civil case *Abu-Jamal v. Price* began, as so many cases, with a small step. As the writer sat on Phase II, with a date to die, a guard sidled up to Cell B-4 and laid a write-up on the opened tray slot. Typed on the pressure sensitive, yellow-tinted paper was a damning indictment: The writing of the book *Live from Death Row*, and of articles for *Scoop* newspaper, *Against the Current Journal*, and other publications, was proof that inmate Jamal [was] guilty of operating "a business or profession" of "Journalism." Also, inmate Jamal was a "professor of economics" for the New York–based Henry George Institute (and thus, perhaps, guilty of the profession of "teacher" of a correspondence course). The June 1995 write-up, served up on the writer's second day on Phase II, made writing (and teaching) an institutional offense, punishable by a sharp reduction in privileges. Sentenced to thirty days in the "hole," with less than sixty days to live, meant no phone calls, no visits, no TV, no radio, and no commissary privileges. It was being placed in a prison within a prison within a prison, for writing. I was sentenced to die in silence.

While waiting for the institutional "hearing," I got word to some friends, and they in turn got in touch with one of the foremost prisoner's rights lawyers, Jere Krakoff, in nearby Pittsburgh.

Krakoff wrote and offered his considerable assistance, which was accepted quickly. As a jailhouse lawyer I was aware of his work, principally the landmark *Tillery v. Owens* case,[23] where the court found, in a conditions-of-confinement case, that double-celling was an element in determining that Western State Correctional Institution at Pittsburgh was being operated in an unconstitutional manner, in violation of the "cruel and unusual" clause of the Eighth Amendment. Given the conservative bent of the judiciary, and the repressive tenor of the times, such a decision was a product of remarkable lawyering, and I realized similar skills were needed in this case.

We went to work.

THE HEARING. When one claims a violation of the First Amendment (regarding freedom of speech, of the press, of religious practice, and to petition the government for redress of grievances) in an institutional misconduct hearing, it may be more fruitful to claim a violation of the Ten Commandments, for it certainly can't go any worse.

Misconduct "hearings" are held before a prison official called a hearing examiner, who is untrained in the law. Prisoners brought before the examiner have no right to legal counsel, and may only be assisted by a willing inmate or staff. All the same, I requested the presence of Jere Krakoff, Esq., to represent me at the hearing, but this was denied out of hand.

Failing this, I presented my written version, arguing that any prison rule must yield to the US and Pennsylvania constitutions, which both had provisions protecting freedom of speech and freedom of the press. No institutional role, I argued, could trump the first article in the Pennsylvania Declaration of Rights, nor the First Amendment to the US Constitution. The hearing examiner disagreed, saying essentially that punishing someone for writing a book, or an article, had "nothing to do with first amendment Rites" (as she spelled "rights"—a Freudian slip?).

On June 9, 1995, she found me guilty of "engaging in the profession of journalism," writing,

> I find an abundance of evidence exists in the misconduct report that Jamal has been actively engaged in the profession of journalism. He has authored a book known

> as *Live from Death Row,* he currently writes columns for different newspapers including, *Scoop USA, First Day* and the *Jamal Journal.* In addition Jamal has made taped commentaries for broadcast over National Public Radio. These undisputed facts combine to establish a clear preponderance of evidence that Jamal has been engaged in both the business and profession of journalism.

And with that, on to court.

THE COURT HEARING. When one enters a US court, in a civil action, the basis for action is claimed violation of the US Constitution. Presumably, any prison rule must fall when it violates what has been called the supreme law of the land (the Constitution). But, as we have learned, courts engage in complex, extensive "balancing tests" when state rules and constitutional rights collide. Our case would prove no different.

In many such civil cases, the case opens with what is called a motion for a temporary restraining order or a preliminary injunction (TRO/PI). These motions, although rarely granted, place cases on a fast track, as it usually requires a prompt hearing to test the claims in a case, and to determine the likelihood of success for the side bringing the suit.

In a case where a person is being punished by the state for writing (a form of speech), the First Amendment comes into play, and a violation of the First Amendment requires what courts have called "strict scrutiny" (or closer than usual judicial attention).

The magistrate judge selected to hear the TRO/PI motion was Kenneth J. Benson, a relatively short, mustached, blue-eyed man. The hearing was held in a carpeted, highly air-conditioned courtroom that had once been assigned to former Third Circuit judge Tim Lewis, in the federal building in central, downtown Pittsburgh. Although this was only sixty-one miles from SCI Greene, the Department of Corrections (DOC) chose to bind me in chains and shackles and to temporarily transfer me to the state prison in Pittsburgh for the duration of the TRO/PI Hearings.

SCI Pittsburgh is one of the oldest prisons in the state, over a century old, situated in the city's north side, a collection of mostly black and ethnic neighborhoods, with some areas zoned for industrial use.

Assigned to a pod of nine other cells, I could easily sense the lower degree of tension on Pittsburgh's death row. Men spoke to each other easily, whether guard or inmate. A thirty-something guard with three chevrons on the shoulders of his gray uniform walked up to the door, identified himself, and gave what seemed to be his standard rap: "Here at Pittsburgh the rules are simple; you don't fuck with us—we don't fuck with you. You treat us like men—we'll treat you like a man. If you give us shit—we'll give you shit."

When I discussed this with guys on the pod, they said everybody got the same rap—and I was assured they meant it. As a rule, I was informed, they didn't harass the men, and they didn't set up and "false-ticket" prisoners (give bogus misconduct reports based on lies or concoctions). That accounted for the low level of tension sensed there. For the duration of the civil TRO/PI hearing, this would be where I slept.

Although the civil court session began at nine o'clock in the morning, court began for me shortly before 5 a.m., with a guard opening the pie slot in the door, and placing a tray therein. A quickly swallowed breakfast, a shower, and it was on to the receiving room. There, a dark suit jacket and trousers would be found, and inseams would be stapled to make the slacks stay up.

By a quarter after six, I would be chained, shackled, and seat-belted in the back of a white DOC vehicle, en route to the federal building. The armed DOC guards were a Mutt and Jeff team, one short, the other tall; one driving, the other riding shotgun. The daily escort was a state trooper, in a marked vehicle, with lights flashing through the streets of the northside.

Arriving at the federal building meant being met by at least twelve U.S. marshals, who took custody of the prisoner. It is difficult to describe the sensation of being "escorted" to and from the courtroom by a phalanx of approximately twelve armed U.S. marshals, but it happened so often (at least four times a day) that it seems it should've become routine.

The magistrate-judge began the day's session by stating, "Good morning, all. Before we begin—and I sincerely want this not to be offensive or insulting to anyone, because no one has given me any reason to believe that there will be any misbehavior or misconduct of any kind—but it is important, I think, that I begin by informing all concerned that I will rigorously enforce . . . the principle that behavior in court must be appropriate at all times. . . .

"Consequently, it is appropriate for me to say at the beginning that if there is any display of emotion, if there is any outburst, if there is any misbehavior or misconduct, then I will ask that the marshals and court security personnel remove the person who engages in that misconduct. There will be no second chance. Once someone is removed from the courtroom, they will not be allowed back in. . . ."

Clearly, the tone was set. The warning seemed virtually to expect some form of disruption, but where did this notion come from? Perhaps the marshals, who seemed to anticipate some form of violence, had whispered such suggestions in the judge's ear? It was unclear.

There was a barely audible grumble of resentment, but it passed quickly. Jere, who visited me briefly down in the holding cell area, accompanied by attorney Rachel Wolkenstein, confided that the magistrate had formerly been in the employ of the Department of Corrections, and as such, might not prove impartial in a case where prison officials were named as defendants. Under the Federal Rules of Civil Procedure, a motion could be brought to recuse him, Jere counseled. After some consideration, this option was rejected. He would do.

As I sat shackled in the plaintiff's seat, I looked at the man, seeking a gestalt-like impression of him. Yet he rarely, if ever, looked in my direction. As the civil TRO/PI hearings took place in the same period as the state PCRA (postconviction) criminal hearings in Philadelphia, I was struck by the apparent differences between this federal magistrate and former common pleas judge Albert F. Sabo. Although both appeared to be relatively short men, Sabo would occasionally glare down at the defendant's bench, his hatred a palpable, tangible thing. Where Benson seemed glacial and professionally distant, Sabo seemed *invested*. His long, baleful, venomous stare, lasting for perhaps a quarter of a minute, was so nasty that I almost prayed someone else took notice of it.

Seeing no such overt expressions of malevolence, I reasoned Benson would be no better [or] worse than any other jurist. The hearing began with attorney Leonard I. Weinglass taking the stand. Speaking of the initial reason the suit was filed, Weinglass spoke of learning that letters he wrote to me were seized, opened, held, and delivered in that state to me over a week later. He spoke of his paralegals being unceremoniously turned away from the prison. He spoke slowly, lawyerly, of learning that my letters to him never arrived at his office. He called this succession of events "unprecedented" and "shocking." In nearly thirty years of law practice,

Weinglass said, he had never seen such interference with his and his client's legal correspondence.

It was for this very reason, he explained, that paralegals were utilized; to provide a channel of communication that was not compromised.

Under prompting by counsel, Weinglass recounted receiving a letter written by me, explaining that the "State has opened and reviewed your letters/documents . . . outside of my presence—there isn't even the pretense of client-lawyer confidentiality." This was confirmed when a photocopy of my letter to Weinglass, and this letter to me, turned up in the Commonwealth's file, found during the course of discovery for the case.

Krakoff continued his examination of Weinglass:

Q: When you wrote Mr. Jamal on August 16, 1994, did you send a copy of the letter to prison officials or to the Department of Corrections personnel?

A: No.

Q: Prior to writing Mr. Jamal on August 16, had you authorized prison Officials or the Office of General Counsel or anyone within the Governor's Office or the Department of Corrections to read your mail?

A: No, hardly.

Q: Had you authorized any of them to photocopy your mail?

A: No.

Q: Had you authorized them to read the enclosed materials that you sent to Mr. Jamal on the 16th?

A: No.

Q: Had you authorized them to distribute your letters to anybody?

A: No.

Q: Had you authorized them to retain your letters in a file?

A: No.

Q: Did you expect that your letter would not be read by prison officials when you sent it to Mumia Abu-Jamal on the 16th of August?

A: In over twenty years of practicing law, to my knowledge no letter that I had ever written to an inmate had ever been opened or read by prison officials. And I expected the same would apply in this instance.

Informed of this breach of confidentiality, neither counsel nor client could dare write the other, for fear such correspondence would find its way into the hands of the state. Similarly, mail from another of my lawyers, Rachel Wolkenstein, was seized by the DOC, photocopied, and forwarded to various government officials. Her letter, properly marked as legal mail, contained a copy of a witness statement that was helpful to the defense. Her mail, she testified, went the same way as Len's mail: out of the prison, out of the DOC, and to various agencies of government.

Like Weinglass, Wolkenstein, an experienced criminal lawyer, found this experience to be "unprecedented." Neither this witness statement, nor a lawyer's memo, were ever returned, nor [were they] acknowledged by the state.

The DOC's attorney, David Horwitz, would attempt to mitigate these actions by prison officials by arguing that the seizure of legal papers was justified by the ongoing "investigation" into whether a rule prohibiting prisoners from engaging in a business or profession was being violated.

In this testimony, Horwitz ordered further investigation even as prison officials announced they had more than sufficient evidence to prepare an institutional misconduct as noted in a memo written by Horwitz liaison and grievance officer Diane Baney:

> It has recently been brought to our attention that Mumia Abu-Jamal, AM-8335, may be violating Department of Corrections policy by accepting payment for interviews, essays, etc. This information came to light when National Public Radio announced that Abu-Jamal had produced 10 three-to-four-minute commentary radio shows which he would be compensated for in the amount of $150.00 apiece. Upon reviewing his account, it was detected that he had received payment from other publications which went unnoticed and were placed in his account. On 5-16-94, NPR issued a decision that the commentaries would not be run. However, they did indicate that Abu-Jamal would be compensated with a standard "kill fee" of $75.00 each, which is given when work is accepted but not used.
>
> It is clear that Abu-Jamal is in violation of Department of Corrections policy...

This Baney memo, sent to Horwitz, was dated May 18, 1994. Yet the so-called investigation continued for over a year, thus allowing the state to peruse my legal mail, dealing with critical issues involving my state court appeals and conviction, with impunity!

The warden at Huntingdon Prison advised his superiors at the DOC Central Office that sufficient information had been gathered to prove a violation of DOC policy, and therefore further mail scrutiny was unnecessary. Horwitz rejected the warden's recommendation and ordered the "investigation" to continue. He admitted at the TRO/PI hearing that he ordered all legal mail intercepted, had its contents removed and photocopied, and sent copies to his office. He copied these items, and forwarded them to Brian Gottlieb, of the governor's office in Harrisburg, and to Cheryl Young, chief counsel. Horwitz testified he had no idea what these persons did with these items of privileged legal correspondence:

[Questions on direct examination by the plaintiff's co-counsel, Timothy O'Brien:]

Q: Now, one thing is clear, Mr. Horwitz, with respect to Mr. Weinglass's letter—to whatever extent you read it—you came to the conclusion, did you not, that only two paragraphs in that entire correspondence could conceivably have anything to do with the investigation that you were conducting, isn't that so?

A: Yes.

Q: With respect to Mr. Jamal's letter to Mr. Weinglass, you came to the conclusion that nothing in that correspondence could be of assistance in your investigation; isn't that correct?

A: That's correct.

Q: So you, before you disseminated this information to anyone else, you had concluded that there was privileged material in the correspondence that had nothing whatever to do with your investigation, correct?

A: That is correct.

Q: You also came to the conclusion that there are materials in the correspondence that had to do with Mr. Jamal's defense of the death penalty case, isn't that correct?

A: That is correct.

He further stated that the invasion of the attorney-client correspondent privilege was needed to determine whether lawyers were helping me to evade the business or profession rules.

Another witness who testified for the defendants was James Hassett, the head of Greene's security staff. It was he who actually opened, read, and photocopied legal letters and documents for forwarding to David Horwitz of DOC central office, and who wrote the misconduct report of June 2, 1995, and signed the document. In the report the writer attempted to explain the delay by claiming "the justification for the timing of the misconduct is that the investigation was not completed until May 19, 1995, and that the assembly of the evidentiary materials in presentation format required additional time." In fact, Hassett's explanation fell flat when he testified at the hearing, for there he admitted that Horwitz had prepared the report, not he. And as we have seen from the Baney memo of May 18, 1994, Horwitz had more than enough "evidentiary materials" to show a violation of the business and profession rule—if that was their actual intent—fully a year before!

Thomas Fulcomer, a former warden at Huntingdon and later deputy regional commissioner of the DOC, advanced the department's justification for their punishment for my writing. The DOC, Fulcomer announced with a straight face and an impressive title, was concerned about what he termed the "big wheel syndrome," or the circumstance where a prisoner "persistently and flagrantly violates Department of Corrections policies," and by so doing becomes a countervailing authority in the prison. Folcomer's testimony was a smart one, as it was designed to tickle a judge's core fear and concern when deciding any prison case: security. It had several key problems, however: (a) Hassett, the DOC's point man during the so-called investigation, and Greene's chief of security, could point to no "big wheel" effects at Greene, and when asked about the impact of the publishing of *Live from Death Row* on the prison, admitted that guards had to field questions from prisoners about how they could put out books; and (b) Ted Alleman, a former teacher at Huntingdon, testified that the prison not only had not opposed the publishing of a book by a prisoner there, but had supported and facilitated it. Alleman set up a small publishing outfit to put out a book written by the late Aubrey "Buddy" Martin, a former death row prisoner at Huntingdon. Guess who was the warden at the time? When testimony was provided showing that the prison had actually allowed and assisted in radio interviews of Martin to promote his book, Fulcomer's "big wheel" theory sprang a major leak, for he never utilized this rationale when he was the warden at Huntingdon. Martin was never given a misconduct for this book, nor even threatened in that regard. In fact, he was praised for it.

Martin, serving several life terms stemming from the January 1970 slayings of United Mine Workers leader Joseph "Jock" Yablonsky, along with his wife and daughter, was an accomplished painter and sculptor. Huntingdon officials provided him studio-like space to do his work, and later applauded the publishing of his book, which featured photographs of many of his works of art. In direct examination by Mr. O'Brien, Alleman testified:

Q: Mr. Alleman, after you came to know Mr. Martin, did you become aware of a book that he was writing?

A: Buddy Martin was a student of mine in my class and I knew him for many years, and over a period of time we started to talk about documenting his life story, and that eventually resulted in a book.

Q: And was this book written by him while he was incarcerated at the State Correctional Institution in Huntingdon?

A: Yes.

Q: And when the book was written and while it was being written, was it understood that this book would be published for purposes of sale outside the institution?

A: Yes.

Q: And did you in fact have a publishing company at that point in time?

A: The publishing company was formed in 1985 and it was formed for the purpose of publishing this book.

Q: And was there a contract between yourself and Mr. Martin with respect to the publishing of the book?

A: Yes.

Q: And could you tell the Court whether, in accordance with the contract, if there were sales of the book in question, whether Mr. Martin was to receive any royalties?

A: The contract was that the publishing company would receive the initial revenue from the book up to the point where the costs of publication were covered, and then there was a fifty-fifty split on royalties of the book.

Q: And could you tell the Court, with respect to any of these efforts to involve the media with Mr. Martin regarding the sale of this book, if there was any involvement whatsoever with SCI Huntingdon?

A: The book was partially promoted through talk shows, and the situation was such that I was live on the air with a talk show host from my office at Tower Press, and the institution provided the capability for Buddy Martin to be in a room with a telephone and he was also live on the air and we answered questions from both the host of the show and the general public that would call in with questions....

Q: Now, aside from these particular interviews, was the institution otherwise aware of this book having been written and published?

A: Yes.

Q: Were there any reviews of the book in the local newspapers, for example?

A: Yes.

Q: What were these?

A: Well, the Huntingdon paper did a review, an extensive review of the book, and also I was on a talk show with the local host in the town of Huntingdon.

Q: Okay. And when the book was published, was there any accompanying public opposition to the book by any influential political group?

A: No, not that I know of.

Q: To your knowledge, from the date that the book was published to the date that Mr. Martin passed away, was he ever disciplined for writing the book on the basis that he had violated a rule at SCI Huntingdon prohibiting the conduct of a business or a profession?

A: No, not at all.

So much for the "big wheel" theory. The trial, like all trials, was only tangentially about truth; central to these public performances is power, and how power is defended, articulated, used, and hidden. The state, of course, is used to exercising power, but it is rarely asked to justify its use. And when forced to answer to its use of power behind prison doors, it resorted to the handiest tool in an age-old arsenal—lies. Nonsense about "big wheels" and "security" and "burdens upon staff" were administrative lies designed to obscure a naked political attack against a radical voice that they opposed.

THE MAGISTRATE RULES. Magistrate Judge Benson heard all of the principals testify at hearings in September and October 1995. Lawyers Jere Krakoff and Tim O'Brien battled in raging paper wars against Thomas Halloran of the attorney general's office.

In early June 1996 Benson issued a remarkable *Report and Recommendation* that was sixty-six pages long[24]. Among the sources quoted or cited from were former British prime minister Winston Churchill and US president Abraham Lincoln. He lauds the defendants as "conscientious" and "scrupulous" men, and goes out of his way to describe one of the defendants: "Superintendent Price appeared to this court to be an estimable man in every way" (Benson, 4). He goes on, however, to point out how they lied either on the stand or in sworn depositions, for example:

> [Finding of Fact #64] Superintendent Price's explanation that requests for interviews with plaintiff were denied due to limited staff resources are not entirely credible.... [T]he decisions to deny plaintiff media interviews were first made immediately after plaintiff's decision to publish his book was communicated to defendants [DOC deputy general counsel David] Horwitz and Price. The decisions continued, with a variety of purported justifications, for several months. These purported reasons are demonstrably false. There is no credible evidence that the conditions at the prison were such that security concerns necessitated denying the requests for interviews (Benson, 25, 56).

Despite the court's finding that prison officials put forth "demonstrably false" evidence in support of their actions, Benson found their "big wheel" defense a "reasonable" one, and a "legitimate concern of the institution" (Benson, 45). He therefore upheld the "business or profession" rule as constitutional and upheld the state's right to open and read privileged legal mail, if that rule was being violated. To this US judge at least, a prison rule was more important than the First Amendment to the US Constitution. If I wrote for publication, I could be punished for doing so, and my legal mail could be rifled. The state was allowed to refuse paralegals if unlicensed, even if no such licensure is now possible. The state was enjoined from denying media interviews, and from disclosing the contents of legal mail to persons outside of the DOC.

After my years of studying civil cases, nothing in the opinion was unexpected to me. Krakoff prepared for appeals.

I resolved to continue writing, no matter what. The district court upheld the main points of the magistrate's recommendation, although expanding the legal mail provisions. We therefore had to go on.

THE COURT OF APPEALS. Although relatively little known in America (quick—name three judges on your circuit court of appeals!) the circuit courts of appeal are the final arbiters of almost every legal conflict in the nation. They are the last court before the US Supreme Court, a body that hears (in the last decade or so) roughly seventy-five cases a year, and as such refuses to hear thousands of cases throughout the court term.

Pennsylvania is the largest state in both population and area in the US Court of Appeals for the Third Circuit. It was to this court, one described as among the most conservative, that the case would be appealed. The panel chosen to hear the case were similarly some of court's more conservative jurists, judges Richard L. Nygaard, Samuel A. Alito, Jr., and Donald P. Lay, a judge from the Eighth Circuit (the southern and midwestern areas of the country) sitting by designation.

Initially, the Court of Appeals noted the "formidable barrier" to a prisoner's claim that a prison regulation is unconstitutional. That "barrier" is a 1987 US Supreme Court case known as the *Turner* ruling.[25] In *Turner*, the nation's highest court ordered deference to prison officials in many of their administrative decisions if those decisions were "reasonable."

Turner established a four-part test as to whether a given prison regulation is reasonable: (1) there must be a valid, rational correlation between the regulation and the government objective at issue; (2) alternative means must exist to exercise the prisoner's asserted right; (3) the impact that accommodation would have on the prison environment, and prison resources generally, must be taken into account; and (4) the existence (or absence) of ready alternatives must be considered.

When the First Amendment is implicated, the regulation, to be approved, must be content-neutral. The Third Circuit panel looked at the appeal through that four-part test, and declared,

> The Superintendent of the S.C.I. Huntingdon was aware of Jamal's writings when Jamal published the Yale article in 1991. An August 16, 1992 letter to the Department noted that Jamal was approaching publishers regarding a book deal. Nevertheless, the Department did not begin to investigate him until May 6, 1994, after National Public Radio sought permission to broadcast Jamal's interviews as regular commentaries. The district court determined that "the investigation was initiated after public complaints concerning Jamal's proposed NPR commentaries were made by the Fraternal Order of Police" and concluded that any delay in the Department's enforcement of the rule was attributable to its investigatory procedures. As a result, it held that Jamal was unlikely to succeed in showing that the action was in retaliation against the content of his writings. WE DISAGREE, AND CONCLUDE THAT THE DISTRICT COURT ERRED (Third Circuit, 10).

Without specifically mentioning the "big wheel" theory, the court's opinion seemed to give this idea little weight, finding the prison could easily accommodate the activities of a writer, because "the record contains no evidence of such a 'ripple effect.' As explained before, Jamal was acting as a journalist from 1986, and the Department did not claim to be burdened by his actions until the Fraternal Order of Police outcry in 1994" (Third Circuit, 12).

The court found the justification for the state's rifling of attorney-privileged mail to be pretextual, writing,

> The district court held that the reading and copying [of] Jamal's legal mail was acceptable if the prison officials had "a reasonable suspicion that plaintiff was violating an institutional regulation by engaging in a business or profession in which wittingly or not one or more of his attorneys was complicit." The Department argues in support that its decision to open Jamal's legal mail was necessitated by its investigation into whether Jamal was conducting a business or profession. THIS ARGUMENT IS NONSENSICAL. We have difficulty seeing the need to investigate an act that Jamal openly confesses he is doing. Jamal's writing is published, and he freely admits his intent to continue. Continued investigation and enforcement of the rule invades the privacy of his legal mail and thus directly interferes with his ability to communicate with counsel (Third Circuit, 14).

We had won two of the three issues appealed to the court, and lost the third. On the state's barring of paralegals, the circuit court agreed. The court determined that a paralegal was also a social visitor (even though she actually did act as a courier for legal papers from counsel), and paralegal visits were pretexts for what were really social visits.

Thus, the court approved the application of a "rule" that had never been applied elsewhere, and was neither written nor disseminated to the general population. As such, it was as much a new "rule" (that is, one never utilized) as the "business or profession" rule, if not more so. For here was a "regulation" that required satisfaction that was impossible to meet: state licensure. SCI Greene's Superintendent Price wrote a letter to my lawyers, dated February 24, 1995, that stated:

> It is not sufficient merely to designate persons as investigators and paralegals unless the identified individuals can produce documentation that they are investigators or credentialed paralegals acting under contract with or as employees of the attorney. Accordingly, please submit copies of the state licensure documents and paralegal credentials under which these individuals conduct business as investigators, or paralegals and such contract or employment documents which verify their relationship with your office as independent contractors or employees.

Krakoff assembled an impressive array of affidavits from another state prison superintendent, secretaries, and other personnel associated with several state legal services programs, which proved these conditions were unprecedented. Indeed, many working paralegals had no such formal training, nor certification, nor degrees. Indeed, at trial the DOC softened its stance, suggesting that some equivalent training would suffice in lieu of credentialing (although Horwitz never communicated this to defense counsel). In fact, in Pennsylvania, no licensure for paralegals is provided.

On this issue, however, the circuit court deferred to the state, reasoning that "visitation—whether it is legal or personal—may jeopardize the security of a facility" (Third Circuit, 15). Thus, the interests of the state prevailed.

AFTER THE COURT DECISION. No case is really over when a court issues its decision. This is especially so in prison civil rights cases, when the winner (a prisoner) goes back into the custody of the loser (the prison). While courts regard prisons as institutions to which they owe deference, prison administrators regard courts as institutions that deserve a barely concealed contempt. They are to courts what pimps are to prostitutes: useful perhaps, but hardly ever respected.

Prison administrators oppose court orders as the work of interlopers, and are sure to undermine such edicts, if not openly. After *Abu-Jamal v. Price* it would seem that if anything is safe, it would be privileged legal mail from lawyers. Several months after the circuit court ruling a letter arrived from a lawyer, with her name, her title (Esquire), her law office address, and the legend "legal mail" stamped on the front of the envelope. The envelope was ripped open and taped shut, and the words "opened by mistake" were scribbled on the envelope face.

Neat, huh?

See with what ease a court's order is made obsolete?

In a nation that claims to be run in strict accordance with the tenets of the Constitution, in which the Constitution and its amendments are termed the "supreme law of the land," what should be the fate of one who violates the "supreme law"?

What about nothing at all?

The prison warden who ordered and participated in some of the unconstitutional acts, and who lied on the stand, James Price, remained prison superintendent, working briefly at SCI Pittsburgh in that role, until his return to Greene, retiring from the post in the spring of 1999. He remains a consultant to the superintendent at Greene.

The deputy commissioner, Thomas Fulcomer, who signed off on some (if not all) of the unconstitutional actions of his subordinates at Huntingdon and Greene, who propounded the preposterous "big wheel" theory in court (while applauding the publication of one of his prisoner's books while warden at SCI Huntingdon) remains western regional deputy commissioner of the DOC.

The Greene head of security, James Hassett, who actually illegally opened, read, and copied legal correspondence from both the court and counsel (and from me to the court and to counsel) was a captain when he testified. He is now a major.

The lesson could hardly be clearer that the DOC regards violations of the so-called supreme law of the land as little more than a mere annoyance.

In such a context, what can the word "unconstitutional" really mean? That term, which seems to go to the core principles upon which the state rests, is instead a minor obstruction, which pales beside the state's coercive powers. It is, in fact, the civil equivalent to the slap on the wrist given to the offender. In the midst of the hearings I asked Jere to speak to the magistrate-judge about wearing the shackles for hours on end in the courtroom. After several long days in shackles, of sitting in pain, I thought it was time for the court to act. Jere did talk to the judge, who said it was out of his hands. It was a decision made by the marshals, and he had no say in the matter.

To sit in pain, for hours, for days, in a U.S. courtroom during a so-called hearing to determine if someone's civil rights were violated months before is an exercise in Kafkaesque absurdity. Is this not an admission of judicial impotence for something that happens right there in the courtroom? "Out of my hands, pally."

Indeed, how can any court that draws its authority and jurisdictional powers from the Constitution decide, in any case, that any administrative regulation, which contemplates punishment for exercise of one's constitutional rights, is superior to the Constitution?

In such a context, how can the Constitution be deemed to be anything other than irrelevant? Courts are inherently conservative institutions that loathe change and defer to the status quo. That is, they tend to perpetuate existing power relations, even though their rhetoric perpetuates the illusion of social equality. In many instances, courts barely conceal their hostility to prisoner litigants, as evinced by increasingly restrictive readings of rights raised in the courts these days.

In that sense then, *Abu-Jamal v. Price* was different from some cases, yet strikingly similar to others.

From death row, this is Mumia Abu-Jamal.

TWENTY-THREE

PBSP-SHU SHORT CORRIDOR COLLECTIVE

California Hunger Striker Statement Agreement to End Hostilities (2012)

THIS STATEMENT, PRODUCED AND DISSEMINATED by prisoners almost a year in advance of the strike they were planning, which occurred in waves, emphasized what they believed would be the essential ingredient to any cohesive coordinated prison action: racial solidarity. Each of the four principal organizers were members of rival affiliations, including Todd Ashker—who at one point was sympathetic to the Aryan Brotherhood, a white supremacist prison gang. Ashker had already endured more than two decades in solitary confinement when the strike was planned. Participation in a political book club transformed the organizers' views on race and politics, inspiring the men to unite as a single "prisoner class." Unity, George Jackson taught years earlier from inside a different California penal facility, is an essential foundation to successful prison organizing, as prison administration intentionally exacerbates racial tensions as a dividing strategy. The strike officially began in July 2013, with an incredible 30,000 prisoners across California's prison system refusing meals to protest the inhumane conditions of long-term, indefinite solitary confinement. The non-violent act of disobedience continued for over 59 days and turned out to be the largest coordinated hunger strike in US history. Organizers were prepared to leave in body bags, but after a judge determined that the prison could use force-feeding, they called off the strike. Their effort stands as a testament that imprisoned people—particularly those who spend twenty-three hours alone in a cage every day—can band together to exert political agency, solidarity, and resistance. This statement went out far and wide to networks on both sides of the wall. It reads as an internal message to other prisoners, as evidenced by the numerous acronyms which have meaning to those accustomed to living beneath the mountain, but it also communicates information to those outside. It stands now as a historical document.

AGREEMENT TO END HOSTILITIES

August 12, 2012
To whom it may concern and all California Prisoners:
Greetings from the entire PBSP-SHU Short Corridor Hunger Strike Representatives. We are hereby presenting this mutual agreement on behalf of all racial groups here in the PBSP-SHU Corridor. Wherein, we have arrived at a mutual agreement concerning the following points:

1. If we really want to bring about substantive meaningful changes to the CDCR [California Department of Corrections and Rehabilitation] system in a manner beneficial to all solid individuals who have never been broken by CDCR's torture tactics intended to coerce one to become a state informant via debriefing, that now is the time for us to collectively seize this moment in time and put an end to more than 20–30 years of hostilities between our racial groups.
2. Therefore, beginning on Oct. 10, 2012, all hostilities between our racial groups in SHU [Special Housing Unit], ad-seg, general population and county jails will officially cease. This means that from this date on, all racial group hostilities need to be at an end. And if personal issues arise between individuals, people need to do all they can

to exhaust all diplomatic means to settle such disputes; do not allow personal, individual issues to escalate into racial group issues!

3. We also want to warn those in the general population that IGI [Institutional Gang Investigators] will continue to plant undercover Sensitive Needs Yard (SNY) debriefer "inmates" amongst the solid GP prisoners with orders from IGI to be informers, snitches, rats and obstructionists, in order to attempt to disrupt and undermine our collective groups' mutual understanding on issues intended for our mutual causes (i.e., forcing CDCR to open up all GP main lines and return to a rehabilitative-type system of meaningful programs and privileges, including lifer conjugal visits etc. via peaceful protest activity and noncooperation e.g., hunger strike, no labor etc.). People need to be aware and vigilant to such tactics and refuse to allow such IGI inmate snitches to create chaos and reignite hostilities amongst our racial groups. We can no longer play into IGI, ISU (Investigative Service Unit), OCS (Office of Correctional Safety) and SSU's (Service Security Unit's) old manipulative divide and conquer tactics!

In conclusion, we must all hold strong to our mutual agreement from this point on and focus our time, attention and energy on mutual causes beneficial to all of us [i.e., prisoners] and our best interests. We can no longer allow CDCR to use us against each other for their benefit!

Because the reality is that collectively, we are an empowered, mighty force that can positively change this entire corrupt system into a system that actually benefits prisoners and thereby the public as a whole, and we simply cannot allow CDCR and CCPOA, the prison guards' union, IGI, ISU, OCS and SSU to continue to get away with their constant form of progressive oppression and warehousing of tens of thousands of prisoners, including the 14,000-plus prisoners held in solitary confinement torture chambers—SHU and ad-seg units—for decades!

We send our love and respect to all those of like mind and heart. Onward in struggle and solidarity!

Presented by the PBSP-SHU Short Corridor Collective:

- Todd Ashker, C-58191, D1-119
- Arturo Castellanos, C-17275, D1-121
- Sitawa Nantambu Jamaa (Dewberry), C-35671, D1-117
- Antonio Guillen, P-81948, D2-106

And the Representatives Body:

- Danny Troxell, B-76578, D1-120
- George Franco, D-46556, D4-217
- Ronnie Yandell, V-27927, D4-215
- Paul Redd, B-72683, D2-117
- James Baridi Williamson, D-34288. D4-107
- Alfred Sandoval, D-61000, D4-214
- Louis Powell, B-59864, D1-104
- Alex Yrigollen, H-32421, D2-204
- Gabriel Huerta, C80766, D3-222
- Frank Clement, D-07919, D3-116
- Raymond Chavo Perez, K-12922, D1-219
- James Mario Perez, B-48186, D3-124

TWENTY-FOUR

RUSSELL "MAROON" SHOATZ

Liberation or Gangsterism (2013)

RUSSELL "MAROON" SHOATZ WAS BORN IN 1943 IN Philadelphia, Pennsylvania. A self-proclaimed "street thug," Shoatz spent his youth in and out of juvenile prison facilities. He later became a founding member of the Black Unity Council and a soldier in the Black Liberation Army. Sent to prison in 1972 for participating in an attack on a police station that resulted in the death of an officer, he made two prison escapes, and endured a total of thirty-three years in solitary confinement. It was within the tortured confines of a 7' x 12' cell—where he was isolated for twenty-three hours a day—that he wrote this essay. Having secured compassionate release from prison, Shoatz experienced fifty-three days of freedom before dying in Philadelphia in 2021.

Shoatz earned his honorary middle name from a fellow prisoner following his second escape. Respectfully bestowed, the nomenclature suggests a historical parallel between the fugitive communities who escaped slavery in the 1700s and 1800s, and more contemporary "prisoners of war" endeavoring to self-emancipate. Throughout nearly fifty years in prison, Shoatz organized and educated generations of men, politicized them to the dynamics of their incarceration, and created a liberation curriculum within one of the most structurally disempowered environments on earth. He encouraged those he mentored to read, analyze, critique, and discuss, but most importantly to apply the theories of liberation to their own life circumstances. This essay, in particular, has been identified by many as the spark that transported them beyond their solitary torture chambers and guided them to become disciplined abolitionists. Human liberation depends on our ability to diagnose the maladies of oppression. Therefore, the essential question Shoatz poses is relevant no matter which side of the prison wall you stand. Does your life further gangsterism or liberation? Slavery or freedom?

LIBERATION OR GANGSTERISM

> "Each generation must out of relative obscurity discover its mission, fulfill it or betray it."
> —FRANTZ FANON

Introduction

Within two generations the youth of this country have come full circle. Starting in 1955, youth were driven by two major motivations:

1. To acquire enough education or training, or through the use of their unskilled labor or street smarts, to land "good" jobs or establish hustles, to make as much money and obtain as many material belongings as possible;
2. To earn, in this way, a measure of respect and dignity from their peers and from society in general. This was the only path open for youth to learn to respect themselves as individuals with self-worth, not just as eating, sleeping, laboring and as sexual beings.

PART ONE

The First Wave: circa 1955–1980

The civil rights movement in the South successfully motivated Black, Puerto Rican, Euro-Amerikan, Native Amerikan,

Chicano/Mexicano/Indigenous, and Asian youth to use their time, energy, creativity and imaginations to discover their true self-worth and earn the respect of the entire world, while struggling toward even broader goals that were not measured by one's material possessions. Over time, each segment cheered on, supported, worked in solidarity with, and/or discovered their common interests and closely linked missions connected to broader goals.

Thus Black youth elevated the civil rights movement to become the Black Power and Black liberation movements. Puerto Rican youth energized their elders' ongoing struggle to win independence for their home island. Euro-Amerikan youth attacked the lies, hypocrisy and oppression that their parents were training them to uphold in the schools, society and overseas. Native Amerikan youth were returning to their suppressed ancestral ways and fighting to regain control over some of their land. Asian youth were struggling to overcome a system and culture that had always used and abused them.

Indeed all of them came to see clearly that [...] education, jobs, money, hustles and material trappings could not—by themselves—win them the victories they needed or the new type of dignity and respect they deserved.

Moreover, from 1955 to around 1975 these youth joined, formulated, led and supported struggles—worldwide—against racial oppression and bigotry, colonialism, and the oppression of women and youth, thus winning themselves the respect, admiration and gratitude of the world's oppressed as well as of their peers. Furthermore, they became people that society had to take seriously, as positive contributors who had much to give and were willing to sacrifice to achieve their goals. These youth were more egalitarian than their parents; more capable of imagining a better world and fighting to realize it—while still remaining youthful and having a good time in the process. This earned them a much-deserved place in history.

From the Mountain to the Sewer

Yet, here we are, thirty years later and the youth nowadays are ridiculed, having been stripped of that hard-earned freedom, self-respect, and dignity. They are being told—over and over—that the only way to regain these things is to acquire education, skills, good jobs, or the right hustle(s), and to once again accumulate as much money and material things as possible. They are told that this is the only way to win respect and dignity from one's peers and society.

How the hell did we get back to 1955?

First off, let me make clear that even with all of the glorious strides that youth made within the first wave, they were not the only ones fighting for radical and in many cases revolutionary change. These young people were usually only the tip of the spear, the shock troops of a global struggle. They were motivated by youthful energy and impatience, with no time or temperament for elaborate theories. They were rushing forward into the fray, ill prepared for the tricks that would eventually overwhelm them.

So to understand what happened, we must examine some of the main "tricks" used to slow down, misdirect, control and defeat them. And without a point, a spear loses all of its usefulness.

Strategic Tricks Used Against the Youth

Understanding these tricks and their various guises and refinements is the key to everything. You will never really understand what happened to get us to the present moment or be able really to move forward until you become a master at recognizing them and at devising ways to defeat them. They remain:

1. Co-option;
2. Glamorization of gangsterism;

3. Separation from the most advanced elements;
4. Indoctrination in reliance on passive approaches;
5. Raw fear;
6. Drugs.

Co-option was used extensively to trick just about all of the first-wave youth into believing that they had won the war. Strategically, among every segment of youth that we can name—university students to lower-class communities—billions of dollars were made available. Supposedly these funds were to enable the youth to determine what should be done to carry out the far-reaching changes they desired. In reality they were being expertly monitored and subtly coaxed further and further away from their most radical and advanced elements, mainly through control of this funding. This was part of the strategy adopted by ruling-class foundations, by government, and by corporate Amerika for defeating the youth with sugar-coated bullets.

In time, consequently, substantial segments of these previously rebellious youth found themselves fully absorbed and neutralized by either directly joining foundations, corporations, university faculties, [or] "approved" community groups, or by becoming full-fledged junior partners after winning control of thousands of previously out-of-reach political offices and government posts. The same trick is still being used today.

Glamorization of gangsterism, however, was then and continues to be the most harmful trick played against lower-class segments of youth. Males in particular were and continue to be the most susceptible to this gambit—especially when combined with a prolonged exposure to raw fear!

Let me illustrate by considering two historic groups which presently enjoy nothing less than iconic status among just about everyone who is aware of them. Yet, their documented history clearly shows how that trick was—and continues to be—played, throughout this country. Therefore, the following is a brief-but-clear history of how the original Black Panther Party (BPP) was bludgeoned and intimidated to the point where its key leader(s) consciously steered the group into accepting the Glamorization of Gangsterism. Because this represented less of a threat to ruling-class interests, the BPP won a temporary respite from the raw fear which ruling circles in the United States had been leveling against them. In the process, however, these leaders who went along with this gangster emphasis totally destroyed the organization. Secondly, we will consider the Nation of Islam–connected Black Mafia, which had a different background. But the same two tricks were played against them. Left in their wake was a sordid tale of young Black men who were—again—turned from seeking to be liberators into ruthless oppressors of their own communities, never once engaging their real enemies and oppressors—the ruling class.

Hands down, the original BPP won more attention, acclaim, respect, support and sympathy than any other youth group of their time. At the same time, they provoked more fear and worry in ruling-class circles than any other domestic group since Presidents Roosevelt, Truman and Eisenhower presided over the neutralization of the labor movement and the US wing of the Communist Party. The BPP was even more feared than the much larger civil rights movement. According to the head of the FBI, they were "the biggest threat to America." That threat came from their ability to inspire other youth—both in the US and globally—to act in similar ways.

Thus, there were separate BPP-style formations among the Puerto Ricans (the Young Lords Party), the Chicano/Mexicano/Indigenous (the Brown Berets), Asians (I Wor Kuen), Euro-Amerikans (Young Patriot Party and White Panther Party), and even the elderly (Gray Panthers). Also there were literally hundreds of other similar but less known groups! Internationally, in Algeria the BPP had the only official embassy established amongst all of the other Afrikan, Asian and South Amerikan refugee groups seeking such a status in that (then) revolutionary country. Astonishingly, Black Panther Parties in India, the Bahamas, and Israel were spawned as well!

On the other hand, the Nation of Islam (NOI) had been active since 1930. Yet it also experienced a huge upsurge in membership in the same period as the BPP, due mainly to the charismatic personality of Malcolm X and his aggressive recruitment techniques. This continued after Malcolm's assassination, fueled by the overall rebellious spirit of the youth looking for some group that would lead them in the fight against the system.

There is a mountain of documents that clearly shows how the highest power in this country classified both groups as class-A threats, ones that they wanted to either neutralize or destroy—even musing that if this goal could be achieved they could then use similar methods to defeat youth in the rest of the country. So how did they do it?

Against the BPP they used a combination of co-option, glamorization of gangsterism, separation from the most advanced elements, indoctrination in passive approaches, and raw fear—*every trick in the book.*

The ruling class's governmental, intelligence, legal, and academic forces were extremely alarmed at the growth and boldness of the BPP and related groups and their ability to win a level of global support. They devised a strategy to split the BPP and co-opt its more compliant elements, while at the same time moving to totally annihilate its more radical and revolutionary wing. In addition, they knew they had the upper hand due to the youth and inexperience of the BPP membership. The government also had a deep well of resources and experience in using counterinsurgency techniques. These were developed and used as early as against Marcus Garvey's United Negro Improvement Association (UNIA) in the early 1900s, during the Palmer Raids against Euro-Amerikans of an Anarchist or left-socialist bent in the 1930s—crushing the Industrial Workers of the World (IWW) and neutralizing other socialists—and in the underground work that contributed to the defeat of Germany and Italy during World War ll, the subsequent destruction of any real Communist power in Western Europe, the total domination and subjugation of the Caribbean (except Cuba), Central and South Amerika (except the fledgling guerilla movements). And they had learned a great deal in their wars to replace the European colonial powers in Afrika and Asia.

Still, the BPP had a highly motivated cadre, imbued with a fearlessness little-known among domestic groups. The ruling class and its henchmen were stretched thin, especially since the Vietnamese, Laotians and Cambodians were kicking ass in Southeast Asia, and the freedom fighters in Guinea-Bissau and Angola had their European allies—whom the United States supplied with the latest military hardware—on the run. So, although inexperienced, the BPP still had a fighting chance.

The co-option depended on the state being able to neutralize BPP co-founder (by that time an icon) Huey P. Newton, and then using him (combined with other methods) to split the BPP and lead Newton's wing along reformist lines, while forcing the still-revolutionary wing into an all-out armed confrontation before it was ready. In this way the repressive forces hoped to either kill, jail, exile or break the BPP's will to resist and send its cadre into an ineffective underground existence. What's more, even with the BPP's extraordinary status globally, no countries seemed to want to risk the wrath of the United States by openly allowing the BPP to train guerilla units on their soil.

Surprisingly, therefore, Huey Newton was allowed to leave jail with a murder-charge for killing a policeman still pending. Thus, the government and courts had him on a short leash. With that leash, they hoped to control his actions, although probably not through any direct agreements. Sadly, the still politically naive BPP cadre and other youth who looked up to Newton could only imagine that they had "forced" his release. Today, some veterans from those times still insist on clinging to such tripe!

Yet it seems Newton had other ideas, and since he was not prepared to go underground and join his fledgling Black Liberation Army (BLA), he almost immediately began to follow a reformist script that was completely at odds with his own earlier theories and writings. This script was also at odds with basic principles that were being practiced by oppressed people throughout the world to good effect. Further, he used his almost complete control of the BPP central committee to expel many veteran and combat-tested BPP cadre in imitation of the Stalinist and Euro-gangster posture he would later become infamous for—involving an all-out shooting war to suppress any BPP members who would not accept his independently derived-at reformist policies.

At the same time, and on a parallel track, US and local police and intelligence agencies were using their now infamous COINTELPRO operation to provoke the split between Newton's wing and other less-compliant BPP members, which was finally consummated in 1971 after Newton's shooting war and purge forced scores of the most loyal, fearless and dedicated aboveground BPP members to go underground. There, they were joined by those other BPP members who were already functioning as the offensive armed wing. They were known by names such as "Panther Wolves," "AfroAmerican Liberation Army," and "Black Liberation Army," but only the last one stuck. The BLA had already become a confederation of clandestine guerilla units of mostly Black revolutionary nationalists from any number of formations, who were willing to accept the BPP's leadership and who also accepted Huey Newton as their minister of defense. But obviously Newton didn't see it that way.

Most telling, it was later learned that Newton's expensive penthouse apartment, where he and other central committee members handled any number of sensitive BPP issues, was under ongoing surveillance by intelligence agents who had another apartment down the hall. Thus, Newton and his faction were boxed in, unable to follow anything but government-sanctioned scripts—unless he/they went underground, which only occurred when Newton fled to Cuba after his gangster antics threatened the revocation of his release on the pending legal matters which the government held over his head.

In addition to the glamorization of gangsterism, there was something else that various ruling-class elements had begun to champion and push on the Black lower classes, especially after they saw how much attention the Black Arts Movement was able to generate. Indeed, they recognized that this new tool could be used to misdirect youth who were attracted to military activities, while at the same time becoming hugely profitable. They had, in fact, already misdirected Euro-Amerikan and other youth with James Bond, *I Spy*, "Secret Agent Man," and other replacements for the "Old West/Cowboys and Indians" racist crap, so why not a "Black" counterpart? Thus was born the enormously successful counterinsurgent genre collectively known as the Blaxploitation movies: *Shaft, Superfly, Foxy Brown, Black Caesar* and their like as well as the wannabe crossovers like *Starsky and Hutch*, with its notorious Black snitch Huggy Bear. This was psychological warfare!

Follow the psychology: You can be "Black," cool, rebellious, dangerous, rich; have respect, women, cars, fine clothes, jewelry, an expensive home, and even stay high—as long as you don't fight the system or its cops! But if you don't go along with that script, get ready to go back to the early days, to shoot-outs with the cops and ending up in the graveyard, in prison, on the run, or in exile! You can still be cool even as a Huggy Bear–style snitch, or his buddy, [a] modern-day/futuristic rat—Cipher of *The Matrix*—who tried to betray Zion in return for a fake life as a rich, steak-eating, movie star. Most importantly, no more fighting with the Agents! Get it?

To bolster the government's assault and to saddle the oppressed with a Trojan Horse that would strategically handicap them for decades to come, the ruling powers began to flood their neighborhoods with heroin, cocaine, marijuana and meth. Yes, all of these drugs had earlier been introduced to the same areas by organized criminals under local police and political protection. But now, intelligence agencies were using them in the same manner that alcohol had long ago been introduced to the Native Amerikans, and with the same intentions: to counter any propensity to rebel against outside control while also profiting from the misery of the ghetto.

So Newton began to indulge in drugs as a way to try to relieve the stress of all that he was facing. He became a drug addict, plain and simple. That, however, didn't upset the newly constructed gangster-cool that Hollywood, the ruling class, and the government were pushing—although many BPP cadre and other outsiders were very concerned about it. But Newton's control was by then too firmly fixed for anyone to challenge, except the BLA, which by then was in full-blown guerilla war with the government.

At the same time, the reformist wing of the BPP did manage to make some noteworthy strides under its only female head, Elaine Brown. Newton's exile, provoked by his addiction/gangster lifestyle, caused him—on his own and without any consultation—to "appoint" Brown to head the Party in his absence. An exceptionally gifted woman, she relied on an inner circle of female BPP cadre, backed up by male party enforcers, to introduce some clear and consistent projects that helped the BPP to become a real local power. However, she pursued a reformist paradigm that could not hope to achieve any of the radical/revolutionary changes the BPP had called for earlier. In fact, within Newton's earlier writings, he had put the cadre on notice that a time would come when the aboveground would have to be supported by an underground in order to keep moving forward. Yet it was Newton who completely rejected that approach on being released from jail—although he still organized and controlled a heavily armed extortion wing called "The Squad" which consisted of BPP cadre who terrorized Oakland's underworld with a belt-operated machine gun mounted on a truck bed. They were accompanied by cadre who were ready for war!

In classical Euro-gangster fashion, Newton had turned to preying on segments of the community that he had earlier vowed to liberate. But, of course, the police and government were wise to him. Since there was no connection to a true underground, there was no rational way to ratchet up the pressure on the police, the government and the still fully operational system of ruling-class control and oppression. Newton's BPP had been reduced to relying completely on methods that were officially sanctioned.

Consequently, we can see all of the government's efforts bearing fruit. Newton's faction of the BPP had limited itself to either a legal or underworld-style approach; "co-optation" and "indoctrination" in reliance on passive approaches that were passive toward the status quo. He fell for the trick of severing all relations with the armed underground—the BLA, which would lead the BPP if it got to the next level of struggle (open armed resistance to the oppressors). This was "separation from the most advanced elements." Because of Newton's control, his faction was immersed in the glamorization of gangsterism. Finally, Newton, his faction, along with activists from other Amerikan radical and revolutionary groups, succumbed to the terror and raw fear that was being leveled on them. All but those who waged armed struggle were killed, jailed, exiled, forced into hiding or into continuing their activism underground.

Epilogue on Huey P. Newton and His BPP Faction

Elaine Brown guided her faction to support Newton and his family in exile, while orchestrating the building up of enough political muscle in Oakland to assure Newton's return on favorable terms. Thus, he did return, and eventually the charges against him were dropped. Newton continued to use his iconic stature and renewed direct control of his faction to play the cool political-gangster role. Like any drug addict who refuses to reform, he kept sliding downhill, turning on old comrades and even on Elaine Brown, who had to flee in fear.

Sadly, for all practical purposes, that was the end of the original Black Panther Party. Check-mate!

Later, as is well-known, Newton's continued drug addiction cost him his life, a sorry ending for a once-great man.

PART TWO

> "When you grow up in situations like me and Cliff... there is a lot of respect for brothers like [drug lords] Alpo and Nicky Barnes, those major hustler-player cats. 'Cause they made it. They made it against society's laws. They were the kings of their own domain."
>
> —TOURÉ

The "Original" Black Mafia (BM)

Albeit a touchy matter to many, it's an irrefutable fact that the original Black Mafia was first established in Philadelphia, PA, in the late 1960s, and has seen its cancerous ideas imitated and lionized by Black youth ever since. Moreover, although it's unclear how much the Nation of Islam (NOI) leadership knew or learned about the BM, there's no question of the local NOI's eventual absorption of the BM under Minister Jeremiah X Pugh. In fact, although the BM was originally just local "stick-up kids" culled from neighborhood gangs, being swallowed up by the NOI eventually turned them into a truly powerful and terrifying criminal enterprise—completely divorced from everything that the NOI had represented since its founding in 1930.

Sadly, most of the high-level tricks used by the government and intelligence agencies against the BPP were used again here—namely, co-option, the glamorization of gangsterism, separation from the more advanced elements, and raw fear. Thus, it must be understood that although the NOI and BPP had different ideologies and styles, most Black youth still saw the same promise in both organizations: the possibility of helping them to obtain the self-respect, dignity and freedom they most desired.

Interestingly, the puritanical NOI's dealings with the founders of the BM were similar to that of the Catholic Church's historical relationship to the Italian Mafia. The BM members who attended NOI religious services did so strictly on that basis, while still coming to the attention of the local NOI leadership as unusually good financial contributors. Within the lower-class Black community, everybody knew that meant that they were hustlers, stick-up kids, or both. So just as the Italian Mafia contributed huge sums to the Catholic Church, the BM eventually did the same thing for Philadelphia's Temple No. 12.

The national NOI, however, had been under close scrutiny and surveillance by intelligence agencies for decades. In fact, by the time of his death, the FBI had in excess of one million pages of files on the Honorable Elijah Muhammad alone!

Consequently, the BM's financial contributors would have come to the attention of the intelligence agencies through this process of monitoring. Nevertheless, overshadowing all of this was the bloody assault the FBI and local police were leveling against other radical and revolutionary Black groups, like the local and national BPP branches, the Revolutionary Action Movement (RAM), and scores of smaller formations. Indeed, FBI agents first tried to recruit Minister Pugh as a snitch against the local BPP by telling him that the BPP was out to get him and supplant the local NOI, which the BPP viewed as competition for the loyalty of Black youth. Pugh, to his credit, didn't take the bait. He also avoided getting his Temple No. 12 involved in a war with the BPP. At the same time, he must have suspected that his taking money from the BM had also come to the attention of the FBI, and that he was therefore vulnerable.

Miraculously, during the same period, Minister Pugh's name was removed from the FBI's "Security Index," which contained all the country's top-level threats—after Pugh had been on this list for years, and immediately following the report on his refusal to be a snitch. Why would they relax the pressure? Co-option! How did they think it would unfold? Was it to give Pugh and his Temple—and their BM followers—enough rope to hang themselves? Or was it to get them addicted to a game that would ultimately be controlled by their professed enemies—the US government and its underlings—thus turning the tables on Pugh and forcing him to be less radical, more compliant, and no longer as significant a threat as the BPP, RAM and company?

For the BM members, the glamorization of gangsterism fit right in. After all, why would a group of Black stick-up kids and gang members call themselves The Black Mafia? This was in the era of "Black is beautiful," when millions of Blacks began wearing afros/bushes and Afrikan clothing, and adopting Afrikan names—completely at odds with aping Italians! Why not name themselves the Zulus, Watusis, or the Mau Mau—like every other street gang was doing? Hollywood's projection of gangsterism was getting through!

Consequently, within a couple of years the BM would uniformly be recognized as expensively dressed, big hat–wearing, Cadillac-driving imitations of the Italian Mafia. And sadly, they turned countless numbers of street gang members, former RAM cadre and militants from dozens of other Philly groups—who were fighting oppression—into pawns who could be then used to further destroy their own communities.

There was a third step in the process of separating these Black youth from the more advanced elements. It operated under cover of Pugh and other insiders continuing to preach Black Nationalist doctrines among the youth in the street gangs and the prisons, never missing an opportunity to hold out the illusion that they could gain pride and respect—while fighting oppression—by joining what they believed to be a rebel group, one that was only awaiting the right moment to throw its lot in with the masses of Blacks who were waging either nonviolent or else bloody battles from coast to coast and on the Afrikan continent. By tricking these youth into diverting their energies toward gangsterism, Pugh and company were effectively separating them from the more advanced elements. True, many, if not most, bought into the rationale: that their extortion and drug-dealing proceeds were a tax that could be used to build the Nation. A few years later, that was dubbed "drinking the Kool-Aid," after Jim Jones and his CIA handlers tricked and forced hundreds of other Blacks to their deaths, committing suicide by consuming poisoned Kool-Aid. And undoubtedly Huey Newton had also tricked his people with a similar game, although decades later it was shown to be completely false! Yes, that money did build or buy some expensive homes, cars, clothing, women, and drugs—as well as a few schools and businesses. But to fight oppression? Please...!

Then, the raw fear being leveled on the entire society had the most devastating effect on the BM as well. Otherwise, how can one account for the hundreds (if not thousands) of BM street soldiers—who were fearless enough to challenge Philly's long-established and ruthless Italian Mafia and other mobs, along with most of its warring street gangs and independents, and who fielded headhunters who literally terrorized the city by decapitations—would demonstrate such a lackluster showing whenever it came to confronting someone in uniform?

I'll tell you how: their leadership had completely disarmed their fighting spirit by always pointing to the gun battles that the BPP/BLA and other Blacks were known for, and telling them not to resist the police until they (the leaders) gave the order—which never came. Ironically, after the police and FBI had succeeded in suppressing, jailing, exiling and co-opting most of the BPP, BLA, RAM and similar formations, they then discovered the BM and attacked it with a vengeance—while none of the BM put up anything resembling real resistance except to go into hiding. Minister Jeremiah also made a 180-degree turn, becoming a snitch after being caught in a drug sting.

Thus, their legacy is one of a ruthless group of Black thugs who have spawned similarly ruthless crews—notably Philly's Junior Black Mafia (JBM) and the latest clone, Atlanta's Black Mafia Family. But the most harmful effect of their deeds and mystique has been to return a huge segment of Black youth to believing that the only way to gain any respect and dignity is through being the best and most heartless hustlers around. Thus, we come full circle back from 1955.

To conclude, I used the BPP/BLA and NOI/BM because they present the best-documented examples. Both are surrounded by so much mythology, that a true analysis is almost never attempted. Except, of course, by government intelligence sources, who use their findings to refine, update, and revise old tricks in order to continue to check and control this country's rebellious youth and persistently oppress the communities they occupy in line with the ruling-class agenda.

Concurrently, the middle- and upper-class youth—from all segments of the first wave—allowed themselves willy-nilly and with few exceptions to be fully co-opted as the new managers of the system they had once vowed to radically change. They became the champions of—and made a doctrine out of the necessity to always use and rely on—passive and legal methods, epitomized by their new saint, Dr. Martin Luther King Jr.

The Second Wave: Circa 1980–2005

Thus, by 1980, the youth from the first wave had, for all practical purposes, been defeated, following which they collectively descended into a long, debilitating, agonizing, escapist period characterized by partying. Not discounting the fringe elements who had their hands full trying to rebuild their sanity and families, or trying to go back to school, or survive in prison or exile, everybody else seemed to be dancing on the ceiling—the shell-shocked vets of World Wars I and II, or the post-traumatic stress sufferers of the Vietnam War.

The most misunderstood victims, however, were the generation's children, the second wave—from 1980 to about 2005. Those are the years when these youth either reached puberty or became young adults. Paradoxically, they were left in the dark about most of what had occurred before. Instead, they were left to the tender mercies of the reformed but still rotten-to-the-core and ruling-class-dominated schools, social institutions, and cultural propaganda machinery.

So among all lower- and working-class segments of the youth, Coolio's "Gangsta's Paradise" fit the bill. They were raised by the state—either in the uncaring schools, juvenile detention centers and homes—or by the TV sets, movies, video arcades, or in the streets. Within the greatly expanded middle classes—most notably among the people of color—the youth were back to the gospel of relying on getting a good education and a good job as their highest calling, intermixed with an originally more-conscientious element, which tackled politics and academia as a continuation of the first wave struggles. The upper-class youth, however, were doomed to follow in the footsteps of their bourgeois parents, since the radical and revolutionary changes the first wave had sought failed to materialize.

Like a reoccurring nightmare, the second-wave youth also fell victim to co-option, glamorization of gangsterism, separation from the most advanced elements, relying on passive methods, the raw fear of an upgraded police state, and drugs. Left to their own devices, the lower-class youth began a search for respect and dignity by devising their own institutions and culture which came to be dominated by gangs and hip-hop. On their own, these things could be used for good or bad. But lacking any knowledge of the first wave's experiences, a new generation was tricked like their parents.

The Gang and Hip-Hop Culture

Gangs are a working- and lower-class phenomenon that dates from the early beginnings of this country. They have also been common overseas. In fact, many of those who joined the first wave were themselves gang members—most notably Alprentice Bunchy Carter, the martyred founder of the Los Angeles Panthers and head of the notorious Slausons, the forerunners of today's Crips. As little as it's understood, the gangs are in fact the lower-class counterpart to the middle and upper classes' youth clubs—Boy Scouts/Girl Scouts, fraternities and sororities. The key difference is the level of positive adult input in the middle- and upper-class groups. Hip-hop is just the latest manifestation of artistic genius bursting forth from these lower-class youth—seeking respect and dignity.

Orthodox hip-hoppers speak about a holy trinity of hip-hop fathers: Herc, Afrika Bambaata, and Grandmaster Flash. But, like moisture in the air before it rains, the conditions were ripe for hip-hop before the holy trinity began spinning. Hip-hop's prefathers or grandfathers are James Brown, Huey Newton, Muhammad Ali, Richard Pryor, Malcolm X, Bob Marley, Bruce Lee, certain celebrity drug dealers and pimps whose names won't be mentioned here, and Al Pacino's *Scarface*.

Alas, hip-hop culture is daily being co-opted in ways so obvious that it needs no explanation. But woe be to us if we don't come to grips with how the second wave's gangs have been co-opted. This is a continuing tragedy, moreover, one that if not turned around will ultimately make the shortcomings of the first wave pale in comparison!

Ronald Reagan and crack were hip-hop's '80s anti-fathers: both helped foster the intense poverty and the teenage drug-dealing millionaires as well as the urge to rebel against the system that appeared to be moving in for the kill, to finally crush Black America.

Certainly the gangs have comprised a subculture that has historically been a thorn in the side of the ruling class, one that either had to be controlled and used or else eradicated. Usually that was accomplished by co-option and attrition, with older elements moving on or being jailed long enough to destroy the group. Our first wave, as noted, was able to outflank the ruling class somewhat, lending their prestige to the rank-and-file's acceptance of radical and revolutionary ideas, which have since been pimped by BM-style groups.

It is fascinatingly simple to understand how the second wave was tricked and continues to be bamboozled into destroying itself. The pillars upholding this giant con-game have become familiar to everyone through the movies, TV, street culture, cops, courts, jails, prisons, death, and our own unfulfilled yearnings for respect and dignity.

Gangstas, Wankstas, and Wannabes

All of these gangstas, wankstas, and wannabes crave respect and dignity more than anything! Forget all of the unformed ideas about the homies wanting the families, fathers and love they never had. That plays a part. But if you think that the homies only need more hugs, then you've drunk the kool-aid! Actually, even if you did have a good father, a loving family and an extended family, everything in society is still geared toward lessening your self-worth because of your youth, race, tastes in dress, music, speech, lack of material trappings, etc.

Therefore, you will still hunger for some respect—because that will give you a sense of dignity within yourself. Even suburban middle- and upper-class youth confront this, although to a lesser degree. All of the beefin', flossin', frontin', set-trippin', violence, and bodies piling up around them comes from that same pursuit of respect and dignity.

This is how 50 Cent put it:

> Niggas out there sellin' drugs is after what I got from rappin'... When you walk into a club and the bouncers stop doin' whatever the fuck they doing to let you in and say everybody else wait. He special. That's the same shit they do when you start killin' niggas in you hood. This is what we been after the whole time. Just the wrong route.

Admittedly, at times this simple—but raw—truth is so intertwined with so many other things that it's hard to grasp. But nowadays the drug game, other get-money games, and most gangs do provide a sort of alternative family as well as a strong cohesion that is mistakenly called love. Let's cut through the distractions, and illustrate my point as follows:

When the second wave was left hanging by the defeated and demoralized first wave, it unknowingly reverted to methods of seeking dignity and respect that the first wave had overcome—through its struggle for radical and revolutionary change during a period during when gang wars and gang-bangin' was anathema! The revolutionary psychiatrist, Frantz Fanon, in *The Wretched of the Earth*, notes that the colonized and oppressed are quick to grab their knives and use them against a neighbor or stranger, thereby in a subconscious way ducking their fear of directing their pent-up rage at those actually responsible for their suffering—their colonial oppressors.

So the primary activity of the notable early gangs like the Bloods, Crips, and Gangster Disciples was bangin', or gang-warring over "turf"—neighborhoods, schools, etc.—as well as over real or imagined slights. But the real underlying motivation was the desire on all sides to build their reputations and earn stripes—meaning to gain prestige in the eyes of fellow bangers. This translated into respect amongst their peers. It also caused these youth to bond with each other like soldiers in combat—the way a family bonds—only more so. Not surprisingly, many outsiders decreed that this bonding was "love," which then caused some youth to parrot that thought. But to exchange love you first have to love yourself. And the gang-banger, by definition, has no love for him- or herself—in fact, these young people are desperately seeking respect, without which anyone's idea of love is fooling itself.

Example: If you "respect" your body you can also "love" your body and you would not dare destroy it with drugs or alcohol. But if you don't respect your body and you go on to destroy it in that fashion, then it follows that you have no love for it either.

The bangin' raged on for years, piling up as many bodies as the Vietnam War—each case elevating the attacker's or victim's stature in the eyes of their peers. During those times the overseers of the oppressive system bemoaned the carnage while locking up untold numbers of bangers for a few years. But overall they did nothing to try to stop the problem.

Now here's where it really gets interesting! Drugs, as noted, had been flooding into these same communities since the 1960s. Back then, however, it was mainly heroin, with marijuana and meth playing relatively minor roles. Remember *Serpico* and *The French Connection*, movies that exposed this? But the early gangs, to their credit, never got deeply involved in that. They saw dope fiends as weak and although they would blow some "sherm" or "chronic," it was just a pastime for them. They were serious about bangin'!

Consequently, the bangers were all co-opted, wedded as they were to their form of fratricidal gangsterism and totally separated from the remnants of the first wave, who they knew next to nothing about. At the same time the "good kids" were being indoctrinated in passive, legal (get a good education) approaches, while both groups were scared to death of the police! Despite the bangers' hate and contempt, any two cops could lay out a dozen of them on all fours at will.

Hence, Tupac's later iconic stature with them, since he could walk his talk:

The fact [is] that while everyone else talks about it, Tupac is the only known rapper who has actually shot a police officer; the walking away from being shot five times with no permanent damage and walking away from the hospital the next day and the rolling into court for a brief but dramatic wheelchair-bound courtroom appearance—it's been dangerously compelling and ecstatically brilliant.

But something was on the horizon that was about to cause a seismic shift in this already sorry state of affairs, altering things in ways that most still cannot or will not believe. Apparently, since this madness was contained in lower-class communities, the ruling classes' henchmen had no desire to do anything but keep their Gestapo-like police heavily armed and fully supported. Technology had made what they dubbed "the underclass" obsolete anyway. See, for example, Sean Penn and Robert Duvall's movie *Colors*.

Peep the Game

The South Amerikan cocaine trade replaced the French Connection and CI-controlled US distribution of Southeast Asian golden-triangle-grown-and-processed heroin as the drug of choice in the early 1980s. Remember *Miami Vice*? As usual, this country's government intelligence agencies and the large banks immediately began a struggle to control this new cocaine trade. Remember, their goal was to control it, not get rid of it, as their lying propaganda projects with the hyped-up "war on drugs"! Thus, they were contending with South Amerikan governments, militaries and large landowners who controlled the raising, processing and shipping of the cocaine although for a few years these South Amerikan elites had to also do battle with a few independent drug lords, most notably the notorious Pablo Escobar and the Ochoa family–dominated Medellín Cartel.

Within this country, the youth gangs had next to nothing to do with the cocaine trade, which was then primarily servicing a middle- and upper-class white clientele. There were a few old-school big-time hustlers, along with some Spanish-speaking wholesalers who also had their own crews to handle things. After the fact, hip-hop favorites such as *Scarface* and *New Jack City* are good descriptions of that period. But both films purposely left out the dominant role that the US government intelligence agencies played in controlling things.

I know you're down with all of that and love it! So let's move on.

In the mid-1980s, the United States began backing a secret war designed to overthrow the revolutionary Sandinista government in Nicaragua. The Sandinistas had fought a long and bloody civil war to rid Nicaragua of its US-sponsored dictatorship in 1979. But after his secret war was exposed for the world to see, the US Congress forbade President Ronald Reagan from continuing it. Like a lot of US presidents, he just ignored Congress and had the CIA raise millions to recruit mercenaries, buy or steal military equipment, and continue the war.

That's how and why crack and the mayhem it has caused came upon us. However, you won't see Hollywood or TV giving up that raw truth—with few exceptions, like Black director Bill Dukes's *Deep Cover*, starring Laurence Fishburne, and *Above the Law* with Steven Seagal. Otherwise, you have to search hard to see the facts portrayed so clearly. Later I'll explain why.

Most people have heard that crack was dumped into South Central Los Angeles in the mid-1980s—along with an arsenal of military-style assault rifles that would have made a first wave BPP member ashamed of how poorly equipped s/he was. Needless to say, the huge profits from the crack sales, coupled with everyone being strapped, magnified the body count! Since crack was also so easy to manufacture locally and so dirt-cheap, just about anybody in the hood could get into the business. Gone were the old days of just a few big-time hustlers—except on the wholesale level.

But, make no mistake, the wholesale cocaine that was sold for the production and distribution of crack was fully controlled by selected CIA-controlled operatives. So, to all of you around-the-way dawgs who have been bragging about how big you were/are, an organizational flow chart would look something like this. At the top would be president Ronald Reagan, vice president and former CIA director George Bush Sr., the national security advisor, the secretary of state, General Secord, Colonel Oliver North, major banking executives, Central and South Amerikan military and government leaders, arms dealers, mercenary pilots, and drug lords like Escobar and the Medellín Cartel (originally), US Customs and Border Patrol officers, state and local police officers, county sheriffs and deputies, and their successors in office. Then, at the bottom of the barrel: you, dawg!

Now, I know that you already understood in your hearts that there were some big dawgs over you, but I'll bet you never guessed that the game came straight out of the White House or that you were straight-up pawns on the board. If that sounds too wild, then tell me why it is harder to find any government, CIA, military, or bankers, like George Bush Sr. and his crew in prison, than it is to win the lottery? Yeah, they double-crossed Noriega, Escobar, and the Medellín Cartel and made Oliver North do some community service, but that's all. The real crime lords—the government, military, CIA, military and banking dons—all got away. True, after Congresswoman Maxine Waters made a stink about it the CIA was forced to launch two investigations, and post its findings and admissions of drug dealing on its official website.

Now, dawg, y'all were played! Face it. That's what happened to you O.G.'s from the '80s. But like Morpheus said in *The Matrix*, let me show you how deep the rabbit hole goes.

Gradually the US government was forced to crack down on the cocaine coming through Florida. By then the South Amerikan cartels and their allies in government and military circles had found new routes through Mexico. At first, the Mexican underworld was just a middleman. But it quickly recognized a golden opportunity and essentially seized control of most of the cocaine trade between South Amerika and the United States. The Mexicans forced the South Amerikans into becoming junior partners, responsible for the less-profitable growing and processing, after which the Mexicans would purchase mounds of cocaine for transshipment overland, smuggling it into the United States and its wholesale markets that produced oil-and-automotive-industry-type profits.

One might wonder how and why the South Amerikans—powerful players—would go for a deal like that? As ever, the answers can be found in the Machiavellian and serpentine maneuverings of the US and Mexican governments. You see, in the 1980s the Mexican government was overseeing an economy that was so bad that for all practical purposes it might have gone belly-up bankrupt. Indeed, the United States and its underlings within the International Monetary Fund (IMF) and the World Bank (WB) were forced to periodically give Mexico millions upon millions in loans in order to save its economy, in return for further unfair trading concessions. Note that the United States was then, and remains today, extremely vulnerable to what happens in Mexico. Common sense and past experience have told its rulers that the worse things got in Mexico, the more destitute its already dirt-poor Mexican majority would become, forcing millions to search for a way into the United States to find the means to feed themselves and their families. Rather than keep prevailing on the IMF to continue lending Mexico money, the rulers of the United States saw another way to temporarily plug up this hole in their control of international finance.

Thus, another unholy alliance was formed. This one was between the US State Department, the CIA, the big banks and other usual suspects on one side, and their Mexican counterparts—including the first fledgling cartels—on the other, with the South Amerikans now in a junior partnership role. However, I don't want to give the impression that it was all arranged diplomatically, neat and tidy. Far from it! It evolved through visionaries among the usual suspects placing their ideas before selected insiders and working to craft an unwritten consensus, the same way that (along with Cuban exiles in Florida) they had earlier created the cocaine trade to fund its growth around Miami. Only this time, it would be Mexico's underworld that would eventually land in the driver's seat due to its ability to take the kind of risks called for, a geographical proximity to the US border, and (most importantly) a strong desire to avoid confronting the US and Mexican governments—as Pablo Escobar had. Thus, the Mexican drug lords were more than willing to guarantee that most of their profits would be pumped back into the moribund Mexican economy through large building projects, upgrading the tourist industry, large-scale farming, and other clearly national ventures. In addition, and on the messy side, their gunmen were becoming experts at making reluctant parties fall into line by offering them a stark choice between gold and lead.

Nevertheless, avoid thinking that the Mexican or South Amerikan underworlds ever became anything more than hired hands of the big dawgs in the US government and their partners in the banking industry, who always remained in control. In fact, under George Bush Sr., the invasion of Panama—a major hub of offshore money laundering—was ordered when their hired hand, Manuel Noriega, became unmanageable in 1989.

Plus, these hired hands would ensure that the chosen corrupt politicians would garner sufficient votes in the Mexican elections by bringing in planeloads of money that the South Amerikan gangsters and government/military partners would make available as part of their overhead expenses. More importantly to the United States, however, a major part of the profits would be pumped into the Mexican economy in order to forestall its looming bankruptcy.

Consequently, by the mid-1990s the Mexican underworld had established the super-powerful Gulf, Juárez, Guadalajara, Sinaloa and Tijuana cartels. Moreover, they had consolidated their power by not only controlling who was elected to key political posts in Mexico, but also [...] perfecting the art of bribing key local, state and regional police heads as well as strategic generals in Mexico's armed forces. Check out the movie *Traffic,* and the Antonio Banderas/Selma Hayek *Desperado* and *Once upon a Time in Mexico*. Again—after the fact—you'll see Hollywood spilling the beans. But don't let the fancy stunt work lull you into thinking that there's no substantive truth to the plots of these films!

Remember, Mexico's cartels would not be able to function without the collaboration and protection of the highest levels within the US establishment. Just as the CIA has openly admitted it was an illegal drug merchant during an earlier period, you can believe nothing has changed—except the partners!

The hilarious part is that none of the wannabe real gangstas in the United States know that in reality they are low-level CIA flunkies. Or else they can't wait to get out of prison and become undercover government agents—slinging crack. Alas, most people think it's crazy to believe that the government of the United States would allow its cities and small towns to be flooded with cocaine. They cling to the illusion that they are something more than pawns on the chessboard.

But you have to go beyond the idea that this whole thing is just a plot to destroy Black and Brown peoples—a favorite though short-sighted theory. Otherwise, there is no way to see just how deep the rabbit hole really is. I repeat: the main objective was to pump billions of dollars into the Mexican economy in order to avoid a complete meltdown and the subsequent fleeing to the United States of sixty million or more Mexicans out of its ninety-plus million inhabitants. It would have been a migration that dwarfed the numbers who actually did cross over, and are just beginning to make their presence felt.

The big dawgs in the United States probably didn't know just how they were going to control the fallout, although they surely knew there would inevitably be some as a result of their cocaine/crack tax. They routinely tax alcohol, gambling (from the lotteries to the casinos), and even prostitution in certain areas, don't they? So yeah, a clandestine operation to use cocaine to rescue Mexico and stave off an economically induced invasion of the United States by a population made poverty-stricken by five hundred years of colonialism, slavery, peonage, neocolonialism, and the theft of one-third of their country by the United States in the nineteenth century was an indirect tax.

Sadly, though, the first wave degenerated into the glorification of gangsterism; the second wave's hunger for respect and recognition fueled the gang carnage; and the hip-hop generation provided youth with vicarious fantasies to indulge their senses with the hypnotic allure of the temporary power that the drug game could bring them. All this led youth in the United States back to emulating the first wave's *Superfly* and *Scarface* days. Others also see that this is true.

My theory is that nine times out of ten, if there's a depression, more a social depression than anything, it brings out the best art in Black people. The best example is Reagan and Bush gave us the best years of hip-hop. Hip-hop is created thanks to the conditions that crack set: easy money but a lot of work, the violence involved, the stories it produced—crack helped birth hip-hop. Now, I'm part conspiracy theorist because you can't develop something that dangerous and it not be planned. I don't think crack happened by accident... Crack offered a lot of money to the inner-city youth who didn't have to go to college. Which enabled them to become businessmen. It also turned us into marksmen. It also turned us comatose.

With the deft moves of a conjurer, the big dawgs in the United States seized upon all of this and began to nudge various elements around on the international chess board—as part of their giant con game. Moreover, these big dawgs in the United States had very little choice regarding who they would sacrifice in order to gain some relief from their manufactured domestic crisis. I'll tell you why!

Cocaine in its powder and crack forms is so addictive with everyone who uses it regularly—the rich and famous, the Hollywood set, corporate executives, lawyers, doctors, weekenders, entertainers, athletes, college kids, suburbanites, hood rats, hustlers, pipers, etc.—that its demand is guaranteed! In this sense, it's just like alcohol and tobacco, which have never been successfully suppressed in the United States for long.

It follows then that despite all of their propaganda about "Just Say No" and the bogus "war on drugs," the big dawgs never had any intention of even trying to eradicate the use of cocaine. At the same time, however, the Black and Brown communities were becoming major headaches that, if left unchecked, could eventually evolve into a real strategic threat. Yes, crack had turned their lower class into lucrative mainstays of the big dawgs alternative taxing scheme. However, the urgency to deal with what happened as a result was graphically driven home by the non-Black/Brown communities' consumption of more (mostly powder) cocaine. And the trade in the Black and Brown hoods and barrios was accompanied by an unforeseen, exponentially rising rate of ever-more-sophisticated drug-related violence, especially once the gangs got seriously involved.

As I've pointed out, the gangs were mainly just pursuing the goal of earning respect prior to getting involved with hustling drugs. The carnage connected with that was not a real concern to the big dawgs. But unlike the earlier dumping of heroin in those communities, accompanied by the comparatively isolated violence of the Black Mafia–style groups, (whose violence, though terrifying, was also more selective) the widespread availability of crack and assault rifles led the big dawgs to understand that this was different. If they did not deal aggressively with the ultraviolent, inner-city politics then, like the Mexican cartels, this reality threatened to become less predictable—once the gangs realized that the money and power they now had would not, of themselves, provide the kind of respect and dignity they sought. To understand why, just consider the rich and famous hip-hop artists who continue to wild-out because they still lack the respect and dignity that comes with struggling for something other than money or power—in short, some type of cause.

Anyway, the hip-hop generational favorite TV drama *The Wire* lays out the entire phenomenon pretty much the way it actually played itself out in Baltimore and other urban areas. In fact, the fictionalized TV series derives its sense of reality from an earlier long-running exposé featured in a Baltimore newspaper. This is another after-the-fact but still-useful piece of work to study. Indeed, the show depicts the earlier years of the Black gangs getting involved in the crack trade and clearly illustrates my point about the gangs evolving into proto-cartels, then getting strategically neutralized.

That's why the "prison industrial complex" was formed! It was set up as a tool to neutralize the second wave before its members woke up to the fact that—despite their money and power—young people were being used and played like suckers. This was an itch that the more astute of the big dawgs feared money would not soothe. Thus, all of our draconian gun-related and mandatory sentencing laws were first formulated on the federal level, where most of the big dawgs have their greatest power. They were then forced upon the states. It was all to ensure that the second wave would never be able to consolidate any real power. Precisely because they were proving themselves to be such ruthless gangstas in imitation of their Hollywood idols, coupled with the potential power derived from their share of the undercover tax being extracted from their communities, the big dawgs chose to step in every time they got too big. This happened on average every one to three years, then everything they acquired was taken. The martyred hip-hop icon The Notorious BIG put it all together in his classic song—rightly titled "Respect":

> Put the drugs on the shelf
> Nah, I couldn't see it
> Scarface, King of New York
> I wanna be it... Until I got incarcerated
> Kinda scary... Not able to move behind the steel gate
> Time to contemplate
> Damn, where did I fail?
> All the money I stacked was all the money for bail.

Let's get another thing straight! I mean the question that continues to have short-sighted individuals chasing ghosts about why powder cocaine and crack are treated so differently. Within the big dawgs' calculations, there was no reason to punish the powder cocaine dealers and users as harshly as they were punishing the crack crowd. Racism was not the driving motive. Rather, it was the potential armed threat within these proto-cartels! The big dawgs witnessed a clear example of what could happen by looking at the Jamaican posses that cropped up in the Black communities at this time. These involved young men from the Jamaican and Caribbean diaspora. Like the second-wave youth from the United States, they were also a product of the degeneration of the attempts by the lower classes to throw off the economic and social effects that were the legacy of slavery and colonial oppression.

Led by the socialist Michael Manley, and inspired by the revolutionary music of Bob Nesta Marley, their activity can be glimpsed in the later Steven Seagal *Marked for Death* and DMX/Nas *Belly* movies. The Jamaican posses were the Black Mafia on steroids!

Moreover, their quasi-religious nationalism, coupled with their ability to operate in Jamaica and in the Caribbean with heavily armed soldiers, put the big dawgs' teeth on edge. Their ten thousand or so were nothing compared to the hundreds of thousands in the wings of the Black and Brown communities!

The cry from the big dawg mouthpieces in Congress was about the gunplay, not so much the drugs. What was not spoken of, however, were the big dawgs' anxieties about stopping these gunslingers before they got over their mental blocks about using their weapons against the police or the system. They wanted to stop them while they were still hung-up on imitating their Hollywood and Euro-Mafia icons—who made a mantra out of instructing their gunmen not to use their weapons against the police. Indeed, with few exceptions, the second wave allowed itself to be disarmed and carted off to prison like pussycats!

Add to all of this the unforeseen windfall of thousands of new jobs in prisons for the rural communities that were being destroyed economically by capitalism's drive for fuller globalization. These conservative rural communities are vital to the big dawgs who needed their fanatical religious support.

We must struggle against the shortsighted view about racism alone being the driving motive that fueled the construction of the prison industrial complex. Instead, if you do a follow-up and add your own research, you'll be able to detect and document the who, when, and where of how the big dawgs set everything in motion, as well as how they continue to use us as pawns in their giant, international con game.

CONCLUSION

Ask yourself the following questions:

1. How can we salvage anything from the way the first and second waves allowed their search for respect and dignity to degenerate into gangsterism?
2. In what ways can we help the next wave avoid our mistakes?
3. What can we do to contribute to documenting who the real big dawgs behind the drug trade are?
4. Why have they never been held accountable?
5. How come our families and communities are the only ones to suffer?
6. How can we overcome our brainwashing?
7. How can we truly gain respect and dignity?
8. In what ways can we atone for our wrongs and redeem ourselves, our families, and our communities?
9. What are some ways to fight for restitution and reparations for all those harmed by the government-imposed (undercover) drug tax?
10. How can we overturn the Thirteenth Amendment of the U.S. Constitution and finally abolish slavery in the United States?

Once you've answered these questions and begun to move to materialize your conclusions, you will then have made the choice between Liberation or Gangsterism: Freedom or Slavery.

TWENTY-FIVE

KEVIN "RASHID" JOHNSON

What Is a "Comrade" and Why We Use the Term

(2013)

HOW SHOULD SOLIDARITY AND RESPECT BE EXpressed toward those we build with in struggle? How can we ensure that oppressive dynamics of hierarchy are not encoded in our personal and political interactions? In this essay, written from the hellhole of prison, Kevin "Rashid" Johnson suggests that the language we use should reinforce our revolutionary ideals. The term "comrade," Rashid asserts, should become our word of choice when referring to those with whom we create communities of justice, freedom, and emancipatory consciousness. Power relations, he reminds us, are constructed and reinforced through interactions, including verbal ones. Johnson knows a lot about the imbalance of power relations, as he has spent decades being transferred from prison to prison, cage to cage, hole to hole, all while striving to deepen his organizing, philosophizing, artwork, and revolutionary awareness. Born in Richmond, Virginia, in 1971, Johnson was in and out of juvenile facilities throughout his youth. At age twenty he was convicted of murder in a case where he was misidentified, he says, and is innocent of the crime. He has spent his numerous years of imprisonment almost exclusively in solitary confinement for various infractions such as organizing fellow prisoners and challenging the abuses they are subjected to.

The genealogy of words is important. Like movements, words don't come out of thin air, they have a history, and in this case "comrade," a term with linguistic roots in French and Spanish, became popularized in communist lexicon following its embrace by Bolsheviks during the Russian Revolution. Adopting it into our contemporary revolutionary traditions establishes the word as an inheritance to be vitalized by another generation in a new historical context. By engaging this lineage, we add something new to the meaning, such as the understanding that we should treat each other with the level of equality and respect that we want to see reproduced in the world. We deserve a better world. Comrade Rashid shows the way.

WHAT IS A "COMRADE" AND WHY WE USE THE TERM

THE CONCEPT of "Comrade" has a special meaning and significance in revolutionary struggle. We have often been asked to explain our use of this term, especially by our peers who are new to the struggle, instead of more familiar terms like "brother," "homie," "cousin," "dog," nigga," etc.

Foremost is that we aspire to build a society based upon equality and a culture of revolutionary transformation, so we need to purge ourselves of the tendency to use terms of address that connote cliques and exclusive relationships. A comrade can be a man or a woman of any color or ethnicity, but definitely a fellow fighter in the struggle against all oppression.

Terms like "mister" or "youngster" imply a difference of social status, entitlement to greater or lesser respect and built-in concepts of superiority or inferiority. Terms like "bitch," "dog," "nigga," "ho," etc., are degrading and disrespectful—even when used affectionately—as some do to dull the edge of their general usage in a world that disrespects us.

"Comrade," however, connotes equality and respect. It implies "I've got your back" and "we are one." Comrades stand united unconditionally and, if need be, to the death. It implies a relationship that is inclusive, not exclusive, and not based on any triviality but [instead] revolutionary class solidarity. It represents the socialist future we seek to represent in the struggles of today, and the eventual triumph of classless communist society.

Most forms of address used by New Afrikans carry subtle implications of differing status and worth, or were originally meant to insult and dehumanize us. Embracing these terms has led to our subconsciously embracing these roles, and feeling and believing we are inferior and treating each other as worth less than others. So, it is definitely important that we remind ourselves constantly that we are equal to, and as good as, anyone else, and address each other accordingly. As Malcolm X put it in an interview with the *Village Voice* in 1965:

> "The greatest mistake of the movement has been trying to organize a sleeping people around specific goals. You have to wake the people up first, then you'll get action."
>
> "Wake them up to their exploitation?" the interviewer asked.
>
> "No," Malcolm replied, "to their humanity, to their own worth."

Conscious use of the term "Comrade" instead of the many disparaging terms of address popular today, explicitly connects all people as humans and equals. It reminds us of our interdependence for survival; promotes relations of equality, friendship and camaraderie between all oppressed and exploited people; it expresses the unified outlook of the proletariat; and it will promote a change in people's outlook and thinking. Its use identifies those committed to the revolutionary struggle and represents the future in the struggles of today.

As Amilcar Cabral expressed in *Our People Are Our Mountains*: "I call you 'comrades' rather than 'brothers and sisters' because if we are brothers and sisters it's not from choice, it's no commitment; but if you are my comrade, I am your comrade too, and that's a commitment and a responsibility. This is the political meaning of 'comrade.'"

In the interpersonal sense, camaraderie binds people by respect, mutual support and trust, making organizations cohesive and stable. It builds and cements unity in the process of struggle, generating mutual confidence between people, affirming that we can rely upon each other regardless of the dangers that come from standing for the people and social justice for all.

Examples of genuine camaraderie are inspirational to the people and build their willingness to make a commitment to the struggle. The development and maintenance of organizational structure depends on the close and genuine camaraderie of the revolutionaries—what we call Panther Love!

TWENTY-SIX

CHELSEA MANNING

Sometimes You Have to Pay a Heavy Price to Live in a Free Society (2017)

AT AGE TWENTY-FIVE, PRIVATE MANNING WAS DEclared guilty on seventeen different charges, including espionage, and sentenced to thirty-five years behind bars. One month later, in August 2013, Chelsea Manning, known to the world as Bradley Manning at the time, came out as transgender while an inmate at a US military prison. Amid a hostile anti-trans political climate, she launched a lawsuit to obtain gender-affirming health care, including hormone therapy. Though her body was confined to a cage, she refused the confinement of misgendering. Like it or not, she was going to tell the truth about her own sexuality, and about the human rights violations that were taking place in Iraq against Iraqi civilians, including media workers and children, and in Guantánamo Bay detention camp where people were being held for years with no due process. Manning believed the public had a right to know what was being done in their name, and her shift from a compliant soldier to a whistleblower—one responsible for leaking more than 700,000 internal classified documents—occurred when she stopped seeing cold data and started seeing people whose humanity was lost in statistics.

Born in Crescent, Oklahoma, in 1987, Manning was bullied for being effeminate and was disrespected in her family for not "measuring up" to cultural expectations of masculinity. Hoping that the military, then operating under "don't ask, don't tell" protocol, could be a way out, she enlisted. Landing in the military brig for releasing classified documents meant months of traumatizing solitary confinement and numerous suicide attempts, which were all met with further isolation. After seven years Chelsea Manning was pardoned by President Obama. She currently resides in Brooklyn, New York, where she continues to work in the field of securities and also DJs on the side. Despite suffering numerous confinements, her life serves as testament that even a single person can stand up to the American war machine, demand accountability and justice, and survive to create a better future for all.

SOMETIMES YOU HAVE TO PAY A HEAVY PRICE TO LIVE IN A FREE SOCIETY

The following is a transcript of the statement made by PFC Bradley Manning as read by David Coombs at a press conference after Manning was sentenced to 35 years in prison.

THE DECISIONS that I made in 2010 were made out of a concern for my country and the world that we live in. Since the tragic events of 9/11, our country has been at war. We've been at war with an enemy that chooses not to meet us on any traditional battlefield, and due to this fact we've had to alter our methods of combating the risks posed to us and our way of life.

I initially agreed with these methods and chose to volunteer to help defend my country. It was not until I was in Iraq and reading secret military reports on a daily basis that I started to question the morality of what we were doing. It was at this time I realized in our efforts to meet this risk posed to us by the enemy, we have forgotten our humanity. We consciously elected to devalue human life both in Iraq and Afghanistan. When we engaged those that we perceived were the enemy, we sometimes killed innocent civilians. Whenever we killed innocent civilians, instead of accepting responsibility for our conduct, we elected to hide behind the veil of national security and classified information in order to avoid any public accountability.

In our zeal to kill the enemy, we internally debated the definition of torture. We held individuals at Guantánamo for years without due process. We inexplicably turned a blind eye to torture and executions by the Iraqi government. And we stomached countless other acts in the name of our war on terror.

Patriotism is often the cry extolled when morally questionable acts are advocated by those in power. When these cries of patriotism drown our any logically based intentions [unclear], it is usually an American soldier that is ordered to carry out some ill-conceived mission.

Our nation has had similar dark moments for the virtues of democracy—the Trail of Tears, the Dred Scott decision, McCarthyism, the Japanese-American internment camps—to name a few. I am confident that many of our actions since 9/11 will one day be viewed in a similar light.

As the late Howard Zinn once said, "There is not a flag large enough to cover the shame of killing innocent people."

I understand that my actions violated the law, and I regret if my actions hurt anyone or harmed the United States. It was never my intention to hurt anyone. I only wanted to help people. When I chose to disclose classified information, I did so out of a love for my country and a sense of duty to others.

If you deny my request for a pardon, I will serve my time knowing that sometimes you have to pay a heavy price to live in a free society. I will gladly pay that price if it means we could have [a] country that is truly conceived in liberty and dedicated to the proposition that all women and men are created equal.

TWENTY-SEVEN

LEONARD PELTIER

Message of Solidarity to Water Defenders (2017)

LEONARD PELTIER WAS BORN IN 1944 IN NORTH Dakota. He worked as a welder, carpenter, and community counselor and co-owned an auto body shop. In his twenties he became involved in Native American activism and joined the American Indian Movement. Based on the testimony of a person who was ultimately found to be mentally unstable and unable to testify at Peltier's trial, Peltier was charged and convicted of murders that occurred at Pine Ridge Reservation in 1975. Peltier escaped from prison in 1979, and was captured five days later. "I'm always on edge here," he writes about being incarcerated, "you never let your guard down when you live in hell." On June 7, 2022, The United Nations Human Rights Council's Working Group on Arbitrary Detention concluded that Peltier's detention is arbitrary and contravenes the International Covenant on Civil and Political Rights.

Peltier penned the following letter of support from Leavenworth Penitentiary, a federal prison in Kansas. His powerful and deeply expressive message functions as an intergenerational handshake extended to young people ready to take up the struggle. Stark are his words, and stark is the grim reality of the carceral landscape that holds him captive. Known as Prisoner #89637-132, Peltier continues his spiritual practices, political advocacy, writing, painting, and drawing from behind bars. His only crime, he says, is simply being an Indian. Though tortured, beaten, falsely accused, and victimized by medical neglect, Peltier remains resolute, claiming: "I will never yield." He characterizes his life in prison as an extended agony, like living a hundred lifetimes. Despite it all, on behalf of his people, he is prepared to live thousands more. In his own words: "We are all leaders. We are each an army of one, working for the survival of our people and of the Earth, our Mother. This isn't rhetoric. This is commitment. This is who we are."

MESSAGE OF SOLIDARITY TO WATER DEFENDERS

GREETING SISTERS and Brothers: I have been asked to write a SOLIDARITY statement to everyone about the Camp of the Sacred Stones on Standing Rock. Thank you for this great honor. I must admit it is very difficult for me to even begin this statement as my eyes get so blurred from tears and my heart swells with pride, as chills run up and down my neck and back. I'm so proud of all of you young people and others there.

I am grateful to have survived to see the rebirth of the united and undefeated Sioux Nation at Standing Rock in the resistance to the poisonous pipeline that threatens the life source of the Missouri and Mississippi Rivers. It is an honor to have been alive to see this happen with you young people. You are nothing but awesome in my eyes.

It has been a long, hard road these 40 years of being caged by an inhuman system for a crime I did not commit. I could not have survived physically or mentally without your support, and I thank you from the bottom of my heart and the depths of my soul for encouraging me to endure and maintain a spiritual and legal resistance.

We are now coming to the end of that road, soon arriving at a destination which will at least in part be determined by you. Along the lines of what Martin Luther King said shortly before his death, I may not get there with you, but I only hope and pray that my life, and if necessary, my death, will lead my Native peoples closer to the Promise Land.

I refer here not to the Promised Land of the Christian bible, but to the modest promises of the Treaties our ancestors secured from enemies bent on their destruction; in order to enable us to survive as distinct peoples and live in a dignified manner. Our elders knew the value of written words and laws to the white man, even as they knew the lengths the invaders would go to try to get around them.

Our ancestors did not benefit from these Treaties, but they shrewdly and persistently negotiated the best terms they could get, to protect us from wars which could only end in our destruction, no matter how courageously and effectively we fought. No, the Treaties were to the benefit of the Americans, this upstart nation needed the Treaties to put a veneer of legitimacy on its conquest of the land and its rebellion against its own countrymen and king.

It should be remembered that Standing Rock was the site of the 1974 conference of the international indigenous movement that spread throughout the Americas and beyond, the starting point for the United Nations Declaration of the Rights of Indigenous Peoples. The UNDRIP was resisted by the United States for three decades until its adoption by the UN in 2007. The US was one of just four nations to vote against ratification, with President Obama acknowledging the Declaration as an aspirational document without binding force under international law.

While some of the leaders of this movement are veterans of the 1970s resistance at Pine Ridge, they share the wisdom of our past elders in perceiving the moral and political symbolism of peaceful protest today is as necessary for us as [it] was necessary for the people of Pine Ridge in the 1970s. The 71-day occupation of Wounded Knee ended with an agreement to investigate human rights and treaty abuses; that inquiry and promise were never implemented [or] honored by the United States. The Wounded Knee Agreement should be honored with a Truth and Reconciliation Commission established to thoroughly examine the US government's role in the "Reign of Terror" on Pine Ridge in the 1970s. This project should be coordinated with the cooperation of the many international human rights organizations that have called for my immediate and unconditional release for more than four decades.

I have to caution you young people to be careful, for you are up against a very evil group of people whose only concern is to fill their pockets with even more gold and wealth. They could not care less how many of you they have to kill or bury in a prison cell. They don't care if you are a young child or an old grandmother, and you better believe they are and have been recruiting our own people to be snitches and traitors. They will look to the drunks, the addicts, and child molesters, those who prey on our old and our children; they look for the weak-minded individuals. You must remember to be very cautious about falsely accusing people based more on personal opinion than on evidence. Be smart.

I call on all my supporters and allies to join the struggle at Standing Rock in the spirit of peaceful spiritual resistance and to work together to protect Unci Maka, Grandmother Earth. I also call upon my supporters and all people who share this Earth to join together to insist that the US complies with and honors the provisions of international law as expressed in the UNDRIP, International Human Rights Treaties and the long-neglected Treaties and trust agreements with the Sioux Nation. I particularly appeal to Jill Stein and the Green Parties of the US and the world to join this struggle by calling for my release and adopting the UNDRIP as the new legal framework for relations with indigenous peoples.

Finally, I also urge my supporters to immediately and urgently call upon President Obama to grant my petition for clemency, to permit me to live my final years on the Turtle Mountain Reservation. Scholars, political grassroots leaders, humanitarians and Nobel Peace Laureates have demanded my release for more than four decades. My Clemency Petition asks President Obama to commute, or end, my prison term now in order for our nation to make progress healing its fractured relations with Native communities. By facing and addressing the injustices of the past, together we can build a better future for our children and our children's children.

Again, my heartfelt thanks to all of you for working together to protect the water. Water is Life.

In the Spirit of Crazy Horse,
Leonard Peltier

TWENTY-EIGHT

FREE ALABAMA MOVEMENT

Let the Crops Rot in the Field (2018)

ON THE 45TH ANNIVERSARY OF THE ATTICA PRISON uprising, members of the Free Alabama Movement (FAM) operating out of the solitary confinement unit in St. Clair Correctional Facility in Springfield, Alabama, called a nationwide strike to protest their unpaid slave labor. The protest that took place as a result involved more than 24,000 incarcerated men and women—the largest labor-related prison strike in history. FAM's statement pays homage to a mélange of movements and insurgent practices, including radical labor, anti-capitalist formations, the great Black radical tradition, and, using Joy James's formulation, the incarcerated Black radical tradition. Although they don't reference W. E. B. Du Bois directly, the collective clearly draws inspiration from his 1935 opus, *Black Reconstruction in America,* which examines the political economy of slaves and newly freed Black people. Because exploiting prisoners' labor is vital to the oppressive system, withholding that labor is vital to abolitionist resistance. The authors note that "letting the crops rot in the field is a proven strategy that was passed down to us from our Ancestors from the slave plantations that was used to disrupt the economics of the field." Through economic revolt, prisoner-slaves are strengthened by recognizing the power of their labor. The Alabama strikers unified around the class conditions common to all trapped in the carceral system. Their tactics emphasize that economic engagement provides points of leverage. Such tactics, moreover, can be waged by movement communities on both sides of the wall.

LET THE CROPS ROT IN THE FIELD

AFTER A period of over 40 years of an accelerated rate of incarceration, the issue of Mass Incarceration and Prison Slavery have now reached its crescendo.

[This has been] spurred on by factors that included racism, capitalism, free labor, and a politically motivated desire to provide jobs to a valued voting block of rural, conservative white citizens by building prisons in rural and agricultural areas that had been decimated by the Industrial Revolution and the outsourcing of jobs to China, India, Indonesia, etc.

Then, once the prisons were built, the government manufactured a "war on drugs" designed to fill those newly built prisons with black, brown and poor whites who had been rendered unemployable by corporate downsizing and outsourcing in the early 1970s, and who were considered a strain on social programs, unwanted competitors for limited jobs, and ideal candidates for corporations that needed a large labor pool for forced slave labor.

Mass incarceration has now culminated in a for-profit Prison Industrialized Complex that now holds over 2.5 million men, women and children hostage for the sole and exclusive purpose of exploitation and free labor.

Today, [in] January 2015, the people in America's prisons, mostly black, brown (and white), and all poor, now make up a free (or penny wages) labor force for a 500-billion-dollar-per-year industry that is producing a range of products and providing services so broad and extensive that it touches every area of the US economy.

Virtually EVERY person in prison, our families, friends and supporters, and even every organization that states that they are against mass incarceration prison slavery, are all contributing financially to the very companies that are exploiting the people through mass incarceration and prison slavery.

Have you eaten at McDonald's or Wendy's lately? Shopped at Walmart or Victoria's Secret? How about that Dell computer? Have you used a customer service center? Where do you bank at, Wells Fargo? Are you in the military? Have you seen a soldier in that finely stitched uniform with night vision goggles? Do you work for a State University or agency that gets its furniture repaired somewhere?? Or that purchases large amounts of cleaning supplies, or hand-made brooms, mops, etc.? How many of these companies do you do business with?

Well, if you get up out of bed and do anything more than breathe, chances are you contribute to the bottom line of a company that is engaged in warehousing millions of people for exploitation through mass incarceration and prison slavery.

"Prison labor—with no union protection, overtime pay, vacation days, pensions, benefits, health and safety protection, or Social Security withholding—also makes complex components for McDonnell Douglas/Boeing's F-15 fighter aircraft, the General Dynamics/Lockheed Martin F-16, and Bell/Textron's Cobra helicopter. Prison labor produces night-vision goggles, body armor, camouflage uniforms, radio and communication devices, and lighting systems and components for 30-mm to 300-mm battleship anti-aircraft guns, along with land mine sweepers and electro-optical equipment for the BAE Systems Bradley Fighting Vehicle's laser rangefinder. Prisoners recycle toxic electronic equipment and overhaul military vehicles."[26] [...]

Don't Trust the Mainstream Media

All across America, one can't turn on the news, read a newspaper, or follow social media without seeing that mass incarceration and prison slavery ("corrections" or "prisons" in mainstream terms) have become a national problem. The 'problem' though, as being reported in the mainstream media (MSM), is not about the human devastation that mass incarceration has wrought, but about the costs associated with maintaining budgets to keep so many people in prison.

The mainstream media, which is controlled by the business elite no less than our current politicians, are reporting on this "problem," but with no real solutions being offered.

CAUTION: I must add that the reason the MSM is reporting on this issue is because the prison profiteers are promoting a "reform" plan to the public that in reality is a new scheme that has been thoroughly exposed by N. Heitzeg and K. Whitlock in their Smoke and Mirrors series,[27] to expand the privatized prison industry directly into the communities with community corrections, privatized parole/probation, drug rehabilitation centers, traffic court, and more, with the sole purpose of releasing low-level offenders, who will then be required to pay a ransom to enjoy a semblance of freedom.

Simply stated, every facet of the criminal justice enterprise will be contracted out to private for-profit businesses, and the human traffickers who own these businesses will become the new slave masters. The businessmen and women will make their campaign contributions, the politicians will ensure that the laws are in place, the police [will] make the arrest, the prosecutors and judges will guarantee the convictions, and the prisoner will be a slave.

The New Strategy: Using Direct Economic Action to Affect Change

When determining the best strategy to challenge Mass Incarceration and Prison Slavery, it is essential that we step back and take a look at the entire system. We must identify the fundamentals of what makes this system work and why this system exists. Once we thoroughly understand the underpinnings of the system of Mass Incarceration we can begin to see why the old strategies and tactics have not [brought] and will not bring about any meaningful change. Then we can begin developing a New Strategy that attacks Mass Incarceration at its core.

Just like the institution of chattel slavery, mass incarceration is in essence an economic system which uses human beings as its nuts and bolts. Therefore, our new approach must be economically based, and must be focused on the factors of production—the people being forced into this slave labor.

Our Three-Part Strategy

1. Organize prison shutdowns at prisons with major economic industries (tag plants, fleet services, food distribution centers, agriculture, etc.)
2. Call for a nationwide leaflet campaign, protests, and boycotts of McDonald's restaurants, which is one of the major corporations that has a national presence and that benefits from prison slavery, in addition to others like Walmart, Victoria's Secret, AT&T, Wells Fargo banks, Wendy's, GEO/CCA private prison companies that are listed on the NYSE, and more.
3. [Have] our families, friends, supporters, activists, and others [hold] protests at the prisons where the people are mass incarcerated and oppressed.

Part 1: Shutdowns/Work Strikes

1. Organize prison shutdowns at prisons with major economic industries (tag plants, fleet services, food distribution centers, agriculture, etc.).

Remember, we are working against a half-trillion-dollar system that is controlled by businessmen and women who are modern-day slave profiteers. And just like any business, their focus is on the bottom line. From this viewpoint, we must organize work stoppages at prisons with economic industries that are operated by slave labor. The impact of a work stoppage is immediate and significant, as production is shut down and profit margins plummet around the country.

Believe me, if you want to have commissioners, politicians and the like hunting you down, organize a strike. You won't have to call them, because they will call you. Prison industry is more than just license plates. Now it includes military, food, clothes, mining, recycling, call centers, car parts, cleaning supplies, printing, and so much more.

And when we organize, we have to demand that real "reforms" take place that will afford everyone an opportunity to earn our freedom, NOT JUST EARN A CHECK FOR OUR LABOR, and that fundamental changes be made throughout the system.

Experience has shown us at FREE ALABAMA MOVEMENT that this approach is more effective than hunger strikes, marching and writing letters combined, as those strategies will only bring publicity, lip service and some changes, while work stoppages shut down the entire economic system and gets directly into their pockets, which brings the movers and shakers to the prison for negotiations.

Part 2: McDonald's

Ronald McDonald: A Slavery Master in Clown's Clothing !!!!

When deciding on which company to protest we have to devise a strategy that we can use nationwide: We can't boycott all companies because there are simply too many corporations involved. What we have to do is focus on just one of them at a time that uses prison slave labor and that is large enough and visible enough to bring a true awareness about prison slavery, and target that one.

Starting off we have identified McDonald's as a company that presents itself as family-oriented, but which uses prison slavery to produce a number of goods:

"McDonald's uses inmates to produce frozen foods. Inmates process beef for patties. They may also process bread, milk and chicken products."[28]

We will start off our McDonald's protest by locating and reaching out to the people in the prisons where McDonald's products are produced. At the same time, we will begin letter-writing campaigns to their investors and shareholders, while also leaving leaflets/pamphlets on the cars of their customers at McDonald's restaurants nationwide, and organize protests at their storefronts, in a mall or headquarters, or wherever we can, and call for boycotts of their stores to force them to stop using products that are manufactured by forced prison slave labor.

But we focus all of our attention on one corporation at a time, instead of using a scattered approach of multiple [organizations] spread out thinly over several corporate fronts.

When one falls, we move on to the next prison profiteer, which can be Victoria's Secret, Walmart, GEO, CCA, JPay, Keefe, or something.

Part 3: Consolidating Our Resources

HAVING OUR FAMILIES, FRIENDS, ACTIVISTS, AND SUPPORTERS ALL GALVANIZED AT A SELECT PRISON TO ENGAGE IN PROTESTS AND TO SHOW SUPPORT FOR THE PEOPLE ON THE INSIDE WHO ARE BEING OPPRESSED

This strategic move is just as important as the strikes, because it brings all of the people together who oppose mass incarceration and prison slavery. We can't have a unified Movement Against Mass Incarceration and Prison Slavery if we are in a long-distance relationship with our supporters, organizers, activists and others who support our cause. We have to get everyone organized at the prisons, so that we can confront the system at the site of its oppression: the prisons.

By having our supporters in one location for each State, we maximize our resources, increase our strength in numbers, and we move with a unified front.

Very little can be done by the State at this point except to meet our demands.

The protests against police brutality are taking place at police stations. The workers at Walmart are protesting at Walmart. The Occupy Wall Street Movement protested on Wall Street. Therefore, the Movement and fight against mass incarceration must take place at the prisons!

"The Old Way"

Now, let's take a look at the familiar strategies of Movement Against Mass Incarceration and Prison Slavery, and see why we need a change in strategy:

1. Hunger strikes
2. Marches and protests at state capitols (as opposed to demonstrations at the prisons where they should be)
3. Letter-writing campaigns, petitions and phone calls, etc.

1) HUNGER STRIKES

The demonstrations put on by the men and women in California (and Georgia, Washington State, and Texas) showed us all that with leadership and unity, we can defeat mass incarceration with the right strategy. But we also learned that, while we did see progress in some areas, it has a minimal impact on the system of mass incarceration.

We have to strategize with the understanding that we are dealing with modern-day slave profiteers. These businessmen will gladly let us die from starvation so long as their assembly lines keep moving.

"Leasing convicts to private businesses made a tidy fortune for both state and local governments, especially after slaves were emancipated. In 1878, 73 percent of Alabama's entire state revenue came from prison labor. Reconstruction-era plantation owners, though, were hardly incentivized to care about their charges: When any of their starving workers died, they simply asked the state for new ones, at no cost to their bottom line."[29]

The net effect on the bottom line from a hunger strike is negligible. This is not going to get the response we need, so we have to do more.

2) MARCHES

Sure, the traditional marches bring attention to issues and they bring people together, but they simply don't bring about much results. If we must march, then let's march at the prisons where mass incarceration and prison slavery are taking place at.

As I said above, when the people protest against police brutality in Ferguson, Memphis, and California, they are doing it at the police stations.

When "BANTHEBOAT" activists protested in support of Palestine, they protested at ports. We have to ask ourselves: If we are protesting against mass incarceration and prison slavery, then why aren't we doing it at the prisons where our economic strength can be felt?

Just like we saw in California with the hunger strikes, the families and supporters showed their support at the prison. The people in the prisons can see that support and receive the boost in morale that will be needed to carry this thing through. The meeting place is at the prisons!

3) LETTER WRITING, PETITIONS, ETC.

Letter-writing campaigns and making phone calls are still effective, but we have to change who we are targeting and what we are attempting to communicate.

Letters/calls help when [targeting] alternative media sources and other activists, organizations and supporters of our Movement, to let them know that we are striking so that we can inform other prisons in other states, so that they can join in also.

Letters/petitions also help when we target companies that are using prison-made goods to let them know that we will boycott them if they don't stop, and it also helps to contact their customers and let them know that they are purchasing slave-made goods. But the old habit of writing politicians and commissioners won't work in today's world, and just [hasn't] produced meaningful results.

It's time to find a new target audience and bring attention to a new strategy and a new message!!

Is the Current Movement against Mass Incarceration Spread Too Thin?

In F.A.M. we strategize around bringing all of the forces and resources together from each individual state into one collective whole. Groups that are fighting against the death penalty, solitary confinement, children in prison, voting rights, mentally ill people in prison, free labor, disenfranchisement, parole reform, and a few other issues. We will address all of these issues in our "FREEDOM BILL," so everyone and every organization that is fighting against these issues should all be fighting together.

Note: Each state should draft their own FREEDOM BILL.

The best way that we see to do this in Alabama is to identify the most economically important prison(s) in Alabama, and start organizing shutdowns until all of the strategically important prisons are shut down. One main prison will serve as the "headquarters" for our families, organizers and supporters, etc. At that point, the negotiations begin as to how to tear down the system of exploitation and create a new system based on the structure as outlined in the FREEDOM BILL, which promotes Education, Rehabilitation and Re-Entry Preparedness.

Take for example the situation that just occurred in California with the various lawsuits that the state fought for over 20 years (see the Plata decision by the US Supreme Court) and passage of the Proposition 47 law that went into effect. Despite the fact of California's prison system being overcrowded with a 160 percent occupancy rate, the state's prison officials and Attorney General's office still refused to budge on releasing people who were eligible.

"Most of those prisoners now work as groundskeepers, janitors and in prison kitchens, with wages that range from 8 cents to 37 cents per hour. Lawyers for Attorney General Kamala Harris had argued in court that if forced to release these inmates early, prisons would lose an important labor pool.

"Prisoners' lawyers countered that the corrections department could hire public employees to do the work."[30]

As for the firefighters, the Attorney General's Office concluded that these men who risked their lives for the state, who saved the state over $1,000,000,000—one billion dollars—annually, were simply too valuable a commodity to release, even though these men worked outside of prison every day and were clearly not a threat to society anymore:

"About half of the people fighting wildland fires on the ground for the California Department of Forestry and Fire Protection (Cal Fire) are incarcerated: over 4,400 prisoners, housed at 42 inmate fire camps, including three for women.

"Together, says Capt. Jorge Santana, the California Department of Corrections & Rehabilitation (CDCR) liaison who supervises the camps, they save the state over $1 billion a year."[31]

While it is extremely rare to receive these types of admissions from the state, what we witnessed in the California litigation is the reality of modern slavery: Yes, the people have an education and are already working in society, but, NO!, they can't be released because it would cost too much to replace their free or penny labor!

This episode highlights why the strategy of work strikes/shutdowns being promoted by FREE ALABAMA MOVEMENT, and now joined by FREE MISSISSIPPI MOVEMENT, is the key to bringing the system of mass incarceration and prison slavery to its death: If we are [being] held solely for our labor and exploitation even after educating and rehabilitating ourselves, then why should we continue to work? If the firefighters in California can't be freed because they save the state a billion dollars that they don't otherwise have, then why don't the firefighters go on a work strike? The fires will continue to burn until they either come up with one billion dollars to train other firefighters, or they can release them and then hire them to do the job at prevailing wages.

Also please note that the state is saving one billion dollars just on the firefighters alone. How much more pressure would a work strike/shutdown put on the CDCR or any other prison system, when all the kitchen workers go on strike?

All the maintenance and electrical workers? All the garbage workers? The yard crew? Gym and library workers? And then the BIG whammy, when ALL of the factory and farm workers in prisons go on strike at one time, and this strike is spread regionally and nationally?

The financial numbers and fallout from such a strike will be felt from Wall Street to Main Street, and every street in between. This is the power of economics at play, and this strategy is the only strategy that will stop mass incarceration in its tracks.

WE MUST LET THE CROPS ROT IN THE FIELD IF WE AREN'T RECEIVING BENEFIT OF THE HARVEST

LET THE CROPS ROT IN THE FIELD is a proven strategy that was passed down to us from our ancestors from the slave plantations that was used to disrupt the economics of the field. The harvest of the planter season was reaped when the crops were picked from the field and sold on the open market. When the slave master had invested all that he owned into his next crop (prison factories), the slaves would wait until just before the harvest and rebel against the slave system by going on strike and causing the crops to rot in the field. This tactic would completely ruin the slave master's investment.

While these crops were rotting in the field, the slave master would come down from the big house, make nice and beg the slaves to go back to work

But when that didn't work, the slave master, just like the modern prison commissioners and wardens, would then result to threats and violence. But those determined for their freedom would resist and fight to the end.

In the end, when the crops were left to rot in the field, the slave master would sometimes lose his plantation if he had used it as collateral to secure a loan from the bank to plant.

This is what happens to a prison system that is built upon the exploitation and free labor of the people incarcerated: when the laborers stop working, the free labor prison system collapses because there isn't any revenue coming in to finance the system of 30,000 people in Alabama, 23,000 in Mississippi, 160,000 in California, or 2.5 million nationwide, who still must be fed, still must be provided medical care, still must have lights, water, and basic hygiene.

These obligations and costs don't stop, but the means to pay for them—the revenue that is produced by our labor—stops when we stop.

In 2014, Alabama has a 400-million-dollar budget to run its prisons, which is paid by the sale of the products and services that are manufactured by the slave labor from the people incarcerated.

All told, Alabama is making anywhere from two to three billion dollars each year from our labor, fines, fees, canteen, phone calls, etc. while over $500,000,000,000 dollars is made nationwide off of prison slave labor.

If we are to end Mass Incarceration and Prison Slavery, which only those caught up in the slave system can do, then we must unify nationwide from inside of these prisons and we must stop our labor and LET THE CROPS ROT IN THE FIELD.

TWENTY-NINE

ED MEAD

Men against Sexism (2023)

ED MEAD, A DEDICATED MEMBER OF THE GEORGE Jackson Brigade, spent eighteen years locked up for the crime of bank robbery, but depending on your political interpretation, you might consider it "bank expropriation." Mead, born in California in 1941, identified as a "godless commie" and "political faggot," and in the following essay he writes about his experiences organizing in Walla Walla State Prison, which followed many years in and out of various prisons since his working-class youth. These earlier stretches of incarceration increased feelings of alienation and anger, and unsurprisingly had a criminogenic impact rather than a rehabilitative one. Mead's life changed profoundly when he stopped identifying as a criminal and started identifying as a radical. His political perspective evolved throughout the 1960s and '70s in the context of deep political unrest, and recognizes armed conflict as a tactic that can at times enable revolutionary movements to win political gains against the forces of empire. He helped found the George Jackson Brigade, which took ideological guidance not only from Jackson but also from many other anti-imperialist thinkers and movements. His prison organizing provides useful lessons for the incarcerated and non-incarcerated alike. Mead's reflections on solidarity, ideological grounding, and serving the most oppressed prisoners, as well as a step-by-step blueprint for prison organizing are some of the gems found within this remarkable account of how incarcerated human beings at Walla Walla Prison came together to create the first openly gay prisoners' organization to be officially recognized by a prison administration.

During a July 2023 interview Mead emphasized the importance of studying historical materialism as the foundation to understanding how to organize in tough places.[32] When it came to Walla Walla Prison, the biggest issue among prisoners was not the power dynamics caused by racial tension but rather the ones caused by sexual violence. Says Mead, "You have to know who you can unite, and how you would go about uniting them. What are the forces opposing you? What are the forces in your favor? Where can you gain an advantage? Those kinds of things, the contradictions, the non-antagonistic contradictions between you and your peers. As well as the antagonistic contradictions between you and your peers and those who are holding you against your will at gunpoint. Now, that might seem to be a pretty easy nut to crack, but you'd be surprised how many prisoners are unable to crack it on their own." Mead passed away shortly before *Beneath the Mountain* went to press. We regret he did not live long enough to hold this book in his hands and are honored to include his words and wisdom.

MEN AGAINST SEXISM

In 1977 the group Men Against Sexism was organized at the Washington State Penitentiary in Walla Walla, Washington. It was the first—and to my knowledge, the only—openly gay organization inside prison walls. What follows is the story of how the group came to be. This is a heavily edited version of a chapter from my book Lumpen. *The original piece is around 33 pages. Accordingly, if the article seems disjointed in places, blame me for poor editing.*

—ED MEAD

THERE WERE between sixteen and seventeen hundred prisoners in the population at the State Penitentiary at Walla Walla back in the day. It was a place where prisoner-on-prisoner rape was rampant. Weaker prisoners were being routinely bought and sold like chattel by the strong; the young and vulnerable ones were raped and then subjected to forced prostitution. It was through this process that stronger prisoners established themselves on the prison's pecking order. Straight prisoners were not going to put their personal safety and status on the line for a bunch of queers. And for the most part gay prisoners were not able to stand up for themselves. The gay population was too demoralized and defeated to stand up for themselves. I became aware of this problem when I first entered the prison.

Because I had been a member of the George Jackson Brigade (GJB) I was immediately placed in segregation upon my arrival at the penitentiary. Being booked into the segregation unit with me was a young prisoner. We did not talk as we were both caught up in our respective dramas of being booked into the unit. He was placed in cell 11 on B tier of Big Red, the name prisoners gave to the segregation unit (it was constructed with red bricks). I was put in the cell next to him, in cell 10. That night a gang of around six predators, with the help of a guard operating the lockbox at the end of the tier, tried to get into my neighbor's cell so they could rape him. He was able to block his door from opening. The rapists failed that night.

The next morning, when I was out of my cell an hour to shower and exercise, I spoke to other prisoners on the tier. One influential old-timer told me that the kid was a punk, and besides, that's the way it is and has always been. His attitude was that if the kid was not having it taken, he'd be giving it away.

While I was on the streets the GJB broke into the headquarters of the Department of Corrections and planted a powerful bomb under the director's desk. The blast did structural damage to the five-story building. We put out a communique saying the bombing was done to focus attention on the segregation prisoners who were being brutalized as a result of their struggle for democracy. I soon learned the victims of that brutalization were living with me on B tier. After talking with these other prisoners, the attempted rapes stopped. The struggle against segregation began. We called ourselves the Walla Walla Brothers. We won the segregation battle. Which is a whole other story.

I was released to Eight Wing. The cells were designed for two people, but they all contained four men. We survivors of the Big Red struggle had our own cell, which was "owned" by Danny Atteberry (we were Danny, Joe Green, Mark Larue, and me, all survivors of the seg struggle). We had a close friend named Blue; after the seg struggle we had a lot of friends. While the decisions we made were not as conscious and straightforward as I might make them sound, those of us in the cell did manage to slowly develop an agenda of sorts. We were going to work with the prison group approved by the warden, called the Resident Government Council (RGC). We would have the RGC sponsor [a] sub-group called the Prison Justice Committee (PJC). The Seattle branch of the American Friends Service Committee (AFSC), a Quaker church group with a long and progressive tradition of involvement in prison issues, agreed to support our organizing efforts.

Building the Prison Justice Committee was not a very difficult task. We were to some extent leaders of the recently victorious 47-day work strike, the longest prison work strike in US history. And I was the guy who bombed the headquarters of the Department of Corrections in the State Capitol over the brutalization of Walla Walla's segregation prisoners. If we believed that an arm of the RGC should be formed that called itself the Prison Justice Committee, then influential members of the population would be more than happy to support the proposal. Most prisoners agreed that it was important to build upon and consolidate the gains and promises achieved as a result of the strike, and that's what the PJC was trying to do.

Leading the PJC was a former segregation graduate named Eddwynn Jordan. He and his two brothers were well respected members of the black prison population. Regular meetings were soon established. From the very start attendance at PJC meetings exceeded that of its parent organization, the RGC. Within a month the PJC was the prisoners' group at the Walls. One of the first things we did was to break ourselves down into much smaller sub-committees, each of which was assigned the responsibility for monitoring specified aspects of the prison experience. On top of that, we had outside guests coming into the prison each week to hold joint meetings with us and to work with us around various prison-related issues.

Just as prisoners in general became increasingly involved in the activities of the PJC, so too did gay and some of the other more vulnerable prisoners. They did not become PJC supporters out of a need for protection, but rather because the group took a firm stand not only against racism, but also against all forms of sexism and homophobia. It was an organization that related to the special needs of gay prisoners. It provided hope for constructive change. Before too long the PJC formed yet another sub-committee, with me as its chairperson, which I called Men Against Sexism (MAS).

The Resident Government Council (RGC) was an officially sponsored group; the PJC was an offspring of the RGC and therefore enjoyed some measure of respectability in the eyes of our captors. Similarly, MAS, because of its relationship to the PJC, while certainly not respectable, did possess a degree of legitimacy sufficient to keep the pigs' boot off our necks for long enough for us to stand on our own two feet. I don't think MAS would have survived that initial phase of development had we not existed under the protective wing of the PJC.

The PJC did its work well and continued to grow; before too long the group was able to cut all ties with the RGC. Now formally sanctioned by the prison administration, given its own meeting space, and with the AFSC as its primary source of outside support, the PJC became an independent organization. The PJC held its weekly meetings in a room on the second floor of the admissions building. This is where our outside guests would come into the prison and regularly meet with us. At these joint gatherings, each sub-director would give a report on the status of the work the sub-committee was doing. The sub-committee on visitation, for example, would report on the progress being made in that area, such as problems with the visiting room staff, expanding the visiting area, the conjugal visitation issues, and so on. I think there were about six different sub-committees, each dealing with issues ranging from racism to legislative action. The MAS sub-committee started out like all the others, but then seemed to quickly develop a life all its own. MAS's membership soon grew to be half the size of the PJC, then grew some more until we slightly outnumbered our parent organization. This difference in growth did not at first create any problems, since we were all marching to the beat of the same drummer.

MAS started having its own separate meetings in the PJC's office (in addition to the weekly PJC gatherings), and at these smaller meetings we invited people from Seattle's gay and lesbian communities inside to meet with us. Before too long firm friendships had been struck between the inside and out. At the same time, we were busily conducting MAS types of activities, which in large part centered on building a sense of pride and community within the walls. This was accomplished through both propaganda and deeds.

There was a rarely published underground newsletter at the penitentiary called *The Bomb,* usually printed only when someone in the population thought it necessary to make a call-to-arms against the administration. We started a monthly newsletter and called it *The Lady Finger* (referring to a very small firecracker). In addition to addressing general issues of sexism and containing news of interest to gays and the somewhat advanced social prisoners, the newsletter was a broadside against the scumbags who were involved in the ongoing rape and the buying and selling of prisoners. Using the PJC's name on my memos, I was able to obtain and screen documentary films with titles like *Men and Masculinity* and anti–Vietnam War themes. We merely had to pay for the postage and insurance costs.

A typical MAS action during this period would be calculated to strengthen gay unity while at the same time working to isolate and expose those powerful elements within the population who believed it was their god-given right to rob, rape, and otherwise pillage their peers. The process was a slow one. If we stuck our collective neck out too far someone would chop it off.

Here is an example of the type of action we'd do back then. There was a nationwide religious organization that primarily ministered to the spiritual needs of gays, called the Metropolitan Community Church. Over a period of time, we had managed to obtain authorization from the administration for an MCC chaplain to come inside the prison and to hold regular services in the prison's chapel. The Catholic priest had no problem with this.

The Protestant preacher, however, who was a right-wing, born-again fundamentalist and Christian nationalist, stooped to petty acts of sabotage against the MCC minister and his congregation. One Sunday morning a prisoner came running up to me and said, Preacher Pig Shit (not his real name) is going to do a sermon this morning on the evils of homosexuality, and specifically targeting the MCC services. I immediately sent runners out to spread the alarm to gays in every cell block; my message was that all MAS members were to attend Protestant services that morning and to be ready to be outrageous.

We were a pretty sight as about twenty of us queers quietly sat in the conservative church that morning, waiting for services to begin. I wore shoulder-length blond hair, with lavender stars for earrings. Others wore facial make up or were in full drag, including colorful dresses. Our quickly arrived at consensus was that our mere presence would be enough to restrain the preacher's bigotry. We were wrong. He started in on the MCC and the evils of homosexuality in general, preaching what a travesty it was that queers would defile the house of the lord with their so-called religion. That was enough for me. He no more than got that filth out of his mouth when I interrupted his diatribe with a speech on the value of religious freedom and tolerance. The other MAS members chimed in with their support for what I was saying. His usual congregation of five or six protective custody candidates and would-be child molesters remained prudently silent, no doubt intimidated by the sight of so many angry faggots.

When the issue was put in a rights context, rather than a religious or moral one, I managed to make the preacher at least pretend to see that his efforts to prevent our chaplain from coming in and conducting services was a denial of our religious freedoms. I made it clear that we would fight hard to defend that freedom. The confrontation seemed to take the wind from his sails. We had no problems with him from then on. After that incident gays seemed to walk around with their heads held a little higher, and with a bit more pride than usual.

As a communist I am of course an atheist. But being a godless commie did not prevent me from defending the democratic right of MAS members to religious freedom. And I exercised that right myself by personally attending each and every MCC service that was conducted at Walla Walla. Wherever you find people who are oppressed and exploited you will find communists there to help them. We defend the rights of poor and working people.

Like the PJC, MAS was also made up of sub-committees dedicated to specific tasks of interest to the gay community on the inside. One such committee worked on getting sewing machines donated, which MAS would use to repair and make clothing for the population. That was a very successful campaign. Another sub-committee was escort duty for the elderly. The commissary shack was where prisoners went to buy their zoos and wham-whams (snacks, personal care items, etc.). It was located in a relatively remote area of the prison. Predators would lay in wait between the cell houses and the commissary shack, looking to rob the weak and elderly of their commissary. We escorted the old convicts from the commissary shack to their cells.

Men Against Sexism continued to build in size and grow in strength. We found safe-cells for victims of rape and physical violence against the weak. We slowly moved in the direction of what we called crisis intervention. A young pedophile named Steve had recently arrived at the prison and was promptly snatched up by predators. When they were done "using" him he was sold into a different cell for three hundred dollars. Where before our intervention tended to come after the incident and would take the form of hand-holding types of support. Now we were moving into the area of direct meddling with the behavior of the prison's *tougheoisie* (tough-wah-zee).

With a combination of bluff and bluster, moral persuasion and dumb luck, we extracted the pedophile from his state of sexual bondage and moved him into one of our safe cells. There was much outrage over this in certain circles. A day or two later I was accosted in the mess hall by one of the tough guys, how, he demanded to know, could I possibly justify standing against solid convicts over a stinking child molester? I stood by my principles and in the end managed to hold firm against the shifting tides of prisoner opinion. We'd lost some support in the population, but won Steve's freedom from sexual slavery.

But the fight was an ongoing one. For every situation we were able to deal with, there seemed to be two others that were beyond our strength to resolve. And so it was that work developed to the point of confrontation with some predatory rapists. We were going to have to fight or back off—that was clear to everyone in the MAS leadership.

At the next Prison Justice Committee meeting, when MAS gave its weekly progress report, I asked for PJC support in a conflict that MAS was about to have with a group of obstinate prisoners over the rape issue. Some other prisoners had captured and enslaved some kid for sexual purposes. We'd talked and manipulated until we were blue in the face, without success. Violence was the next option. It was my feeling that the more of us who confronted them, the less likely it would be that physical conflict would be necessary.

The PJC would not back our play, saying it was a matter for us to resolve on our own. In retrospect they were probably right. Blacks must be their own liberators, just as gays must free themselves. As appealing as the prospect is, we cannot rely on anyone else to do our fighting for us. But at the time we did not see it that way; we were outraged that our parent organization would cut us loose to fend for ourselves in the violent seas that surrounded us. MAS thereupon quit the PJC. The breakup was a rather acrimonious one. MAS was reduced to an underground group. Without a sponsoring group we could no longer bring in our outside support folks. Yet our inside membership was still intact.

The "breezeway" was a term I'd not heard of before my arrival at the Walls. There were a number of these roofed walkways at the penitentiary, only these, unlike those on the streets, had chain-link fencing from top to bottom on each side. Walking from the block to the mess hall, for example, required one to traverse one of these open tunnels both ways. It was on these breezeways that much of the violence took place. In fact, there were so many stabbings in one area of the breezeway that it became known as "Blood Alley" by both prisoners and guards. The breezeway was the place of choice for prison hustlers to hang out. They would sell used street clothing, drugs, and even pimp their punks from these areas. The breezeway was, in short, a commercial and social hangout for much of the joint's riffraff. And MAS was no exception. In the absence of an office, we met with each other and conducted the group's day-to-day business from the breezeway.

The entire prison was not dirty and ugly; there was a lone lovely island of beauty and tranquility in the form of Lifer's Park. Set on two sides by huge cellblocks, Seven Wing on one side and Eight Wing on the other, and a breezeway fence in front and the lifers' clubhouse in the rear, the park was an exclusive island of manicured grass and carefully cultured flowers. There was always an inmate guard at the gate leading to the park; no one got in unless they were a lifer or the escorted guest of a member. At the other end of their rectangular park was a large, two-story brick building. This was the lifers' clubhouse. The Lifer's Club was run by a large Black man named Tommy Thomas and his two white lieutenants, both of whom were young and tough. Tommy was a well-built ex-boxer who liked having sex with men.

Tommy fancied himself a progressive, on occasion going so far as to let it slip that he considered himself to be another George Jackson. While I found that laughable, I nonetheless tended to overestimate Tommy's level of political development. Tommy had ongoing problems with other elements of the population, like the Chicanos, but these were nothing he could not handle himself, should it ever come to that. Still, like any leader, he could always use additional strength. Tommy [...] wanted more political and military strength. MAS consisted mostly of people who liked doing sex with men, it had some strength, and it needed a home. An implicit agreement was reached. The Lifer's Club soon became the new, if unofficial, MAS headquarters.

MAS's eventual takeover of the Lifer's Club was not a sudden one, nor was it deliberate. We slowly started spending less time on the breezeway and more time in the comfort of Lifer's Park. Tommy made us feel welcomed. At a subsequent Lifer's meeting it was proposed that MAS, who had been orphaned by the mean ol' PJC, be loaned just a tiny little corner of the big Lifer's meeting room, and this only for as long as it took MAS to be recognized by the administration and given a space of its own. With MAS present and Tommy and his goons ramrodding the motion through, the membership somewhat agreed. We set up an office and from under the protective wing offered by the Lifers, we started inviting our outside guests back into the prison.

Lifer's and MAS members were also able to have sex with outsiders in a specially prepared downstairs room. It was a soundproof room that prisoners once used for reading books for the blind on cassette tapes. But at that point it was empty and unused, with only a mattress tossed on the floor. The members of the Lifer's would take their woman friends into the little room, MAS would take their men friends. I was lovers with a beautiful black man on the inside, and with Robert, who was a white leader of the gay community on the outside.

As attrition slowly took the officers of the Lifer's Club, by release, transfer or whatever, they would most often be replaced by MAS members. This was not because of some grand conspiracy or master plan, but simply because we were hard workers who did have the interests of the Lifer's Club at heart. Gradually, the line between the Lifer's and MAS blurred, in our minds as well as in the thinking of the other officers of the Lifer's Club. I was the chairperson of MAS, and Danny Atteberry, Mark La Rue, and Carl Harp were my officers. I was also the treasurer for the Lifer's, and Danny, Mark, and Carl were all on the Lifer's executive board as well. While I had all but lost sight of the distinction between the two groups, others, those on the outside of our gate, had not.

MAS had contributed a lot to the Lifer's Club. We implemented a candy sales program in which all prisoners could trade prison script money for our specialized candies. The candy business was highly successful. The Lifer's Club was making money for the first time in a long time. We bought a pool and foosball tables and other games for the members; we made many improvements to the club. I put an end to Tommy's looting of the club's treasury and made regular and accurate financial reports to the membership. Decisions on what to spend the profits on were democratically arrived at by the members. The Lifer's Club was doing better than at any time in recent history. MAS was doing well too. We'd obtained lots of support from Seattle's gay and lesbian communities and were in the process of pressuring the administration, both directly and indirectly, to recognize MAS and to provide us with a space of our own.

Rape had been all but stopped and prisoners were no longer being bought and sold. Nobody was particularly happy about this, except of course for the weak and vulnerable. Most other prisoners had not seen it as a problem. Worse, our having sex with each other and with male outsiders was freaking out many lifers. On the breezeway people started referring to the Lifer's Club as "the faggot club." I heard these complaints but felt we would have our own space before too much longer, and besides, we were doing a lot of good for the club itself—something lifers would eventually come to respect. We had made the club even nicer. What I didn't see was the new financial success of the Lifer's Club that made the opportunists want it back. And I must also confess to having paved the way for their return.

The time for the annual election of officers for the Lifer's Club was at hand. The prison's lifer population was being agitated by two dope fiends who pretty much ran the prison, Kenny and Al. Kenny was a heroin addict who was going to run for the office of Lifer president, and Al the tough rapist helped him by stirring things up against MAS in the population. It did not take me long to see that the lifer population was going to vote for Kenny. And it was also clear that once elected he would kick MAS out of the Lifer's Club.

On the surface all was civil and polite, but beneath the surface the struggle was [being waged]. The day-to-day pressure of this polite-to-your-face-stab-you-in-the-back became too much for Tommy. One night he and his two sidekicks went to the pigs and told them everything they wanted to know in exchange for a transfer to what was then the kids' joint at Shelton. The administration agreed. They were gone the next morning, and so was our weapons stash. There was MAS, now weaponless and by default in total control of the Lifer's Club.

There's an old Kenny Rogers song about gambling that has a line saying something like this, "you got to know when to hold 'em, know when to fold 'em, know when to walk away, and know when to run." It was time for MAS to fold 'em, to pack our bags, and walk away from the plush comfort of the Lifer's Club and back to the harsh realities of existence on the breezeway.

Nearly all MAS members came with me as I left the Lifer's Club. Danny, Blue, and Mark, most of the leadership, stayed behind. They were not going to run in the face of danger. They were not concerned with whether it was right or wrong for us to be there or whether it was politically correct for us to take a step back before advancing again. They were only concerned with losing face in the eyes of other prisoners. After the election Mark and Danny were driven out of Lifer's Park at knifepoint, with the loss of much face in the process. Blue, who was a lifer, quit MAS and became a part of the new Lifer's clique, or at least he was tolerated by them.

MAS went back to seeking sanctioning from the administration and its own meeting space. I gave up the position of MAS president, turning the job over to a more "respectable" person, a guy more likely to win recognition than my friends and I would have been. Buying and selling of weaker prisoners had been stopped, and rape had gone from a traditional test of manhood to a very rare incident. An unarmed MAS would do fine, and most of us would continue to be active in the group's meetings and activities.

What was permitted to develop was little more than a social club for gays. MAS started working on inoffensive projects like collecting newspapers for recycling [and] doing sewing and mending jobs for the population. We put forward a harmless face. Some thought we should have fought Kenny and Al over control of the Lifer's Club, but most of MAS's membership consisted of non-lifers who didn't belong there anyway. Besides, I did not want to hurt anyone. The bottom line was that we were unarmed and without allies. I had pretty much spent the political capital won as a result of the successful work strike.

There was always a high level of tension at the Walls. People were unceremoniously tossed out of their cells for one reason or another, and no other cells would be willing to take them in. There were frequent fights; stabbings took place often, and occasionally these would lead to death. Often the death could have been avoided had it not been for the incompetency of the prison's medical staff. I'll give you an example:

On May 23, 1978, a black prisoner named Robert Redwine was stabbed in the side by another black prisoner. The stabbing was over nothing of consequence—another senseless act of violence. The victim went to the prison hospital where he was given a cursory examination by a doctor who diagnosed the wounds as "superficial." The treatment did not include the standard practice of x-rays or probing the depths of the wounds. Redwine was sewn up and then locked in a hospital isolation room and left alone. After a while the victim started to protest by banging on the solid door at the front of his room, yelling for help from the hospital staff. His demands attracted the attention of one of the hospital porters, an inmate who inquired about the problem. Redwine told the porter that he was in pain and needed to see someone on the medical staff. When the porter delivered this information to

Chief Nurse Eva Nelson, he was told to ignore the victim's cries, as he was only "playing for drugs." The victim's cries went unanswered. He died alone and ignored, from internal bleeding. The doctor and Ms. Nelson were never so much as questioned or suffered any [...] consequence for their incompetence.

After many long months of work, including the submission of numerous proposals, revisions of those proposals, pressure from outside supporters, the dogged persistence of MAS workers, and the passage of time, the prison administration finally sanctioned our organization. This time we'd been on the breezeway for about two or three months. Now we were official. We were given a meeting space, which just happened to be the air-conditioned offices of some counselors who'd moved to another area of the prison. We thought we were in fat city. MAS was the first openly gay prisoner's organization to be officially recognized by a prison administration. As far as I know, no such group has been so recognized since then.

Our organized existence was the result of our determination as a group, the pre-AIDS era in which we existed, the strength of our community support, the good work we'd done on the inside, and of course the existence of the then relatively liberal prison administration. What official sanctioning meant to us, in addition to having a nice office to work from, was that we could once again invite our outside guests back into the prison. And bring them in we did. We'd have good meetings in our new office, with lots of singing songs together, hugs, and general closeness. One thing we did not do, however, is have sex in the office. There was always pressure from the social gays to exploit what we'd gained, using guests to smuggle drugs for us, or to turn tricks for the population in the club's new office. We always had to guard against these opportunistic tendencies. As far as I was concerned, if something was going to be smuggled into the prison, it would be explosives, not dope.

Prison is always a terrible place to be. But within that context the degree of terribleness can vary considerably from one day to the next. On some days, particularly when MAS was doing well, the relative level of pain was not too great. At times we were almost happy. At other times the fear and tension were so heavy in the air that we never knew from one hour to the next if we'd continue to live. There would be senseless killings, racial conflicts, and other forms of violence.

It was during one of these oppressive periods that Al raped a young kid in the Lifer's office. Rape had all but stopped taking place, and now here it was again, being rubbed in our faces by our old lifer foes. I began to wonder if the sickness of this place would ever be changed. We took the rape victim into our cell, as Mark had moved out and his bunk was still empty. Danny and I all tried our best to help heal the kid. The next day I had a talk with Al, who I found lounging about in front of the Biker's Club. When I confronted him over the rape he lied to me, saying the incident did not happen. Now what? I'd talked to the kid and knew all the intimate details surrounding the rape; I'd seen the youngster's bruises. He had no motivation to lie. I was inadequately armed for a showdown with Al and the growing gang of killers who now ran the Lifer's.

When tension built up in seg I would try to aim or direct prisoner anger against their captors and to educate them about the nature of their real enemies. Our cell tried to do the same thing with the whole population. The drug dealing and murders were getting out of hand. MAS would still escort older prisoners to and from the inmate store to keep them from being robbed, but others were victimized. It was going to take more than a finger in the dike to slow this flood of predatory behavior. We organized a prisoner work strike, putting all our effort into making it a success, only to discover that Kenny and Al had become the administration's first line of defense. They threw their energy into preventing the protest. They were successful, too. They had a vested interest in the status quo; their candy scam (the one MAS started) and other schemes were needed to support their growing heroin addiction. Their narrow self-interests led them to a consistent pattern of opportunism and collaboration with the pigs.

Our cell had knives, just as nearly every other cell did. Indeed, I always carried a 12-inch spring steel shank with me. But knives were not enough to meet the arms race that was taking place on the inside. Kenny and Al had a .38 caliber pistol, and information reached us that they were building bombs. The beatings, robberies, and killings that were going on, most of it directly or indirectly connected with Lifer's leadership as well as the violent mood of the whole prison, dictated that we also arm—for self-defense if for no other reason. We smuggled in a pistol with eighty rounds of ammunition. We also brought in four pounds of gunpowder, which we used in our homemade pipe bombs.

The construction of these bombs in the cell was a rather different experience. On the streets Brigade bombs were made by rotating teams—the bomb-maker and an assistant (or a trainee)—and for safety's sake everyone else would leave the house until the task was completed. Doing this job in the cell was a dangerous challenge. These bombs were electromechanical hand grenades. Flash bulbs wired in parallel were used as detonators. One of the wires coming out of the cap of the pipe (the nipple) was soldered to one pole of a small 9-volt battery then onto one side of a mechanical stopwatch. The other wire went to a small screw placed in the plastic face of the watch at the five second mark. In between all this wiring was a small automotive safety (toggle) switch. For safety's sake, all wiring connections were soldered.

If assembled properly, the bomb would not go off unless the safety switch was thrown into the "armed" position and the stopwatch activated, after which the user would have five seconds to dispose of the device before it exploded. Making these bombs in the cell was a unifying experience, one that required a great deal of trust among the cell's occupants. We used toilet paper, rolled up into tight doughnut-like balls and lit on fire to create heat for our little home-made soldering iron. There was much cooperation throughout the whole process. When we were finally done, we tore the guts out of my stereo radio and stashed the gun, ammunition, bombs, and related contraband inside of my huge boom box. While it took some time to gather all those materials and put them together, once it was finally done, we felt considerably more secure. We were now prepared to meet any emergency.

And an example of that sort of emergency soon materialized. The Chicano Club made a move on the joint's most attractive and desirable gay prisoner, a feminine appearing young homosexual I'll call Sally. Sally was not a member of MAS and was one of the few gays who had not contributed anything toward the building of the group. One day the leadership of the Chicanos snatched her up and told her she was theirs now. They told her she would be living with them and dancing in their club house. She had previously been living in a cell with a man of her choice. Upon learning of this, we older MAS officers went into the Chicano Club and tried to persuade them to free Sally. They told us to get our faggot asses out of their clubhouse.

Mark, Danny, and I discussed the situation and concluded we would go back into their club, fully armed with our gun, ammo, and three hand grenades. We would pull Sally out and then lay waste to everyone else in the club. We wanted our membership to see the road that needed to be taken.

I called an emergency meeting of all of MAS. With members assembled in our office I explained the situation. I told them we were going to fight for Sally. I did not tell them we had a gun and grenades; if anything, they probably thought we had knives. I told the members not to go into the Chicano Club. They were to gather in People's Park, an area well outside the Chicano Club and to demonstrate against sexual slavery. The membership did not know the true extent of the violence we were about to wage.

Mark, Danny and I were just about to walk from our office to the Chicano Club. Our common headset was to walk in and start killing the slavers—the time for talking was over. The gun and bombs were concealed on our bodies. As we were getting ready to march, Blue, who clearly saw that the attack was actually going to happen, said he wanted to give the Chicanos one more chance. I told him to be quick. He was. Upon his return he told us the situation was resolved. It was. Sally was promptly returned to her lover.

We packed up our weapons and went back to our cells. I never asked Blue what he told them. I didn't care. There was a near certainty in my mind that we would kill several people that afternoon. I saw it as necessary to deliver the message that rape and slavery would not be tolerated. I was fully prepared to write that message in the blood of my fellow prisoners. We escaped committing mass murder on that day, but there was always tomorrow. When I think about that afternoon today, I ponder the great educational value our trial would have been if we had killed a few of the slavers.

During this period we found it necessary to move bombs and to gather materials to make more. We briefly stored several small pipe casings in Sally's cell. We would later learn that she reported this fact to the pigs. We were prepared to kill and perhaps die for her right not to be forced into sexual slavery, and she rewarded us by turning our tools in to the prison administration. This kind of thing happened more than once in my life as a professional prisoner.

There was much we might have been able to do with MAS if given time and favorable circumstances. We had a liberal warden and liberal director of corrections in the state capitol. They didn't care what we did so long as we made them look good. If we had won control of the population, a big "if," we could have introduced mandatory reeducation classes for sex offenders, where they would study feminist literature and theory. They would not have to internalize it, but they would be required to adequately verbalize its subtleties. In male prisons anything feminine is demonized. Women are referred to a bitches, cunts, etc. On the inside, the worst thing you can call a man is one of these derogatory terms for women. That whole culture could have been reversed.

Classes on dialectical and historical materialism might have been offered, so as to help transform the prisons into universities of liberation. With the necessary strength, we would have started many vocational classes. The donated sewing machines were just a start. Tattooing was popular on the inside; we could have [had] tattoo artists come in and teach safe skills so prisoners could get work doing tattoos on the streets. We could have brought in computer nerds to teach building and maintaining computers, network administration, database management, spreadsheets, and word processing, high-demand skills prisoners could use to get decent paying jobs. It would cost less a year to make the prisoner a rocket scientist than it does to keep him in prison.

But instead, Danny, Mark, and I were subjected to involuntary out-of-state transfers to prisons in other states. Blue and some 50 others soon followed. I wound up in the federal prison in Marion, Illinois, a maximum-security facility constructed to replace the aging Alcatraz. While MAS accomplished a lot; it had the potential to achieve a great deal more.

THIRTY

SAFEAR NESS

Phone Resistance (2022)

A SINGLE SPARK CAN START A FIRE, AND SAFEAR Ness's account of a successful prison campaign around the issue of phone usage provides insurgent inspiration. Ness was born in 1990 in New Jersey and raised in Philadelphia. In this piece he sidesteps abstract ideology and platitudes, delivering practical strategies for winning basic freedoms through solidarity, avoiding "physical and interpersonal walls," minimizing administrative repercussions, and maximizing leverage from outside supporters. Ness advances the model of the hydra, a concept also identified by Russell "Maroon" Shoatz in "The Dragon and the Hydra," as a way to be innovative and undefeatable even when up against a formidable and intimidating opponent. Just as colonialists and oppressors have borrowed strategies from each other through the ages and fine-tuned their methods of domination and coercive power, so too do we share and refine models of resistance. Ness tells us, "Incarcerated people are not only separated from the free world, we are separated from each other." Yet he also demonstrates that the antidote to the alienation that results from such separation is solidarity. "Prison censorship is a nefarious tool that administrators use to keep incarcerated people from organizing," writes Ness, "and those outside from knowing we're always resisting." Politicized on the streets of Philadelphia during the height of the Occupy Movement, Safear Ness spent the first eleven years of his adult life in prison, where he became an abolitionist in part due to exposure to the writings of Martin Sostre and the mentoring of fellow prisoners. Since his release in 2023, he has been living in central Pennsylvania, where he writes and produces "In the Mix Prisoner Podcast" and organizes around issues of abolition. Free now, he no longer has to worry about the repercussions of his prison organizing. Writing this article put him in the hole. Therefore, the least we can do is read it, learn from it, and share it far and wide.

PHONE RESISTANCE

Could you live without your cell phone? How would you function? Most people in the free world couldn't imagine life without it. Prisoners don't have that privilege. Cell phones are prohibited in Pennsylvania State Prison. But for those locked away, there are few things more precious than the phone. It's mounted on the wall, costs a dollar for 15 minutes, and is limited to 20 numbers that must be pre-approved by the prison. Despite its limitations, it's our lifeline to the free world. We live our lives through it. Some get married on it, others divorced. Parents raise children. Children care for parents. We laugh, scream, and cry through the receiver. In prison, a phone is much more than a phone. The mission of the Pennsylvania Department of Corrections (PA DOC) is to "reduce criminal behavior by providing individualized treatment and education to offenders, resulting in successful community reintegration through accountability and positive change." The emptiness of their words is crushed by the hypocrisy of their actions. Studies show that one of the most effective means of decreasing recidivism is a strong support system and building connections in the community. While the PA DOC seems to support this in speech, their policy often reflects differently.

During the COVID-19 pandemic, in direct opposition to the mission of "successful community reintegration," the administration at SCI Fayette decided to limit incarcerated people to one 15-minute phone call per day. This essay is how a rainbow coalition of prisoners at Fayette fought the phone restriction policy. And how, despite the mountain of opposition, we won.

When the pandemic first started and prison officials restricted our movement, abolished the chow hall, canceled programming and confined us to our cells, we openly speculated that the prison would use this medical emergency to their advantage and continue these restrictions as a means of control.

As incarcerated people, our communication with the outside world mostly depended on phone calls and video visits. We struggled to maintain relationships with our loved ones on a limit of four 15-minute phone calls each day.

The administration at Fayette asked us to comply with COVID precautions to make the transition easy. Most of us were worried about catching the virus, so we complied. At that point violence among prisoners was almost non-existent. As time passed they told us to take the vaccine to open the prison back up. We were tired of being locked down so most of us complied with that too. Then they offered the booster. We took that too. After all that, the prison administration repaid us by implementing a new policy limiting us to just one 15-minute phone call per day.

News of the phone restriction first came from a video recording posted on a television channel the prison hosts. An administrator announced the new policy in a condescending tone. He claimed that he previously warned us that if we couldn't work out the phone situation ourselves that they would do it for us. He said they were still getting complaints. Now they were taking it into their own hands.

The policy was to implement a phone sign-up sheet. Each prisoner would be limited to sign up for one 15-minute slot during their recreational time each day. If there was time left, discretion would be left to the block sergeant to allow further use of the phone. There was no guarantee we could make more than one call.

But it was the administration that created the stressful phone environment in the first place. They split the block into cohorts, only allowing a limited amount of time for everyone to get on the phone. There were too many people, not enough phones, and not enough time. Instead of extending our time out, or adding more phones to the block, they decided to punish us for a situation they created.

I was heated. My comrades were furious. Everyone that used the phone, which is almost every prisoner, hated the idea of the upcoming restriction. We had already done the best we could to make the phone situation as safe as possible. We created our own phone lines. I was on three different blocks during the lockdown. On each block the lines would be long, and sometimes we couldn't get on at the exact time that we wanted, but everyone eventually had time to get on the phone more than once. To us, the administration was flexing their power. But what, if anything, could be done? Would we take this sitting down? Or would the people finally say enough is enough and stand up to fight?

Prison twitter was ablaze with speculation. A group of us understood that a revolution needs organizers. We had the anger of the people. Now we just needed to channel it. But we had to work fast. The administration announced that the restrictions would be implemented in about a week. First stage: planning.

The planning began with a small group of us housed together on the same block. We came from various social groups in the prison: Muslim, Christian, Black nationalist, white, and "gang" affiliated. Using our networks we checked the pulse of the people. Not a single person wanted the restriction. Most were ready to take a stand. There was a hurdle to overcome, however. Even amongst those ready, many expressed doubt whether other people would ride or if they [would] fold when the pressure came.

Our group quickly developed a plan of action. The public action itself was pretty straightforward: We would boycott the phone list and refuse to sign. We anticipated that the prison [might] counter by preventing us from using the phone so we decided we would boycott the phone altogether. If the restriction continued, we would then increase our resistance with a food boycott and send our trays back to the kitchen.

Most social groups have a leader or leaders that they look to for guidance. Some are explicitly labeled a leader, others act in that capacity without the title. Regardless, to be as effective as possible we targeted leaders of the various groups throughout the prison. Once we got them active in the resistance, they influenced others.

Spreading our message as a group to those with influence over large numbers of people allowed us to share some of the risk. Now there was an army of organizers. That made it much more difficult for the administration to identify the initial organizers. And even if they did by sending us to solitary confinement it wouldn't neutralize the resistance. It's not that we were leaderless. Instead, our leaders were embedded with the people, taking direction from the people, and directly accountable to them. This is called building a hydra. When you chop a dragon's head off, it dies. A hydra has multiple heads and when you chop one off, two more grow in its place.

A debate occurred over whether we should write a pamphlet to distribute. The writing would be a reminder to the people of all the things the prison had taken from us over the years, their plans for the phone restriction, and our plan to fight back with help from outside accomplices. It would serve as an encouragement to stand up to our oppressors. Some people felt that a pamphlet would make it back to the administration. If that happened, they argued, someone [might] go to the hole. Others felt like the administration was going to hear about our plans through their informants anyway. Besides, this group said, we want the administration to feel the pressure; we want them to know we don't plan on taking this lightly. Everyone understood that, pamphlet or not, some of us [might] end up in the hole. In the end it was decided to go forward with distributing it to select organizers who would show it to other people, but take it back when they were done reading it.

Some of us had been developing friendships with free world abolitionists. We knew that if we wanted to pull this off we would need people attacking from the outside in as well. Our outside accomplices were delegated two tasks. First, a phone campaign would be developed on social media. An inside comrade wrote a short description of the restriction and asked anyone concerned to call the prison and complain. And of course, we were advising all incarcerated people to contact their families and inform them of the phone restriction. This would let the administration know we were not alone inside. We relayed this information over a video visit. At the time video visits were less than the phone. And because we were on a time crunch, we couldn't use snail mail. If you have the time, the safest method is snail mail and having a person who is not under surveillance mail it out.

Second, our outside accomplices set up a smart communications account, perhaps multiple accounts, to communicate with prisoners throughout the prison. A prisoner managed to get a list of the names and numbers of incarcerated people throughout the compound. Over 100 prisoners located on different blocks received a message about the upcoming phone restriction and our planned resistance to it. There were some security concerns about taking this step. We didn't want the administration to think they were responsible for organizing on their block. However, we determined that since COVID restrictions might prevent some people being informed, the benefits outweighed the risk. We advised that they send a message back saying that they would not be able to participate in the phone boycott because it was against the rules and to block the sender. That way they would be able to use that as evidence if they ever received a misconduct. War is deception. This method was only used by necessity and should be avoided if you can.

They made an announcement, "If you want to use the phone tomorrow, sign the sheet in the dayroom." Everyone's eyes darted around the block. Who would make the first move? A few comrades and I walked over to the table. There was a memo next to the sign up explaining the policy. We sat near the table and kept watch.

The people were hype about the unity we were witnessing. At one point someone walked over to the desk and signed the list. Before he had a chance to walk away a comrade approached him and explained that we weren't signing the list, that we were protesting the policy. How is it, he explained, that the mission of the DOC is supposed to be rehabilitation and making prisoners productive members of society, but they do nothing to actually make that happen? Studies show that building community support is one of the most important factors to reduce recidivism, yet the administration wants to block our connection to the street. Ain't that fucked up? We were tired of them oppressing us. This time we were standing up. The person agreed and immediately scratched his name off the list.

Out of everyone on the block, there was one person who refused to join the resistance. He was a known bootlicker and suspected informant. His block worker job made him feel like he ran the block with the COs. He found more joy in conversing with them than us. It wasn't a surprise that he continued to sign the list. Some suggested we get him out [of] the way. But the situation didn't really call for that. We advised the people to abandon him. He didn't have any influence so it was safer to just leave him.

Not every block participated in the boycott. For example, one block with low participation houses the majority of workers in the Correction Industries (CI) shop. They are the highest paid positions in the prison, averaging $150 a month. These are mostly older men who have come to cherish the money. Many of them are white. This privilege affects their unity with other prisoners.

Many of them confine themselves to the block, never going to the yard where prisoners congregate. What's more concerning is that most of them are buddy-buddy with the COs and staff. It's almost as if they relate more to the administration than the people they are locked up with. This dynamic deserves a more substantial analysis, but at the very least I can say that the administration uses their job as leverage over them. They resemble the petty bourgeois in the free world. Rarely do any of them support collective liberation. They sold their revolutionary impulse for some soups and cookies.

Our outside accomplices continued to call the administration. I don't know what response they received. For us, it was enough that the prison knew we were supported, that they couldn't hide behind their veil of secrecy as they normally [did]. Some outside organizers might see social media posts asking them to call prison administrators and think it isn't important: what can my call do? They are wrong. Inside organizing is strengthened by outside support.

On the second day, they came around with the phone list at night again. Only one person signed the list. You know who. The next day the phones ran as normal. The third night was the last time they tried the list. After that there was never a list again. We were surprised no one got locked up. They didn't lock us down either. Perhaps the administration couldn't identify the organizers. Maybe our outside accomplices kept them in check. It could be that their superiors at central office told them to stand down. It's hard to say for sure.

Our war was not decided in an epic battle. There were no victory celebrations. The administration announced no defeat. Instead, they let the phone restriction quietly fade away. But we know what happened. We came together; we organized; we fought the phone restriction; we won. Despite everyone that said it would never work, we won.

Incarcerated people are not only separated from the free world, we are separated from each other. Prison erects both physical and interpersonal walls. More modern prisons favor smaller blocks and smaller yards to keep social interaction to a minimum. If the heart of organizing is relationship building, then how do you organize if you don't have the opportunity to socialize? Incarcerated people must be creative in overcoming these barriers. Prison-prescribed programming can become subversive bases. The law library, school rooms, and religious spaces can become gatherings for organizing. With more time and opportunity, we could have utilized these "legitimate" prison spaces to spread word about the phone boycott.

When you find yourself in these spaces, step out of your comfort zone and extend yourself to meet new people. Instead of leading with a statement, throw a question out there. It could be as simple as, "Hey did you hear about such and such news? What do you think about that?" Starting conversations for the phone resistance was usually as easy as, "Hey did you hear about the upcoming phone restriction? What do you think about that?" Even people that didn't use the phone often hated the idea of the administration taking more from us. Why? Because they keep taking shit from us and "no one stands up." Anticipate that response. Why is this time different?

Before the phone resistance we spent a lot of time building study groups, connecting incarcerated people with outside activists and increasing our political education collectively. These groups were integral to our resistance. If there are no study groups where you're at, start one right now. Grab a book, take it to the dayroom and start a conversation. It can be as simple as that.

The administration's plan to restrict the phone backfired in ways they couldn't have imagined. Instead of isolating us from the free world, they brought us together. And when we come together collectively, we win.

THIRTY-ONE

SALEEM HOLBROOK

Dismantling the Master's House (2023)

BORN TO POLITICALLY ACTIVE PARENTS IN PHILAdelphia in 1974, Saleem Holbrook came of age—and came to political consciousness—in a cage. A casualty of tough-on-crime measures and the "lock 'em up and throw away the key" mentalities of the 1990s, he was condemned to a life sentence as a sixteen-year-old and spent the next twenty-seven years locked up in various prison facilities throughout the state of Pennsylvania until a new law passed allowing juvenile lifers the right to be resentenced. A youth condemned to die in prison, Holbrook benefited tremendously from the tutelage of a handful of older men who helped raise him. One such mentor was Russell "Maroon" Shoatz, who provided a political education that helped Holbrook and others navigate their political and personal realities while in prison. Most important, Holbrook did not just study the freedom curriculum that he was exposed to, he applied those theories and became an actor in the advancement of his own freedom dreams. Holbrook became a revolutionary in the hole, and from that place of total repression he manifested an emancipatory consciousness that empowered him. Within three years of returning to his Philadelphia community, he became executive director of the Abolitionist Law Center and Straight Ahead, two influential anti-prison organizations dedicated to statewide abolition.

Every prisoner wants to be free, but free toward what end? Having secured his own release from prison, today Holbrook works fervently to ensure that no human be subjected to what he went through. It is from this vantage point that we appreciate this text and witness his effort to reconcile a path forward. However, the tools that served well for his survival in prison might not be the same tools needed to advance the abolition agenda in communities of resistance outside of prison. This writing exhibits a genealogy of abolitionist thought, theory, and practice while simultaneously advancing this radical tradition. Revolutionary consciousness can emerge even when forged in the desolation of prison hell. When cultivated, such consciousness advances an agenda of freedom that honors those who came before, while serving generations yet to come.

DISMANTLING THE MASTER'S HOUSE

> "The master's tools will never dismantle the master's house."
>
> —AUDRE LORDE

I WAS struck by Audre Lorde's quote a couple days ago during a conversation around decarceration and abolition. I came to abolition by necessity, not by choice. When I was 16 years old, I was arrested and subsequently sentenced to life without parole. A death by incarceration sentence. My options were limited, and at the time seemed confined to overturning my sentence on appeal or commutation by the governor. Both options had odds of around 1 percent at the time. I buried myself in the law library, teaching myself how to navigate court opinions, statutes and rules of procedure. From behind razor wire and gun towers I experienced firsthand the impact of the 1993 Crime Bill that birthed mass incarceration on steroids. I became frustrated at realizing how the state weaponized the law against Black and Brown communities—specifically Black and Latinx youth. Laws were never used to make our communities safer.

It was during this time that I found law can be used as conduit for resistance, and how oppressed peoples have historically used the law as a tool to aid in their liberation. This brings me to Audre Lorde's statement and how, to sound blasphemous, as an abolitionist I don't completely agree with it. I came to this observation in the most unlikely places, the state's Special Management Unit: a "hole" within the "hole" in the Pennsylvania Department of Corrections. This was a twenty-three hour a day lockdown, where I remained for close to three years. In an environment designed to lay dormant the human soul is where the seeds of abolition were planted. It is there that I found the historical tracts on rebellion and abolition like *American Negro Slave Revolts*, *David Walker's Appeal*, and *The Black Jacobins*. It is there I discovered the fighting history of the Maroons who carved enclaves of free and abolitionist societies out of the slave regimes in the Americas. It was there that I discovered the story of the Amistad. It is where to my delight, as a born native of Philadelphia, that our city was a key station on the abolitionist underground railroad and produced abolitionists like William Still and Octavious Catto.

It was also there that I learned of the heroic anti-colonial struggles of the colonized and oppressed peoples around the world. Particularly in Africa and Asia. I discovered how colonized peoples waged wars of national liberation on the battlefield of their homelands and within the halls of the United Nations and its International Human Rights Charter, a world body that was established by the Colonial Powers. To read how African and Asian liberation movements used a body of law promulgated by colonial powers to liberate themselves from colonial oppression resonated with me. What resonated more was how, despite using it, they did not, for one minute, believe in the body of laws created by the colonial powers. To them, it was just another tool in their war chest.

It was in the abolitionist programs of the Black Radical Tradition, that I found that the master's tools in fact have been used to dismantle the master's house. Slave rebellions have always held special places in the consciousness of Black political prisoners and politicized prisoners. George Jackson, Malcolm X, Assata Shakur, and Safiya Bukhari all speak to the inspiration slave revolts had on their thinking and politics. But abolition in the cage is different than the envisioning of abolition out here in the free world.

It wasn't long ago that the seminal books I named above on slave revolts were banned by the Department of Corrections. Prison bureaucrats realized that the system they operated had too many similarities with the plantation system, and books on slave rebellions were banned as "subversive and/or disruptive to the orderly operation of the institution." Those words are seared in my memory today, even though I've been home for three years. As a prisoner agitator and abolitionist, I fought the censorship regime and prevailed by using the "master's law" to dismantle the DOC's mail policies that allowed censorship. Other comrades and I viewed our campaign on prison censorship as a plantation rebellion. We filed grievance after grievance on every denial, had people on the outside challenge the censorship and organize direct actions against it. As organizers and abolitionists, we weren't trying to make our imprisonment more comfortable. For us, it was a matter of survival and an organizing strategy. Books on slave rebellions were political education for us, and the ability to hold political education multiplied our numbers.

When it comes to the law, the same applies, it can be an organizing strategy. We certainly didn't believe in the law[,] and all of us at one time or another during our imprisonment spent time in the hole for attempted escape or suspicion of escape. We didn't pin our hopes of freedom in the law; our motto was we'd either get out the "white way" or the "right way," the white way being the law and the right way meaning going over or under the wall. For us it was using the tools or weapons at our disposal to gain our freedom. The inspiration for this again was found in the courage, audacity and tools of our ancestors.

The machete. Our ancestors throughout the Western Hemisphere worked the fields with this tool, night and day, young and old, all genders. Calloused hands whipped it from sunup to sundown, the blade cutting through stem and root. This tool built the wealth of Europe and the Western Hemisphere at the expense of the African people wielding it. Yet this same tool during times of rebellion was wielded with a fury that laid waste to entire plantations and in the case of Haiti, liberated and created a nation. The same blade that ripped through sugar cane crops to enrich slave owners was just as quickly used to rip through their bodies to enrich the ground with their blood. Thinking about the uprisings of our ancestors, uprisings for freedom and dignity, the words of Fidel Castro echoed in our minds, "*We were taught that liberty is not begged for but won with the blade of a machete.*" This is US history for us—and our founding mentors were: Nat Turner, Denmark Vesey, David Walker, Dessalines, Granny Nanny, and Harriet Tubman.

Abolition in the cage is different from the envisioning of abolition out here in the free world. Inside it is the machete, with the capacity to cut through the repression, trauma and harm of a system that since its inception, has pulverized Black, Brown and poor communities beneath its weight. The law is a tool that, along with other tools, we will use to dismantle the master's house. The law that is used to oppress us, we will use to defend ourselves. It is part of the theory of change that I bring to the outside at the Abolitionist Law Center, and we will use its full disposal. We also recognize that the law is not the solution, it is just one tool in our Abolitionist Toolbox.

We utilize the law to liberate ourselves, and erode the pillars of the carceral state, the same way water seeps into and erodes the foundation of a wall. It exploits gaps, and when we use the law, we use it to exploit gaps in the system. An example of this is the campaign to end life without parole sentences for child offenders. International law long held that children could not be sentenced to life imprisonment (or death) without the possibility of release. We seized on that and built a national and international campaign challenging the sentencing of children to life without parole. We seized the momentum, and when the reactionary United States Supreme Court ruled that the practice was unconstitutional, we exploited that gap[,] and as a result hundreds of prisoners in Pennsylvania who were sentenced to die in prison as children were released.

But we knew we had to move quickly because several years later the Supreme Court rolled back its ruling and shut the door once again. We knew that was going to happen because we studied law, not because we believed in it. In America, victories won one day can be rolled back by the state the next day. The thing is: what position are you in when the ruling comes, and can you seize the momentum? Therefore, we approached the litigation and subsequent ruling as a prison break, not a legal victory[,] and our tools were organizing people and law books, not hacksaw blades.

As I look out at the abolitionist landscape today, I am not sure if I can recognize or can even relate to many of the spaces dedicated to "envisioning" and "envisioning practices." Abolition on the inside is a brick-and-mortar abolition, a thrashing abolition. Despite my reservations, I feel comfortable in it, as comfortable as a new pair of slippers. But that's my problem, because the other side is comfortable in boots; and so am I. I can't envision abolition as a garden, flourishing and growing. I can only envision abolition as brick-and-mortar, as something that is built with calloused hands. Yet, I have seen the calloused hands of gardeners and realize that there is a place for both, the garden needs water, flowers and pollinators as much as it needs a machete. As some are working the garden planting seeds of change, others will be in the field cutting and harvesting the crop and uprooting the weeds. Sometimes it's just a matter of finding one's place in the world we are building.

JULIA WRIGHT

AFTERWORD

Towards an Ecology of Hope

hope-rooted
a fragile sapling
splits a brick

Dear Mumia,

When invited to write the afterword to your collection of prison voices, my first reaction was to decline, on the grounds that I have never been incarcerated. Unless one counts the car arrest at gunpoint by Ghanaian soldiers as my late husband, my arm-held baby, and I were driven to Accra's international airport after we had gone underground following the CIA-engineered coup against President Kwame Nkrumah in early 1966. Then again, I wondered, what is being underground if not self-restriction of freedom that has become more dangerous than danger itself?

After a moment I thought to myself, "Wait a minute, Julia, you *are* incarcerated." That is the message of this book: that the whole ploy of the empire that is grinding our bones is to make us believe we are free. In fact, if I was deluded enough to imagine I was free, sitting here unshackled and undeterred, outside prison walls writing to you, then I have two sets of bars to break out of. So thank you, Comrade Brother, for offering me the opportunity to write this message to you, because I know that at least you will get to read it, unlike dozens of censored letters I sent to you.

I have just reluctantly reached the end of *Beneath the Mountain,* in which you and Jennifer Black give space and deep listening to your brothers and sisters in incarceration, and all I want to do is go back to the beginning and start reading all over again with the hard-hitting and challenging hindsight of all I have just read.

I am no arborist, but I am reminded of how a healthy tree trunk grows in a circular fashion around its pith. Each first-person singular who bears witness to what it is like to live beneath the mountain thickens the trunk of the tree of Abolition. The first-person singular of the very singular experience of these US prisoners is not narcissistic, even though the pronoun "I" is used. It is not the Cartesian *"Je pense, donc je suis"*—I think, therefore I am. Quite the opposite—it is the finding of one's voice despite having one's vocal cords torturously choked. It is the discovery that we can know our name and that, through literacy acquired in prison, each newfound voice is the echo of countless others. "The song that I sing is part of an echo," Assata says in this book. And Leonard Peltier recently said that, fearing a loss of his identity in the hole, he wrote his name on a piece of paper and slipped it under his mattress so he could remind himself that he had a name if his mind went dark.

So, back to the pith. What could it be? Each voice in this book has slightly different words for it, and each pith has its intrinsic identity. When you, Assata, Che Guevara, and others speak of Revolutionary Love, that is the pith, the very center of our collective birth and growth. But when we learned that Ruchell Magee would be freed—that it would be a few days, and he would return home—my own belief in Revolutionary Love was put to the test. And since so many of us had laid small stones to the edifice of his release, we could not help hoping. We could not help our hope being explosive, pent up as it had been for over half a century. We could not help letting off spiritual fireworks. But caution also whispered to us to beware, to self-censor our hope, because there had been

Veronza Bowers.[33] It was a difficult twilight period where we remained reluctantly in the trenches even as we wanted to dance and sing on the rooftops.

Would we still have the audacity to hope? Just as Che told us not to be ashamed of Revolutionary Love, we should not be ashamed of the Hope that is the soil or compost in which Love grows best. Because Hope is not L. Frank Baum's craving for an over-the-rainbow illusion or a nostalgia-tinted vision of the future.[34] Because Hope is not Pollyannaish or akin to the magical thinking of white supremacy. Rather, our Black Hope is hard-earned, gritty, messy, and painful, like birth labor. Hope is an upside-down blues sung by Cesária Évora. Hope is the awareness that we are so much wealthier than we know. As Joy James says, we are the heirs to ancestral wisdom, heirs to a whole history of resistance and suppressed slave narratives.

The theme of Hope runs through this book like a thread of revolutionary glue. As Assata and Angela teach us, Hope unbreaks the spirit. Hope is agency, the opposite of an absence of self-reliance. As George Jackson shows us, Hope is the courage to be alone, and as Safiya Bukhari instructs us, Hope is knowing that "we too can slay the beast." Hope is "the callous hands of the gardener," as Saleem Holbrook writes. Hope is victory, a movement grown in a resistant soil, a resilient plant.

On putting the book down, we each might ask ourselves: what is Hope to me? Hope to me is Kwame Nkrumah's spirit of "Forward Ever." Hope was such a difficult exercise for Richard Wright, my father, that he preferred to speak of "hope-prints." Hope is the fact that because I am wounded, I can be a better healer. Hope is visualizing all the things that made my day, not the things that unmade it.

My elder's memory goes back to the very day of the coup d'état in Ghana—February 24, 1966. In 1963, Nkrumah had offered my late husband and me jobs as the French editors of *Spark,* the Ghana-based newspaper that served anticolonial and anti-neo-colonial liberation movements in Africa and beyond. After the dawn coup, we huddled in fear in our living room with some of the freedom fighters. We were mostly silent, speaking sporadically, tersely. We knew we were all on the list of "Nkrumaists" being hunted down. We were waiting for a call from the Cuban embassy in Accra. Then S. G. Ikoku, a Nigerian freedom fighter and opponent of neocolonialism, broke yet another long spell of trench-like silence.

"I will tell you an African folktale," he offered in that moment. It felt incongruous at the time, but we listened. He proceeded to recount how a turtle on its way through the forest encountered a very hungry lion who informed the turtle that it would be his next meal. The turtle acquiesced, asking for only one thing: thirty minutes to pray before its impending doom. The lion, amused and confident his meal was a done deal, agreed. The turtle then proceeded to carefully and methodically scratch the soil all around the clearing where they had met.

The lion, puzzled but also amused, asked the turtle, "What does all this scratching mean? I thought you were going to pray."

The turtle replied, "When you have swallowed me, all the animals of the forest who pass through this clearing will comment in admiration about the dauntless fight I put up before my demise."

The turtle was passing on its legacy like the revolutionary voices you have allowed us to hear in your book, Mumia.

Either my memory fails me, or we were not told that morning how the tale ended, whether the turtle was indeed eaten like Malcolm X, Martin Luther King, George Jackson, and others. Or whether the white-supremacist lion, given to instant gratification, couldn't wait out the thirty minutes and gobbled up a different fast-food prey too illiterate to leave scratchings behind. Or whether the scratchings represent the law, and were successfully weaponized against a lion who had not mastered the constitution of the forest. Or... We can choose the narrative that best matches our level of hope and love.

Mumia, there are those who would classify me as an Afro Optimist. I am no expert in isms or whatever so maybe I just try to be an Afro Existentialist, in the same way Fanon had the lucidity to foresee that there would be post-colonial betrayal but that the choice remains firmly in our hands.

The voices you have chosen, Mumia, form a master class of political and spiritual abolitionist scratchings. There are those who have been devoured, but also those who have survived and live among us. And we will make sure that there are fewer and fewer martyrs and more and more survivors. And as we on the outside learn liberation techniques from all of them, fewer and fewer prisoners will be devoured on the inside.

As the decades passed and the ecological struggle intersected increasingly with the abolitionist movement, we realized that scratching Mother Earth had a powerfully symbolic meaning when we learned of another turtle's killing, Tortuguita's, as he sat cross-legged, meditating in another forest clearing.[35] Tortuguita left the human animals of Weelaunee Forest with the indelible traces of their smiling, hopeful legacy.

And, Mumia, before your final brief was brought in front of blackface Judge Lucretia Clemons, thousands of us sent her scratchings of our own within the legal deadline, the parable's thirty minutes. And you added to all your commentaries and books yet another prose scratching when you spoke eloquently before the United Nations "Expert Mechanism to Advance Racial Justice and Equality" on April 26, 2023, in Atlanta. The United Nations Human Rights Council had already sent a landmark amicus curiae in your defense. On March 31, 2023, the cowardly lioness swallowed you nonetheless, sending you back to death by incarceration, but those reams of paper sent to her have become revolutionary compost for the soil to grow the trees of a rekindled liberation movement.

Like Nelson Mandela before you, you will be released, Mumia.

To borrow Amilcar Cabral's own parable in his iconic speech at Kwame Nkrumah's funeral in 1972, there is a cancer of betrayal. And that betrayal sooner than later will lead to a tsunami, and the people will be its waves.

This book is a richly sown field. Its harvest is our birthright—pages we will share and teach and pass on. Our prisons are built on the land that was stolen from us and on the forgotten cemeteries of our ancestors—our inner Middle Passage. The prisons belong to us. The prison lore too. Until we reclaim the walls, we are all incarcerated with you and we all write on the same page.

Towards an Ecology of Hope,

JULIA

ACKNOWLEDGMENTS

THIS BOOK PROJECT WOULD NOT HAVE BEEN POSsible without a squad of supporters who rallied to provide suggestions, services, inspiration, and guidance. It was a combined labor of love, proffered by those who hold the belief that together we can interrupt our current carceral reality and positively impact our futures by altering the function of prisons in our society. We are profoundly beholden to each contributor, some among the living, others our venerated ancestors. Many went to prison for advocating for the least among us, and they stood up to the monstruous and terrorizing American Empire. The sacrifices they made on our behalf, and the detriments their families were also forced to endure, contribute toward cultivating the vital resources of love and hope that the visionary writer Julia Wright unearths in her afterword. It is to them—and to those still caged beneath the mountain—that we dedicate this book.

We thank the remarkable and talented team at City Lights Publishers. They have been exceptional to work with and we are grateful for that. Most significantly, we thank Greg Ruggiero, who was committed and worked very hard to make this the best book it could be. His breadth of experience, vision, and consistent approachability was a reservoir we drew from again and again. We would also like to highlight the significant contributions of our friend and comrade Noelle Hanrahan, Esq., co-director of Prison Radio. This project would have been no more than a fleeting, bright idea without Noelle, our midwife, who went above and beyond in every way imaginable to help us birth this book into the world. Our entire Prison Radio family was supportive, and we thank all the interns who conducted research and transcribed texts for us, especially Bea Phi, for their coordinating effort in helping us put together the manuscript. It is also important to highlight the support of Dr. Michael O. West, aka "small axe." A staunch comrade, he performed many services such as driving to and from the prison, being part of our earliest strategy sessions, offering feedback, and extending social solidarity in the form of shared meals, including vending machine vittles from the prison visiting room.

Mumia wishes to specifically thank our encaged sisters and brothers, who, like Malcolm X, have so thirsted for knowledge in these places of darkness, that they read beloved texts by the dim light of the prison corridors or the glow from the full moon. These stories, drawn from many works and written over many years, remind us all of the strength of social movements to challenge unjust systems of power and to create movements from below. But we must remember not only that we are all beneath the mountain, but that here, in this dark abode, dwells an abundance of riches—community, solidarity, affection—and, yes, even love. What crowns it all is our undying capacity for love.

In addition, Jennifer would like to express her appreciation to all the resolute, bold, and brave organizers in central Pennsylvania, including this current generation of Penn State activists, for providing inspiration and reason to "keep on keeping on." Those who humbled the Proud Boys, who stood in support of justice for Osaze Osagie, unjustly murdered by Officer Michael Pieniazek on March 20, 2019, who coordinate efforts to challenge genocide against Palestinians in the Middle East, and who study, struggle, sacrifice, and strive to build a world we all deserve to live in. To them, she echoes the assuring words inscribed on Jess X Snow's beautiful mural in Philly: "The coming years will be hard, but the future is worth the fight, just hold on and you will see." And when it comes to her co-editor, the mighty Mumia Abu-Jamal, there aren't words adequate to convey her immense respect and gratitude. If you know, you know. Simply put, Mumia is unparalleled, unmatched, and unequaled. He is one of one, and the breadth and scope of his enormous influence will be felt for a thousand generations.

ENDNOTES

1. "Ona Judge," George Washington Library at Mont Vernon, Center for Digital History.

2. "Ona Judge," George Washington Library at Mont Vernon, Center for Digital History, quoting T. H. Adams, "Washington's Runaway Slave, and How Portsmouth Freed Her," *Granite* (N.H.) *Freeman*, May 22, 1845, reprinted in Frank W. Miller, *Portsmouth* (N.H.) *Weekly*, June 2, 1877.

3. Lindsay M. Chervinsky, White House Historian, "The Remarkable Story of Ona Judge," White House Historical Association, quoting "Washington's Runaway Slave," *Granite* [NH] *Freeman*, May 22, 1845.

4. Douglass refers here to Edward Covey, a malicious farmer with a reputation for his brutal and dehumanizing treatment of enslaved people. Douglass details his experiences of working under Covey's tyrannical control and the physical and psychological hardships he endured in *Narrative of the Life of Frederick Douglass, an American Slave*, first published in 1845.

5. The term "squaw" is now considered to be an offensive, racist, and misogynistic pejorative after decades of disrespectful usage. At the time of this testimony, it was commonly used to denote a North American Indian woman or wife.

6. Debs refers here to the embalmed-beef meat scandal of 1898 in which Armour & Company, an American meatpacking company, supplied tons of rotting, canned meat preserved with formaldehyde to Cuba and the US Army during the Spanish-American War.

7. "We Shall Remain: Geronimo," *American Experience*, PBS, May 4, 2009.

8. Jesse Kratz, "Geronimo, Apache Chief," *Pieces of History* (blog), National Archives, November 22, 2022.

9. Ibid.

10. Victoria, chief of the Hot Springs Apaches, met his death in opposing

the forcible removal of his band to a reservation, because, having previously tried and failed, he felt it impossible for separate bands of Apaches to live at peace under such arrangement.

11. Geronimo's whole family, except his eldest son, a warrior, was captured.

12. This statement was so controversial that the Superintendent of Education who originally produced this transcript felt compelled to reiterate that the assertion recorded was "Geronimo's exact words."

13. In this context, "jail delivery" suggests the illicit or unauthorized release of prisoners from confinement, such as through escape, but it can also refer to a legal process or official action by which imprisoned people are released from jail or prison.

14. Robert Lester Jackson, George Jackson's father. Throughout *Soledad Brother*, Jackson refers to him sometimes as Lester and sometimes as Robert.

15. California prison regulations limit the length of convict letters to both sides of one standard 8.5-by-11-inch sheet of paper.

16. George Davis, the author's grandfather.

17. Angela Davis, Bobby Seale, Erika Huggins, Ruchell Magee. Los Siete de la Raza are the seven Chicanos who were acquitted in San Francisco of the charge of killing a police officer, and who continue to be harassed by the police. Reis Tijerina was a Chicano leader imprisoned for his attempt to reassert Mexican-American ownership by right of treaty grant to large tracts of land in the Southwest. James Carr was with George Jackson during most of his years in prison. While on parole, he reportedly attempted to come to George's assistance during the violent aftermath of the Soledad Brothers' hearing. Carr was murdered April 6, 1972, outside his home in San Jose.

18. Billy Dean Smith was born in Bakersfield, California, in 1948. Though he was morally opposed to the war, he was drafted into the US Army in 1969 and sent to fight in Vietnam in 1970. Accused of "fragging," the act of intentionally killing or intending to kill a superior officer by grenade, Smith was accused and held in military prison with no physical evidence to support the accusation. His case became a cause célèbre, highlighted to demonstrate the racial tensions and unequal treatment of African American soldiers. Smith was eventually acquitted of murder

charges after spending over a year in solitary confinement but found guilty of assault and given a bad-conduct discharge.

19. CIW refers to the California Institution for Women

20. See Sections 851–854, New York State Correction Law, McKinney's Consolidated Laws.

21. Robert McKay, dean of the Law School at New York University, was appointed by Governor Rockefeller to prepare a report on the rebellion at Attica. Published in September 1972, by Bantam Books and titled *Official Report on the New York State Commission on Attica.*

22. Vernon Jordan, *The State of Black America* (New York: National Urban League, 1979).

23. *Tillery v Owens*, 907 F. 2nd 41 g (3rd Cir. 1990).

24. *Abu-Jamal v. Price,* No. 95-cv-00618, U.S. District Court, West. Dist., Pa.

25. *Turner v. Safley*, 482 U.S. 78, 107 S.Ct. 2254 (1987).

26. Sara Flounders, "The Pentagon and Slave Labor in U.S. Prisons," Global Research, June 2011.

27. Truthout Staff, "Smoke and Mirrors: Inside the New "Bipartisan Prison Reform," *Truthout*, October 29, 2014.

28. Ricky Riley, "13 Mainstream Corporations Benefiting from the Prison Industrial Complex," *Atlanta Black Star*, October 10, 2014.

29. Amanda Chicago Lewisby, "The Prisoners Fighting California's Wildfires," *Buzzfeed News*, October 30, 2014.

30. Paige St. John, "Federal Judges Order California to Expand Prison Releases," *Los Angeles Times*, November 14, 2014.

31. Amanda Chicago Lewisby, "The Prisoners Fighting California's Wildfires," *Buzzfeed News*, October 30, 2014.

32. Stroud, p.240 2 Brevard's Digest, 241.

33. Veronza Bowers Jr. is a former member of the Black Panther Party serving a life sentence since 1973 after being convicted with questionable evidence and compromised witnesses in the murder of a US park ranger, a crime he vehemently denies committing. In 2005, after serving more than thirty-one years in prison, following a successful parole vote, Bowers was to be released from prison. Shockingly, on the day of his release, a petition filed by US Attorney General Alberto Gonzales requested that the National Appeals Board reconsider its decision. Bowers remains incarcerated in North Carolina, one of the longest-held inmates in US history.

34. L. Frank Baum is an American author and the creator of *The Wonderful Wizard of Oz* series. However, as the editor of South Dakota's *Aberdeen Saturday Pioneer* newspaper, he wrote this a week and a half before the Battle of Wounded Knee in 1890: "The Whites by law of conquest, by justice of civilization, are masters of the American continent, and the best safety of the frontier settlements will be secured by the total annihilation of the few remaining Indians."

35. "Tortuguita" refers to Manuel Esteban Paez Teran, the 26-year-old Indigenous Venezuelan environmental activist who was fatally shot by law enforcement in Atlanta, Georgia, on January 18, 2023. Tortuguita was part of the Stop Cop City activists who organized an initiative to defend Atlanta's Weelaunee Forest from the construction of a $90-million state-of-the-art police-training facility aimed at teaching counterinsurgency techniques. The word "tortuguita" means "little turtle" in Spanish.

SOURCES AND PERMISSIONS

WE ARE GRATEFUL FOR THE PERMISSION TO PUBLISH the documents listed below. All good-faith efforts have been made to clear permissions for copyrighted material. We will gladly rectify any omissions in a future printing.

Chapter 1: Ona "Oney" Judge Staines, *Response to George and Martha Washington, Her Enslavers*
Interview with Ona Judge Staines (1846) by the Rev. Benjamin Chase. Letter to the editor, *Liberator*, January 1, 1847. Public Domain.

Chapter 2: Nat Turner, *Pre-Trial Confessions*
Nat Turner and Thomas Gray, *The Confessions of Nat Turner, the Leader of the Late Insurrection in Southampton, Virginia* (Baltimore: Thomas R. Gray, Lucas & Deaver, 1831). Public Domain.

Chapter 3: John Brown, *Last Letter to His Family*
John Brown, November 30, 1859. John Brown ms. collection, Kansas State Historical Society. Public Domain.

Chapter 4 : Frederick Douglass, *The Runaway Plot*
Frederick Douglass, *Life and Times of Frederick Douglass, His Early Life as a Slave, His Escape from Bondage, and His Complete History to the Present Time* (Hartford, CT: Park Publishing, 1881), 9–21. Public Domain.

Chapter 5: Crazy Horse, *"I Have Spoken"*
Statement made to Lieutenant Jesse M. Lee, September 5, 1877, Fort Robinson. Public Domain.

Chapter 6: Eugene V. Debs, *Prison Labor, Its Effect on Industry and Trade*
Eugene V. Debs, "Prison Labor, Address Delivered before Nineteenth Century Club at Delmonico's, New York City, March 21st, 1899," *Progressive Thought*, no. 4, April 1899. Public Domain.

Chapter 7: Geronimo, *In Prison and on the Warpath*
Geronimo, *Geronimo's Story of His Life*, edited by S. M. Barrett (New York: Duffield, 1906), 79–82. Public Domain.

Chapter 8: Mother Jones, *Early Years, The Haymarket Tragedy,* and *In Rockefeller's Prison*
Mother Jones, *The Autobiography of Mother Jones*, edited by Mary Field Parton (Chicago: Charles H. Kerr, 1925), 23–27. Public Domain.

Chapter 9: Nicola Sacco, Letter to His Son Dante
Nicola Sacco and Bartolomeo Vanzetti, *The Letters of Sacco and Vanzetti* (New York: Penguin Classics, 2007), 28–33. Public Domain.

Chapter 10: Angelo Herndon, *You Cannot Kill the Working Class*
Angelo Herndon, *You Cannot Kill the Working Class* (New York: International Labor Defense and the League of Struggle for Negro Rights, 1937). Public Domain.

Chapter 11: Ethel and Julius Rosenberg, *Selected Letters*
Michael Meeropol, editor, *The Rosenberg Letters: A Complete Edition of the Prison Correspondence of Julius and Ethel Rosenberg* (New York: Garland, 1994), 48–62. Reproduced by permission of Taylor & Francis Group. Copyright © 1994 Michael Meeropol.

Chapter 12: Martin Luther King Jr., *Letter from Birmingham City Jail*
Reproduced by permission of the Heirs to the Estate of Martin Luther King Jr., c/o Writers House as agent for the proprietor, New York, NY. Copyright © 1963 by Dr. Martin Luther King, Jr. Renewed © 1991 by Coretta Scott King.

Chapter 13: Malcolm X, *Saved*
Alex Haley and Malcolm X, *The Autobiography of Malcolm X: As Told to Alex Haley* (New York: Ballantine Books, 1992), 77–90. Copyright © 1964 by Alex Haley and Malcolm X. Copyright © 1965 by Alex Haley and Betty Shabazz. Used by permission of Ballantine Books, an imprint of Random House, a division of Penguin Random House LLC. All rights reserved.

Chapter 14: Elijah Muhammad, *Message to the Blackman in America*
Elijah Muhammad, *Message to the Blackman in America* (Chicago: Muhammad's Temple No. 2, 1965), chapters 19, 28, 124. Copyright © 1965 Elijah Muhammad. Permissions requested.

Chapter 15: George Jackson, *Selected Prison Letters* and *Toward the United Front*
George Jackson, *Soledad Brother: The Prison Letters of George Jackson* (New York: Coward-McCann, 1970), 49–51, 51–53, 61–62, 64–65, 67–68, 69–70, 85–86, 107–109. Copyright © 1994 by Jonathan Jackson Jr. c/o Chicago Review Press, Susan Schulman Literary Agency. "Toward a United Front" excerpted from George L. Jackson, *Blood in My Eye* (Baltimore: Black Classic Press,1990), 105–113. Used by permission of Black Classic Press.

Chapter 16: Angela Y. Davis, *Jail Letter* and *"Beneath the Mountain" Victory Speech*

Jail letter (Marin County Jail, 1971) and "Victory Speech" delivered June 9, 1972 at the Embassy Auditorium, Los Angeles, California, Copyright © 1971 & 1972 Angela Y. Davis. Used by permission of the author.

Chapter 17: Martin Sostre, *The New Prisoner*

Martin Sostre, "The New Prisoner," *North Carolina Central Law Journal* 4, no. 2 (Spring 1973), 242–254. Copyright © 1973 Martin Sostre. Used by permission of Vincent Sostre.

Chapter 18: Assata Shakur, *Women in Prison: How It Is with Us* and *Two Poems*

Assata Shakur, "Women In Prison: How It Is with Us," *Black Scholar* vol. 9, no. 7, April 1978, 8–15. Copyright © 1978 Assata Shakur. Used by permission of Black Scholar/Taylor Francis. "Affirmation," 1, and "Left Overs, What Is Left?" 146–147. *Assata: An Autobiography* Copyright © 2001 Lawrence Hill Books. Permissions requested.

Chapter 19: Rita Bo Brown, *Court Statement*

Sentencing Statement, February 2, 1978, by Rita Bo Brown, in *Queer Fire* (Bloomington, IN: Untorelli Press). Copyright © 1978 Rita Bo Brown. Used by permission of Etang.

Chapter 20: Safiya Bukhari, *Coming of Age: A Black Revolutionary*

Safiya Bukhari, *The War Before: The True Life Story of Becoming a Black Panther, Keeping the Faith in Prison, and Fighting for Those Left Behind* (New York City: Feminist Press, 2010). 1–11. Copyright © 2010 by the Estate of Safiya Bukhari. Reprinted with the permission of The Permissions Company, LLC, on behalf of the Feminist Press at the City University of New York, www.feministpress.org.

Chapter 21: Eve Goldberg and Linda Evans, *The Prison Industrial Complex and the Global Economy*
Excerpt from Eve Goldberg and Linda Evans, *The Prison Industrial Complex and the Global Economy* (Oakland: PM Press, 2009). Copyright © 2009 Eve Goldberg and Linda Evans. Used by permission of PM Press and the authors.

Chapter 22: Mumia Abu-Jamal, *An Uncivil Action*
Mumia Abu-Jamal, *All Things Censored* (New York: Seven Stories Press, 2000), 76–93. Used with the permission of Seven Stories Press and the author.

Chapter 23: Pelican Bay State Prison SHU Short Corridor Collective, *California Hunger Striker Statement, Agreement to End Hostilities*:
Todd Ashker, C-58191, D1-119
Arturo Castellanos, C-17275, D1-121
Sitawa Nantambu Jamaa (Dewberry), C-35671, D1-117
Antonio Guillen, P-81948, D2-106

And the Representatives Body:
Danny Troxell, B-76578, D1-120
George Franco, D-46556, D4-217
Ronnie Yandell, V-27927, D4-215
Paul Redd, B-72683, D2-117
James Baridi Williamson, D-34288. D4-107
Alfred Sandoval, D-61000, D4-214
Louis Powell, B-59864, D1-104
Alex Yrigollen, H-32421, D2-204
Gabriel Huerta, C-80766, D3-222

Frank Clement, D-07919, D3-116
Raymond Chavo Perez, K-12922, D1-219
James Mario Perez, B-48186, D3-124

All names and the foregoing statement must be shown verbatim when used and posted on any website or other publication. Public Domain. Retrieved from https://ccrjustice.org/sites/default/files/attach/2015/07/Agreement%20to%20End%20Hostilities.pdf.

Chapter 24: Russell Maroon Shoatz, *Liberation or Gangsterism*
Russell Maroon Shoatz, "Liberation or Gangsterism," *Utopian* 6 (July 16, 2007). Copyright © 2007 Russell Maroon Shoatz. Used by permission of the author's family.

Chapter 25: Kevin Rashid Johnson, *What Is a "Comrade" and Why We Use the Term*
Originally published on rashidmod.com, May 20, 2013. Copyright © 2013 Kevin Rashid Johnson. Used by permission of the author.

Chapter 26: Chelsea Manning, *Sometimes You Have to Pay a Heavy Price to Live in a Free Society*
Copyright © 2013 Chelsea Manning. Reprinted by permission of the author. The statements and expressions are Chelsea Manning's and not the opinions of the US Disciplinary Barracks, the US Army, the Department of the Army, the Department of the Defense or any other US government department or agency. Chelsea Manning was not compensated for use of her expressions here.

Chapter 27: Leonard Peltier, *Message of Solidarity to the Water Defenders*
Originally posted on lrinspire.com on January 5, 2017. Copyright © 2016 Leonard Peltier. Used by permission of the author.

Chapter 28: Free Alabama Movement Collective, *Let the Crops Rot in the Field*
Copyright © 2016 The Free Alabama Movement Collective. Used with permission of the authors.

Chapter 29: Ed Mead, *Men against Sexism*
Text is an expanded version of an essay of the same title in Ed Mead, *Lumpen: The Autobiography of Ed Mead* (Montreal: Kersplebedeb, 2015). Copyright © 2015 Ed Mead/Kersplebedeb Publishing. Used by permission of the author.

Chapter 30: Safear Ness, *Phone Resistance*
Originally published by www.studyandstruggle.com. Copyright © 2023 Safear Ness. Used by permission of the author.

Chapter 31: Saleem Holbrook, *Dismantling the Master's House*
"Dismantling the Master's House, Brick and Mortar Abolition," by Robert Saleem Holbrook. Copyright © 2023 Robert Saleem Holbrook, Abolitionist Law Center. Used by permission of the author.

Afterword: Julia Wright, *Towards an Ecology of Hope*
Copyright © 2023 Julia Wright. All rights reserved. Used by permission of the author.

ABOUT THE EDITORS

MUMIA ABU-JAMAL IS AN AWARD-WINNING BROADcast journalist, essayist, and author of thirteen books. Abu-Jamal has lived the last forty-three years in state prison, Twenty-eight of those years were spent in solitary confinement on death row. Currently, he's serving life without parole at SCI Mahanoy in Frackville, Pennsylvania. Abu-Jamal's 1982 trial and its resultant first-degree murder conviction have been criticized as unconstitutionally corrupt by legal and activist groups for decades, including Amnesty International, and by Nobel Laureates Nelson Mandela, Toni Morrison, and Desmond Tutu. His demand for a new trial and for freedom is supported by the European Parliament, and he has been made an honorary citizen of Paris, France. Abu-Jamal earned his BA at Goddard College in 1996; his MA from California State University, Dominguez Hills in 1999; and an honorary Doctorate of Law from the New College of California in 1996. He is currently pursuing a PhD in the History of Consciousness at the University of California, Santa Cruz. The unified theme of his career has been to expose and disrupt the long train of oppression, to document the resistance of the oppressed, and to celebrate the inherent drive for human liberation from all systems of domination over the minds, movements, and spirits of humankind.

JENNIFER BLACK holds an MA in African American Studies and a PhD in Comparative Studies, both earned at the Ohio State University. Hailing from a background in both activism and academia, she focuses her research on high-risk activism, state-sponsored terror against political insurgents, and the impact of mass incarceration on marginalized communities. Black currently lives in State College, Pennsylvania, where she divides her time between teaching classes in the English department at Penn State University and working directly with incarcerated writers and political prisoners.

ALSO AVAILABLE IN THE OPEN MEDIA SERIES

Writing on the Wall
Selected Prison Writings of Mumia Abu-Jamal
Edited by Johanna Fernández, foreword by Cornel West

Have Black Lives Ever Mattered?
By Mumia Abu-Jamal

Jailhouse Lawyers
Prisoners Defending Prisoners v. the USA Paperback
By Mumia Abu-Jamal, foreword by Angela Y. Davis

Death Blossoms
Reflections from a Prisoner of Conscience, Expanded Edition
By Mumia Abu-Jamal, foreword by Cornel West

Twenty Dollars and Change
Harriet Tubman and the Ongoing Fight for Racial Justice and Democracy
By Clarence Lusane, foreword by Kali Holloway

Build Bridges, Not Walls
By Todd Miller

Rising Up
The Power of Narrative in Pursuing Racial Justice
By Sonali Kolhatkar, foreword by Rinku Sen

No Fascist USA!
The John Brown Anti-Klan Committee and Lessons for Today's Movements
By Hilary Moore and James Tracy, foreword by Robin D. G. Kelley

Narrative of the Life of Frederick Douglass, an American Slave, Written by Himself
A New Critical Edition
By Angela Y. Davis

CITY LIGHTS BOOKS | OPEN MEDIA SERIES